DETECTING EARNINGS
MANAGEMENT

GARY GIROUX

Texas A&M University

WILEY

www.wiley.com/college/giroux

This book is dedicated to
Naomi Giroux, Renee Ward, Tommy Giroux, and Josh Emerson

Executive Editor   *Jay O'Callaghan*

Marketing Manager   *Steven Herdegen*

Editorial Assistant   *Brian Kamins*

Managing Editor   *Lari Bishop*

Illustration Editor   *Benjamin Reece*

Cover Design   *Kris Pauls*

Cover Images   *Front cover Top: PhotoDisc, Inc.; Middle: PhotoDisc, Inc.; Bottom: Corbis Digital Stock; Back cover: Corbis Digital Stock*

This book was set in Minion by Leyh Publishing, LLC and printed and bound by Malloy Lithographers. The cover was printed by The Lehigh Press.

This book is printed on acid free paper. ∞

ISBN 0-471-47086-4

Printed in the United States of America
10 9 8 7 6 5 4 3 2 1

Contents

Preface

The United States survived Y2K, only to be hit with the stock market collapse, recession, and then a series of big-time corporate scandals. At Texas A&M University, we were hit hard by the Enron debacle because the accounting department had close ties with the Houston office of Arthur Andersen. I was teaching financial analysis at the time, and it occurred to me that I didn't have a clue about the problems that existed at Enron or how any outsider could possibly figure it out in advance. I'm supposed to know something about exactly that—evaluating financial information and the earnings quality of large corporations.

A little career soul-searching led to the decision to try and figure it out. How are scandal, bankruptcy, and fraud possible in a highly regulated environment filled with intelligent people and a seemingly endless supply of financial data on the Internet? The first step was trying to understand the financial environment. The accounting department ran a program called "Profession at the Crossroads," inviting experts from the major professions and regulators involved. Some chastised the system; others defended their industry as doing no wrong. Regulators speculated about the Sarbanes-Oxley Act and its potential impact. It was all very confusing, but it was a start.

Actually, I wrote the rough drafts of the first two chapters of this book to help me untangle the circumstances involved. As I researched the scandals, the regulations, and the roles of auditors, boards of directors, regulators, attorneys, and so on, I gained confidence that detecting earnings management was a viable goal and spent the next several months trying to prove it. This book is the result. The analysis won't lead to pinpointing specific fraud or other problems, but it provides signals that an earnings management environment exists and manipulation (or possibly worse) is possible. The basic advice: do the analysis, evaluate the major concerns, and, as an investor, get out when problems exist.

ORGANIZATION OF THE BOOK

This book is relatively short, given the topic; a comprehensive analysis would have been encyclopedia-sized. It includes three sections, each with a different objective. The first part involves the attempt to understand the environment and put it into perspective. The second is the nasty accounting stuff, literally using the financial statements to evaluate the reporting and the quality of the disclosures and identifying the potential signals of manipulation. The third section discusses particularly difficult issues, which include business combinations, executive compensation, and the relationships to corporate governance, retirement plans, and other factors such as evaluating risk, derivatives, and special purpose entities. The Appendix puts it all together in an evaluation checklist on earnings management detection. The findings for Apple Computer are reviewed with the checklist, as well as the case on Hilton Hotels.

Section 1 describes the environment. Chapter 1 attempts to explain what earnings management is (at least, according to my definition) and the relationship of earnings management to the current business and regulatory environment. This is a moving target, as regulations are changing and companies are improving corporate governance. Chapter 2 puts the current scandals in historical perspective, comparing them to those of the 1990s, the earlier 20th century, and previous eras. In some ways, the current mess is unique: new financial toys such as special purpose entities and executive compensation fit for sultans and rock stars. In other respects, it's the same old thing. Scandals from the 1990s and 1930s look strangely familiar. Chapter 3 introduces accounting and financial reporting, how this system is supposed to work, and how the earnings management environment and manipulation strategies can be detected. Apple Computer is used throughout the book to illustrate reporting and potential concerns. Apple is used because it is well known and has a relatively simple reporting structure, not because of massive fraud. However, massive problem and fraud cases will be presented throughout the book.

Section 2 focuses on financial statements, describing the earnings management potential and detection strategy by topic associated with the three major financial statements. Chapter 4 covers the balances sheet. A two-tier strategy is suggested: (1) a detection overview considering the major issues and the interrelationships across accounts and (2) a detailed evaluation of individual accounts, beginning with cash and working through to treasury stock.

Chapters 5 and 6 use the same perspective on the income statement. With the focus on earnings, this would seem to be the best place to find manipulation. Since the most significant problems relate to revenue recognition, allocation of costs, and problems with nonrecurring and special items, these topics are given considerable coverage. Chapter 5 presents a detailed overview of revenue recognition issues. Chapter 6 analyzes expenses, nonrecurring items, and other issues associated with the income statement.

Chapter 7 considers the statement of cash flows and compares alternative bottom-line definitions of earnings, including cash from operations. The final chapter in this section covers trend and quarterly analysis, an extension of techniques from the previous three chapters, but specifically using multiperiod techniques. Trends in quarterly and annual data can be powerful signals of potential manipulation.

Section 3 reviews various special topics. Chapter 9 considers business combinations and related issues. Acquisitions and divestitures can be part of a viable business strategy for economies of scale and expanding lines of business. On the other hand, accounting allows for incredible earnings management possibilities. Unfortunately, the accounting issues are complex, and the ability to see through potential manipulation during and after the acquisition is limited. Companies also can maintain control with less than 50% ownership. Accounting requirements change dramatically in such cases, allowing additional opportunities for earnings management. This chapter highlights the manipulation potential and the detection strategies available. Other related topics include segment reporting and the use of divestitures. Integrating the analysis of these interrelated topics is suggested.

Chapter 10 combines the intertwined issues of compensation and corporate governance. Proxy statement disclosures are a significant part of the investigation. Compensation packages of senior executives are summarized and can be evaluated in relation to corporate performance. If the members of the board of directors are pals of the chief executive officer and the compensation package seems particularly attractive, this is not expected to be a manipulation-free corporation. Stock options seem to be a particularly troublesome issue associated with an earnings management environment, and performance ratios will be restated for the impact of stock option expense and potential stock dilution. Pensions and other post-employment benefits issues also are described in this chapter, as are the additional combined earnings management–economic reality concerns they present. Current generally accepted accounting principles for both defined benefit pension plans and other post-employment benefits require smoothing techniques, which essentially represent "enforced earnings management." While they are not indicators of manipulation, pensions and other post-retirement employee benefits require recalculations to better approximate financial reality.

Derivatives in the context of risk management and special purpose entities (SPEs) are reviewed in Chapter 11. These are areas of considerable complexity and concern for the analyst. It can be extremely difficult to determine earnings management strategies when evaluating these items. The stated purpose of derivative use by most corporations is hedging to reduce risk; in fact, it is difficult to determine under what circumstances a firm is hedging (reducing risk) versus speculating (increasing risk). SPEs are used primarily to move obligations and assets off balance sheets and to limit disclosures on the activities accounted for by these entities. SPEs are evaluated skeptically because of the off-balance-sheet reporting and lack of complete disclosures.

A complete earnings management detection sheet that summarizes all the issues raised is presented in the Appendix. The results from the analysis of Apple Computer are summarized and concerns are highlighted. Another earnings management detection case features Hilton Hotels.

TEXTBOOK FEATURES

End-of-chapter materials include: (1) questions, (2) problems, and (3) cases. The questions are designed to encourage discussion about thought-provoking issues associated with chapter information. All the problems involve Hilton Hotels, a service company, usually compared to competitors Marriott and Mandalay Resorts. These include both quantitative analysis and qualitative issues related to earnings management and generally parallel the chapter discussions presented on Apple Computer. Cases are more detailed and include a variety of companies. These are more challenging and cover a wider variety of issues.

End-of-book materials include a glossary and a list of references and useful Web sites. All terms in bold in the text are defined in the glossary.

A complete support Web site appears at www.wiley.com/college/giroux. The site will include an instructor's Solutions Manual, Test Bank, PowerPoint slides, Web appendix, and a list of common financial ratios. The financial ratios are significant quantitative financial analysis tools. Although the book generally does not focus on these quantitative techniques, they are reviewed in detail in standard financial analysis textbooks (see, for example, Giroux 2003, especially chapter 4).

About the Author

Gary Giroux is Shelton Professor of Accounting at Texas A&M University. He received his Ph.D. from Texas Tech University and has been at Texas A&M for about twenty-five years. He teaches financial analysis and other financial and governmental courses in the undergraduate program. He also teaches research methods in the Ph.D. program.

Dr. Giroux has published over fifty articles, including publications in *Accounting Review, Journal of Accounting Research, Accounting, Organizations and Society, Journal of Accounting and Public Policy,* and numerous other journals. He is the author of three earlier books, including *Dollars & Scholars, Scribes & Bribes: The Story of Accounting* and *Financial Analysis: A User Approach.* His primary research areas are governmental and financial accounting. He also is interested in accounting and business history.

He has a number of outside interests, including collecting revenue documents and stamps, reading, golf, and scuba diving. He and his wife Naomi travel regularly, in part based on international research projects and presentations.

Acknowledgments

My thanks to Rick Leyh for encouraging me to write this book on a difficult but important topic. I thank the Leyh Publishing editorial staff for their hard work, including Kevin Dodds, Lari Bishop, Kris Pauls, Jennifer Wasson, and Benjamin Reece. Also the talented people at Wiley, including Jay O'Callaghan, Steve Herdegen, and Brian Kamins. I benefitted from the evaluations of several colleagues who reviewed various chapters, including Don Deis at Missouri, David Hurtt at Western Michigan, Stan Kratchman at Texas A&M, Marti Loudder at Texas A&M, Andy McLelland at Auburn, Lynn Rees at Texas A&M, Ed Swanson at Texas A&M, Val Vendrzyk at Richmond, and Mike Wilkins at Texas A&M. Special thanks to Wig DeMoville at Texas, Pan American and Steve Grossman at Texas A&M, who read the entire manuscript and provided detailed reviews.

1

What Is Earnings Management?

Enron was an incredible success story at the start of 2001. It was the seventh largest American company by market value, with substantial profits. It had a new-economy business strategy, focusing on energy trading and novel uses for derivatives. The stock price started falling in mid-2001 for seemingly unknown reasons. Management restated earnings in the third quarter 10-Q, issued in November 2001. The centerpiece was the restatement of three special purpose entities (SPEs), which required lowering stockholders' equity more than one billion dollars. Then the company declared bankruptcy in early December. What happened? Investors were stunned.

This was the first big financial fiasco of the new century. Congressional hearings would follow. The auditor, Arthur Andersen, would claim innocence and then be ruined by criminal prosecution. Executives would be indicted and face serious slammer time. Other big companies would fall like dominoes, in part for accounting irregularities: Global Crossing, WorldCom, Adelphia, and Tyco. A central theme to all these failures was aggressive earnings management, in which firms misstated earnings and presented misleading accounting information. Earnings manipulation, driven by corporate greed in a permissive environment, led to stock price and financial collapse for many corporations when the economy turned south.

There's nothing new about corporate bankruptcies or accounting debacles. The shock apparently was that with improved disclosure requirements, more stringent regulation, and high expectations from corporate governance and auditing, these scandals could still happen. As with all periods of fiscal fiascos, the results must be evaluated to consider appropriate changes in the accounting and regulatory environment that will make these scandals less likely in the future.

No matter what regulatory improvements occur, the financial analyst should assume *caveat emptor*—let the buyer beware. **Earnings management** is part of the accounting system. The basic question for the analyst is how much faith to place in the disclosures of specific firms and other public information. When is it likely that manipulation or fraud exists? Certain tools and techniques give the analyst a fighting chance to spot earnings management and perhaps restate financial data as more realistic information. That is the fundamental purpose of this book.

DEFINING EARNINGS MANAGEMENT

Given that it may be the scourge of modern American accounting, what exactly is earnings management? There is less than total agreement on how the term should be defined, and my own definition differs from much of the literature (Appendix 1.1). Consider the following continuum:

Conservative Accounting	Moderate Accounting	Aggressive Accounting	Fraud

My perspective is that earnings management includes the whole spectrum, from conservative accounting through fraud, a huge range for accounting judgment, given the incentives of management. Management takes a relative position on accounting issues, based on its perspective. This can be conservative, with few if any nonrecurring or unusual items and complete disclosure. The result should be a close approximation of economic reality and suggest high **earnings quality.** On the other hand, the perspective can be much more aggressive or even fraudulent.

Examples of the range of alternatives and the fit to this perspective include those in Table 1.1. As shown in the table, there are few limits on accounting creativity. Unfortunately, financial reality is based on following the rules, not avoiding them.

The objective of accounting information is to explain financial and economic reality, including both the performance and the relative financial position of a company. The chief financial officer (CFO), in conjunction with executives and board members, develops a perspective on what this economic reality is (or how to deviate from it in the case of earnings manipulation) and how it should be reported. This is a dynamic process that may change from quarter to quarter, because meeting financial analysts' expectations is important. With this approach, earnings management is the planning and control of the accounting and reporting system to meet the personal objectives of management. The objective of management may include meeting analysts' expectations, reporting sustained earnings growth, or achieving a performance goal of an incentive compensation plan. A definition I have previously proposed (Giroux 2003, p. 280) captures this as the use of "operating and discretionary accounting methods to adjust earnings to a desired outcome."

TABLE 1.1	EARNINGS MANAGEMENT IN RELATION TO COMPANY OBJECTIVES			
	Conservative	Moderate	Aggressive	Fraud
Revenue recognition, products	After sale, delivery, and acceptance	After sale is made	Bill and hold	Fraudulent sale
Revenue recognition on services	Services prepaid and performed	Services prepaid and partially performed	Services agreed to but not yet performed	Fraudulent scheme
Inventory	LCM faithfully followed	Slow to write-down slow-moving inventory	Obsolescent inventory still on the books	Sham rebates on purchased inventory; non-existent inventory
Asset reserves	Conservative use	Liberal use	Adjusting reserves to meet earnings targets	Releasing large reserve amounts to boost income
Accounts receivable	Conservative credit terms and bad debt allowance	Liberal credit terms and bad debts allowance	Liberalizing credit policies to expand sales and reduce bad debts by ignoring likely defaults	Fictitious receivables established to support nonexistent sales
Software development	Expensed as incurred	Limited capitalization	Extensive capitalization	Non-software development costs capitalized under this category
Depreciation	Conservative useful life and residual value	Liberal useful life and residual value	Restate useful life and residual value upward	Change estimates or principles to meet earnings targets
Advertising, marketing	Expensed as incurred	Expensed based on a formula; perhaps sales-based	Marketing costs capitalized	Costs capitalized and manipulated to meet earnings targets; other costs treated as marketing and capitalized

This definition of earnings management is designed to be a neutral one. The CFO, in conjunction with the chief executive officer (CEO) and other senior executives, has accounting choices and incentives for presenting financial performance. A research staff often determines these alternatives on the basis of industry practices or the opinions of various third-party experts. Earnings management can focus entirely on the most accurate presentation and full disclosure of financial and economic reality. Aggressive earnings management may be subtle, such as manipulating the allowance accounts or providing for additional tax reserves.

Most of the emphasis on earnings management problems focuses on **aggressive accounting** and **fraud,** the deliberate misstatement of financial information for the personal benefit of the managers. The term **earnings manipulation** will be reserved for these two categories, defined as "opportunistic use of earnings management to effectively misstate earnings to benefit managers" (Giroux 2003, p. 280).

WHY EARNINGS MANAGEMENT?

Economists claim there are three levels of individual behavior: obedience, self-interest, and opportunism. Obedience made sense to Karl Marx, but the capitalist system focuses on individual self-interest. **Opportunism** is "self-interest with guile." In other words, people are willing to violate normal ethical boundaries for personal benefit. Financial analysts should be on the lookout for opportunistic behavior. It's not clear where the boundary is between simple self-interest and opportunism, and that distinction probably differs with each individual. Earnings management strategy relates to self-interested behavior, from manipulation to opportunism.

Managers in their fiduciary role are expected to be corporate stewards, running the company in the best interests of the shareholders. Presumably, the firm should maximize long-term economic earnings. More immediate goals include a pragmatic business strategy; successful long-term relationships with suppliers; a focus on employee competence, welfare, training, and career opportunities; innovative customer products and services; and the use of new technologies and media such as the Internet to enhance the productivity and image of the company.

One of the potential problems inherent in the corporate form is that managers may focus on short-term personal incentives rather than the long-term economic success of the firm. Managers may attempt to maximize salary, bonuses, and other short-term compensation. This can be accomplished through improved business strategy and successful operations. It can also be accomplished, at least in the short term, through aggressive earnings management.

Most earnings management decisions represent relative timing differences. Revenues and expenses can be increased or decreased in the current period rather than in future periods. Revenues can be increased through aggressive revenue recognition, while expenses can be avoided temporarily by capitalizing certain costs. Gains can be recognized immediately and losses can be postponed. Troubled companies likely use earnings manipulation techniques to indicate they are still solvent. However, even successful companies are tempted to manage operating numbers when quarterly earnings are not up to analysts' forecasts.

A number of recent examples of earnings manipulation have led to considerable distrust of corporate financial information. WorldCom announced that it had wrongly capitalized some $3.85 billion in operating expenses and then declared bankruptcy in July 2002. The actual amount ballooned, with more recent estimates approaching $10 billion. Enron hid a multitude of its operating problems by using SPEs to keep liabilities, losses, and other bad news off the financial statements. Global Crossing sold fiber cable capacity to other telecommunications companies with use of long-term contracts, booking the prospective proceeds immediately as operating revenues. Dynegy was subjected to a federal probe based on sham trades, again used to boost revenues. Just when it appeared that the run of scandals had ended, HealthSouth erupted in another billion-dollar scandal, in 2003.

Given management incentives for self-interest or opportunism, executives can manipulate accounting earnings to achieve their personal agenda, such as bonuses. The basic incentive could be to raise current bonuses by increasing accounting earnings. Aggressive revenue recognition (e.g., recognizing revenues early in the operating cycle), capitalizing rather than expensing operating costs, and allocating costs over longer periods (e.g., increasing the expected useful lives of fixed assets) are common examples of potential earnings management techniques. Since many accounting techniques allow alternatives and professional judgment, **accounting choice** is an important component of earnings management. Inventory methods, depreciation, and accounting for marketable securities are examples of areas that allow accounting choice. Management can also use accounts involving estimates to manage earnings, such as the provision for bad debts or providing reserves for tax exposure.

A potential component of earnings management is **income smoothing,** attempting to generate consistent revenue and earnings growth rather than erratic changes. Generally, accrual accounting promotes income smoothing, such as capitalizing costs and allocating these costs over time as expenses with use of a straight-line method. Companies also can categorize accounting errors or misapplications of **generally accepted accounting principles** (GAAP) as "immaterial" and can effectively hide them as part of "other expenses." This helps give the appearance of high earnings quality or earnings persistence (indicators that core earnings are likely to continue).

The CFO may manage earnings to "just meet" analyst expectations, which may call for an "adjustment" of as little as a penny per share. Bonuses and other incentive compensation may be based on some non-GAAP formula approved by the board of directors. For example, unusual or infrequent items may be excluded from determining bonuses. The use of **stock options** has been more pronounced since the 1990s, with a couple of interrelated problems. First, options normally are not expensed on the income statement, understating real compensation expense. (Note that companies also receive a tax break when options are exercised.) Second, the options generate big incentives to drive up the stock price, whether justified by economic performance or not.

At some point, the line is crossed to opportunistic behavior. For example, when obvious operating expenses are capitalized, this is earnings manipulation. Generally, when earnings manipulation is detected, the earnings quality of the firm is questioned and analysts may have to reevaluate and restate financial information (a process called **normalizing income**).

Techniques to decrease current earnings also can be used. This can be part of an income smoothing strategy. Examples include extremely conservative revenue recognition (e.g., delaying recognition of sales) and expense recognition (e.g., immediate expensing of items that typically are capitalized). Also included in this category are **cookie jar reserves** to "store away" extra earnings for recognition in down periods. As a high-profit company with antitrust problems, Microsoft has used multiple methods to keep down current earnings. Microsoft usually expenses software development costs that other software providers capitalize. Microsoft also has used several categories of reserves, such as operating reserves based on contingencies, "marketing accruals" resulting in lower-than-budgeted advertising expenses, and reserves associated with reducing the useful lives of fixed assets. Microsoft agreed to "cease and desist" certain of these practices following a 2002 **Securities and Exchange Commission** (SEC) Administrative Proceeding.

An extreme example of loss recognition is the **"big bath" write-offs.** AOL Time Warner wrote off $54 billion in goodwill in the first quarter of 2002, the largest such write-off ever.

Why would managers do this? When the corporation is losing money in the current period and, therefore, no cash bonuses will be paid, it may be a good time to take a large write-off. This is especially effective when the company is in the process of reorganizing. Generally, these write-offs are nonrecurring items that are not considered part of continuing operations (and may be ignored by some analysts). These losses highlight the reorganization attempt, and because they are recorded in the current year, it is more likely that profitability will occur in future years—allowing the managers to get larger bonuses in the future. Better yet, when new managers are in place, they can blame all the problems on the old team.

Potential areas of earnings management often are industry-specific: the understatement of warranty liabilities for manufacturers; credit losses and loan loss provisions of banks; contingencies for tobacco litigation or environmental damage due to industrial waste; technological change, especially important in high-tech companies (e.g., as potential for inventory losses); high receivables and bad debts in retailing; and product liabilities for chemical or drug companies.

THE EARNINGS MANAGEMENT ENVIRONMENT

It's tempting to use just two words: corporate greed (that is, CORPORATE GREED!). Schilit (2002, p. 28) put it this way: "(1) It pays to do it, (2) it's easy to do, and (3) it's unlikely that you'll get caught." But the story gets more complicated. In terms of the institutional structure involved, it seems incredible that scandal is possible. Granted, managers do have self-interest incentives, but their employment contracts are structured to reward outstanding operating performance.

Each company should have a review structure in place to monitor the actions of the CEO, CFO, and other executives, designed to ensure compliance. Executive performance should be reviewed by a compensation committee, made up of independent members of the board of directors. Equally important is a separate audit committee made up entirely of independent and financially competent board members and an independent auditor, usually one of the **Big Four** accounting firms. New securities issues and other financial instruments are handled primarily on Wall Street, with the investment bankers highly regulated by the SEC.

Financial reporting is complex and governed by the extensive standards of the **Financial Accounting Standards Board** (FASB) and the SEC. There also are industry-driven standards by other regulatory agencies, such as the Federal Energy Regulatory Commission for regulated utilities and the Comptroller of the Currency for financial institutions. Accounting regulatory oversight is extensive. In addition to the regulations associated with specific industries, the SEC is directly and aggressively involved. All actively traded corporations must submit extensive reports to the SEC: the annual **10-K,** the quarterly **10-Q,** and the annual **Proxy Statement,** along with more technical reports such as the **8-K,** for significant events outside the normal reporting periods. Given this extensive institutional structure, how is noncompliance, let alone fraud and other criminal acts, possible?

The institutional environment related to earnings management has several significant factors, listed in Table 1.2.

CORPORATE GOVERNANCE

The starting point for analysis is corporate governance, essentially the relationships among the board of directors, management, and investors. The board should be composed primarily of

TABLE 1.2	SIGNIFICANT INSTITUTIONAL-ENVIRONMENTAL FACTORS RELATED TO EARNINGS MANAGEMENT
Corporate governance	The governance structure includes the board of directors, the functions of the committees, the interaction of the board with management, compensation issues, and auditing.
Auditing	The external auditors evaluate appropriate financial accounting and reporting according to generally accepted accounting principles (GAAP). Auditors must have the ability to discover significant discrepancies with GAAP (competence) and willingness to report the discrepancies to the audit committee or other relevant bodies (independence).
Accounting regulation and standard setting	The SEC regulates the equity capital market structure, including the stock exchanges and financial reports of some 17,000 public companies.
Earnings restatements	An earnings restatement is the revision of public financial information that was previously reported. It represents real evidence of past earnings manipulation.
SEC enforcement actions	The SEC's Division of Enforcement investigates possible violations of accounting issues and other violations of securities laws. Accounting enforcement actions often indicate earnings manipulation.
Attorneys	Attorneys often write and review contracts, particularly those that are complex and controversial. Other law firms write legal opinion letters. The auditor can normally approve complex contracts on the basis of attorney opinion letters.
Investment bankers	Investment banks issue new securities and other financial instruments. Financial analysts provide research on equity investments, including earnings forecasts and buy-hold-sell recommendations. Analysts have incentives to recommend buys on investment banking clients, and brokers are encouraged to sell the new issues.
Whistle-blowers	Prosecutors in many cases of fraud and other deceptive practices have depended on whistle-blowers to come forward.

outside and independent directors. In 2001, an average 77 percent of board members were outsiders (Levitt 2002). For example, the 2002 Proxy Statements from General Electric (GE) listed 16 directors, only three of whom were GE executives. Board committees should include an audit committee (required by the stock exchanges since 1999), made up entirely of outside directors capable of evaluating the effectiveness of the audit, and a compensation committee. GE included both, plus a nominating committee and a management development and compensation committee. The audit committee comprised nine independent members, and their duties were explained in the proxy statement.

Important considerations include the members of the board and their relationships to the CEO, the corporation, the board committees, the senior executives, and the structure of their compensation packages. Executive compensation at major corporations is extensive and is reported in the annual proxy statement. The compensation package summarizes the incentive structure of the key executives. Pay should be based on real performance, but this is somewhat a judgment call.

Jack Welch retired as chairman and CEO of GE in 2001. The 2002 GE Proxy Statement reported that Welch received a salary of $3.4 million, a bonus of $12.7 million, and total compensation (including other items) of $16.2 million. In addition, he received retirement-related compensation of $2.6 million. At his retirement, he had a total of 13.7 million exercisable stock options, worth a quarter of a billion dollars. That's compensation for a job well done (according to GE), and the rationale for the compensation is explained in some detail in the proxy statement. Welch made the news in 2002 for additional lavish retirement perks. For some reason, many viewed this compensation as excessive.

The point is not to pick on Jack Welch but to indicate the levels and types of compensation available to executives. There are real incentives to perform well or to at least give the appearance of performing well. In addition, there are the executives of the companies that flopped. Thanks, in part, to Congressional hearings, the faces on the Enron scandal include Chairman Ken Lay, CEO Jeff Skilling, and CFO Andrew Fastow. Then there are Dennis Kozlowski of Tyco and Bernie Ebbers of WorldCom. The standard image is corporate fat cats enriching themselves, while investors lose. Thus, the relationship of executives to the board of directors and how compensation is determined become important.

Levitt (2002) referred to the board of directors at Apple. He was initially asked to be a board member after his retirement as chairman of the SEC. But after Apple CEO Steve Jobs read a Levitt speech on corporate governance, Levitt was "disinvited." Steve Jobs received 20 million stock options in 2000. As Levitt stated (p. 205): "Apple's board did not meet a number of the good governance litmus tests I had highlighted. It did not, for example, have a separate compensation committee (although it does now). ... One member of Apple's audit committee, Jerome York, is the CEO of MicroWarehouse, Inc. ... York's relationship as a major reseller of Apple products meant that he could no longer be considered an independent board member." As summed up by Levitt (p. 206): "So what's the problem? Small, insular boards lack the outside perspective that is necessary in case a company finds itself in trouble."

Business Week (January 13, 2003, p. 78) picked Sanford (Sandy) Weill of Citigroup (Citi) as one of the worst managers of the year for 2002, largely for corporate governance problems. Weill and ATT CEO Michael Armstrong were on each other's board of directors. Citi stock analyst Jack Grubman was asked by Weill to "take another look at ATT"; Grubman did and issued a more favorable opinion. ATT then used Citibank for investment banking business. Citi would later pay $400 million in fines as part of a settlement with regulators. Citi then took $1.5 billion in charges, largely to cover expected contingencies associated with Enron and other investment banking shortcomings.

Corporate governance should improve largely because of increasing regulatory requirements by the SEC, the stock exchanges, and others. The **Sarbanes-Oxley Act (SO)** of 2002 also initiated new corporate governance requirements. SO increases the responsibility of the board's audit committee (which becomes responsible for appointing the auditor, compensation and oversight, and approval of any nonaudit services performed by the auditor). The auditor must report to the audit committee on any critical accounting issues. The act requires the CEO and CFO to certify that the annual and quarterly reports are "fairly presented." Under SO, executives and board members must reimburse any compensation based on accounting and other misconduct. Criminal penalties for white-collar crime are increased under SO. SO also requires the SEC and other regulators to issue new conflict-of-interest rules, including those associated with investment banking and analyst recommendations.

AUDITING

The external auditors are the experts on appropriate financial accounting and reporting according to GAAP. Audit quality reflects the auditors' ability to discover significant discrepancies from GAAPs (competence) and the ability or willingness to report the discrepancies to the audit committee or other relevant bodies (independence). According to the SEC, the audit firm works for the interests of the public, not the client. In a Supreme Court decision (*U.S. v. Arthur Young,* 1984), it was stated that the auditor's "ultimate allegiance" is to "a corporation's creditors and stockholders, as well as to the investing public." Of course, it's the client that pays the fees.

The Big Four (KPMG, PricewaterhouseCoopers, Ernst & Young, and Deloitte & Touche—with Arthur Andersen notably absent, unable to survive Enron) are the major accounting firms and audit most large corporations. They have the competence to conduct thorough audits (with an occasional misstep). A major question has been independence, a particular concern when much of their revenue comes from nonaudit services provided to audit clients. The auditors will argue that this is not a problem for a couple of reasons. There is a separation of duties between auditors and tax and consulting services experts. The audit partners in charge know the credibility of the audit firm must be maintained and have substantial power to make corporations toe the line. The companies can fire the auditors, but this results in an 8-K filing to the SEC, a major blemish on the corporation's own credibility if this is due to disagreements with the auditor. In addition, the revenue generated from any single client is a miniscule percentage of the audit firm's overall revenue, and retaining a single client is just not a reasonable incentive for violating independence standards.

Unfortunately, there have been violations of independence standards. Levitt (2002, pp. 124–125) stressed the importance of an earlier SEC investigation of Coopers & Lybrand to document real independence abuse. The SEC investigated Coopers & Lybrand with regard to its ownership of stock in companies it audited—an independence violation. Coopers & Lybrand then merged with Price Waterhouse to form PricewaterhouseCoopers (PwC), which complicated the investigation. Ultimately, the SEC uncovered some 8,000 violations (many of which were trivial) involving about half the PwC partners.

The SEC and other outsiders have been concerned with the nonaudit fees charged to audit clients. According to Levitt (2002, p. 116), audit fees, which represented 70 percent of audit firms' revenues in 1976, dropped to 31 percent in 1998. Particularly since the late 1970s, corporations have spent more time on auditor procurement, with more emphasis on low cost. The financial audit was viewed more as a commodity than a high-quality, product-differentiated service. Consequently, audit firms have focused on nonaudit services as a means of maintaining and increasing revenues. The perception is lack of independence. As pointed out by FASB member John (Neil) Foster (2002), the Big Four firms have become "advocates for their clients," attempting to get the resolutions the clients want rather than the most appropriate answer.

GE's 2002 proxy statement shows that KPMG charged $23.5 million for the audit, $2.1 million for financial information systems, $17.5 million for tax, $13.8 million for "non-financial statement audit services," and $3.7 million for other services. Thus, only 38.8 percent of total fees came from the audit. However, most of the other fees would be considered common services performed by an accounting firm. The recent corporate collapse of Enron again raised the issue of auditor independence. Enron paid Arthur Andersen $25 million for audit services and $27 million for nonaudit services. Critics claim a lack of auditor independence as a major factor.

The Sarbanes-Oxley Act of 2002 substantially increased audit-related regulations. The act established the Public Company Accounting Oversight Board (PCAOB), which has broad regulation powers, including the establishment, adoption, and modification of audit-related standards. The PCAOB has five members: four were selected in late 2002, and William McDonough (former President of the New York Federal Reserve Bank) was nominated as chair in April 2003. Fees charged to registered public companies and auditors will fund the PCAOB. The act increases the responsibilities of management for internal control, expands the role of the audit committee, requires auditor and audit committee independence, and has additional financial disclosure requirements. The specific SEC regulations required to implement the act and the actual functions of the PCAOB were finalized in April 2003.

WHAT IF THE AUDITOR FINDS FRAUD?

Auditors usually do a pretty good job of discovering material accounting misstatements, detecting fraud, and uncovering other white-collar criminal acts. In most cases, the executives and board agree with the auditor and make appropriate changes and decisions about the perpetrators and when to contact appropriate regulators. But not always. Executives and board members may be in on the deceptions and/or criminal acts. What then? When that's the case, it's not clear that the auditors can come out "winners," no matter what they do.

When auditors discover a potential problem, generally a detailed analysis goes to the managing partner in charge of the audit. For highly technical issues, involving the technical staff at the headquarters is required. A resolution usually is sought with key corporate executives. If the matter is not resolved at this level, the auditor may take it to the audit committee of the board.

According to Statement on Auditing Standards (SAS) No. 99 (2002): "The disclosure of possible fraud to parties other than the client's senior management and its audit committee ordinarily is not part of the auditor's responsibility and ordinarily would be precluded by the auditor's ethical or legal obligations of confidentiality unless the matter is reflected in the auditor's report" (paragraph 82). There are exceptions for some legal or regulatory requirements, such as a response to a subpoena.

If no resolution is possible at this level, then what? The auditor can: (1) back down, perhaps conceding the issue is "immaterial," (2) resign from the audit, and/or (3) notify the SEC and other regulators. Notifying regulators, unless specifically required by regulation, is not an option, according to SAS No. 99. On the other hand, the company's board can fire the audit firm (see Case 1 on SAS No. 99 issues).

Under current rules, resignation is the obvious answer, but that doesn't mean the auditor is off the hook. Presumably, the SEC will investigate the circumstances of the resignation (based on the required 8-K filing), but that's up to the SEC. With an ongoing investigation, the audit firm can point the SEC in the right direction. The auditor has lost a client, but that doesn't necessarily mean that's the end of the story. If fraud and criminal acts are found, corporate executives may be fired and prosecuted. The stock price will almost certainly drop substantially, and if the problems are severe, bankruptcy is a possibility. Investor and other lawsuits likely will include the auditors (they have "deep pockets"), in addition to the corporation and its former executives. That's a reward for acting responsibly. Obviously, there are incentives to make different decisions.

Waste Management had a long history of improper accounting practices. These were well known by auditor Arthur Andersen (AA) by the mid-1990s. AA summarized these problem areas and annually presented a summary with "proposed adjusting journal entries" to correct these issues. When the problems were not corrected, AA still issued unqualified opinions, apparently considering these problems as immaterial. In 1999, Waste Management issued restatements for years 1992 through 1999. Regulators and shareholders sued both Waste Management and AA. AA paid a $7 million settlement to the SEC, then the largest SEC penalty against a major accounting firm (General Accounting Office or GAO 2002, pp. 214–224).

Orbital Sciences, a space technology company (yes, this is rocket science) trading on the New York Stock Exchange, had accounting issues with auditor KPMG on capitalized costs and revenue recognition. KPMG disagreed with the company in 1999 on the treatment of these accounting issues. Although it had objected in earlier years (documented by confidential letters to the company's board and SEC), KPMG had signed off and issued unqualified opinions. Orbital fired KPMG in 1999 and hired PricewaterhouseCoopers (PwC). PwC required the company to restate the financial statements for 1997 through 1999. Investors' lawsuits in 1999 were filed against both Orbital and KPMG (GAO 2002, pp. 171–175.)

Rite Aid is a large retail drugstore chain. The company had numerous accounting issues associated with inventory and cost of goods sold, adjustments to property, plant and equipment, leases, acquisition accounting, and various operating expenses. KPMG was the auditor in 1998 and 1999. KPMG met with the audit committee in June 1999 and described material weaknesses in internal controls. Without resolution of these issues, KPMG resigned later in 1999. Deloitte & Touche replaced KPMG, and Rite Aid subsequently restated the financial reports for 1997 through 2000. A securities class-action lawsuit against Rite Aid, its officers and directors, and KPMG followed.

Adelphia Communications kept billions of dollars of liabilities off the balance sheet by having them recorded by nonconsolidated affiliates. Auditor Deloitte & Touche (DT) discovered these by 1999 and recommended that they be included on the firm's balance sheet. When management disagreed, DT backed off. In 2002, DT advised Adelphia that it was suspending the audit for fiscal year 2001 primarily because of the off-balance-sheet liabilities (presumably now material). Adelphia then fired DT and hired PricewaterhouseCooper. Lawsuits followed, accusing Adelphia of financial fraud.

ACCOUNTING REGULATION AND STANDARD SETTING

It's an oversimplification to view the regulators as the good guys. They regulate what they think is important and within their budgets. However, if Arthur Levitt (2002) had been able to put into place the regulatory structure he sought, many of the excesses might have been avoided or at least discovered earlier. Significant issues include full funding of the SEC and the political process involved in standard setting and other regulatory issues.

The SEC is responsible for regulating the entire equity capital market structure. That includes the stock exchanges and the accounting records of some 17,000 public companies. The SEC lacks the funding to conduct a thorough review of all the filings. Critics say the SEC overregulates, and, indeed, many of the enforcement actions of the SEC seem inconsequential. On the other hand, Enron was not on the SEC's radar before the collapse. Opinions differ on the role of the SEC and its relative competence, but increased funding has been recommended.

The setting of accounting standards is a political process. On the surface, it would seem that the FASB would be concerned only with attempting to structure standards based on its definition of economic reality. Thus, new issues would be added to the agenda as the role of business technology and business contracting expands. But the story is more complicated. There is no single view of what economic reality means, and many participants in the process have other agendas. And it's a moving target, both because of the dynamic economic and business environment and because board members change.

Standard setting lags corporate developments. That is, it is reactive and not proactive. Business innovations and new financial instruments are introduced; then a new accounting problem is recognized and investigated by the FASB. Typically, agenda items are current issues on which the literature is unclear and subject to interpretation. Due process means that the interval from the introduction of a new agenda item to a new standard typically is a long time, usually three to five years (Foster 2002). The greater the controversy, the longer the process and the greater the need for compromise. The FASB has looked at SPEs for the last twenty years, without much success. Part of earnings management can be considered political gamesmanship by corporate executives: how to best influence new standards or maintain the existing standards.

One of the most contentious recent issues involved stock options, also a major concern for executive incentives and corporate governance. Generally, stock options are ignored in the financial statements and essentially treated as "costless" compensation (with a tax benefit as an additional bonus). In 1993, the FASB proposed that stock options should be expensed, on the basis of a calculated fair value. Corporate America went ballistic and geared up for crush-our-regulator-foes mode. Computer-related and other high-tech companies were particularly incensed, since options were the preferred form of compensation. Lobbying of Congress (note that campaign contributions make access easy) and the SEC was extensive. Senator Joe Lieberman led the fight and was willing to threaten to limit future FASB authority (Levitt 2002). There was even some talk of eliminating the FASB. The FASB backed down, and in its final form the stock option standard required only footnote disclosure of existing options and a *pro forma* calculation of net income, as if options were expensed. (Reporting options as an expense is allowed but not widespread.) In March 2003, the FASB put stock options back on its agenda, with a new pronouncement expected in 2004. The FASB again claims that expensing options will become GAAP.

U.S. GAAP is generally considered rules-based, whereas European and international standards are considered principles-based (that is, based more on general concepts than on specific rules). For example, Foster (2002) referred to SFAS No. 13 on lease accounting as "the poster child of rules-based accounting." Whether a lease is categorized as an operating lease depends exclusively on rigid numerical or yes-no rules. However, most U.S. standards are relatively flexible and state specific accounting and reporting objectives (one definition of principles). In addition, U.S. standard-setting relies on the seven concept statements that represent the FASB's Conceptual Framework. Foster (2002) pointed out that airlines record almost all airplanes as operating leases under SFAS No. 13 but did the same under the previous "principles-based" standard. It appears that many CFOs have the perspective that unless a particular practice is specifically prohibited, then it's doable, a practice called "gaming the system." According to Don Warren, Director of the Center for Continuous Auditing at Texas A&M University, "Analysts drive entities to keep obligations off the balance sheet. Companies are penalized for reflecting a debt/equity ratio unacceptable to Wall Street" (personal communication).

EARNINGS (FINANCIAL STATEMENT) RESTATEMENTS

Financial restatements often present crucial evidence of earnings manipulation. An **earnings restatement** is the revision of public financial information that was previously reported. Only three companies restated earnings in 1981, in comparison with more than 200 in 2002. According to Levitt (2000, p. 117): "The restatements came at a tremendous cost to investors, whose shares would lose tens of billions of dollars in market value."

A GAO report on restatements (GAO 2002) examined restatements from 1997 through 2002 and discovered 919 restatements from 845 companies on the New York Stock Exchange, NASDAQ, and the American Stock Exchange, with the annual breakdown (p. 16) as shown in Table 1.3.

Over this five-year period, almost 10 percent of listed companies restated earnings or other financial statement information. The problem has been growing, with the restatement rate rising from less than 1 percent in 1997 to almost 3 percent in 2002. The GAO report also noted that the number of restatements for larger companies has been rising. Five of the thirty firms comprising the Dow Jones Industrial average (AOL, McDonald's, Alcoa, Hewlett-Packard, and Du Pont) restated, as did 72 S&P 500 firms (14.4 percent).

The issuance of an earnings restatement is a potential red flag for analyzing earnings management and should be part of the qualitative analysis process (see Chapter 3). The GAO research staff did a computer search with Lexis-Nexis of the word *restatement* and similar terminology and reviewed various research articles on this issue. The resulting list of restatements is presented by year (GAO 2002, Appendix III, pp. 88–112).

TABLE 1.3	THE NUMBER OF COMPANIES ISSUING EARNINGS RESTATEMENTS DURING 1997 THROUGH 2002							
	1997	1998	1999	2000	2001	2002 (6 months)	Total no.	Total %
DJ*	1	1	0	0	2	1	5	16.7
S&P 500	4	4	19	12	25	16	80	16.0
Total	92	102	174	201	225	125	919	10.0

*Firms in the Dow Jones Industrial Average (30 firms).

The GAO report partitioned restatements into nine categories. The categories and the percentages of restatements in each (GAO 2002, pp. 21–22) are shown in Table 1.4.

These all are earnings management items of concern and suggest areas that should attract analysts' attention. Revenue recognition problems are the number one restatement issue by far, at almost 40 percent, and this category represents the most significant area of earnings management concerns, followed by cost or expense issues (more on these in Chapters 5 and 6).

SEC ENFORCEMENT ACTIONS

The SEC's Division of Enforcement investigates possible violations of accounting issues and other violations of securities laws. The division also recommends SEC action when appropriate, either in a federal court or before an administrative law judge, and negotiates settlements. The description of the division on the SEC Web site (www.sec.gov) includes the following:

TABLE 1.4	CATEGORIES OF EARNINGS RESTATEMENTS AND PERCENTAGES ISSUED	
Category	Description	Percentage
Revenue	Improper revenue accounting: improperly recognized, questionable revenues, other misreported revenues	37.9
Cost or expense	Improper cost accounting: improperly capitalized expenses and other misreported costs, includes improper treatment of tax liabilities, income tax reserves, and other tax items	15.7
Restructuring, assets or inventory	Asset impairment, errors related to investments, timing of asset write-downs, goodwill, restructuring activity and inventory valuation, and inventory quantity issues	8.9
Acquisition or merger	Wrong accounting method used or losses or gains were understated or overstated	5.9
Securities-related	Improper accounting for derivatives, warrants, stock option, and other convertible securities	5.4
Reclassification	Improperly classified accounts, such as debt payments classified as investments	5.1
In-process research and development	Improper accounting to value in-process research and development at time of acquisition	3.6
Related-party transactions	Inadequate disclosure or improper accounting involving transactions or relationships with related parties, including SPEs	3.0
Other	Any other restatement, including inadequate loan-loss reserves, delinquent loans, loan write-offs, or accounting irregularities left unspecified	14.1

The Division of Enforcement was created in August 1972 to consolidate enforcement activities that previously had been handled by the various operating divisions at the Commission's headquarters in Washington. The Commission's enforcement staff conducts investigations into possible violations of the federal securities laws, and prosecutes the Commission's civil suits in the federal courts as well as its administrative proceedings.

The division has four categories of enforcement actions (see www.sec.gov), as shown in Table 1.5. These enforcement actions are listed chronologically on the SEC Web page. The SEC's search engine can be used to find pending actions. About 20 percent of the SEC's enforcements in 2001 were accounting-related (GAO 2002, p. 44). As with earnings restatements, enforcement actions are a red flag in earnings management analysis. A search on Enron, for example, identified 345 matches.

ATTORNEYS

Attorneys play a crucial role in writing and reviewing contracts, particularly those that are complex and controversial. Many of Enron's complicated structured-finance deals using SPEs were written or reviewed by Houston law firms Vinson & Elkins and Andrews & Kurth. These deals were lucrative to attorneys, accountants, and bankers, all charging substantial fees. Enron's third quarter 2001 10-K indicated over $2 billion in off-balance-sheet debt associated with these structured-finance deals.

Attorneys might create an SPE and then build a series of corporate transactions using the SPE and other corporate entities. Other law firms would write legal opinion letters. After a "due diligence investigation" and a review by a special partner committee, the opinion letter is signed by the law firm, indicating legal compliance. The auditor can normally approve the transaction with a couple of opinion letters, based on SFAS No. 140 (France 2002). Both Vinson & Elkins and Kirkland & Ellis have been subject to shareholder class action suits associated with the use of SPEs by Enron. The Sarbanes-Oxley Act of 2002 added additional regulations on the lawyers, including possible reporting of wrongdoings to top management, the board of directors, or the SEC (subject to new SEC regulations).

Attorneys cite attorney-client privilege (forbidding attorneys from disclosing clients' secrets, including illegal acts) to avoid disclosing corporate wrongdoings. But rules vary

TABLE 1.5	SEC ENFORCEMENT ACTIONS FOR VIOLATIONS OF FEDERAL SECURITIES LAWS
Federal court actions	Litigation releases concerning civil lawsuits brought by the SEC in federal court
Administrative proceedings	Orders and related materials released by the SEC when administrative proceedings are instituted and/or settled
ALJ initial decisions and orders	Opinions issued by Administrative Law Judges (ALJs) in contested administrative proceedings
SEC opinions	Opinions issued by the SEC on appeal of initial decisions or disciplinary decisions issued by self-regulatory organizations (e.g., NYSE or NASD)

by state, and four states (Florida, New Jersey, Virginia, and Wisconsin) require lawyers to turn in clients when fraud is discovered. By comparison, nine states forbid lawyers from whistle-blowing, whereas the remaining thirty-seven allow attorneys to report wrongdoings but do not require it. As stated by France (2003, p. 54):

> The SEC's proposed change will make lawyers think twice before blessing dubious tax shelters or trading strategies. And despite the ABA's [American Bar Association] hysteria, it won't subvert the legal system by making businesspeople too frightened to confide in their attorneys. The fact is, execs can't draft legal documents. They have no choice but to talk to lawyers.

INVESTMENT BANKERS

Investment banking is a small part of the earnings management story but a major component of the corporate greed story. Investment banks are active in issuing new equity and debt securities, as well as assisting with mergers and acquisitions, divestitures, spin-offs, joint ventures, derivative instruments, SPEs, and so on. The bankers have incentives to develop new financial instruments that have unique characteristics sellable to corporations. These are major revenue-producing items for the bankers. Their incentives are to get as much of the business as possible at a premium price and to keep the corporate clientele happy. And many of these products have earnings management issues (more on that in future chapters).

Stockbrokers and equity financial analysts also are part of the investment banking industry. Financial analysts provide research on equity investments, including quarterly and long-term earnings forecasts and buy-hold-sell recommendations. Prior to 1975, brokers sold securities on a fixed commission, and broker commissions were the largest revenue source to investment bankers. The lucrative fixed-commission system also funded financial analyst research. Without fixed commissions, investment bankers turned increasingly to the securities deals already mentioned and to very large investors such as pension plans and mutual funds. Equity financial analysis conducted by the large investment banks lacked funding and, according to critics, independence when evaluating investment banking clients.

Although a complete separation is supposed to exist between investment banking (that is, the securities deals) and brokers and analysts, the incentives are for analysts to recommend buys on investment banking clients (not necessarily on the basis of corporate fundamentals) and for brokers to sell the new issues. Eliot Spitzer, the New York attorney general, sued investment banker Merrill Lynch for this type of behavior, and evidence indicated that some analysts were recommending buys on stocks they disparaged privately. In mid-2002, Merrill Lynch paid a $100 million fine and watched its stock price plummet after the announcement. Similar investigations of other investment banks followed. In December 2002, ten investment banks agreed to pay a combined fine of $1.4 billion for similar activities.

Companies pay particular attention to analysts' quarterly earnings forecasts, and evidence exists (see Appendix 2) that they attempt to meet or beat these forecasts (and seldom just miss the forecasts). This has been partly driven by bonuses and stock options, because share price (which drives the value of the options) can continually increase if analysts' expectations are met. The problem is the potential for earnings management specifically designed to meet these forecasts. Meeting forecasts suggests high-quality earnings persistence, but the existence of earnings management suggests that the term *high quality* may be suspect.

WHISTLE-BLOWERS

At the end of 2002, *Time* named the whistle-blowers as the persons of the year. These included Sherron Watkins of Enron, Coleen Rowley of the FBI, and Cynthia Cooper of WorldCom. Thus, Watkins and Cooper were important players in the two biggest scandals of 2001–2002.

Cooper was Vice President of Auditing at WorldCom and uncovered some $3.8 billion of operating expenses that were capitalized (the actual amount proved to be close to $10 billion). Her heroism was to ignore CFO Scott Sullivan and external auditor Arthur Andersen and report her findings to the audit committee. Sullivan was fired shortly after that and later charged with securities fraud.

Enron Vice President Sherron Watkins worked directly for CFO Andrew Fastow. She found unusual arrangements associated with structured-finance deals. She wrote up her finding to Chairman Kenneth Lay and recommended to Lay that independent attorneys review the partnerships. The company restated earnings for the third quarter of 2001 and declared bankruptcy in December 2001.

The role of the whistle-blower is ambiguous, particularly relative to individual incentives, timing, and appropriate actions. However, investigators have depended on them to crack many cases of fraud and to find the "smoking gun." The Sarbanes-Oxley Act of 2002 makes federal regulations more whistle-blower-friendly.

A SUMMARY OF EARNINGS MANAGEMENT INCENTIVES

In summary, this is the environment facing the investor and financial analyst attempting to determine the financial and economic reality of major corporations. There are a multitude of complex and interrelated incentives for corporations to "play with the numbers." Therefore, a major component of analysis is to see through potential earnings management and attempt to determine more realistic values. Table 1.6 summarizes conditions that promote earnings management.

QUESTIONS

1. Earnings management is a major issue in evaluations of financial accounting. Why?
2. What is the difference between earnings management and earnings manipulation?
3. Are cookie jar reserves and income smoothing related? Explain.
4. What is the relationship between corporate greed and opportunistic behavior?
5. Do earnings restatements always indicate earnings manipulation? Explain.

TABLE 1.6	CONDITIONS THAT PROMOTE EARNINGS MANAGEMENT

Condition	Description
Strong CEO with substantial perks	A strong CEO, with only limited control from the board of directors and others, has incentives to favor his or her own interests, often to the long-term detriment of the company.
Board of directors made up of insiders	Lack of independence means little control over the performance of top executives and incentives to promote managers' interests.
"Interlocking directors"	Directors that are friends of the CEO and often "trade" board seats; suppliers and major customers on the board; lack of independence and incentives to promote the interests of the CEO.
Poor board committee structure	Board committees are nonexistent or poorly structured; audit committee made up of nonindependent members without specific knowledge of accounting issues; executive compensation committee also made up of insiders.
Weak audit linkages	Both internal and external auditors report directly to the CFO, and the external auditors are chosen without formal procurement practices; nonaudit services by the external auditors are substantial and not subject to audit committee oversight.
Executive compensation extensive without being tied directly to performance	Lack of executive compensation information in the annual proxy statement or disclosures indicates that compensation is not tied to performance.
"Insider" relationships with investment banks	Recent litigation indicates that investment banking relationships contributed to an earnings management environment, including "strong buy" recommendations for banking customers, irrespective of the investment fundamentals.

CASES

Case 1: Audit Regulations

Statements on Auditing Standards (SASs) are issued by the Auditing Standards Board (ASB), a committee of the American Institute of Certified Public Accountants (AICPA). Thus, audit standards represent self-regulation by the industry. SAS No. 99 on auditor responsibilities for fraud precludes auditors from reporting evidence of fraud to the SEC or other regulators in most cases. The standard cites ethical considerations associated with confidentiality.

    a. Give the justification for supporting the ASB position on reporting fraud to regulators.

    b. Given the potential for lawsuits, why is it in the best interests of auditors to be required to disclose potential fraud to the SEC and other regulators?

   c. Is it in the best interests of investors for auditors to report suspected fraud to the SEC? Explain.

   d. Should all future auditing standards be issued by the Public Company Auditing Standards Board (PCABO), the new regulatory board established by the Sarbanes-Oxley Act of 2002? Explain.

Case 2: Serial Earnings Restaters

Given in Table 1.7 are the eight S&P 500 companies that restated earnings more than once in the past five years.

   a. To what extent do restatements affect the perception of an environment of earnings manipulation by these firms?

   b. Do the categories of restatements suggest that these firms are similar in their attitudes on financial reporting or that each firm should be evaluated separately? Explain.

   c. Does the fact that these firms restated more than once influence your evaluation relative to firms that restated only once during this period? Explain.

TABLE 1.7 — COMPANIES ISSUING MORE THAN ONE EARNINGS RESTATEMENT IN A 5-YEAR PERIOD

Company	Reason for Restatement					
	1997	1998	1999	2000	2001	2002
Avon				Expenses	Revenue recognition	
Lucent				Revenue recognition		
Northrop Grumman			Restructuring		Revenue recognition	
PNC Financial Service						Loan losses; revenue recognition
Thomas & Betts			Restructuring	Restructuring		
Tyco					Mergers, restructuring	Revenue recognition
Waste Mgt.	Assets		Revenue recognition			
Xerox					Related-party expenses	Revenue recognition

Appendix 1.1: Definitions in the Professional Literature

Considerable information in the professional and academic literature on accounting and finance is related to earnings management. Several definitions exist, but they vary substantially.

Two common definitions of earnings management come from academic accounting. Shipper (1989, p. 92) defines it as "a purposeful intervention in the external financial reporting process, with the intent of obtaining some private gain." The Healy and Wahlen definition (1999, p. 368) is "Earnings management occurs when managers use judgment in financial reporting and in structural transactions to alter financial reports to either mislead some stakeholders about the underlying performance of the company, or to influence contractual outcomes that depend on reported accounting numbers."

In their book *The Financial Numbers Game* (2002, pp. 15–16), academics Mulford and Comisky define earnings management as

> … the active manipulation of earnings toward a predetermined target. That target may be one set by management, a forecast made by analysts, or an amount that is consistent with a smoother, more sustainable earnings stream. Often, although not always, earnings management entails taking steps to reduce and "store" profits during good years for use during slower years. This more limited form of earnings management is known as income smoothing.

Mulford and Comisky (p. 157) also refer to abusive earnings management as "a characterization by the Securities and Exchange Commission to designate earnings management that results in an intentional and material misrepresentation of results."

Philip Livingston of Financial Executives International (FEI), on the FEI Web page, defines earnings management as: "the process of establishing stakeholder expectations and achieving the result through legitimate and/or illegitimate methods."

Fields et al. (2001, p. 256) define accounting choice as "any decision whose primary purpose is to influence (either in form or substance) the outcome of the accounting system in a particular way, including not only financial statements published in accordance with GAAP, but also tax returns and regulatory filings." By this definition, accounting choice is clearly a significant part of earnings management. Inventory methods, when to use operating leases, and the timing of revenue recognition are all accounting choices.

Also important is financial **fraud,** defined by the National Association of Certified Fraud Examiners as "the intentional, deliberate misstatement or omission of material facts, or accounting data, which is misleading." Note that this defined action is well short of being a criminal act but is consistent with earnings manipulation. The Treadway Commission (1987, p. 2) defined fraudulent financial reporting as "intentional or reckless conduct, whether act or omission, that results in materially misleading financial statements."

The definitions generally differ on the basis of whether normal financial decisions are part of the definition or the purpose is entirely to mislead. An advantage of a broader definition is the difficulty of determining the initial purpose of specific accounting and reporting decisions, especially the intent to deceive.

Appendix 1.2: Academics to the Rescue?

Earnings management has been an important topic for academic researchers in accounting and finance. However, their perspective has differed from that of the profession. A key point is whether the academic approach represents a useful perspective in the evaluation of earnings management issues. Most professionals and regulators review earnings management on a case-by-case basis. Many of these cases involve specific criminal investigations and proceedings. With use of this approach, lots of specific information is available. However, academic research has a different perspective. As stated by Dechow and Skinner (2000, p. 236): "First, because academics usually wish to make general statements about earnings management, they often choose to examine large samples of firms, and so tend to use statistical definitions of earnings management that may not be very powerful in identifying earnings management. Second, academics have focused on particular samples and management incentives that (1) are not of a great deal of interest to practitioners, and (2) *ex post*, have not been very fruitful in terms of identifying earnings management behavior."

McNichols (2000) identified 55 earnings management articles published in the academic accounting literature in the 1990s. Publication of this literature started well before 1990 and continues in the 21st century. Thus, there has been no lack of effort to study this issue. McNichols identified three categories of models: (1) aggregate accrual models, (2) specific accrual models, and (3) frequency distribution models.

Aggregate accrual models assume that accounting choice can be captured with use of "discretionary accruals" that are proxied by looking at some definition of total accruals or changes in total accruals. Healy (1985), for example, looked at bonus contracts of executives, which could have upper and lower bounds, and speculated that managers had incentives to lower earnings outside the bounds with use of discretionary accruals. His empirical findings supported these results. At the lower bounds (essentially a zero bonus), Healy suggested the incentives for "big bath" write-offs, since there are no bonuses anyway. Jones (1991) looked at companies seeking import relief from the federal government and used "accrual residuals" from regression analysis to provide evidence that these "accrual residuals" fell in the year the firms were seeking relief (implying income-decreasing discretionary accruals).

Specific accrual studies focused on specific accounting items in specialized industries. Prominent examples included loan loss reserves for banks to meet capital adequacy requirements and claim loss reserves for insurance companies. Thus, a bank struggling to meet the minimum capital requirements has incentives to manipulate reserves until requirements are met.

A particularly interesting area is the frequency distribution approach. The basic rationale is that managers will use earnings management around specific **benchmarks.** The common benchmarks considered in the literature (and in this priority) are (1) around 0, in other words, to make sure the company does not report a loss; (2) last period's earnings; and (3) analysts' forecast expectations. The findings from this perspective support the importance of these benchmarks. Results indicated that companies are likely to report a small net income but seldom record a small net loss; are likely to report income at or slightly above last period but seldom slightly below; and are more likely to meet or exceed analysts' expectations than just miss them. The interpretation from this literature is that earnings management was used to nudge earnings just over these benchmarks.

Healy and Wahlen (1999) also published a literature review, but it had a perspective different from that of McNichols. Here, the three categories of research were (1) capital markets, (2) contracts (called an agency theory perspective in accounting), and (3) regulation. Thus, Healy (1985) used the contracts perspective and Jones (1991) used a regulation perspective. Cross-classifying the two approaches (McNichols vs. Healy and Wahlen) suggests certain "holes" in the literature. For example, no research is cited under either approach based on evaluation of stock options.

Fields et al. (2001) reviewed the accounting choice literature primarily from the 1990s. The types of research reviewed were similar to those of Healy & Wahlen (1999) and were divided into three categories: (1) efficient contracting and agency theory (mainly managerial opportunism), (2) asset pricing and the cost of capital and the related issue of information asymmetries, and (3) externalities (the impact on third parties). Asset pricing included disclosure levels related to the cost of capital. Both Botoson (1997) and Sengupta (1998) found an inverse relationship (increased disclosures relate to a lower cost of capital). One conclusion from these findings is that full disclosure is an important component of efficient contracting.

Investigators in other earnings management-related studies considered segment reporting, describing environmental liabilities and disclosure by foreign firms to U.S. stock markets to stock prices or valuations. Externalities (third parties) include research on taxes and tax rates, industry-specific regulations, and SEC enforcement actions. Results suggested that corporations have multiple incentives for disclosure levels and various types of accounting choices related to these incentives. Fields et al. (2001) indicated a multitude of problems associated with these multiple motivations and choices as well as with various statistical and theoretical limitations.

This brief review suggests that academic research contributes to the analysis of earnings management and offers at least limited insight to financial analysts and other professionals. For example, the benchmark perspective associated with a "frequency distribution" approach suggests that the analyst should be on the lookout for earnings management techniques around the benchmarks cited, such as analysts' forecasts. There is evidence that actual earnings management uses (or abuses) can be predicted on the basis of specific management incentives. These include compensation-based and various contract-based incentives (especially debt covenants). In addition, certain types of earnings management tend to be industry-specific, such as manipulating loan-loss reserves in banking.

CHAPTER 2

Companies in Trouble— A Historical Perspective

The Enron scandal! Earnings manipulation on a vast scale, corporate greed at the top of the organization, charges of fraud and criminal behavior. Investors lost billions in a company that appeared a brilliant success until just before the fall. There's been nothing like it in America's business history. Right? Nope. It seems strangely similar to earlier business debacles in the 1990s, or, for that matter, the 1890s. This chapter takes a historical perspective, comparing the recent problems to those of earlier eras. Reactions to these fiascos included new laws and regulations, and these are described in Appendix 2.1.

CURRENT CORPORATE TROUBLES

Corporate troubles are nothing new. Every time a company is in trouble it is shocking, but business history records dozens of major failures, frauds, and corruption each decade. We'll start with the recent ones and then compare them to earlier decades. Table 2.1 shows some of the recent corporate problems that made the nightly news.

To put a few faces on these scandals, CNNMoney.com came out with a top-ten list of scoundrels in December 2002. These are shown in Table 2.2.

TABLE 2.1		CORPORATE SCANDALS AND PROBLEMS OF THE 21ST CENTURY	
Company	Year	Auditor	Description
Enron	2001	Arthur Andersen	Declared bankruptcy on December 2, 2001, after restating earnings in the third-quarter 10-Q, indicating major problems with SPEs; ongoing investigations by the SEC, Justice Department, and others; executives indicted and class action lawsuits filed
Cisco Systems	2001	PricewaterhouseCoopers	Inventory write-downs of $2.8 billion, based on take-or-pay supply contracts when demand for products didn't materialize
Lucent Technology	2001	PricewaterhouseCoopers	Restructuring charges initially of $1.2 billion but eventually reaching $11.4 billion, while share price dropped from $75 in 1999 to $5 in fall 2001
JDS Uniphase	2001	Ernst & Young	Fiber optics manufacturer with acquisition accounting problems, particularly involving long-lived assets and goodwill; $40 billion write-off of goodwill & long-lived assets required; class action lawsuits filed in 2002
Global Crossing	2002	Arthur Andersen	Overstated revenue and earnings over network capacity swaps and then declared bankruptcy; under investigation by SEC and FBI
WorldCom	2002	Arthur Andersen	Recorded improper expenses of $3.8 billion and then declared bankruptcy; under investigation for accounting fraud and other violations; the amount of improper expenses uncovered approached $10 billion
Tyco	2002	PricewaterhouseCoopers	Conglomerate with questionable practices on accounting for acquisitions and other issues; restated 1999–2001 financials on the basis of merger-related restructurings plus other problems with reserves; CEO and CFO indicted
Qwest	2002	Arthur Andersen	Subject to criminal investigation by Justice Dept. and accounting practice probe by the SEC, associated with "hollow swaps"
Adelphia	2002	Deloitte & Touche	Cable TV operation charged with overstating earnings; former CEO John Rigas charged with looting the company, which went bankrupt
Xerox	2002	KPMG	Restated earnings by $6 billion in pretax earnings (revenues overstated over 5 years) after an SEC investigation and a $10 million fine
Bristol-Myers Squibb	2002	PricewaterhouseCoopers	Restated sales by $2 billion after inflating sales through inventive offers to wholesalers
Merrill Lynch	2002	Deloitte & Touche	Paid a $100 million fine to settle New York charges of hyping stocks analysts knew to be dogs in order to win investment banking business
Citigroup	2002	KPMG	Paid a $240 million fine to settle a predatory lending practice charge made by the Federal Trade Commission

(Continued)

TABLE 2.1			CATEGORIES OF EARNINGS RESTATEMENTS AND PERCENTAGES ISSUED (CONT.)
Company	**Year**	**Auditor**	**Description**
Dynegy, El Paso Corp., and others	2002	Arthur Andersen, PricewaterhouseCoopers and Arthur Andersen, respectively	Investigated for charges similar to those against Enron, related to questionable accounting and energy trading practices; these include sham trades and securities fraud
Imclone	2002	KPMG	Insider trading charges against former CEO for selling stock after FDA rejected a new drug; alleged to have tipped off Martha Stewart and other friends and relatives
AOL-Time Warner	2002	Ernst & Young	Wrote off $54 billion in goodwill from the recent merger, about a third of the company's book value; total loss for the year totaled almost $100 billion, another record!
Honeywell, Halliburton	2002	PricewaterhouseCoopers and Arthur Andersen, respectively	Finally settled asbestos litigation, at losses of $2 billion and $4 billion, respectively; Halliburton also being investigated for booking cost overruns on big construction projects as revenue before approval by customers
Salomon, Smith Barney, Credit Suisse, Goldman Sachs, J.P. Morgan, and others	2002	Various	Ten investment banks settled in December with the New York Attorney General, SEC, and other regulators on charges of deceptive stock analysis and other brokerage-related practices, similar to Merrill Lynch earlier. The total fine was a combined $1.4 billion, plus other sanctions and agreement to correct deceptive practices
HealthSouth	2003	Ernst & Young	Accused of accounting fraud involving $1.4 billion in earnings and $800 million in overstated assets; former CFO and others pleaded guilty to fraud charges

TABLE 2.2		THE TOP TEN SCOUNDRELS OF 2002, ACCORDING TO CNNMONEY.COM
1.	Dennis Kozlowski	Former CEO of Tyco—indicted on 34 felony counts
2.	Andrew Fastow	Former CFO of Enron—indicted
3.	Scott Sullivan	Former CFO of WorldCom—indicted
4.	Bernard Ebbers	Former CEO of WorldCom—resigned
5.	Jack Grubman	Former Salomon Smith Barney telecom analyst—resigned for tainted analysis; settled with New York Attorney General; $15 million fine; the Salomon Smith Barney fine would total $400 million
6.	Samuel Waksal	Former CEO of Imclone—pleaded guilty to securities fraud
7.	Martha Stewart	CEO of Martha Stewart Omnimedia—denied insider trading, later indicted
8.	John Regas	Former CEO of Adelphia—indicted
9.	Henry Blodget	Former Merrill Lynch analyst—Merrill Lynch paid a $100 million fine for conflict of interests
10.	Joe Nacchio	Former CEO of Qwest—sued by New York Attorney General

Although the problems are diverse, a few common characteristics pop out. The first is the obvious corporate greed. Why do this stuff? Presumably, the perpetrators expected to get away with it. They also fit the financial-corporate culture described in Chapter 1. And earnings manipulation is part of (and central to) most of the scandals. Some of them (such as WorldCom) used brazen and unsophisticated approaches, whereas others (like Enron) used new, sophisticated devices to defraud. Others just had major accounting problems, like AOL-Time Warner's massive write-off of goodwill. Determining how much of this involved criminal acts may take years. More on these fiascos in later chapters.

Two industries were particularly prominent in the scandals: energy and telecommunications. The stodgy energy companies that performed such basic operations as transmitting natural gas became high-tech energy traders using sophisticated derivatives and structured-finance deals. Continued giant profits meant increasing risks and more complex deals. For Enron and others it also meant hiding the losses in controversial (and perhaps fraudulent) off-balance-sheet schemes. The telecommunications industry transformed from monopolist AT&T in the 1970s to a group of dynamic and competitive high-tech giants, all trying to integrate and dominate with new telecommunications methods. Overcapacity led to shady capacity-trading schemes booked as revenues and, despite the deceptive accounting, big losses and bankruptcies.

The various investment bank scandals are included in this discussion because their deceptive practices encouraged earnings management and an environment of fraud. Rather than emphasizing financial and economic reality, analysts and brokers were encouraged to push stocks of companies doing investment-banking business with the parent company, irrespective of the underlying performance potential.

The pace of scandal slowed down but did not disappear. The most recent scandal (early in 2003) involved HealthSouth, which runs outpatient surgical centers. The company and senior executives were charged with accounting fraud related to deals with MedCenterDirect and Source Medical. The stock was downgraded by S&P to CCC, and the NYSE suspended trading following an SEC order to halt trading. CEO and founder Richard Scrushy and several other senior executives were fired, as was auditor Ernst & Young.

SCANDALS IN THE 1990S

Several major events happened in the 1990s that changed the financial world. The collapse of the Soviet Union about 1989 meant the end of the Cold War and a new political-economic system. Friedman (2000) called this new system "globalism," stressing worldwide interrelationships of economies. On the technological front, the major development was the Internet. The technology companies were major factors in the economic boom of the later 1990s and the stock market bubble.

Scandals during this period (Table 2.3) represented both the standard U.S. corporate greed story (e.g., Waste Management, Sunbeam, and Cendant) and unique "globalism-related" problems (Barings, Thailand, Russia, and Long-Term Capital Management). Lots of U.S. and European capital went to developing countries in Asia and elsewhere, driven in part by high interest rates. This represented another type of speculative bubble subject to collapse. On the financial side, considerable interest developed in derivative instruments, including those dealing with foreign currencies and relative interest rates. Hedge funds supposedly were well-hedged and low risk, but increased earnings required speculation. Wrong bets meant catastrophe.

The 1990s became a boom decade after a slow economic start. Many of the seemingly unique cultural characteristics that led to catastrophe started in the dot-com environment of

TABLE 2.3	SCANDALS AND CORPORATE PROBLEMS IN THE 1990s	
Name	**Year**	**Description**
Chrysler	1990	The Big Three couldn't seem to compete with the imports, which were perceived as higher in quality and lower in price. On the verge of bankruptcy, Chrysler had to be bailed out by the federal government. It successfully restructured.
IBM	1991	After FASB issued the other post-employment benefit obligation (OPEB) standard 106 in 1990, IBM made a "big bath" write-off of $3.4 billion to recognize liabilities as part of a restructuring plan; IBM was a big, bureaucratic company in trouble.
Barings Bank	1995	Baring Brothers was one of the early British private banking companies and the oldest existing bank in the world. A single rogue trader, Nick Leeson, who speculated on the Japanese Nikkei 225 stock market and lost $2.2 billion, brought down the company. Too bad no one in charge had a clue what he was doing.
Thailand	1997	The Thai baht collapsed because of over-borrowing and currency speculation against the baht. The result was the bankruptcy of most Thai banks and recession. Like dominoes, South Korea, Malaysia, and Indonesia collapsed.
Waste Management	1997	In 1997, Waste Management had the largest earnings restatement up to that time, $1.4 billion, for the 1992–1997 period, associated with understated expenses (including inflated useful lives and salvage value of fixed assets). Arthur Andersen was the auditor.
Russia	1998	The collapse of the Asian Tigers led to falling commodities prices, including oil prices. Russia depended on oil to finance its massive debt, and the country defaulted on its debt, followed by the massive devaluation of the ruble.
Long-Term Capital	1998	Arbitrage kings of the 1990s, but competition forced them to take increasing risks; they failed when their trading strategies went awry and could have taken down the financial markets without the intervention of the Federal Reserve. It was the collapse of the Russian debt and ruble that caught them on the wrong side of their derivative speculation.
Sunbeam	1998	Al Dunlap was hired in 1996 to turn the company around. Sunbeam was profitable by 1997, due to premature revenue recognition, channel stuffing, bill and hold, ignoring returned merchandise, and other problems. After an internal investigation, Dunlap was fired and Sunbeam wrote-off $1.2 billion in earnings. Arthur Andersen was the auditor.
Cendant	1998	Conglomerate that gobbled up many well-known firms, including Ramada, Coldwell Banker, and Avis. HFS acquired CUC International to form Cendant, but after the acquisition, fraud was discovered in sales and receivables. Cendant lost billions in market value and eventually settled a shareholder suit for $2.8 billion.
New York Stock Exchange	1998–1999	Floor brokers convicted of trading for their own profit. SEC enforcement action against NYSE for failure to supervise floor brokers.
Rite Aid	1999–2000	Retail drugstore chain with a multitude of accounting issues, many related to acquisitions; auditor KPMG resigned in 1999; misstatements related to maintenance costs capitalized; leases recorded as sales; compensation costs capitalized; charges for store closures not expensed; improper inventory and cost of goods sold; SEC investigation and class-action lawsuits filed.

the 1990s. This decade also saw its share of scandal and corporate problems. These made much less overall impact, in part because none of them caused more than a ripple in the booming economy. Rising stock prices typically were seen as the proper response to an incredible economy transformed by technology, not an irrational bubble. Many investors were shocked to learn that the business cycle still existed and that stock prices could actually go down.

At the start of the 1990s, U.S. firms were considered uncompetitive in comparison with Japanese and other foreign giants, especially in "rust belt" manufacturing such as automobiles. Chrysler could survive only with a federal government bailout. But the company restructured and ultimately did well in the 1990s. Like Chrysler, IBM had a vast, slow bureaucracy that adapted to change slowly. IBM had set the standard for personal computers in the early 1980s, only to be pummeled by small, dynamic companies like Compaq and Dell. IBM's business strategy of leasing mainframes and changing technology slowly was not a winner. The company almost collapsed in the early 1990s, in part because it was unable to develop a competitive personal computer.

During the 1980s to 1990s, big, centralized companies with huge bureaucracies were increasingly uncompetitive. Revenues and profits declined as competition increased. Restructuring was virtually nationwide, thanks in part to improved productivity related to the information revolution. Sophisticated technology, including the continued advances in personal computers, played a central part in the vast restructuring.

Corporate problems in the later 1990s were often similar to the current scandals, and corporate greed and earnings management were widespread. Scandals included the traditional fraud stories of Waste Management, Sunbeam, and Cendant. However, derivative instruments also caused fiascos, partly because senior management did not understand what junior-level staff was doing. Countries saw currencies collapse and both corporate and government debt repayment problems. Mexico's peso collapsed in 1995, and Thailand's baht in 1997. After the monetary collapse in Thailand, investors and currency traders bailed out of Asia. Russia would follow in 1998.

Then it got interesting. Long-Term Capital Management bet on Russia and against the U.S. Treasury to the tune of hundreds of billions of dollars, which it figured was a perfect hedge. It bet wrong and lost billions. It took the intervention of the Federal Reserve to avoid a complete collapse of the world's economy. As it turned out, the U.S. economy hardly skipped a beat. The moral of the story was that massive speculation and high risk are long-term losing strategies. Apparently, investors viewed the moral as anything goes—you can't lose given government bailouts.

In addition to scandals involving companies, regulatory problems popped up with investment bankers, brokers, stock exchanges, and others involved in financial transactions. Such was the 1998 case against New York Stock Exchange (NYSE) floor brokers trading for their own profit. Floor brokers handle transactions for institutional traders and are not allowed to trade for their own accounts because of access to customer order-flow information. Nine brokers pleaded guilty and were sentenced to prison. Then in 1999, an SEC enforcement action was filed against the NYSE for failure to supervise the floor brokers adequately (Weiss 2003, pp. 66–67).

EARLIER TWENTIETH-CENTURY SCANDALS AND CORPORATE PROBLEMS

The twentieth century has been considered America's century. The United States became the biggest economic power before World War I and was the only superpower (economically, politically, and militarily) at the end of the century. There were many ups and downs, and history shows that both are important long-term. Needed regulations came out of chaos, not prosperity.

These ninety turbulent years saw immense economic and technological progress in America, but also two world wars, the Cold War (which included two particularly nasty foreign wars), and the Great Depression. The role of the federal government and public policy changed dramatically because of the Depression, including the regulation of securities markets and accounting and reporting by corporations. The current regulatory environment was shaped in this period, from the formation of the Federal Reserve and the Federal Trade Commission before World War I and the formation of the Securities and Exchange Commission (SEC) in reaction to the corporate scandals before and during the Great Depression (Table 2.4). Accounting standards and audit regulations were a direct result of the formation of the SEC and specific corporate scandals (especially that involving McKesson & Robbins).

At the start of the twentieth century, Democrats and progressive Republicans such as Theodore Roosevelt wanted reform. The Food and Drug Act of 1906 was a milestone for sanitary food packaging and effective drugs. The decade following the Panic of 1907 and the recession that followed was one of reform legislation. The Money Trust Investigation of Congress (Pujo Hearings) of 1912–1913 discovered the use of interlocking directorships, trusts, and other means of controlling credit and business. NYSE abuses discovered included price manipulation, speculation, and lending for short sales. The Taft administration brought antitrust suits against U.S. Steel, International Harvester, Standard Oil, and American Tobacco. In 1913, the Clayton Act prohibited interlocking boards of competing companies, the Federal Reserve Act established the Federal Reserve System as the central bank, and the Federal Trade Commission (FTC) Act created the FTC. However, the major securities regulations were the ineffective state Blue Sky Laws (which were unable to regulate interstate commerce).

The Roaring Twenties didn't roar for everyone, but the stock market boomed in the late 1920s, fueled by margin buying. Without effective regulation, stocks were openly rigged. A recession starting in the summer of 1929 eventually led to the crash in October; after that, the market and the economy continued downward for the next four years. The market structure, relying on massive speculation and debt, was a major factor that led to the Great Depression. The poor performance of the Hoover administration, Congressional legislation (such as the infamous Smoot-Hawley Act, which substantially raised tariffs), and monetary policy of the Federal Reserve (which tried to preserve the gold standard) also were significant factors.

The Democratic presidential platform of 1932 promised federal assistance and regulation—a New Deal. Franklin Roosevelt won, and he delivered. The federal government assumed the responsibility for protecting investors against malpractice in the investment market with the Securities Act of 1933. Initially under the FTC, the Securities and Exchange Commission Act of 1934 created the Securities and Exchange Commission (SEC). The market and accounting structure established by the SEC is the basic regulatory framework existing today. The rules are complex, and companies have to file annual and quarterly reports to the SEC soon after the end of the accounting period (see Chapter 3). The SEC delegated both financial accounting standard setting (now under the Financial Accounting Standards Board) and financial auditing (now under the Auditing Standards Boards of the AICPA) to the private sector. However, auditing rules are expected to change because of the Sarbanes-Oxley Act of 2002.

| TABLE 2.4 | CORPORATE PROBLEMS AND SCANDALS OF THE EARLY TWENTIETH CENTURY |

Company	Year	Description
Standard Oil	1911	Rockefeller's Standard Oil became one of the first giant industrial firms and held a monopoly position; sued for antitrust violations and convicted by the Supreme Court; broken up into separate oil companies primarily geographically, most of which were highly successful and are still around.
NYSE	Before 1930	Insider trading was common and not illegal; "preferred list" sales of new securities at discount prices before the public issues were the norm; stock pools existed (syndicates established by investment bankers and brokers to manipulate stock price); before the Great Depression, prices of at least 100 stocks were openly rigged; information was considered a private matter, and this allowed companies to manipulate, misrepresent, and conceal information.
The Crash	1929	By the summer of 1929, the economy was in recession, with industrial production peaking in June. Stock prices continued to new highs and the Great Bull Market continued into September. The first panic occurred on October 24, Black Thursday. Prices continued down: from a peak of 386 the Dow tumbled to 41 in 1933. The market had no credibility with the public. From 1929 to 1932, 11,000 banks failed, gross national product (GNP) declined 10 percent annually, steel production fell to 12 percent of capacity, and unemployment hit 25 percent.
Krueger & Toll	1920s and 1930s	Ivar Krueger refused to disclose financial information. It was discovered that this was a bankrupt company. Interest and dividend payments were paid regularly from the cash receipts of new securities issues. Krueger's suicide followed the financial collapse of his empire in the early 1930s.
Samuel Insull	1920s	Utility pyramid. Insull's holding company acquired utilities with limited equity, only enough to acquire control. It was a pyramid, since there were several layers of acquisition, again with just enough equity to maintain control. Ultimately, only a small amount of equity held the empire together. The debt was paid by the continued dividends from the utilities up to the holding company. When the economy collapsed in 1929, the pyramid collapsed. Insull's was the most infamous utility pyramid, and there was a similar scheme in railroads by the Van Sweringen brothers.
McKesson & Robbins	1937	Massive fraud by the president (Philip Musica), involving bogus receivables and inventory, were missed by the auditor, Price Waterhouse. Audit procedures changed as a result of this case, and audit regulation was considered essential.
Penn Central	1970	Merger in 1968 of New York Central (part of Cornelius Vanderbilt's empire in the mid-nineteenth century) and Pennsylvania Railroad (the "training ground" of Andrew Carnegie)—two of the oldest railroads, but failing. After the merger, dividends continued and the board was well paid, but rising debt and declining cash led to bankruptcy. The bankruptcy was long and difficult, but service continued—eventually by the federal government through Amtrak.
LTV	1970s	One of the original conglomerates from the 1950s, which seemed successful because of accounting gimmicks associated with acquisitions and divestitures. The firm appeared very profitable, but the "magic" profits came from the accounting tricks associated with business combination accounting. Ultimately, new acquisitions became impossible and the company was forced into bankruptcy.
Equity Funding	1972	Massive computer fraud of insurance company. Financial statements for 1964 were fraudulent, followed by coverup using false insurance policies and inserting bogus data into computer system. Finally shut down by SEC in 1972, on the basis of whistle-blower information.

(Continued)

TABLE 2.4		CORPORATE PROBLEMS AND SCANDALS OF THE EARLY 20TH CENTURY (CONT.)
Company	**Year**	**Description**
ZZZZ Best	1980s	ZZZZ Best went from virtually nothing to a giant in the insurance restoration business; records showed tremendous growth. However, most of the actual restoration projects did not exist. It turned out, like McKesson-Robbins, that many executives were crooks. This suggested the importance of background checks on new audit clients as well as confirmation of construction projects.
Lincoln Savings	1980s	Part of the savings and loan scandal of the 1980s; deregulation of this industry and ongoing interest rate problems led to massive fraud and other problems, requiring a federal bailout. Charles Keating was one of many executives convicted and sent to jail.
Drexel & Milken	1980s	Michael Milken discovered that non-investment-grade debt (junk bonds) was not that risky and quite profitable. He created a massive junk bond market that fueled leveraged buyouts and acquisitions. Overspeculation and shady practices forced Drexel into bankruptcy and put Milken in jail.
Johns Manville	1982	Filed for bankruptcy because of litigation about asbestos (used since 1858). Other asbestos manufacturers also would declare bankruptcy. Honeywell and Halliburton settled their asbestos litigation in late 2002 (with losses of $2 billion and $4 billion, respectively).
EMS Governmental Securities	1986	A CPA audit partner was convicted of accepting bribes to falsify financial statements of EMS Governmental Securities, which defrauded Home State Bank in Ohio.
The Crash of '87	1987	Another stock price bubble, which burst on a single day—October 17; not a problem with the economy but with the market—perhaps program trading, perhaps just unjustified speculation.
BCCI Scandal	1988	Criminal corporate structure centered in Abu Dhabi, beginning in the 1970s. Acquired U.S. banks and used American politicians as front men. Criminal behavior included global drug money laundering, bribery, arms trafficking, and tax evasion, not to mention a multitude of financial crimes. Layered corporate structure including shell corporations. U.S. indictments started in 1988, and the firm collapsed in 1991.

The post-World War II/Cold War period (roughly 1945–1989) has been one of economic dominance and continued economic growth and innovation for the United States. The Cold War tensions meant high military spending and a foreign policy focusing on the "Evil Empire" rather than on economic values. The Korean and Vietnam Wars caused additional disruptions. Until the 1970s, the major focus of monetary policy was inflation-avoidance, and recessions were common. Still, it was a good environment for economic growth and corporate profitability. Conglomerate mergers became a major fad beginning in the late 1950s, and major conglomerates like LTV achieved stock prices at substantial premiums to earnings. Accounting manipulation associated with conglomerate acquisitions led to new accounting pronouncements, beginning with Accounting Principles Board Opinions 16 and 17 in 1970.

The 1960s saw the simultaneous Vietnam War and war on poverty, both quite expensive and federal budget busters. Rampant inflation, beginning in the 1970s, caused a host of problems, including high interest rates, "stagflation" (inflation with low economic growth and high unemployment), and relatively poor corporate performance. Adding to the corporate woes was increasing foreign competition. It was feared that the Japanese in particular could build products both better and cheaper, and major industries like auto-mobile manufacturing and steel faced ruin. About this time, it was demonstrated that conglomerates generally didn't work that well except for the manipulative power of business combination accounting, and several bit the dust, including LTV.

Probably the whole post-World War II period was part of the Information Revolution (perhaps it started with Gutenberg), but rapid advances were made in the 1980s. The personal computer was introduced in the mid-1970s, and the power of computers and potential of software became apparent in the 1980s. Key parts of the Internet also were developing nicely but wouldn't be commercially usable until the mid-1990s. American industry was recovering and restructuring. Inflation was harnessed in the 1980s. The tax cuts of the Reagan Revolution probably represented a minor, although important ingredient of future corporate success.

Company bankruptcies continued throughout this period. "Old industries" such as railroads were particularly susceptible. The biggest railroad of the time, Penn Central, declared bankruptcy in 1970. Corporate scandals continued throughout the post-World War II period. Mainly, these involved basic fraud and abuse. The fraud scandals were particularly troublesome to the accounting community, because they had some responsibility for detecting fraud. Corporate bankruptcy following fraud often brought lawsuits against the auditors, at least in part because of their "deep pockets."

There were a number of corporate fraud cases. Among the most infamous were those involving Equity Funding, National Student Marketing, Continental Vending, EMS Governmental Securities, ZZZZ Best, Silverado S&L, and Lincoln Savings. Congressional hearings followed many of these cases, including those conducted by Congressman John Moss and Senator Lee Metcalf in the 1970s and Congressmen John Dingell and Jack Brooks in the 1980s. Following the Moss & Metcalf hearings, an attempt at federal regulation of auditors was attempted but failed. The legislation would have to wait for Enron and the Sarbanes-Oxley Act of 2002. However, partly as a response to some of the audit failures, auditing standards improved over the years. To what extent the improvements helped investors is a debatable point.

THE FIRST HUNDRED YEARS

The business history of the United States from the Revolution to the start of the twentieth century had several distinct periods and important elements related to current business practices. The first was the establishment of the rule of law and a reasonably powerful federal government. The Constitution of 1787 gave the United States a democratic political structure and virtually no business regulation beyond the common law traditions adapted from Britain. Next was the growth of an agricultural and mercantile system and the related continuing expansion of the United States to the Pacific Ocean.

Manufacturing and industry started in New England with mechanization of the textile industry, beginning at the turn of the 19th century. Transportation with canals and then railroads gave the country its first major corporations and related commercial stock market. Innovation and entrepreneurship continued throughout the century; Eli Whitney introduced the cotton gin and the use of interchangeable parts for gun manufacturing, and Thomas Edison introduced inventions such as electric power and the light bulb.

Really big industrial business started with the economic boom of the Civil War and ruthless entrepreneurs like John D. Rockefeller, famous for his relentless pursuit of monopoly power. The lack of government regulation saw corruption on a vast scale (Table 2.5) and little regard for individual rights to health, safety, or even much protection of business property. A large percentage of politicians were more likely on the take than sponsoring reform legislation. It was a century of immense success, but at a price of vast corruption and individual ruin for those not powerful or ruthless enough to succeed.

TABLE 2.5	CORPORATE SCANDALS OCCURRING BEFORE ESTABLISHMENT OF GOVERNMENT REGULATIONS	
Company/Scandal	**Period**	**Description**
Robert Morris	1800	Robert Morris, the Superintendent of Finance late in the Revolutionary War, probably saved the newly independent country from bankruptcy. But land speculation on a vast scale forced him into bankruptcy in the Panic of 1797, and he was in debtors prison in 1800.
Collapse of the Second Bank of the U.S.	1837	For the second time, Congress authorized a central bank in 1817. It functioned reasonably well and kept the otherwise unregulated (actually state-regulated) banking system in check. But farmers detested the "hard money" currency that kept inflation low, and competing banks opposed it also. President Andrew Jackson vetoed its renewal. The result: the Panic of 1837 and no other attempt at a central bank until the Federal Reserve in 1914.
Drew, Gould, and Fisk	1840s to 1890s	Daniel Drew, Jay Gould, and Jim Fisk could be considered the original Robber Barons. They manipulated stocks, caused "bear runs" to collapse stock prices, and cornered markets. They could get control of companies, pilfer them internally, and then sell out at inflated prices. They spent no time in jail, partly from bribing judges and politicians but mainly because there were few laws dealing with corporations and markets that could be broken.
Raiding the Erie	1860	Commodore Vanderbilt, after an illustrious career in shipping, decided late in life to go into railroading and acquired the New York Central. He went after the Erie Railroad, a close competitor then controlled by Jay Gould and Jim Fisk. When Vanderbilt tried to corner the market in Erie stock, Gould & Fisk issued massive amounts of new securities (probably illegally). Vanderbilt ultimately "surrendered" and reached an accommodation with Gould & Fisk. They would loot the railroad, which collapsed in 1873.
Munitions manufacturers	1861	Northern munitions manufacturers sold vast quantities of munitions to the Confederacy before war was declared. In addition to lack of patriotism, this was shortsighted, because the Confederate military or companies paid on credit—which was uncollected. They would fleece the Union military after that.
John D. Rockefeller	1860s and beyond	Rockefeller obtained secret rebates from the competing railroads to transport his refined oil to markets from Cleveland. With the lowest production and transportation costs, Rockefeller forced all competitors to combine with his (for cash or stock) at his rates or face ruin through cut throat competition. Standard Oil became a trust and eventually had a virtual monopoly on the oil industry. Other industries followed Rockefeller's lead. He is viewed today either as one of the great entrepreneurs in American history or as a ruthless robber baron. In any case, he became the richest man in America.

(Continued)

TABLE 2.5	CORPORATE SCANDALS OCCURRING BEFORE ESTABLISHMENT OF GOVERNMENT REGULATIONS (CONT.)	
Company/Scandal	Period	Description
Credit Mobilier	1862 to 1872	The Central Pacific and the Union Pacific were awarded lucrative contracts to build a railroad line that connected all the way to California. Credit Mobilier was contracted to build the line for the Union Pacific. It was actually a front for the Union Pacific promoters, and they enormously overcharged the railroad for construction costs. Congressional investigations in 1872 demonstrated that huge payments in cash and stock to politicians led to federal legislation generous in land grants and government loans (at $16,000 to $48,000 per mile of track).
Cornering gold	1869	Jay Gould and Jim Fisk attempted to corner the gold market; Treasury Secretary George Boutwell released gold from the federal stock, foiling their plans. After that, Gould bribed judges to void contracts he broke.
Boss Tweed	1872	William Tweed ran Tammany Hall, the corrupt Democratic machine that ran much of New York City. Corruption and bribery existed on such a vast scale that Tweed was eventually tried and convicted of bribery and was actually one of the few corrupt politicians to die in jail.
Black Friday	1873	Jay Cooke was a "hero" of Civil War financing, selling a vast amount of Treasury securities to "average Americans." The collapse of Cooke & Co. after railroad speculation led to the Panic of 1873.
Depression	1893	The last great panic of the nineteenth century started with the failure of the Philadelphia & Reading Railroad. Democrats had a small window of opportunity for reform legislation, but reform efforts were short-lived as Republicans regained control.
Bankruptcy of Edison General Electric	1893	Thomas Edition was a cofounder of the original GE, which included his inventions of electric power. Unfortunately, Edison backed DC rather than AC power (which worked better over long distances), and the firm failed. J.P. Morgan reorganized the firm in combination with other competitors, and GE has been around ever since.
Northern Pacific	1890s	The two most powerful financial groups in the nation fought for the Northern Pacific Railroad (and thus domination of transportation in mid-America): J.P. Morgan and James Hill versus Edward Harriman and Standard Oil money. It ended in a draw, and they colluded to dominate railroad rates across the nation. By 1900, virtually all railroads were organized into six trust systems controlled by Morgan and other New York bankers. Teddy Roosevelt established his trust-busting credentials by breaking up the Northern Pacific Trust, which was held up by the Supreme Court—a small victory for the government regulation of monopolies.

The nineteenth century saw the United States overtake Britain as the leading industrial power in the world after 100 years of unrestricted capitalism: inventors and entrepreneurs flourished, from Fulton and Whitney to McCormick, Bell, and Edison, as well as financiers, culminating in the power of J. P. Morgan. Banking (and the related issue of printing paper money) was problematic, and bank corruption and failures contributed to the frequent depressions during the century. The Robber Barons thrived in an unregulated economy— an era of Darwinian brutality. Financial markets developed to provide capital to the large corporations, but with few regulations. Insiders grew rich from price-fixing, stock manipulation, and outright fraud. The "Banking Trust" centered on Morgan and dominated investment banking. Morgan perfected the use of interlocking directorships to maintain monopoly power over most major industries. By 1890, 300 trusts controlled 5,000 companies. Accounting aided insiders, while assistance to outsiders was problematic.

SUMMARY: THE LESSON OF HISTORY

That completes a quick rundown of U.S. business history, focusing on crisis and scandal over the past two centuries. The good news is that current scandals are nothing like the incredible corruption of nineteenth century American business and politics, although the dollar amounts involved are now much larger. The bad news is that opportunism and corruption still function fairly well after decades of increasingly complex business regulation and substantial monitoring. The motivations of individual and institutional greed seem basically the same. If there seem to be more violators, it's probably because there are more laws to be broken, more executives with ambiguous ethical standards, an increasingly complex environment, and more regulators to investigate. Some specific lessons are summarized in Table 2.6.

QUESTIONS

1. Twenty-five companies are involved in the list of "twenty-first century scandals." How many of these companies were involved in fraud? Explain.

2. Dennis Kozlowski, Andres Fastow, and Bernie Ebbers are closely associated with the scandals at Tyco, Enron, and WorldCom, respectively. Are senior executives usually associated with earnings manipulations and fraud? Discuss.

3. Compare the similarities and differences of Waste Management and Sunbeam (scandals of the 1990s) with Enron and WorldCom.

4. Review the scandals of the twentieth century. Do they seem less or more disastrous than Enron and the other twenty-first century scandals?

5. The original Robber Barons were Daniel Drew, Jay Gould, and Jim Fisk. How do they compare with modern Robber Barons?

6. (See Appendix 2.1.) The Sherman Act of 1890 was federal legislation aimed at the perceived major business of the time, monopolies. Other federal laws included the Federal Trade Commission Act of 1914, the Securities Acts of 1933–1934, and the Sarbanes-Oxley Act of 2002. Review the impact of federal regulations on business practices over the past 100-plus years.

CASES

Case 1: Financial Analysis of the 1850s

Figure 2.1 contains the financial statements presented for the Minehill & Schuylkill Haven Railroad from 1850. This was a small Pennsylvania Railroad used to transport coal, mainly to Philadelphia. Stockholders primarily were managers of the railroad and Philadelphia businessmen. This was one of the few annual reports of the railroad (or any railroad) that actually presented all three financial statements that are recognizable today. Can a reasonably thorough financial analysis be conducted on the basis of these financial statements?

TABLE 2.6	LESSONS LEARNED FROM HISTORY OF U.S. BUSINESS VIOLATIONS
It's the incentives, stupid	Corporate actions follow the incentives, particularly compensation, to some extent based on the risk-reward tradeoff.
Irrational exuberance	Scandals seem to be more pronounced after an economic boom, usually associated with speculation and a stock market that seems only to go up.
Corporate culture	A permissive culture can develop in companies, industries, or entire sectors. The 1990s can be described as a period of high-tech, dynamic, sophisticated trading, out-of-control investment banking, accountants and attorneys interested more in accommodating clients than public policy, and lax governance structures.
Regulation follows the business environment	The economy, technology, and business community can change rapidly, and regulations follow with a lag (sometimes a long lag) and often inadequately.
Regulations are not foolproof	Even stringent regulations can be violated, either by blatant manipulation and criminal acts or by skirting the regulations with the help of attorneys, accountants, and investment bankers.
The political environment	The political environment largely determines the extent of reform regulations and stringency of monitoring and review.
Financial, operating, and credit risks	The risk/reward tradeoffs are always present, and some individuals and institutions push these to the limit. Incentive structure is a prominent component in behavior.
The economy is global	Just to make the environment even more complicated are the global economy and global strategies used by big business. Business cultures and ethical boundaries also differ across the world.

a. What is the amount of net income for the company? It's not the $157,153 actually listed as net income. Calculate return on sales, return on equity (include the Depreciation Fund), and return on total assets (use the debit total from Schedule B).

b. How important is the cash statement (Schedule A) for this analysis? Remember that nothing like GAAP existed at the time, and railroads were trying to figure out what an expense was, especially because of the vast infrastructure that existed and that had to be continuously repaired.

c. Notice the substantial payment of dividends (which also were taxed at 5 percent) to investors. This was the common practice during the nineteenth century. Why did the railroad do this, and what are the implications for the continued survival of the railroad?

d. The company struggled with the concept of depreciation. Roadbeds, rolling stock, and other fixed assets were recorded at cost and not depreciated. A depreciation fund was established and worked something like retained earnings. Explain this. Was this a viable solution to the depreciation problem?

e. Stock of $2,500 is listed as a debit on Schedule B. What is stock? Hint: it has nothing to do with equity investments.

Case 2

Is the system fixed? Given the historical perspective, can investors have confidence that the regulatory system is essentially fixed?

a. Assume you're an advocate for the position that the system is indeed fixed. Present your arguments to substantiate the case.

b. Assume the opposite. The system is still broken. Why?

c. Given the arguments on both sides, how does this affect the financial analysis of these firms? What strategic changes in analysis are recommended based on the current regulatory environment?

FIGURE 2.1	FINANCIAL STATEMENTS FOR THE MINEHILL & SCHUYLKILL HAVEN RAILROAD, IN PENNSYLVANIA, FROM 1850 (GIROUX 1998, P. 31)

A. *Statement of the Receipt and Payment of Cash by The Treasurer of the Mine Hill and Schuylkill Haven Rail Road Company, from Jan. 1, to Dec. 31, 1850.*

RECEIPTS		PAYMENTS	
Balance on hand Jan. 1, 1850	$ 18,819.85	Expenses of motive power dep't	$ 37,851.79
Received for new stock issued	80,000.00	Machinery for shop	302.70
for bills receivable taken for tolls	142,292.39	Paid order in favor of Sup't, for disbursements on account	
from Wm. Newell, coll'r,	6,729.85	new road, re-location of old road, and current expenses	52,178.57
for iron rails and c. sold	1,120.87	Iron rails purchased	23,754.87
for bills payable	19,880.00	Engines bought	3,829.99
for dividend and interest	257.89	Bills payable, note discounted	20,000.00
for locomotive engine sold	9,300.00	Dividends and interest	83,033.59
for advance (on account water		State taxes on dividends of 1849	3,600.00
station: returned	100.00	Real estate to straighten road	2,440.00
		Spikes	715.32
		Trucks	500.00
		Note discounted	991.50
		Expenses, damages, and sundry claims paid in Phila.	4,888.01
		Balance of cash on hand, Dec. 31, 1850	44,414.51
	$278,500.85		$278,500.85

E.E.

SAMUEL MASON, Treasurer

B. *Summary Statement of Debits and Credits or Ledger Balances, January 7, 1850.*

DEBITS		CREDITS	
Cost of road and laterals	$742,582.07	Capital Stock	$800,000.00
Cost of engines and trucks	76,335.23	Depreciation Fund	31,332.58
Real estate	8,442.93		
Machinery for shop	2,433.90		831,332.38
Stock	2,500.00	Philadelphia and Reading Rail Road	1,250.00
		R.A. Wilder, for Iron sold	2,761.05
	832,294.13	R.A. Wilder, Superintendent motive	
Cash on hand	44,414.51	power department	2,699.89
Bills receivable	14,756.89	Dividends and Interest	56,412.34
Due by Collector	5,232.35	State Tax	4,600.00
Due by Superintendent	2,218.89	Relief Fund	189.95
Amounts due by sundry persons	1,359.06	Unpaid Tolls	1,030.02
	$900,275.83		$900,275.83

C. *Statement showing the Income of the Company for the year 1850, and the expenditures chargeable thereto.*

RECEIPTS		PAYMENTS	
Amount charged for tolls		On account of motive power department.	
and use of motive power, & c.	$157,095.22	Fuel, repairs and other expenses	$ 39,830.28
Collections from old dues	120.87	On account of wages, materials and other expenses	
Rents of tenements	138.53	in the repair and maintenance of the road	11,806.65
For loan of engines	372.50	Old claim for materials	102.19
		Expenses of office, salaries, & C. in Philadelphia	4,467.18
	157,727.12	Interest allowed upon installments for new stock	1,167.78
Less tolls likely to be lost	574.42	Dividend No. 33, August, 1850, on $7,200,000, 5 p.c.	36,000.00
		Dividend No. 34, January, 1851, on $800,000, 7 p.c.	56,000.00
Net income for the year	$157,152.70	State tax on dividends	4,600.00
		Balance appropriated to the depreciation fund	3,178.62
			$157,152.70

Appendix 2.1: Laws and Regulations, Often Following Fiscal Fiascos

The United States started with the Constitution as a basic framework, and the system of laws and regulations has evolved since then (Table 2.7). Virtually the whole business and political structure had to be developed from scratch, often starting from Colonial counterparts and British precedent. The Colonies had no banks. The post-revolutionary period saw an economy in depression, a weak government structure, a country that was bankrupt, with a substantial war debt, and facing hostile foreign powers. As Treasury Secretary, Alexander Hamilton established a strong monetary and fiscal policy in the early 1790s. A banking system was established and changed radically over the next 200 years. The government established a tariff and tax system that put the government in surplus, at least most of the time. The country was agrarian and mercantile, with little experience in industry. That would change.

Industry came and regulation followed at a substantial lag, in an attempt to maintain a structure of fair practices and appropriate taxes and dealings with customers, suppliers, investors, and creditors. Industry would explode and transform into Big Business with monopoly power and immense political influence. Regulation would eventually follow in an attempt to stop at least the most blatant practices. This started at the state level, which was fought by business successfully. Prompted by the Granger movement around the 1870s, western and Midwestern states passed Granger laws to regulate railroads and other businesses that preyed on farmers.

The turning point was *Munn v. Illinois* in 1876 (the opinion was released in 1877). Munn & Scott owned grain elevators (warehouses) in Chicago and charged monopoly prices through conspiracy with the other elevator owners. They also engaged in other corrupt practices, such as claiming that farmers' grain was spoiled and then buying it cheaply. Illinois' Warehouse Act regulated grain elevators. When the elevator operators ignored the law, they were sued by the state and the case went up to the Supreme Court. Morrison Waite, Chief Justice of the Supreme Court, wrote the opinion that allowed the state to regulate the grain elevators. The crux of the argument was an obscure British common law case that established the public-interest doctrine, subject to state control. In other words, public interest outweighed private property considerations (regulation represented confiscation of private property, impaired contract obligations, and interfered with interstate commerce). With the Warehouse Act sustained, cases involving railroads could be settled. Within states, the railroads could be regulated up to a point. Interstate commerce was still a sticking point, requiring federal regulations.

Federal regulation began with the Interstate Commerce Commission (ICC) Act of 1887, which established the ICC to regulate railroads. The ICC had only limited authority until the Hepburn Act of 1906 gave the ICC authority to regulate rates. The Sherman Antitrust Act of 1890 outlawed conspiracies in restraint of trade but proved of only limited

TABLE 2.7	REGULATION BY GOVERNMENT AND THE PRIVATE SECTOR

Issue	Period	Description
Constitution, new government	1787, 1788–1796	Following victory and the Treaty of Paris in 1783, the country did poorly under the Articles of Confederation. The Constitution established the federal system still in place today. George Washington proved to be a great leader in establishing precedents for a successful federal government. Alexander Hamilton established a tax, banking, and credit system that favored merchants and industry.
Taxation and banking systems	1790 and beyond	Important to the new country was a revenue source to fund government and pay the national debt, most of which was a holdover from the Revolutionary War debt. Customs duties were the primary revenue source, and this would continue until the 16th Amendment of 1913. Hamilton established the First Bank of the United States, which worked as a central bank, and a state banking system essentially was built around it. After 20 years, the charter was not renewed.
Second Bank of the United States	1816–1836	After the fiasco of the War of 1812, the country learned its lesson that a government bank was essential in times of trouble. So the Second Bank was chartered after the trouble was over. It functioned well, except its "hard money" policies angered farmers and its competitive position against the state banks angered them. Andrew Jackson apparently hated all banks and refused to renew the charter in 1836.
Civil War legislation	1861–1865	The Union was financially unprepared for the Civil War. New emergency legislation included issuing government paper money ("greenbacks"), new tax laws that included the first federal income tax, and the creation of the national banking system, regulated by the Treasury Department.
Munn v. Illinois	1876	Munn was a grain elevator operator with monopoly power to set outrageous prices (and also engaged in other corrupt practices). Illinois passed legislation to regulate and set grain-warehousing prices, which was challenged in the courts (part of the Granger laws trying to get farmers relief from railroads and other big business). The Supreme Court, on the basis of the "public interest" argument, upheld the state law. This was the start of the relatively successful regulation of business by both state and federal governments.
Interstate Commerce Commission	1887	The Interstate Commerce Commission Act created the ICC in an attempt to regulate railroads engaged in interstate commerce. It was only modestly successful until the ICC was given authority to regulate railroad rates.
Sherman Antitrust Act	1890	The Sherman Act was the first attempt to regulate monopoly practices of Big Business through federal regulation. The Act outlawed price-setting conspiracies, but it initially proved rather ineffective in court.

(Continued)

TABLE 2.7	REGULATION BY GOVERNMENT AND THE PRIVATE SECTOR (CONT.)

Issue	Period	Description
CPA licensing	1896	The state of New York was the first to license accountants, calling them certified public accountants. Existing auditors were "grandfathered in," but others would be tested for competence.
Clayton Act, 16th Amendment, Federal Reserve Act, Federal Trade Commission Act	1913, 1913, 1914, and 1914, respectively	Following the Congressional (Pujo) hearings of 1913, the federal government passed these key acts to regulate business and banking. The Clayton Act was an antitrust law that attempted to tighten requirements beyond the Sherman Act. The 16th Amendment allowed federal income taxes (essential for financing World War I), after being ruled unconstitutional in the 1890s. The Federal Reserve Act created the Federal Reserve System as a central bank regulating monetary policy and banks, as well as printing paper money. The FTC Act created the FTC, again primarily for antitrust purposes (e.g., price-fixing).
Securities Act and Securities Exchange Commission Act	1933 and 1934	Following Congressional hearings (Pecora Commission), the SEC was established as part of FDR's New Deal. The SEC regulates the securities markets and has authority over financial reporting.
Committee on Accounting Procedure	1938–1959	The CAP was established in the private sector to set financial accounting standards. It published Accounting Research Bulletins that established generally accepted accounting principles, first codified in ARB 43 in 1953.
Committee on Auditing Regulation	1939	The McKesson-Robbins case demonstrated the need for audit regulations. The Committee on Auditing Regulation was established. Its Statement on Auditing Procedure No. 1 required inventory verification, confirmation of receivables, and other procedures found deficient in the McKesson-Robbins case.
Accounting Principles Board	1959–1973	The APB replaced the CAP as the standard-setting body, presumably with an improved structure. It had problems with the SEC and other political difficulties.
Financial Accounting Standards Board	1973	The FASB replaced the APB as the standard-setting body, with a much-improved structure to promote independence, a research staff, and substantial due process (the public is involved). It has had continued political problems with auditors, business, and Congress but is still in business.
Public Oversight Board	1977	Independent private body to oversee SEC company-related auditing, including peer reviews of firms and investigation of wrongdoings by auditors. It voted itself out of existence in 2002.
Foreign Corrupt Practices Act	1977	Forbids payment of bribes in foreign countries to promote business activity. Most other developed countries passed comparable legislation.
Regulation FD	2001	SEC regulation that requires "full disclosure" when companies talk to financial analysts. The company must make earnings announcements (and other disclosures) available to the public at the same time such disclosures are made to analysts. Usually, the companies simulcast the announcement on the Internet.

(Continued)

TABLE 2.7	REGULATION BY GOVERNMENT AND THE PRIVATE SECTOR (CONT.)

Issue	Period	Description
Corporate governance regulations	Since Enron	Minimum corporate governance requirements have expanded since Enron, based on federal laws (Sarbannes-Oxley), SEC regulations, and new stock exchange requirements.
Sarbanes-Oxley Act	2002	Federal legislation after Enron and related Congressional hearings. The Act establishes a new Public Company Accounting Oversight Board (PCAOB), essentially to regulate auditors. New SEC and PCAOB rules to implement the Act's provisions are in process.
Statement on Auditing Standards (SAS) No. 99	2002	The most recent audit standard on fraud requirements during a financial audit, which include identifying risks of fraud and guidance on communicating fraud evidence to management, the board's audit committee, and others.

effectiveness in the courts. However, it did limit some extreme antitrust practices. Teddy Roosevelt would lead the Progressive Movement soon after 1900, and federal regulations began to have more bite, including antitrust prosecutions under the Sherman Act. The Food and Drug Act of 1906 began the federal regulation of food sanitation and required verification of claims on pharmaceutical products.

After the Panic of 1907, the Progressive Movement became more widespread—eventually leading to the election of a Democratic president, Woodrow Wilson. There was a rush of federal legislation in 1913–1914, including the Clayton Act, Federal Trade Commission Act, and the Federal Reserve Act. The Sixteenth Amendment allowed the income tax, just in time for World War I funding, and has continued ever since as the major revenue source of the federal government.

The 1920s reverted to Republican control, and regulation of business and markets was put on hold. The stock market crash of 1929 put an end to the speculative bubble of the late 1920s, but the result (largely due to the inept response of government) was the Great Depression. President Herbert Hoover had no effective solutions and was defeated in 1932 by Franklin Roosevelt, who did. The New Deal included massive new federal programs, including the new Securities and Exchange Commission to regulate the stock markets.

The SEC Acts required companies to prepare registration statements offering stocks, bonds, and other securities to make "full and fair disclosure" of financial data. All information relevant to a "prudent" investor was to be contained in the registration statement. Antifraud and liability sections increased the legal risks to accountants, who now became accountable to the public as well as to the firms they audited. The SEC has the specific authority to regulate financial accounting and reporting for commercial firms. This authority was implicitly delegated to the private sector only after some debate. In 1938, the SEC issued Accounting Series Release (ASR) No. 4, which stated that accounting standards would be issued by the organization with "substantial authoritative support."

In 1938, the Committee on Accounting Procedure (CAP) was given the authority by the American Institute of Accountants (AIA, later the American Institute of Certified Public Accountants) to issue pronouncements. (The CAP was established in 1936 with limited authority.) The CAP issued Accounting Research Bulletins (ARBs), with ARB No. 1 describing goals, procedures, and presumed authority following ASR No. 4.

In twenty years (1938–1959), the CAP issued fifty-one ARBs. In 1953, ARB No. 43 codified the earlier statements. Despite the limitations, today's basic accounting procedures follow these early bulletins. The profession, for several reasons, increasingly criticized the CAP. There was no overall framework of principles, little research effort, and an ad hoc focus on pronouncements. In 1959, the AICPA (which changed its name from AIA in 1957) replaced the CAP with the Accounting Principles Board (APB), also made up of a large part-time committee of accountants. Over fourteen years, the APB issued thirty-one opinions, many still in force, while essentially carrying on the tradition of the CAP.

Unfortunately, the APB had the same weaknesses as the CAP. There was no accepted framework of accounting principles; the board was a committee of the AICPA and was not independent of the accounting profession; no direct research staff was available; and due process was not formalized. In 1971, the AICPA appointed the Wheat Committee, which recommended a framework that was adopted to establish the Financial Accounting Standards Board (FASB). For the first time in forty years, GAAP was established by a committee separate from the AICPA.

A three-body organizational structure was established to claim independence. The Financial Accounting Foundation (FAF) was established as a nonprofit organization to provide financial support and oversight for the FASB and, later, a Government Accounting Standards Board. Financial support was initially provided by five organizations: AICPA, American Accounting Association (AAA), Financial Analysts Federation (FAnF), Financial Executive Institute (FEI), and National Association of Accountants (NAA). Other sponsoring organizations joined later. The FASB is a seven-member board appointed by the FAF. The board members are full-time, well-paid, and appointed for five-year terms, and they can be reappointed for an additional term. The board has a Director of Research and a staff of about forty professionals. The mission of the FASB is "to establish and improve standards of financial accounting and reporting for the guidance and education of the public, including issuers, auditors, and users of financial information" (Facts About FASB, p. 1).

The FASB's Rules of Procedure require extensive due process that allows public observation and comment. After the board agrees to add a topic to its agenda, an advisory task force is appointed under a project manager for each major project. An appointed staff usually prepares a discussion memorandum (DM), which defines the problem, the scope of the project, issues involved, a research analysis, and alternative solutions. The DM is distributed and public hearings are held. The staff analyzes the oral and written comments for the meeting of the board. When the board reaches a conclusion, the staff prepares an exposure draft (ED), which is the proposed standard. The ED includes a discussion of the problem, a proposed solution and effective date, and the rationale for the decision. Five affirmative votes of the board are required to issue the ED, which is publicly exposed and open to public hearings. The staff again analyzes the comments. If major controversy is avoided, a final statement is prepared, usually with modifications to the ED. A super majority of five affirmative votes is required for approval, and the statement becomes GAAP as a Statement of Financial Accounting Standards (SFAS) at an effective date established by the SFAS. Members dissenting from the majority are identified, and their perspective is written up in the document.

The FASB did not solve all the problems of accounting and certainly did not stop fraud and corruption, as demonstrated by the fraud cases mentioned earlier. Complex areas are difficult to deal with—business combinations involving huge multinationals, just to name one. With competing interests and different perspectives, compromise is as good as it gets. New issues keep popping up, as both technology and contracting get more sophisticated. For example, combining the Internet and new derivative instruments creates trillion-dollar markets where global trading can be instantaneous. This is not an area where annual financial reporting works particularly well.

Standard setting is a political process in addition to being one seeking a reasonable approach to identifying economic reality. Business interests want specific accounting outcomes and can buy political influence. That was demonstrated with the FASB's attempt to require expensing of stock options in 1993. Corporate interests, especially in high-tech industries that paid employees mainly in options, opposed this position and lobbied both the SEC and Congress. After considerable pressure, the FASB backed off and required only footnote disclosure to report the change in net income, as if options had been expensed. Under the Sarbanes-Oxley Act, the FASB will be funded by mandatory payments from corporations, rather than from "contributions" from the AICPA, Big Four, and other organizations. The result should be increased independence from the professional accounting and business communities.

Former SEC Chairman Arthur Levitt pushed for new requirements on public disclosure by corporations, which resulted in Regulation Full Disclosure (over the loud objections of the business and investment banking communities). Regulation FD requires that all material information be released to all investors at the same time. The threat from Levitt's perspective was the vast amount of insider information given to "selected" or "favored" analysts. Related to that was the difficulty of prosecuting investors for **insider trading.** Thus, Regulation FD was seen as a strategy to limit Wall Street's cozy relationships with business and corresponding potential for profitable insider trading. As stated by Levitt (2002, p. 101), "In some ways, Regulation FD has reduced the quarterly earnings numbers to a commodity, something that is easy to obtain and available to all."

Congress passed the Sarbanes-Oxley Act in 2002, which increases audit requirements plus additional financial reporting and other requirements. The act established the Public Company Accounting Oversight Board (PCAOB), which will have broad powers to regulate the audit process of public companies. Both public companies (essentially those that are regulated by the SEC) and auditors must register with the board. The registered auditors and companies will pay fees to fund PCAOB, as well as the FASB. Although the board has met and PCAOB has a spiffy Web site (www.pcaob.com), the specific role of the board has not yet been finalized.

Sarbanes-Oxley requires companies to maintain adequate internal controls and report annually on management responsibility for internal controls and their effectiveness. The auditor also must attest to the effectiveness of internal controls annually. The act requires complex rules on auditor independence and audit committee independence and expertise. Certain nonaudit services to audit clients are prohibited or curtailed, such as bookkeeping, financial information services, and internal auditing. Additional disclosures include a thorough discussion of off-balance-sheet arrangements as part of MD&A. Certain "non-GAAP financial measures" (mainly *pro forma* earnings measures, such as income before special charges or earnings before interest, taxes, depreciation, and amortization) are prohibited if misleading.

The scandals of the new century involved big corporations and a corresponding need to regulate corporations from the top; that is, to increase the roles and responsibilities of the board of directors. Increased regulations have been coming from the stock exchanges and the SEC, as well as from the impending implementations of the Sarbanes-Oxley Act. Simultaneously, corporate boards are beefing up their own written charters and making more rigid requirements for director independence and the roles of directors on audit, compensation, and nominating committees. Finally, the Auditing Standards Board issued SAS No. 99, providing new guidance on fraud requirements during a financial audit.

Throughout the whole post-World War II period, corporate fraud and audit failures plagued the accounting industry. Major fraud cases were often followed by Congressional hearings, blue ribbon committees to research the shortcomings, and new regulations. However, auditing regulations stayed in the private sector and appeared to benefit the profession rather than fix fundamental problems with audit failures. This environment continues. However, the PCAOB may issue auditing standards in the future rather than the Auditing Standards Board.

The key question is whether this new framework is adequate for the future. Important elements seem to be in place. Corporate governance rules have been tightened; the SEC has somewhat greater powers; the new PCAOB may be effective; the biggest violators seem to have been "caught"; many corporations are strengthening their procedures to ensure greater compliance; and investment bankers, auditors, and lawyers may have been sufficiently chastised to perform in the public interest. On the other hand, incentives still exist to "game the system," including continued bonus and stock option payments to key executives; auditors still get paid by the corporations, and their incentives remain basically unchanged, as do the incentives of investment bankers and attorneys.

CHAPTER 3

What's in a Financial Report and What to Do with It

Companies are required to submit an annual report, Form 10-K, to the Securities & Exchange Commission (SEC) within ninety days of the end of the fiscal year. A company can also issue a separate annual report that has most of the information in the 10-K plus lots of pretty pictures. The quarterly report, the 10-Q, is submitted within forty-five days of the end of the fiscal quarter. These reports are almost immediately made available to the public over the Internet from the SEC's EDGAR system or from the companies' Web sites. Usually within a few weeks of the end of the quarter, companies issue earnings announcements that often include an income statement and balance sheet. Consequently, this level of information generally is available quickly. Thanks in part to Regulation FD, companies are expected to "simulcast" their earnings announcements and other financial press releases that are presented to analysts and other financial specialists.

The financial statements and the explanatory notes represent the most significant disclosures of these reports and will be the central focus for analyzing earnings management. These financial statements are based on **generally accepted accounting principles** (GAAPs), primarily established by the Financial Accounting Standards Board (FASB). In addition to the financial statements are the Management Discussion and Analysis (MD&A) and additional explanatory materials such as a CEO's letter.

These are primarily used to explain the company's current operations, business strategy, market and business risks, and future expectations.

Corporations also issue **proxy statements** annually, issued before the annual stockholders' meeting. These statements concern issues to be voted on by the stockholders and are useful to evaluate corporate governance. Stockholders vote on directors, and considerable information is given on each director or prospective director. Proxy statements also include information on board committees, which must include audit committees and compensation committees. Important information is presented on the audit, including auditor, audit cost, and nonaudit fees. Executive compensation is presented in some detail, which is particularly important to understand management performance incentives. As more disclosures on corporate governance are required, the proxy statement becomes increasingly important to evaluate the earnings management environment.

The purpose of financial accounting is to provide financial information to internal and external parties to enable them to make reasonable decisions on investment, credit, supply, and so on. The FASB not only establishes GAAP but also continues to develop a conceptual framework to determine the objectives and fundamental "theory" on which financial information should be incorporated and how it should be measured. The basic financial reports and other relevant information are described in this chapter. Also included is a discussion of earnings quality and an earnings management detection strategy.

THE CONTENTS OF THE 10-K

The basic format of the 10-K is governed by SEC requirements. Most components are required, whereas others are common but voluntary. Table 3.1 shows the major components of the 10-K, presented in typical order. The more significant categories are reviewed in detail in separate subsections. Terminology and specific content will vary by company.

MANAGEMENT DISCUSSION AND ANALYSIS (MD&A)

MD&A is designed to be a near-complete source of the company's business strategy. This includes an analysis of the corporation's operations and financial position, existing business risks and steps to control the risk, and various management policies. Specific content required by the SEC is stated in Regulation S-K, Item 303, on financial condition. Specific items mentioned are liquidity, capital resources, and results of operations.

A brief history and description of the company can be presented to highlight its development over time and perhaps to indicate the founder's values and beliefs, for example, this statement from GE's 2001 10-K:

> GE is one of the largest and most diversified industrial corporations in the world. GE has engaged in developing, manufacturing and marketing a wide variety of products for the generation, transmission, distribution, control and utilization of electricity since its incorporation in 1892. Over the years, GE

TABLE 3.1	BASIC COMPONENTS OF THE 10-K

Section	Description
Management letter	Optional section that could be from the President, CEO, Chairman, founder, or others. It's usually optimistic and presents the most cheerful information possible.
Financial highlights	Optional summary, usually focusing on operations (income statement) information for two or more years.
Mission statement or objectives statement	Occasionally stated separately from the MD&A, presumably to emphasize the distinct business strategy of the corporation.
Various types of management reports	The executives' responsibility for financial statements is presented, often next to the auditor's report; other reports are common for some companies and industries.
Management discussion & analysis (MD&A)	Required extensive analysis of business strategy, current operations, business risks, and future projections (which can be presented in a separate "forward-looking statement").
Financial section	The financial section includes all financial statements, the auditor's report, and notes to the financial statements. This is the heart of the annual report.
Auditor's report	The auditor's report is a standard opinion related to the financial audit. It is signed in the name of the audit firm (usually one of the Big Four), dated at completion, perhaps within a month after the end of the fiscal year, and states an opinion in one or more paragraphs. Almost all opinions are "clean," meaning there are no exceptions (audit problems usually lead to a qualified opinion—essentially the auditor disagrees with the client).
Income statement	Comparative analysis for the past three years, explaining the operations over each year associated with sales and other revenues, operating expenses and various nonoperating gains and losses (most of which are considered nonrecurring items), resulting in net income. Earnings per share on a basic and diluted basis also are presented.
Balance sheet	The position statement at the end of the fiscal year, listing the book values of the major categories of assets, liabilities, and owners' equity, compared to the previous year.
Statement of cash flows	Comparative statement over the past three years explains the changes in cash of the period in three major categories (indirect method): (1) cash flows from operations starts from net income and adds back depreciation and other accruals (plus changes in other current items); (2) cash from investing, including capital expenditures; and (3) cash from financing, including sale or purchase of stock, debt instruments, and dividend payments.
Statement of stockholders' equity	This statement (also called statement of changes in stockholders' equity or something similar) comes in a variety of formats and generally presents three years of changes in equity by categories, including other comprehensive income.

(Continued)

TABLE 3.1	BASIC COMPONENTS OF THE 10-K (CONTINUED)
Section	**Description**
Notes	The notes explain the accounting policies used by the corporation and present detailed information on various accounts and categories of financial information. These can be extensive and important for analyzing earnings management potential.
Operating summary	Company must present a five-year summary (many companies extend this to ten or more years) of significant financial and nonfinancial information. Financial data include operations (sales, net income, earnings per share, and so on), balance sheet items (working capital, assets, equity, various ratios), and cash flow items. Nonfinancial information tends to be industry-specific.

has developed or acquired new technologies and services that have broadened considerably the scope of its activities.

Dell, a more recently established company, stated the following:

Dell is the world's leading computer systems company and a premier provider of computing products and services. ... The Company was founded in 1984 by Michael Dell on a simple concept: by selling computer systems directly to customers, the Company could best understand customer needs and efficiently provide the most effective computing solutions to meet those needs.

MD&A includes an in-depth analysis of operations and financial position for the fiscal year, usually compared to the previous two years. Dell's "Fiscal 2002 Overview" included sections entitled (1) Results from Operations (including Net Revenue, Gross Margin, Operating Expenses, Investment and Other Income, and Income Tax) and (2) Liquidity, Capital Commitments and Other Financial Arrangements. An analysis of market risk described Dell's major categories, which include foreign currency and the hedging activities the company uses; cash and investments, including equity securities; and debt, including interest rate swaps. A paragraph explained "Factors Affecting the Company's Business and Prospects," such as the level of product demand, technology competition, and managing operating costs. As a smaller company than GE, Dell's MD&A was covered in thirteen pages in the 2002 10-K (pp. 17–29).

As a bigger and more complex company, GE had a more comprehensive MD&A for fiscal year 2001 (nineteen pages, from 48–66). A major factor was the discussion of the various operating segments, which included aircraft engines, appliances, various industrial projects, NBC, power systems, and GE Capital Services. Liquidity analysis included discussions of global commercial paper markets and off-balance-sheet arrangements, including SPEs (for account and other receivables and various securitized assets and investment-related vehicles by GE Credit).

FINANCIAL SECTION

The financial statements represent the heart of financial accounting. Four statements are required: Balance Sheet, Income Statement, Cash Flow Statement, and Statement of

Stockholders' Equity. The statements compare the current year to the previous year (balances sheet) or two (income statement, cash flow statement, statement of stockholders' equity). These statements usually are relatively abbreviated, and additional details are presented in the notes at the end of the financial statements. The financial statements for Dell are presented in Appendix 3.1. The specific contents of the financial statements will be reviewed in detail in later chapters of the book. Also included in the financial section is the auditor's report, usually a **"boiler plate"** paragraph or two indicating conformance with GAAP (a clean opinion). Finally, an operating summary includes a set of operating and balance sheet numbers and ratios for at least five years and often longer.

The balance sheet shows the financial position of a company at the end of the fiscal year. It is composed of assets, liabilities, and stockholders' equity. The assets are the resources of the firm. The liabilities and equity are the "sources" of assets, explaining how they were financed by creditors or owners (also called the stakeholders). This is demonstrated in the following accounting equation: Assets = Liabilities + Stockholders' Equity. Current assets usually are disclosed separately from long-term assets, as are current and long-term liabilities.

An income statement summarizes the relative operating success of business performance for the fiscal year. The statement is comparative, including figures for the current year and the two previous years. Basically, the form is sales and other revenue less all expenses (plus and minus gains and losses), to arrive at net income. Major categories of expenses include cost-of-goods-sold (for manufacturers) or cost of sales (for service and financial firms), other operating expenses, and nonoperating expenses (nonrecurring items and others). Net income is then stated on a per-share basis as earnings per share. The format is more or less standardized on the basis of GAAP to include several basic components. However, there are substantial differences in reporting format, usually by industry.

The statement of cash flows evaluates cash receipts (inflows) and cash payments (outflows) for the year into three categories: operations, investing, and financing activities. The focus of cash flows from operations (CFO) is cash effects of all transactions that involve net income. The indirect method starts with net income and then adds back noncash items such as depreciation and amortization as well as changes in noncash current items (receivables, inventory, payables, and so on). Most often, CFO is positive because net income is normally positive and noncash expenses such as depreciation increase CFO. Cash flows from investing (CFI) include capital expenditures and investments. Generally, CFI is negative because investments are uses of cash. Cash flow from financing (CFF) includes the acquisition or disposal of equity and debt as well as the payment of dividends. Then cash is reconciled from the beginning balance to the ending balance.

The final required statement is the statement of stockholders' equity, which reconciles the various components of equity for three years. Alternative formats are allowable. In most cases, the beginning equity balances are stated for the beginning of the year and additions and deletions presented for each of the three years, to arrive at current year-end balances for all major components. Particularly important is the reconciliation of other comprehensive income items, because these gains and losses are not part of net income.

NOTES

The Notes section may be the longest part of the 10-K. The first note is "The Summary of Significant Accounting Policies" and reviews specific accounting policies (essentially how GAAP is being applied) for each major income statement and balance sheet category. Much of this is a summary of basic GAAP requirements. All firms are required to use lower-of-cost-or-market (LCM) for inventory, for example. The important information is the specific accounting choices made; e.g., first-in first-out for inventory rather than last-in first-out or another method.

The remaining notes review specific reporting areas in detail. Unique items the company uses during the current year, such as restructuring or specific nonrecurring items, usually come next, followed by detailed disclosures item by item. Format differs. Most often, companies start with either the balance sheet or income statement and disclose major categories down that statement. The last item presented tends to be quarterly information.

THE CONTENTS OF THE 10-Q

The quarterly report is an abbreviated report, usually much shorter than the annual report and less regulated. For example, quarterly reports are reviewed by the auditors but not audited. For the most part, GAAP is associated with annual reporting and the assumption of a complete financial audit to verify the contents. Much of the content of the quarterly report is based on estimates and assumptions associated with annual reporting (e.g., obvious accruals for the annual report can be less obvious quarterly). In summary, it can be considered less accurate but more timely. For most of the year, it represents the most recent detailed financial information available. It is also presented relatively sooner. The 10-Q must be submitted to the SEC within forty-five days of the end of the fiscal quarter. Major information usually included is shown in Table 3.2.

Earnings management strategy is expected to differ in a 10-Q from that of an annual report. First, there are some accounting and reporting differences. Second, quarterly

TABLE 3.2	MAJOR COMPONENTS OF THE 10-Q
Section	**Description**
Income statement	Results for three months and six months, compared to same-quarter results from the previous year (plus nine months' results for third quarter)
Balance sheet	Current quarter compared to previous year-end balances
Cash flow statement	Year-to-date results, compared to year-to-date results from the previous year
Notes	Notes are abbreviated relative to the annual report but are usually extensive
Other information	Additional data can be presented voluntarily, such as MD&A

statements are more subject to estimates, based on expected annual results. Third, the 10-Q is unaudited and there is more leeway in what's reported. Fourth, there is the continued incentive to meet quarterly analysts' forecasts of earnings. Earnings manipulation is relatively easier in quarterly versus annual reports.

THE USEFULNESS OF THE PROXY STATEMENT

The proxy statement is an SEC-required annual report, in advance of the corporation's annual stockholders' meeting. The stockholders will be expected to vote on directors and various other issues. On the basis of current SEC and stock exchange requirements (especially NYSE, AMEX, and NASDAQ requirements), stockholders vote on executive compensation issues and the selection and fee structure of the auditor. The purpose of the proxy statement is to present the stockholders the information they need for informed voting. There is considerable information on the existing and proposed board of directors, information on board and executive compensation, and information on the auditor, including fees charged and nonaudit services provided. Consequently, the proxy statement can be extremely useful in evaluating corporate governance and the overall earnings management environment. More on this in Chapter 10.

ADDITIONAL SOURCES OF INFORMATION

Thanks largely to the Internet, there are many additional sources of information related to the operations, financial position, forecasts, and analysis of business strategy success. Some useful items appear in Table 3.3.

Business news is updated regularly, and most breaking stories become available quickly and often in considerable detail. Company press releases can be particularly important, and thanks to Regulation FD, the announcements or conferences are available live (see, for example, www.bestcalls.com). The use of search engines also can be useful when information is needed on a specific topic or company.

REPORTING QUALITY

What characteristics are most useful in evaluating the reporting quality and, implicitly, the potential earnings quality of a corporation? Six categories seem particularly important: (1) a well-defined business strategy; (2) a reasonable corporate governance structure; (3) report completeness and timeliness; (4) transparency; (5) conservative accounting; and (6) evidence of earnings manipulation. The reporting quality results are not obvious at the start of analysis but should become clearer as the analysis continues.

WELL-DEFINED BUSINESS STRATEGY

Evaluating the business strategy of a corporation is part of the qualitative analysis to determine the relative effectiveness of strategy relative to the industry and economic conditions the firm

TABLE 3.3	ADDITIONAL SOURCES OF INFORMATION ABOUT COMPANIES

Source	Description
Additional SEC reports, other information	Companies issue 8-K for certain types of events that could be important to investors, such as a change in auditors. If an auditor resigns or is fired, this is a strong signal of accounting problems. The SEC also lists ongoing investigations and findings. All are available on-line at www.sec.gov.
Analysts' forecasts	Analysts issue quarterly EPS forecasts and longer-term forecasts. Consensus forecasts are available on a number of sites, including Zacks (www.zacks.com), which is summarized at Quicken (www.quicken.com).
Stock prices and stock charts	Current stock prices, historical stock prices, and stock charts are available from many financial sites, including Quicken and Yahoo! (finance.yahoo.com).
Business press	Important sources of current information include the *Wall Street Journal, Fortune, Business Week, Forbes,* and many others. Some of these have Web sites with selected articles. Hoovers (www.hoovers.com) is a good choice.
Bond ratings	Moody's, Standard & Poors, and others issue bond ratings and other credit information. An investment grade rating is expected and the higher the rating the better. Detailed information requires a subscription to these services.
Internet searches	Substantial information is available on virtually any subject, including all the items mentioned above. This can be a great place to begin looking for the bad stuff.

faces. If the company can't articulate a viable business strategy in its MD&A and other sources, it's unlikely that the financial reporting will demonstrate current and continued operating success. Did Tyco's conglomerate strategy of acquiring unrelated companies make sense?

This is called qualitative analysis for a reason. The analyst must make a viability judgment. For several years, AT&T attempted to enter virtually all telecommunications markets. The concept was fully integrated telecommunication, in which consumers could come to AT&T to solve their communication needs. This AT&T strategy meant buying a bunch of high-priced firms in various telecommunication segments or developing these segments internally. Unfortunately, technology problems (integration is still a long way off) and competition almost brought AT&T to financial ruin. This strategy proved to be a failure, but it looked like a winner at the start.

Conversely, Dell has a relatively simple business strategy of cost leadership. Through a variety of efficiency measures (e.g., selling directly to the customer online or over the phone), Dell is the low-cost producer of PCs and has used a low-price strategy to increase market share and enter new business hardware areas such as servers.

CORPORATE GOVERNANCE STRUCTURE

The corporate governance structure is the basis for the financial environment of a company. The board of directors and its committees should provide an objective review of corporate strategy, compensation and compensation incentives, financial audit decisions and review, and overall evaluation of the success for the executives and corporate operations. A high-quality, independent board that takes its roles seriously and is not beholden to the CEO and other executives provides considerable ensurance that earnings manipulation and other mischief will not be tolerated. By the same token, a board composed largely of insiders or friends of the CEO and members interlocking with other company boards, particularly those of suppliers and customers, signals significant concern. The corporate scandals reviewed in Chapter 2 almost always involved the second variety.

Corporations are improving corporate structures, partly in response to new rules by stock exchanges and other bodies. But the specific characteristics need to be reviewed, with considerable information on the board detailed in the Proxy Statement. The review should include compensation agreements and audit characteristics, also found in the Proxy Statement.

REPORTING COMPLETENESS AND TIMELINESS

Financial reports can be over 100-page monsters based on accounting standards that require computer storage rather than paper because they're so long and complex (and tend to be updated often). How can reporting be incomplete? The companies have strict SEC guidelines for when reports must be issued. How can they be untimely? Granted, completeness and timeliness are relative terms. Some companies always wait to the last acceptable date to file. Many companies present no more than the minimum acceptable information and then present it in a confusing fashion. Some companies miss the deadlines and present reports that violate GAAP disclosure standards.

The reporting completeness and timeliness include the following. The earliest financial information is the earnings announcement at the end of each quarter. The faster companies announce earnings within a couple of weeks of the end of the period. In addition, the information is relatively complete, including almost complete financial statements and substantial discussions of operations and any issues of concern, such as restructuring or nonrecurring items of any kind. The 10-K and 10-Q are filed early, and they tend to provide detailed information on key operating and financial items.

Other companies follow with a considerable lag. Typically, relatively little is disclosed in earnings announcements, and it may be deceptive, such as focusing on *pro forma* earnings rather than net income and earnings per share on a GAAP basis. Quarterly and annual reports tend to follow this same pattern, with the companies often filing on the last possible day.

Reporting completeness means including all necessary information to make informed judgments on financial and economic reality. Consider special purpose entities (SPEs). Thanks to Enron, SPEs went from an obscure type of structured financing contract used for ordinary operating purposes to the well-known means of pulling virtually anything off the balance sheet. Normally, SPEs don't have to be reported (although this is changing somewhat with new accounting standards), and most companies don't report any. But the business press suggests that the vast majority of major companies use SPEs routinely. There should be a statement from companies in the notes or MD&A on SPEs, whether they use them or not. If they use them, the discussion should be thorough.

TRANSPARENCY

Transparency means that all financial information is observable and fully reported, at least within reason. Financial information is based primarily on annual and quarterly reports that present summarized information based on existing standards and available with a lag of up to ninety days for a 10-K. The basic concept of transparency is captured by Friedman (2000, p. 172), using the metaphor of the African plain:

> When a wildebeest on the edge of the herd sees something move in the tall, thick brush … that wildebeest starts a stampede. They stampede to the next country and crush everything in their path. So how does one protect your country from this? Answer: You cut the grass, and clear away the bush, so that the next time the wildebeest sees something rustle in the grass it thinks, "no problem, I see what it is."

Opaque reporting in good times can lead to optimistic illusion that can bid up stock prices (think Enron). When the bad news hits, nothing can be believed and prices collapse. "You go from believing everything to believing nothing" (Friedman 2000, p. 173).

Several areas of disclosure can be frustrating (potentially opaque), starting with the previously mentioned SPEs. A related area of concern is derivative accounting. Derivatives are usually reported in the financial statements on the basis of fair value. However, it is difficult to determine if a company is, in fact, hedging (the usual claim) or speculating.

Another example is segment reporting. Limited segment reporting is required by GAAP, and reporting is often very limited. Major corporations are complex and global. Consequently, industry and geographic segments are widespread and usually complicated. The first problem is the extreme flexibility in defining a segment. There is no obvious standardization, and complexity doesn't help. At a minimum, revenues and operating income should be stated for each segment, but often they are not. Disney, for example, has extensive information on the four operating segments it reports; however, if you want to evaluate the Mighty Ducks or the Anaheim Angels (which Disney owns), you're out of luck—they're part of Parks and Resorts and not reported separately. Consequently, an area extremely important to analysts can lack usefulness.

CONSERVATIVE ACCOUNTING

A key question in determining earnings is, When does accounting accurately reflect economic timing and reality? Under conservative accounting, the answer is usually on a timely basis, sometimes late, but never early. Revenue recognition can be relatively late in the operating cycle, when there is no question that the revenue was earned and collection is assured; losses are recognized as soon as possible; gains are often not recognized until cash is received.

Conservative accounting errs on the side of lower relative earnings. Many costs that result in real assets (such as research and development) are expensed rather than capitalized, because of the difficulty of actually measuring value. The result should be high-quality earnings, that is, earnings numbers that may be understated but not overstated.

Conservative accounting is not the same as what is sometimes called "aggressive conservative accounting": understated revenues and earnings during good years and offsetting them (essentially overstating them) in bad years. This is called **income smoothing** (a form of earnings management) because it attempts to smooth out the normally occurring ups and downs in the operating cycle and earnings. Income smoothing gives the appearance of high-quality earnings, but this is based on accounting flexibility rather than economic reality.

Evidence of Earnings Manipulation Companies don't admit to manipulation. They have to be caught in the act. The primary method of gathering evidence is a relatively detailed analysis of the financial statements and related information to look for manipulation signals. Alternatively, the evidence comes from external sources. The SEC initiates investigations of unacceptable practices with some frequency, but the number of companies it can fully investigate is limited because of funding constraints. The business press also reviews company problems and can highlight potential manipulation.

Companies can restate earnings from previous periods. Enron, Xerox, and others did exactly that in the past couple of years. As demonstrated in the GAO report on earnings restatements (2002), restatements have become increasingly common. About 15 percent of S&P 500 firms restated at least once from 1997 through 2002, with revenue recognition and expensing the most common categories. Restatements can signal past earnings manipulation. Whether that environment still exists becomes an important test during the qualitative analysis.

SEC litigation summaries are available on the SEC Web site (www.sec.gov/litigation), another good place to start for finding those companies caught in the act. For example, recent findings included the following: (1) in December 2002, five major banking firms were fined for destroying e-mails, in violation of the SEC Act of 1934 and NYSE rules (administrative proceedings), (2) in November 2002, WorldCom was issued a permanent injunction on various governance practices and operations (civil lawsuits), and (3) in November 2002, an investigation of Motorola was conducted with regard to sales orders. The major cases make the headlines, including fines issued to Deutsche Bank, Goldman Sachs, Morgan Stanley, Solomon Smith Barney, and U.S. Bancorp's Piper Jaffray for e-mail destruction.

Certain practices suggest attempts to camouflage information. For example, airlines and various types of retail stores often use massive amounts of operating leases, clearly to keep the debt of fixed asset acquisition off the balance sheet. Practices like off-balance-sheet reporting, massive stock options (they represent "unreported compensation"), and extensive use of business combinations signal management incentives for potential manipulation.

The major reporting-quality components are summarized in Table 3.4.

AN EARNINGS MANAGEMENT DETECTION STRATEGY

Most large American corporations are probably run by competent, relatively honest and trustworthy executives that use earnings management conservatively. U.S. GAAP tends to be conservative, and most firms follow conservative options (such as delaying revenue recognition until the earnings process is definitely complete). Most CFOs probably attempt to smooth earnings over time and perhaps tweak quarterly earnings to meet analysts' forecasts. However, when evaluating a particular company, there is no reason to assume anything. Earnings management can be rampant even if difficult to detect,

TABLE 3.4	FACTORS INVOLVED IN REPORTING QUALITY

Component	Discussion
Well-defined business strategy	The corporation's operation and accounting policies are derived from the business strategy, relative to competitors and industry.
Corporate governance structure	Corporate governance provides long-range leadership and monitoring of the corporate executives and business strategy effectiveness. If the structure is loose, earnings management is a greater concern and reporting quality more suspect.
Reporting completeness and timeliness	The 10-K and 10-Q must be available to the SEC (and the public) within 90 days and 45 days, respectively. Early reporting of these—and of earnings announcements and other reports—is an indicator of timeliness. GAAP establishes certain reporting requirements and minimum reporting. Actual reporting should meet and is expected to exceed the minimum requirements.
Transparency	Financial information and results of operations should be clear to the reader and in a form that is both simple to analyze and complete.
Conservative accounting	GAAP usually encourages conservative alternatives, but aggressive and manipulative policies may exist (and may or may not violate GAAP). Conservative accounting may result in the reporting of lower short-term results but is necessary for long-run high reporting quality.
Evidence of earnings manipulation	Evidence of earnings manipulation substantially reduces reporting quality, because of the specific manipulation practices but also the lack of credibility of the entire report.

corruption and greed could be on a vast scale, and fraud and other criminal acts may be the norm. This can be true even for well-known companies with a long history. Consequently, an earnings management detection strategy should be comprehensive and thorough. However, like a financial audit, the focus should be on areas of greatest risk for earnings management potential.

An earnings management detection (EMD) strategy should be part of a thorough financial analysis of a company. Note that the detailed quantitative financial analysis tools are not emphasized in this book (see Giroux 2003 or other financial analysis texts for thorough coverage). A comprehensive financial analysis that includes both quantitative financial statement analysis and market analysis gives a first pass on the operating and reporting quality of a company and the market response to the financial information. Now the question is how much to believe. That's the role of EMD.

A QUALITATIVE ANALYSIS

The first step in EMD is a thorough subjective or qualitative analysis. This follows from the reporting quality characteristics, which are (1) a well-defined business strategy; (2) a reasonable corporate governance structure; (3) report completeness and timeliness; (4) transparency; (5) conservative accounting; and (6) evidence of earnings manipulation. Financial operations should follow from the business strategy. For example, acquisition and various partnership arrangements fit some business strategies but not others. Corporate governance is particularly important. The board should be independent and competent, have necessary committees, and be compensated appropriately. If not, this may be an environment for deceit and manipulation. Red flags and questionable results will suggest areas of particular concern. In summary, this qualitative analysis suggests the initial expectations and level of skepticism. Within a basic EMD structure, a particular analytical strategy can be designed.

Now comes the detailed EMD strategy. This can cover specific categories or be quite comprehensive. For example, consider Maytag as a possible equity investment. The company has a dividend yield over 2.5 percent, has fair earnings, and seems to be undervalued. However, Maytag has total stockholders' equity of less than one percent of total assets. Evaluating this equity position may be the focus. That is, the analysis would go forward only if the investor would still consider Maytag a viable investment candidate after this preliminary analysis of equity.

General Electric is one of the largest, oldest, and most respected American companies. It is a huge, global conglomerate but has suffered some bad press over former CEO Jack Welch's retirement package and a number of accounting practices. The global operations are complex, as are the business strategy and financial operations. Just to make things particularly difficult, a large part of GE's operations is GE Credit, with quite different practices from the various industrial segments. The analysis of GE will have to be thorough.

A COMPREHENSIVE QUANTITATIVE DETECTION STRATEGY

The comprehensive EMD strategy can be built around the financial statements and then address a number of additional issues of concern. Arbitrarily, coverage begins with the balance sheet and then the income statement. Thus, the analysis starts with cash and other current assets and liabilities related to liquidity and then moves on to property, plant and equipment, and other long-term assets. Leverage concentrates on liabilities (primarily long-term liabilities) and then "hidden" liabilities, potential liabilities such as contingencies as well as off-balance-sheet liabilities. Stockholders' equity includes several "cross-over" areas such as treasury securities, comprehensive income, and relationships to stock options and dividends. The statement of stockholders' equity will be evaluated at the same time.

Analysis of operations starts with revenues and works down the income statement to net income and earnings per share. Also considered are alternative bottom-line measures, including earnings before interest and taxes (EBIT), comprehensive income, and *pro forma* earnings. Related to performance are cash flows from operations. The cash flow statement includes investing and financing activities, which provide information useful for the evaluation of the overall business strategy relative to operations.

A long list of separate items includes pensions and other post-employment benefits, stock options, business combinations and divestitures, derivatives and special purpose entities, and segment reporting. These are difficult issues to evaluate and have considerable earnings management potential. Consequently, these will be evaluated in greater detail.

INTERRELATIONSHIP OF FINANCIAL STATEMENTS AND OTHER ITEMS

When EMD concerns pop up, they often show up in bunches, because the financial statements are interrelated. Thus, Maytag has an extremely low level of stockholders' equity, which is obvious from a brief look at the balance sheet. It shows up in standard leverage ratios. It also shows up when evaluating income statement performance with a large return on equity. The cash flow statement shows an acquisition of treasury stock as a negative cash flow item under financing activities. A more detailed analysis indicates the importance of treasury stock for reducing equity, and the stock options note indicates the relationship of options to treasury securities. And so on.

Companies with poor operating performance, especially net losses after a period of profitability, usually have concerns pop up like mushrooms. Gateway Computer started running net losses in the December 2000 quarter after years of high-tech success. Performance ratios were large and negative for 2001–2002, as were cash flows from operations. Stockholders' equity continued down as losses increased. Corporate announcements, MD&A, and various footnotes detailed the multiple approaches to restructuring. The company attempted to control cost, shut down foreign operations, and beef up cash and liquidity. The potential areas of earnings management shifted accordingly, with particular emphasis on how the restructuring activities were accounted for and if the company was boosting performance through manipulation.

Gateway did not meet the ninety-day deadline for filing its 10-K. Instead, it petitioned the SEC for an extension. The 10-K filing was issued on April 15, 2003, two weeks late. The net loss for 2002 was $298 million. The EMD strategy for Gateway shifted from evaluating the real growth potential of the company to evaluating survival probabilities.

Key components of an earnings management detection strategy are summarized in Table 3.5.

SUMMARY

This chapter reviewed financial reporting topics and provided a brief summary of the information to be found in various reports and other sources. Of particular concern when evaluating earnings management is reporting quality and special characteristics that suggest high-quality earnings. Finally, an overview of the earnings management detection strategy is presented. The strategy is derived from the characteristics of high earnings quality.

QUESTIONS

1. Why would management have different disclosure objectives than stockholders?
2. What is the mission of the SEC? The FASB? Why are these organizations important to financial reporting?
3. Why is the Proxy Statement important for evaluating corporate governance?
4. Why is management discussion and analysis (MD&A) important for evaluating earnings management?

TABLE 3.5	COMPONENTS OF QUALITATIVE AND QUANTITATIVE ANALYSES FOR DETECTION OF EARNINGS MANAGEMENT

Analysis	Description
Qualitative	
Evaluate business strategy	Business strategy must be reasonable, given direct competitors and industry characteristics.
Evaluate economic and industry conditions	The potential success of operations, given the existing business strategy, depends on current economic conditions, especially those that are industry-related.
Review corporate governance	The looser the corporate governance structure, the more likely the potential for earnings manipulation.
Review the monitoring structure	Review the board of directors' committees, the external auditor, and other potential monitors. Evaluate specific committees (especially the composition and workings of the audit committee and compensation committees). Evaluate the auditor, the auditor's report, and nonaudit services performed by this firm.
Evaluate findings from the SEC, other regulators, and the business press	The SEC reports current investigations and findings on the SEC Web page. Evaluate other regulatory information, especially for firms in highly regulated industries such as utilities and banks; also consider such factors as potential antitrust problems. Refer to the business press for evidence of wrong-doings.
Quantitative	
Balance sheet	Standard financial analysis using common size, ratios, trends, and quarterly analysis. See Chapter 4.
Income statement	Standard financial analysis using common size, ratios, trends, and quarterly analysis. Review in detail restructuring information and the use of nonrecurring items. See Chapter 5.
Cash flows	Review cash flow statement, evaluate cash from operations and other cash-related evidence, and compare with accrual accounting practices. See Chapter 6.
Bottom-line measures	Evaluate net income, earnings per share, earnings before income and taxes (also EBITDA), income from continuing operations, comprehensive income, pro forma income numbers, and other possible measures. See Chapter 6.
Time series measures	Consider financial statement and other information items from a multiperiod perspective. Long-term trends and quarterly results may provide additional signals of possible manipulation. See Chapter 7.
Specific problem topics	Several topics that have earnings management potential are complex and need further analysis. These include business combination and divestitures, corporate governance, compensation topics such as stock options and retirement-related plans, derivatives, and off-balance-sheet items.

5. What is transparency and why is it important?

6. Why is an earnings management detection strategy a necessary component of a comprehensive financial analysis?

PROBLEMS

Problem 3.1: Where Is This Information Found?

You're ready to start a financial analysis of Hilton Hotels. Where would you find the information shown in Table 3.6? In the 10-K or another source?

Problem 3.2: Financial Accounting Overview

A review of Note 1 (Accounting Policies) of three hotel and resort companies provides the following information for fiscal year 2002 (Table 3.7). Are there substantial differences in accounting policies across these companies? Explain. Does this information suggest earnings management or the need for further analysis? Explain.

TABLE 3.6	FORMAT FOR ANALYSIS OF FINANCIAL DATA FOR HILTON HOTELS				
	MD&A	Financial Statements	Notes	Proxy Statement	Market (Internet)
Business strategy					
Next year's expected performance					
Retained earnings					
Earnings per share					
Operating leases					
Cash from operations					
Board of directors					
Number of common shares outstanding					
Board committees					
Executive compensation					
Analysts' forecasts					
Contingencies					
Audit fees and nonaudit fees					
Use of special purpose entities					

TABLE 3.7 | **FISCAL YEAR 2002 DATA FOR THREE MAJOR HOTEL/RESORT COMPANIES**

	Hilton	Marriott	Mandalay
Revenue Recognition	Recognized as services are performed; management fees and franchise fees based on contract	Management fees based on contract; distribution services when shipped and title pass to customer; timeshare when 10 percent of sales price received	Casino revenues, cash basis less incentives; hotel services as performed, less complementary allowances
Special Charges	Not mentioned	Not mentioned	Abandonment loss in 2000
Nonrecurring Items	Not mentioned	Not mentioned	Accounting change in 2000 (preopening expenses)
Marketable Securities	Held-to-maturity	Trading, held-to-maturity, or available-for-sale	Held-to-maturity
Accounts Receivable (bad debts, percent)	$17 million allowance allowance for uncollectible accounts for 2002	$12 million of accounts receivable, which we deemed uncollectible	Bad debts of $20.4 million for 2002
Inventory	Timeshare properties	Not mentioned	FIFO and average (e.g., food, (beverages)
Property, Plant, and Equipment	Recorded at cost, straight-line depreciation	Recorded at cost, straight-line depreciation	Recorded at cost, straight-line depreciation
Long-term Investments	Unconsolidated affiliates, including hotel joint ventures	The majority of our equity method investments are investments in entities that own lodging properties	Yes, for unconsolidated affiliates
Acquisitions (list for 2002)	Hilton, Waikoloa Village, acquired the remaining 87 percent interest for approximately $155 million; total $285 million for investments accounted for under equity method	Assumption of $227 million debt associated with the acquisition of 14 senior living communities	No recent acquisitions
Divestitures (list for 2002)	Spin-off of Park Place	Three lodging properties and six pieces of undeveloped land for $330 million in cash, two of them accounted for under cost recovery method; 11 percent investment in Interval International	None
Use of Equity Method, Joint Ventures	Yes, for companies we own with more than a minimal investment but less than 50 percent ownership interest	Yes, when we exercise significant influence over the venture	Yes, for unconsolidated affiliates

(Continued)

TABLE 3.7	FISCAL YEAR 2002 DATA FOR THREE MAJOR HOTEL/RESORT COMPANIES (CONT.)		
	Hilton	**Marriott**	Mandalay
Insurance	Self-insured	Self-insured for certain levels of property, liability workers' compensation, and employee medical coverage	Not mentioned
Warranties	Not mentioned	Not mentioned	Not mentioned
Use of Treasury Stock	Stock repurchase program	Yes, compute the effect of dilutive securities with use of the treasury stock method and average market prices during the period	Yes, valued at cost, with use of FIFO
Pension Plans	Defined benefits plan	Profit-sharing plan	Defined benefit plan (underfunded) and supplemental executive retirement plan (unfunded)
Hedging	Forward, exchange contracts, interest rate swaps	Not mentioned	Interest rate swaps
Special Purpose Entities (SPEs)	Not mentioned	Periodically sell notes receivable through SPEs	Not mentioned

Problem 3.3: Hilton's Business Strategy

The following are excerpts from various sources.

> Industry: The hotel, casino and resort industry includes nine companies on Fortune's 1000 list, with Hilton at #499 based on revenue. Total revenues for the group were $35 billion in 2001, with income down substantially to $791 million. Marriott is the largest of the group, at #189. These companies have global operations, although their primary focus usually is in the U.S. The corporations operate in somewhat different sectors, although all have major hotel operations. This is a capital-intensive industry and depends on tourism for most of its revenue and growth. They were hard hit by the recession of 2001 and the September 11 attacks.

From Hoover's Company Capsule (www.hoovers.com):

> The company's lodging empire includes some 2,000 hotels (about 80% are franchised), mostly located in the U.S. Hilton operates 21 vacation resorts [but] has completely cashed out of the gaming industry.

History from Hoover's Handbook (1993, p. 326):

> Conrad Hilton got his start in hotel management by renting rooms in his family's New Mexico home. [He bought] his first hotel in Cicso, Texas. He

survived the Great Depression. He began buying hotels again. He founded Hilton International to manage his foreign business (1948) and realized his ambition to run New York's Waldorf-Astoria (1949). The company began to franchise in 1965. Conrad's son Baron became president in 1966.

From the company's MD&A, 2002 10-K:

We are primarily engaged in the ownership, management and development of hotels, resorts and timeshare properties and the franchising of lodging properties. Our brands include Hilton, Hilton Garden Inn, Doubletree, Embassy Suites, Hampton, [and] Homewood Suites by Hilton. In addition, we develop and operate timeshare resorts through Hilton Grand Vacations Company.

Our operations consist of three reportable segments, which are based on similar products or services: Hotel Ownership, Managing and Franchising, and Timeshare. The Hotel Ownership segment derives revenue primarily from the rental of rooms as well as food and beverage operations at our owned, majority owned and leased hotel properties and equity earnings from unconsolidated affiliates. The Management and Franchising segment provides services including hotel management and licensing of the Hilton family of brands. This segment generates its revenue from management and franchise fees charged to hotel owners. The Timeshare segment consists of multi-unit timeshare resorts.

Development: We intend to grow our hotel brands primarily through franchising and the addition of management contracts, which require little or no capital investment. In addition, we will continue to invest in normal capital replacement and select major renovation projects at our owned hotels, and we may seek to acquire hotel properties on a strategic and selective basis.

Below is a financial summary (Table 3.8) of 2002 in comparison with fiscal 2001. Revenue is down, as are EBITDA and operating income; however, net income is up because of increased efficiency.

From Hilton's Web page (www.hilton.com):

Conrad Hilton purchased his first hotel in Cisco, Texas, back in 1919. The first hotel to carry the Hilton name was built in Dallas in 1925. In 1943, Hilton became the first "coast-to-coast" hotel chain in the United States, and in 1949, opened its first hotel outside the U.S. in San Juan, Puerto Rico.

TABLE 3.8 | **HILTON FINANCIAL SUMMARY (MILLIONS OF DOLLARS)**

	2001	2002	% Change
Revenue	3,993	3,847	−4%
EBITDA	1,072	990	−8%
Operating income	632	603	−5%
Net income	166	198	19%
EPS, basic	0.45	0.53	−18%

Hilton went on the New York Stock Exchange in 1946, and Conrad Hilton purchased the Waldorf Astoria in 1949. Hilton has several world-renowned, marquee properties, some of which are [the] Beverly Hilton, Cavalieri Hilton in Rome, Hilton Athens, Hilton San Francisco, Hilton New York, Hilton Hawaiian Village, Hilton Waikoloa Village, Paris Hilton, and others.

Hilton Hotels Corporation is recognized around the world as a preeminent lodging hospitality company, offering guests and customers the finest accommodations, services, amenities, and value for business or leisure. While the Hilton brand has, for more than 80 years, been synonymous with excellence in the hospitality industry, our acquisition in 1999 of Promus Hotel Corporation expanded our family of brands to include such well-known and highly respected brand names as Hampton Inn®, Doubletree®, Embassy Suites Hotels®, and Homewood Suites® by Hilton. Through ownership of some of the most recognized hotels in the world and our newly enhanced brand portfolio, Hilton is now able to offer guests the widest possible variety of hotel experiences, including four-star city center hotels, convention properties, all-suite hotels, extended-stay, mid-priced focused service, destination resorts, vacation ownership, airport hotels, and conference centers.

Today's Hilton can be viewed as a major industry competitor in a number of areas:

Owning hotels. Hilton owns such unique, irreplaceable hotel assets as New York's Waldorf-Astoria, The Hilton Hawaiian Village® on Waikiki Beach, Chicago's Palmer House Hilton, and the Hilton San Francisco on Union Square. These large-scale properties occupy the best locations in the nation's best markets.

Managing/franchising hotels. The company is a prominent franchisor of hotels across its entire brand family, with income from management or franchise fees accounting for some 30 percent of Hilton's total cash flow. The company [opened], through its franchisees, approximately 430 hotels and 63,000 rooms in 2000–2001, consisting primarily of Hampton Inn, Homewood Suites by Hilton, and Hilton Garden Inn hotels.

Vacation ownership. Hilton Grand Vacations Club, the company's vacation ownership business, operates properties across the country, including such desirable locales as Las Vegas, Orlando, Miami, and Honolulu.

International. A global strategic alliance with Hilton International, the London-based company [that] owns the rights to the Hilton brand outside of the U.S., brings to customers a single, seamless Hilton system of 2,000 hotels in more than 50 countries throughout the world. Additionally, Conrad International offers five-star luxury hotels in England, Ireland, Belgium, Hong Kong, Singapore, Turkey, and Egypt.

Use this information (plus information from other Internet searches) to write a one-page Business Strategy for Hilton. Be sure to answer the following questions:

1. What is the industry?
2. Give a brief historical perspective on Hilton.
3. What is the primary focus of operations of this company?
4. What is the most important strategy used by Hilton (e.g., low-cost producer, product differentiation, quality, service)?
5. What are the major operating segments?
6. What is the outlook (operating forecast) for this company (for 1–5 years)?
7. What is the impact of the business cycle on Hilton? Future potential?

CASES

Case 1: Sources of Information for Qualitative Analysis—Dell Computer

The information in Table 3.9 is summarized from Dell's 2002 proxy statement. Qualitative information from the company's 2002 10-K is shown in Table 3.10. Table 3.11 includes further information.

a. On the basis of this limited information, summarize key qualitative characteristics associated with Dell.

b. Describe any concerns (especially red flags) associated with Dell's corporate governance, auditing, or other qualitative characteristics.

c. What additional information is needed for a thorough qualitative analysis, and where would it be found?

Case 2: Dell's Business Strategy

The following information is summarized from Dell's 2002 10-K on business strategy. It's not complete, but it indicates the basic strategy used by the company.

> The Company's business strategy is based upon the direct model. The direct model seeks to deliver a superior customer experience through direct, comprehensive customer relationships, cooperative research and development with technology partners, use of the Internet, computer systems custom-built to customer specifications, and service and support programs tailored to specific customer needs.

> The Company believes that the direct model provides it with several distinct competitive advantages. The direct model eliminates the need to support an extensive network of wholesale and retail dealers, thereby avoiding dealer markups; avoids the higher inventory costs associated with the wholesale/retail channel and the competition for retail shelf space; and reduces the high risk of obsolescence associated with products in a rapidly changing technological market. In addition, the direct model allows the Company to maintain, monitor, and update a customer database that can be used to shape future product offerings and post-sale service and support programs. This direct approach allows the Company to rapidly and efficiently deliver relevant technology to its customers.

> The Company has successfully developed cooperative, working relationships with many of the world's most advanced technology companies. Working

TABLE 3.9	QUALITATIVE INFORMATION ON DELL COMPUTER
Board of Directors	Eleven directors; two insiders include founder Michael Dell and former Counselor to the CEO Morton Topfer. Compensation for independent directors includes an annual $40,000 retainer, expense reimbursements, and stock options.
Board Committees	Audit, Compensation, Finance and Nominating. All are made up of independent directors.
Audit	Audit committee made up of four outside directors and chaired by Donald Carty, CEO of AMR Corp. PricewaterhouseCoopers reappointed as auditor. Audit fees, $2.3 million; nonaudit fees paid to PWC include financial information services of $1.1 million and other (audit-related and tax) of $3.1 million.
Compensation	Compensation committee made up of three outside members. Executive compensation includes base salary, bonuses (percent of net income), stock options, and other perquisites. Actual compensation reported for five executives. Michael Dell for 2002 received base salary of $925, 962, bonus of $347,236, options to 500,000 shares, and other of $35,499.
Timing	Proxy statement was issued May 28, 2002, for annual meeting on July 18, 2002; fiscal year ended February 1, 2002.
Other	Founder Michael Dell owns 11.8 percent of outstanding shares.

TABLE 3.10	FURTHER INFORMATION FROM DELL'S 2002 10-K
Audit	Audited by PWC; report date February 14, 2002 (two weeks after the end of the fiscal year); unqualified ("clean") opinion
Executives	Biographies of top eleven executives presented
Related-party	Related-party transaction reported with Tyco International to form joint venture Dell Financial Services

TABLE 3.11	PERTINENT DELL FILINGS	
Topic	**Source**	**Analysis**
10-K filing	Lexis-Nexis	2002 10-K filed May 1, 2002, for fiscal year-end February 1, 2002
10-Q filing	Lexis-Nexis	Third-quarter 10-Q filed December 16, 2002, for period ended November 1, 2002
Earnings announcement	Dell Web page (press releases)	February 13, 2003, earnings announcement (for January 31, 2003, fiscal year end); includes both income statement and balance sheet, reporting increase in revenues of 14 percent and EPS of 23 percent

with these companies, the Company's engineers manage quality, integrate technologies, and design and manage system architecture. This cooperative approach allows the Company to determine the best method and timing for delivering new technologies to the market. The Company's goal is to quickly and efficiently deliver the latest relevant technology to its customers.

The Company's primary product offerings include enterprise systems, notebook computers, and desktop computer systems. Enterprise systems include PowerEdge servers; PowerApp server appliances; PowerVault storage products; PowerConnect network switches; and Dell Precision desktop and mobile workstations. The Company also markets and sells Dell/EMC storage products under a long-term strategic relationship with EMC Corporation. The Company offers Latitude and Inspiron notebook computers and Dimension, OptiPlex, and SmartStep desktop computer systems.

The Company enhances its product offerings with a number of specialized services, including professional consulting services, custom hardware and software integration, leasing and asset management, network installation and support, and onsite service.

The Company has established a broad range of customers based on continuing relationships with large corporations, governmental, healthcare and educational institutions, and small-to-medium businesses. The Company maintains a field sales force throughout the world to call on business and institutional customers. The Company develops marketing programs and services specifically geared to meet the needs of these relationship customers. Dedicated account teams, which include field-based system engineers and consultants, form long-term customer relationships to provide each customer with a single source of assistance and to develop specific marketing programs for these customers.

The Company's product development efforts are focused on designing and developing competitively priced computer systems that adhere to industry standards and incorporate the technologies and features that the Company believes are most desired by its customers. To accomplish this objective, the Company must evaluate, obtain, and incorporate new hardware, software, storage, communications, and peripherals technologies that are primarily developed by others. The Company's product development team includes programmers, technical project managers, and engineers experienced in system architecture, logic board design, sub-system development, mechanical engineering, manufacturing processing, and operating systems. This cross-functional approach to product design has enabled the Company to develop systems with improved functionality, manufacturability, reliability, serviceability, and performance, while keeping costs competitive. The Company takes steps to ensure that new products are compatible with industry standards and that they meet cost objectives based on competitive pricing targets.

The Company encounters aggressive competition from numerous companies in all aspects of its business. The Company competes on the basis of price, technology availability, performance, quality, reliability, service, and support. The Company believes that its cost structure and business model creates a competitive advantage over its competitors. However, the Company cannot provide any assurance that it will be able to maintain this advantage if its competitors alter their cost structure or business model or take other actions that affect the Company's current competitive advantage.

The Company's direct business model gives it the ability to operate with reduced levels of component and finished goods inventories. The Company's financial success in recent periods has been due in part to its asset management practices, including its ability to achieve rapid inventory turns. However, temporary disruptions in component availability can unfavorably affect the Company's short-term performance. Supply conditions have generally been favorable both to the Company and to the industry in recent years. However, less favorable supply conditions, as well as other factors, may require or result in increased inventory levels in the future.

The Company's manufacturing process requires a high volume of quality components that are procured from third-party suppliers. Reliance on suppliers, as well as industry supply conditions, generally involves several risks, including the possibility of defective parts (which can adversely affect the reliability and reputation of the Company's products), a shortage of components, and reduced control over delivery schedules (which can adversely affect the Company's manufacturing efficiencies) and increases in component costs (which can adversely affect the Company's profitability).

The Company has several single-sourced supplier relationships, either because alternative sources are not available or the relationship is advantageous due to performance, quality, support, delivery, capacity, or price considerations. If these sources are unable to provide timely and reliable supply, the Company could experience manufacturing interruptions, delays, or inefficiencies, adversely affecting its results of operations. Even where alternative sources of supply are available, qualification of the alternative suppliers and establishment of reliable supplies could result in delays and a possible loss of sales, which could affect operating results adversely.

a. On the basis of this limited review of Dell's basic strategy, evaluate its relative competitive position. If possible, review the complete annual reports of Dell, as well as direct competitors Apple and Gateway. Both have somewhat different strategies.

b. "Part a" was difficult because perspective is needed to evaluate the effectiveness of business strategy, especially as compared to direct competitors. What information would you need to be confident in undertaking an effective evaluation of business strategy?

c. Dell's business strategy has, in fact, proven to be highly effective in an extremely competitive industry subject to constant technological change. Turn to competitors Gateway and Apple, both of which have had substantial operating difficulties, and evaluate why Dell's strategy has been effective and theirs have not.

Appendix 3.1: Dell Computer Corporation

Dell Computer Corporation
Consolidated Statement of Financial Position (in millions of dollars)

	February 1, 2002	February 2, 2001
ASSETS		
Current assets:		
Cash and cash equivalents	$ 3,641	$ 4,910
Short-term investments	273	525
Accounts receivable, net	2,269	2,424
Inventories	278	400
Other	1,416	1,467
Total current assets	7,877	9,726
Property, plant, and equipment, net	826	996
Investments	4,373	2,418
Other noncurrent assets	459	530
Total assets	$13,535	$13,670
LIABILITIES AND STOCKHOLDERS' EQUITY		
Current liabilities:		
Accounts payable	$ 5,075	$ 4,286
Accrued and other	2,444	2,492
Total current liabilities	7,519	6,778
Long-term debt	520	509
Other	802	761
Commitments and contingent liabilities (Note 7)	—	—
Total liabilities	8,841	8,048
Stockholders' equity:		
Preferred stock and capital in excess of $.01 par value; shares issued and outstanding: none	—	—
Common stock and capital in excess of $.01 par value; shares authorized: 7,000; shares issued: 2,654 and 2,601, respectively	5,605	4,795
Treasury stock, at cost; 52 shares and no shares, respectively	(2,249)	—
Retained earnings	1,364	839
Other comprehensive income	38	62
Other	(64)	(74)
Total stockholders' equity	4,694	5,622
Total liabilities and stockholders' equity	$13,535	$13,670

Dell Computer Corporation
Consolidated Statement of Income (in millions of dollars, except per-share amounts)

	Fiscal Year Ended		
	February 1, 2002	February 2, 2001	January 28, 2000
Net revenue	$31,168	$31,888	$25,265
Cost of revenue	25,661	25,445	20,047
Gross margin	5,507	6,443	5,218
Operating expenses:			
Selling, general, and administrative	2,784	3,193	2,387
Research, development, and engineering	452	82	374
Special charges	482	105	194
Total operating expenses	3,718	3,780	2,955
Operating income	1,789	2,663	2,263
Investment and other income (loss), net	(58)	531	188
Income before income taxes and cumulative effect of change in accounting principle	1,731	3,194	2,451
Provision for income taxes	485	958	785
Income before cumulative effect of change in accounting principle	1,246	2,236	1,666
Cumulative effect of change in accounting principle, net	—	59	—
Net income	$ 1,246	$2,177	$ 1,666
Earnings per common share:			
Before cumulative effect of change in accounting principle:			
Basic	$0.48	$0.87	$0.66
Diluted	$0.46	$0.81	$0.61
After cumulative effect of change in accounting principle:			
Basic	$0.48	$0.84	$0.66
Diluted	$0.46	$0.79	$0.61
Weighted average shares outstanding:			
Basic	2,602	2,582	2,536
Diluted	2,726	2,746	2,728

Dell Computer Corporation
Consolidated Statement of Cash Flows (in millions of dollars)

	Fiscal Year Ended		
	February 1, 2002	February 2, 2001	January 28, 2000
Cash flows from operating activities:			
Net income	$1,246	$2,177	$1,666
Adjustments to reconcile net income to net cash provided by operating activities:			
Depreciation and amortization	239	240	156
Tax benefits of employee stock plans	487	929	1,040
Special charges	742	105	194
(Gains)/losses on investments	17	(307)	(80)
Other	178	13	56
Changes in:			
Operating working capital	826	642	812
Noncurrent assets and liabilities	62	274	82
Net cash provided by operating activities	3,797	4,195	3,926
Cash flows from investing activities:			
Investments:			
Purchases	(5,382)	(2,606)	(3,101)
Maturities and sales	3,425	2,331	2,319
Capital expenditures	(303)	(482)	(401)
Net cash used in investing activities	(2,260)	(757)	(1,183)
Cash flows from financing activities:			
Purchase of common stock	(3,000)	(2,700)	(1,061)
Issuance of common stock under employee plans	295	404	289
Other	3	(9)	77
Net cash used in financing activities	(2,702)	(2,305)	(695)
Effect of exchange rate changes on cash	(104)	(32)	35
Net (decrease) increase in cash	(1,269)	1,101	2,083
Cash and cash equivalents at beginning of period	4,910	3,809	1,726
Cash and cash equivalents at end of period	$3,641	$4,910	$3,809

Consolidated Statement of Stockholders' Equity
(in millions of dollars, only current year shown)

	Common Stock and Capital in Excess of Par Value		Treasury Stock		Retained Earnings	Other Comprehensive-Income	Other	Total
	Shares	Amount	Shares	Amount				
Balances at February 2, 2001	$2,601	$4,795	—	—	$ 839	$62	($74)	$5,622
Net income	—	—	—	—	1,246	—	—	1,246
Change in unrealized gain on investments, net of taxes	—	—	—	—	—	(65)	—	(65)
Foreign currency translation adjustments	—	—	—	—	2	2		
Net unrealized gain on derivative instruments, net of taxes	—	—	—	—	39	—	39	—
Total comprehensive income for fiscal 2002								
1,222 Stock issuances under employee plans	69	843	—	—	—	—	10	53
Purchases and retirements	(16)	(30)	52	(2,249)	(721)	—	—	(3,000)
Other	—	(3)	—	—	—	—	—	(3)
Balances at February 1, 2002	$2,654	$5,605	$52	($2,249)	$1,364	$38	($64)	$4,694

4

The Balance Sheet

The balance sheet displays the productive (and not so productive) assets of the firm and how they were financed (debt and ownership). The basic components and interpretation of how these items are reported are reviewed in Background. The approach to be followed for detecting earnings management is described in An EMD [Earnings Management Detection] Balance Sheet Strategy. The first step (or level) is an overview of all the accounts, with particular emphasis on relative composition, the adequacy of working capital, and evaluating leverage. The second level is the review of individual accounts by major categories: (1) current assets and liabilities, (2) long-term assets, (3) long-term liabilities, and (4) stockholders' equity. The analysis will focus on Apple Computer (Apple's 2002 balance sheet is presented in Appendix 1) and various companies where particular concerns exist.

BACKGROUND

The balance sheet represents the statement of position at the end of the fiscal period. It balances because assets = liabilities + stockholders' equity. In this sense stockholders' equity essentially is a "plug figure" (equity = assets – liabilities)—also known as book value or net assets. Thus, earnings management issues focus more on assets and liabilities than equity.

Accounting standards emphasized historical cost accounting from the start of standard setting in the United States, as well defended by Paton and Littleton (1940). Historical (acquisition-based) values are easily verified, tend to be conservative (e.g., book values are not raised to current values), and emphasize the income statement rather than the balance sheet. The ultraconservative concept of lower-of-cost-or-market (LCM) also permeated accounting thinking (partly because of the experience of the Great Depression), requiring write-downs if fair value was less than book value, but these were never written up if fair value was greater than book value.

The conceptual framework of the Financial Accounting Standards Board (FASB), as stated in *Statement of Financial Accounting Concepts No. 6*, defined the balance sheet categories as shown in Table 4.1.

According to the FASB's conceptual framework, assets have probable future economic benefit, whereas liabilities are probable future economic sacrifices. A basic problem is the poor match of this definition to how assets and liabilities are recorded under GAAP. The definition suggests that some measure of current or market value should always be stated. But accounting standards are pragmatic, and alternative approaches are used. The FASB now uses fair values where market or fair values can be reasonably determined (basically financial assets and liabilities, particularly when a formal market exists). If not, historical cost is most likely used. However, several key categories that meet the FASB definitions, especially human resources and research and development (R&D), are expensed and don't show up on the balance sheet (except through business acquisitions).

The present GAAP structure can be defended, and it can be argued that GAAP provides a reasonable starting point for approximating economic reality. The historical cost process (including depreciation and other allocations) is conservative. The dollar amounts can be verified and defended as "real costs," whereas valuations based on current cost often cannot. Human capital is expensed, although companies spend considerable sums on employee training and development. Again, this is conservative. The costs are expensed as incurred, reducing current earnings. They are not capitalized, in part because they are difficult to value. For example, employees can leave the firm at any time, making it difficult to capitalize training or experience costs. Internal R&D costs may be the most important spending categories by high-tech companies and result in real economic assets (patents, new products, improved processes, and so on). These are expensed, largely because it is difficult to measure specific benefits. One of the reasons why the market value of a major corporation is much higher than book value is because these "intangible assets" have real value recognized by the market.

Some assets are recorded at fair value. Inventory is recorded at LCM, a "one direction current cost." Marketable securities (if trading or available-for-sale securities) are recorded at fair value, because market values are easily determined (and verifiable). Derivatives must be stated at fair value, a complex calculation based on economic models such as

TABLE 4.1	BALANCE SHEET CATEGORIES
Assets	Probable future economic benefits obtained or controlled by a particular entity as a result of past transactions or events.
Liabilities	Probable future sacrifices of economic benefits arising from present obligations of a particular entity to transfer assets or provide services to another entity in the future as a result of past transactions or events.
Equity (or net assets)	Residual interest in the assets of an entity that remains after deducting its liabilities. In a business enterprise, the equity is the ownership interest.

Black-Scholes—values that change continuously and can move swiftly. The result is that, despite the conceptual framework, there is little consistent guidance from accounting theory to financial practice on valuing assets—potentially an earnings management nightmare.

Assets and liabilities are divided into current and noncurrent categories. The usual rule of thumb is current items are converted (received or paid) into cash or otherwise eliminated within one year. This is important to evaluate the relative liquidity of a company. Assets can be categorized as physical, financial, or intangible. Physical assets include property, plant, and equipment (PPE) and inventory. Assets and liabilities also can be categorized as monetary (stated in specific monetary terms such as accounts receivable or payable or bonds) or nonmonetary (such as inventory or property, plant, and equipment). Financial assets (debt instruments are monetary, equity instruments are not) include cash, investments, and accounts receivable. Intangible assets include goodwill, patents, trademarks, etc. Most liabilities are financial.

In most cases, liabilities are payables with a due date and payable in specific monetary amounts (dollars in the United States, euros in much of Europe, and so on). For these items, the criteria for recording have been met: (1) an obligation has been incurred and (2) the amount and timing are measurable. Except for the time value of money, there are few conceptual problems between GAAP and the conceptual framework for these items. Note that deferred revenue items also are categorized as liabilities.

Obligations exist that are difficult to quantify. Product warranties are obligations, but specific timing and dollar amounts can be difficult to determine. Generally, companies use experience to determine probable costs. Judgment is involved—and judgment means earnings management issues. Insurance premiums prepay insurance coverage. The amount and timing of claims have to be estimated by insurance companies to record insurance reserves (a liability): judgment again.

Other categories of potential obligations are problematic. A major category is contingencies, potential obligations recognized by rules established in SFAS No. 5. To record a contingency as a liability, the loss must be probable and the amount reasonably estimated. Litigation is a primary example, because major corporations are subject to government regulations and lawsuits of various kinds. Another category is environmental hazards that impact certain industries such as chemicals and utilities. Some companies record losses and reserve accounts for estimated contingencies (common for chemical companies, for example). In most cases, companies claim that the SFAS No. 5 criteria are not met and the contingent liabilities are unrecorded but described in a contingency note.

Stockholders' equity can be considered a plug figure. That is, equity must equal assets minus liabilities, and equity also is called book value and net assets. The composition of equity is reasonably complex and needs reconciliation with net income (through retained earnings), cash dividend payments, the purchase of the company's stock in the open market (treasury stock), other comprehensive income, and other items. The evaluation of equity generally ties into other aspects of earnings management.

AN EMD BALANCE SHEET STRATEGY

The earnings management detection (EMD) balance sheet strategy will incorporate two levels of analysis for amounts on the current financial statement (trend and quarterly analyses will be described in Chapter 7). First is a balance sheet overview, looking at the interrelationship between all major accounts. As a first step, a common-size analysis is useful, that is, a restatement of all the major balance sheet accounts as a percentage of total assets. Simultaneously, these percentages are compared with those of the corporation's direct competitors. The amounts and percentages for the current year, previous year, and direct competitors give a general indication of any unusual balances. Determining working capital (current assets minus current liabilities), debt to equity (at this point, total liabilities divided by stockholders' equity), and other "overview" ratios is a starting point.

The second level is the evaluation of each category, starting with cash. Arbitrarily, this analysis will work down the balance sheet and end up evaluating equity. First is a common-size review (from level one) to spot any items of particular concern. Further ratio analysis and other quantitative techniques indicate basic relationships related to liquidity and leverage (activity and profitability will be analyzed in the next chapter). See, for example, Chapter 4 of Giroux (2003) for an overview of quantitative financial analysis. Then an accounting-related analysis will be completed, with use of primarily the balance sheet accounts and appropriate notes that provide the details on accounting policies (primarily found in note 1 of most annual reports).

LEVEL 1 ANALYSIS

A summary of EMD overview concerns (level 1) appears in Table 4.2.

This is a straightforward and quick overview, primarily to determine where to spend the most time in level 2 analysis. There are basic rules of thumb, but experience is the best instructor. Thus, a current ratio of at least two (current assets divided by current liabilities) and equity equal to 50 percent or more of total assets are standard examples. However, more companies have levels below these rules of thumb than in the past. Comparisons to the previous year and competitors are most likely useful, although negative working capital and very low equity would be concerns in any case.

TABLE 4.2	EARNINGS MANAGEMENT DETECTION OVERVIEW CONCERNS	
Topic	**Concern**	**Detection Strategy**
Relative balances	Unusual amounts may indicate potential problems.	Common-size percentages for the current year that are substantially different from the previous year and/or competitors'.
Working capital	A reasonable level of overall liquidity is expected. Negative working capital is a particular concern.	Compute working capital (current assets minus current liabilities) and evaluate. Inadequate working liquidity suggests further analysis.
Leverage	Comparison of liabilities to equity, looking for a reasonable level; high leverage (too little equity) is a particular concern.	Evaluate equity common-size percentage plus leverage ratios. There is particular concern if they are higher than previous year's and competitors'.
Composition issues	Balance sheets may not conform to industry standards; important information may be hidden under "other assets" and "other liabilities."	Review for conformity; check magnitude of other assets and liability accounts; review footnote disclosures associated with "other categories."

A simplified common-size balance sheet summary for Apple for 2002, showing comparisons with figures for 2001 and for competitors Dell and Gateway, is presented in Table 4.3.

On the basis of the common-size statement, with comparisons to the previous years and Apple's competitors, a level one analysis can be summarized. All three companies have high levels of cash, current assets, and current liabilities. Apple's cash balance ($2.3 billion) includes cash equivalents, which are high-quality debt instruments that mature within 90 days. Included as "near cash" are marketable securities that mature within 1 year (listed as short-term investments of $2.1 billion). Apple's cash position is 68.9 percent for the current year, which is above average for the three companies and below the previous year's 84.3 percent. Apple has a relatively low level of receivables at 9.0 percent and an extremely low inventory level at 0.7 percent. Current assets represent over 85 percent of total assets, comparable to last year's figures and higher than those of both Dell and Gateway. With current liabilities of 26.3 percent, working capital is quite high ($5,385 – $1,658 = $3,727 million), resulting in a current ratio of 3.2 ($5,385/$1,658). This is higher than the competitors' figures. Liquidity does not seem to be a problem, unless it can be demonstrated that the company has too much cash that is not productive (an unlikely outcome, given the dynamic nature of the industry and the high cash levels of Dell and Gateway).

Total liabilities of Apple are 35.0 percent of total assets, usually considered relatively low leverage (e.g., based on the rule of thumb of 50 percent or less of assets). The other two competitors have higher leverage ratios, and Dell's debt level of 65.3 percent is considerably higher. Apple's property, plant, and equipment represents less than 10 percent of total assets, a very low level for a manufacturing company. However, Dell's is lower at 6.1 percent, and Gateway's is less than 20 percent. Given the nature of the business, which concentrates on assembly rather than complex manufacturing, this is probably reasonable. This overview suggests that Apple has no obvious problems associated with the balance sheet.

The balance sheet of Hilton Hotels for 2001 illustrates a service company. The composition is quite different from that of Apple and the other PC companies. Hilton has rela-

TABLE 4.3	**COMPARISON OF SUMMARIZED BALANCE SHEETS**				
Account	Apple 2002 (Millions of $)	Apple 2002—CS	Apple 2001—CS	Dell 2002—CS	Gateway 2001—CS
Cash*	4,337	68.9%	84.3%	28.9%	39.0%
Receivables	565	9.0	7.7	19.5	7.4
Inventory	45	0.7	0.2	2.1	4.0
Current assets	5,388	85.6	85.4	58.2	71.1
Property, plant, and equipment	621	9.9	9.4	6.1	20.4
Total assets†	6,298	100.0	100.0	100.0	100.0
Current liabilities	1,658	26.3	25.2	55.6	38.4
Total liabilities	2,203	35.0	34.9	65.3	47.6
Total equity	4,095	65.0	65.1	34.7	52.4

* Includes cash equivalents and short-term marketable securities.
† Does not add up to 100% because certain accounts are excluded.
CS = common-size.

tively less in current assets (11.3 percent of total assets; cash is only 0.4 percent), the remainder being long-term assets. Property, plant, and equipment were the largest category at 44.5 percent of total assets. Hilton was highly leveraged, with a debt-to-equity ratio of 3.9× ($7,002/$1,783). Long-term liabilities were 87.1 percent of total liabilities. Thus, Hilton's cash position and leverage would be two key areas of concern. (Hilton's level 1 analysis for 2002 is presented as Problem 4.1.)

Consider the common-size analysis of some extreme examples (Table 4.4) in comparison with Apple (all of these companies have a December 31, 2001, year end).

Given these percentages, one can calculate working capital, current ratio, and leverage (Table 4.5; the debt-to-equity ration used is total liabilities/total assets).

There are problems with regard to working capital and leverage. Gillette, Kellogg, and TXU Corp. have negative working capital (equivalent to a current ratio less than one), an automatic red flag (RF) for this analysis. Negative working capital is an area of concern, because the company does not have enough current assets to cover current liabilities. This does not mean eminent insolvency, but it necessitates further analysis to explain why. Note that some analysts believe that current assets should be kept low and current liabilities should be paid as late as possible.

Maytag has a debt-to-equity ratio greater than 100, an obvious red flag (Kellogg with debt-to-equity greater than ten also could be a red flag). This means the ownership interest represents less than 1 percent of total assets, virtually no cushion against insolvency should additional financial problems strike. These problems were demonstrated with ratios; however, they also are obvious on the basis of common-size analysis.

The level 1 analysis points out some obvious areas for extensive investigation in the level 2 analysis for the four companies above. However, the simplified balance sheet analysis for Apple does not indicate obvious problems. If anything, the numbers for cash and

TABLE 4.4   **COMMON-SIZE (CS) ANALYSIS EXAMPLES FOR COMPARISON**

Account	Maytag—CS	Gillette—CS	Kellogg—CS	TXU—CS
Cash	3.5%	9.5%	2.2%	2.7%
Receivables	19.6	17.9	7.3	6.0
Inventory	14.2	10.1	5.5	1.2
Current assets	43.4	44.7	18.3	15.5
Total assets	100.0	100.0	100.0	100.0
Current liabilities	34.1	48.5	21.3	23.5
Total liabilities	99.2	78.6	91.6	81.2
Total equity	0.8	21.4	8.4	18.8

TABLE 4.5   **FINANCIAL CALCULATIONS, SOME OF WHICH MAY REQUIRE FURTHER ANALYSIS**

	Maytag	Gillette	Kellogg	TXU
Working Capital	$295 million	$–383 million (RF)	$–306 million (RF)	$–3,418 million (RF)
Current Ratio	1.3×	92.1% (RF)	86.1% (RF)	65.7% (RF)
Leverage	130.5× (RF)*	3.7×	10.9×	4.3×

RF = red flag/area of particular concern (requiring further analysis).

inventory look "too good" (very high and very low, respectively). The "too good" amounts need explanation also, particularly with regard to business strategy.

Composition will vary by company and industry. Balance sheet format is relatively standardized, and most deviations are industry-based; that is, industries have unique items and format procedures. A particular concern is when complex companies have oversimplified balance sheet presentations and large balances stated as "other assets" or "other liabilities" (either current or long-term). These "other" balances should be well explained in the footnote presentation. If not, disclosure is incomplete and the reporting quality is suspect. Apple has other current assets of 4.4 percent and other assets of 2.1 percent of total assets, not large enough to be considered concerns. General Motors had over $17 billion of other assets under "Automotive" (13.3 percent of Automotive assets, down from $32 billion the previous year) and $37 billion under "Financing" (19.1 percent of Financial assets) for 2001. The categories making up "Other" were listed in Note 11. "Other" liability amounts were comparable ($14 billion for Automotive and $16 billion for Financing, listed in Note 12).

EMD concerns for individual accounts (level 2 analysis) are separated into four categories for review: (1) current assets and liabilities, (2) long-term assets, (3) long-term liabilities, and (4) stockholders' equity. The primary analysis continues for Apple.

CURRENT ASSETS AND LIABILITIES

A summary of EMD current asset and liability concerns is given in Table 4.6. The focus of analysis is on liquidity and specific issues by account.

CASH AND CASH EQUIVALENTS

Cash is one of the most important balance sheet accounts, partly because of the economic focus on cash flows (more on this in Chapter 6). Cash equivalents are highly liquid short-term-interest-bearing debt investments, usually defined as high-quality-debt marketable securities due within ninety days. Managing cash is part of financial planning and easier if it's a big pile of cash. At $2.3 billion or 41.8 percent of current assets, Apple has a big pile of cash and cash equivalents, as do the two competitors. Note that there is some difference of opinion among analysts as to the proper amount of cash. The alternative to the "big pile of cash" perspective is that better investment alternatives should be available.

MARKETABLE SECURITIES

Marketable securities are investments that are traded on financial markets. They can be debt or equity, short- or long-term. Short-term investments are debt investments maturing beyond ninety days but within one year. Accounting options make them a potential earnings management concern. The three accounting options (which apply to all marketable securities) are based on how they're categorized, as shown in Table 4.7.

The major earnings management concern is the different recognition requirements, since judgment is involved in the accounting choice. The reasonableness of the category choice is based on the investor's judgment. The problem is that this decision can be based on results rather than intentions. Thus, holding losses could be avoided by treating them as held-to-maturity; alternatively, available-for-sale treatment would keep the losses off the income statement. Detailed information should be available in the notes. Note one states accounting policies used, and that is where to find which option(s) the company is using.

TABLE 4.6	CONCERNS AND DETECTION STRATEGIES REGARDING CURRENT ASSETS AND LIABILITIES		
Topic	**Concern**		**Detection Strategy**
Cash and cash equivalents	What is the appropriate balance and how is it proportioned between cash and interest-earnings equivalents?		Relative levels compared to previous year and competitors; footnote analysis of cash equivalents and any relevant MD&A discussion
Marketable securities, short-term	Relative amounts, distribution across categories, and which accounting method was used		Ratio analysis of levels; footnote analysis of composition and accounting method(s) used
Inventory	Relative amounts, including considerations of efficiency and potential obsolete or hard-to-dispose-of items		Ratio analysis of levels; footnote analysis of accounting method(s) used, write-downs, composition, and evaluation of obsolescence potential
Accounts receivable	Balances and changes in balances; importance of credit terms and the relationship to sales; potential for misstating bad debts; factoring and related techniques		Relative levels, with particular concern about changes over time (trend and quarterly analysis important); look for notes or MD&A discussion on factoring or special purpose entities to eliminate receivables from the balance sheet
Accounts payable	Company policy may be to pay these quickly or put it off as long as possible to "conserve" cash; companies may avoid recording payables near end of the period to understate liabilities		Relative levels; look at notes or MD&A for evidence of firm's payables policy
Reserve accounts	"Cookie jar" reserves to smooth income		Evaluate amounts for doubtful accounts and large changes in percentages to receivables; other reserve accounts often not reported and difficult to evaluate; review notes and MD&A
Other	Deferred tax practices; prepaid items; large accumulated balances reported as "other"		Tax strategies could be problematic, so review tax note; review policies for prepaid items; review "other" notes— lack of disclosure is a particular concern

TABLE 4.7	ACCOUNTING OPTIONS FOR MARKETABLE SECURITIES	
Type	**Definition**	
Trading securities	Debt and equity instruments are trading securities if the investor expects to sell them before maturity. They are stated at fair value, with holding gains and losses recorded as part of operations on the income statement.	
Available-for-sale	Investors may hold them to maturity or sell them sooner. They are recorded at fair value, but holding gains and losses are recorded directly to stockholders' equity as part of "other comprehensive income."	
Held-to-maturity	Investors are not planning to resell them; therefore, they are recorded at amortized cost. This category applies only to debt securities.	

The numeric details should be in a marketable securities note. Apple has short-term investments of $2.1 billion or 38.7 percent of current assets. They are categorized as available-for-sale.

INVENTORY

In many industries, inventory is the most critical asset for analysis. Retail firms can have large inventory levels on store shelves and in warehouses. Wal-Mart is considered one of the most efficient retailers, but inventory was 84.8 percent of current assets and 30.8 percent of total assets for the October 2002 quarter. Manufacturing firms accumulate three levels of inventory: raw materials, work in progress, and finished goods. These three categories are usually stated in an inventory footnote. The relative level of inventory is a sign of manufacturing efficiency (the lower the better), and inventory levels vary by company and industry.

The method of inventory (or multiple methods by complex multinationals) can be considered an earnings management decision, and the method can be changed (called a change in accounting principle)—another factor of potential concern. FIFO (first in, first out) is the most common technique used, and companies tend to follow the industry. Inventory methods that differ from the rest of the industry, a change in inventory methods, and certain specific practices are causes for concern.

When inventory costs are rising or falling relatively quickly, the inventory method used becomes important. Table 4.8 summarizes the basic effects involved.

When costs are rising, LIFO (last in, first out) usually results in higher cost of goods sold. Taxes would be lower, but so would earnings, while inventory levels also would be lower. When inventory costs are falling, FIFO gives the same result. When inventory costs are rising, than parts of LIFO inventory may be stated much below current inventory costs. Cash flows represent the "real economic effect" and usually go up when prices are rising, with use of LIFO (because lower taxes are paid).

Companies that use LIFO typically have "old inventory" costs very much lower than current costs. These are referred to as LIFO reserves and may be disclosed under the inventory note. When reported, the LIFO reserve can be added to the LIFO inventory balance to approximate current costs. LIFO companies can work down to these "old layers," called LIFO liquidation, which lowers cost of goods sold (thus increasing income). Generally, substantial information is available in the inventory footnote to determine the impact of

TABLE 4.8   EFFECTS OF INVENTORY METHOD

	Rising Prices		Falling Prices	
	LIFO	**FIFO**	**LIFO**	**FIFO**
COGS	Higher	Lower	Lower	Higher
Income before tax	Lower	Higher	Higher	Lower
Income tax	Lower	Higher	Higher	Lower
Net income	Lower	Higher	Higher	Lower
Cash flows	Higher	Lower	Lower	Higher
Inventory level	Lower	Higher	Higher	Lower
Working capital	Lower	Higher	Higher	Lower

COGS = cost of goods sold; LIFO = last in, first out; FIFO = first in, first out.

these potential earnings management devices. For example, Sunoco reported petroleum and other inventory of $652 million on a LIFO basis for 2001, but the LIFO reserve was higher by $515 million. Thus, replacement cost was $1,167 billion or 79 percent higher than reported.

Apple uses FIFO, appropriate when inventory is more likely to decline in value than increase. Year-end inventory was $9 million in purchased parts and $36 million in finished goods, for a total of $45 million. This was a low 0.8 percent of current assets. By comparison, Dell is considered one of the most efficient manufacturers, and inventory was 3.5 percent of current assets for the October 2002 quarter. Inventory levels vary by industry and company. Boeing had inventory of 35.5 percent of current assets for the September 2002 quarter. Service companies generally don't have inventory.

A measure of inventory efficiency is inventory turnover, measured as cost of goods sold/average inventory. Apple's inventory turnover for 2002 was 147.8 ($4,139/½(45 + 11). In other words, inventory turned over almost 148 times during the year. This can be converted to days (called average days inventory in stock) by dividing inventory turnover into 365: 365/147.8 = 2.5 days for Apple. This is the average length of time Apple holds inventory, assuming that year-end figures are representative. A sophisticated "just in time" inventory system is necessary at Apple to speed production and control costs. By comparison, Boeing had 53.2 days of inventory for fiscal year 2001, and Wal-Mart had 217.3 days. Generally, the higher the number of days, the greater the concern for earnings management potential. This is tempered by industry characteristics and specific firm trends. For example, Boeing has a long operating cycle and days of inventory higher than Apple is expected. As a retailer, Wal-Mart must maintain high inventory levels to ensure adequate customer selection. A combination of high number of days, an increase in inventory over time, and poor numbers in comparison with close competitors and industry averages raises a potential red flag (see Chapter 7).

A key area of concern is obsolete inventory items and goods that are slow sellers. GAAP requires inventory to be stated at lower-of-cost-or-market, which means that inventory dogs need to be written down and an operating loss taken. Companies have considerable flexibility here, especially before year end. Once the auditors arrive, flexibility diminishes. Unless it is specifically discussed in the annual report, determining overstated inventory is difficult, but this can be attempted by looking at inventory levels over time.

Inventory changes should be proportional to sales changes. If sales go up 10 percent a year, it is reasonable to expect inventory also to rise about 10 percent a year. Unusually large inventory levels on quarterly statements without comparable sales growth may indicate problems. These may be corrected at year end to pass the annual audit. With luck, additional inventory information may be available from the MD&A or inventory footnote. Business publications and SEC investigations also may indicate inventory problems.

Certain fashionable items are vulnerable to slow selling and potential write-downs, such as toys and apparel. Hot items can make a bundle for the manufacturers and retailers. Mistakes can mean large losses and massive write-offs. High-tech hardware and software are subject to quick obsolescence. Corporations may not be quick to write these off and take the losses, especially if the lower income affects bonuses and other compensation rewards.

In 2000, Cisco Systems overcommitted to purchase manufacturing components (the pressing problem seemed to be to maintain enough inventory to meet demand). Inventory rose in each quarter, from $695 million in January 2000 to $2,533 million in January 2001. Inventory rose from 16 percent of sales to 38 percent. Then sales dropped. The company took a $2.5 billion write-down of inventory as a special charge in April 2001 (the total charge-off was $3.9 billion, including various restructuring costs). Since the write-down dropped the inventory balance essentially to zero, the gamesmanship seemed to change. Now if these items were actually sold, cost of goods sold would be close to zero, and gross margin and net income would be up accordingly.

The extreme problem is outright fraud. There is a long and infamous history of fraudulent overstatements of inventory. McKesson-Robbins in the 1930s was the classic case, before audit standards required physical counts by the auditors. However, the potential never disappeared, although it is much less common because of better controls and audit requirements. The analyst cannot determine fraud. The best that can be hoped for is observing where an environment for possible fraud exists, on the basis of corporate governance, compensation packages, current executives, and history. Fraud detection would have to come from the internal or external auditor, whistle-blowers, the SEC, or others. When discovered, the interpretation is usually massive earnings manipulation and likely earnings quality of close to zero.

ACCOUNTS RECEIVABLE

Accounts and notes receivable represent the amounts due on credit sales. Receivables are reported on the balance sheet net of an allowance for doubtful accounts, an estimate of bad debts. Several earnings management techniques are possible. The relative magnitude of receivables and their relationship to sales are the first consideration. Unlike inventory, "smaller is better" is not necessarily correct. Apple's receivables at the end of the 2002 fiscal year end were 10.5 percent of current assets, compared to 9.1 percent the previous year and 17.6 percent in 2000. Since much of Apple's sales are for cash (usually by credit card), a relatively low balance is expected. Apple's receivables turnover (sales/average accounting receivable) for 2002 was 11.1 [$5,742/½($565 + $466)], or 32.9 days (365/11.1). Thus, on average, accounts were paid in just over a month. These numbers were almost identical to Dell's.

The expected balances and ratios depend on competitor and industry averages as well as comparisons over time. In the same industry, IBM had a much higher 122.9 days. This would be a concern for the evaluation of IBM. Why does it take over four months to collect the average account? (Note that IBM has many lines of hardware, software, and information services available, in addition to PCs.) Wal-Mart's was a low 3.2 average days receivables (associated with few direct credit sales), and Boeing's was 31.7 days.

What is not apparent are the relative credit terms given by the corporations. Relaxing credit standards can increase sales. However, bad debts would increase. The optimal level of credit sales is difficult to determine; however, extreme decisions and changes in credit terms can be recognized. Large and growing receivables are a clear indicator of declining credit terms or related problems (e.g., potential problems with a specific large customer). The key indicator is a receivables balance growing at a much higher rate than sales. The balance sheet or a receivables footnote should give gross receivables (usually by operating category) and the allowance, plus additional information that might be useful. The bad debts percentage, when compared over time and to direct competitors', indicates the relative level of credit terms and changes in credit terms.

Apple had an allowance for bad debts of $51 million for 2002, 8.3 percent of gross receivables of $616 million. The 2001 allowance also was $51 million. By comparison, Dell's bad debts were 2.9 percent of gross receivables. Apple's receivables for one customer (Ingram Micro) represented 10.8 percent of total receivables, suggesting the importance of the credit-worthiness of this company. Apple also had nontrade receivables associated with the sale of components to vendors of $142 million (2.6 percent of current assets), recorded as other current assets.

Corporations that use aggressive revenue recognition will have relatively higher receivables, because the offset to sales usually is accounts receivable. When a company shifts to a more aggressive revenue recognition policy, the result should be higher sales but also higher receivables. In addition, the receivables will tend to grow faster than sales and the average days receivable will increase.

Companies can dispose of their receivables. The most common method is factoring, essentially selling a portfolio of receivables to a financial intermediary specializing in factoring. This has the advantage of removing some percentage of the receivables from the balance sheet, but it is a relatively expensive form of financing. A more recent alternative is to transfer the receivables to a special purpose entity (SPE), essentially a mechanism to maintain some level of control of the receivables but removing them from the balance sheet. It has essentially the same effect as factoring for removing the receivables from the balance sheet but at a lower cost. Since the purpose of both approaches is to "hide" the real receivables' balances, these are examples of earnings management. That is, factoring or transferring to an SPE lowers the receivables balance and thus reduces the receivables turnover. This information may or may not be disclosed in the annual report.

Kohl's reported receivables of $836 million for fiscal year 2002 (the allowance was 2.1 percent of gross receivables). Prior to 1999, Kohl's "sold" credit card receivables to an SPE (Kohl's Receivables Corporation). Since 1999, Kohl's has "sold" these receivable to Preferred Receivables Funding Corporation and others (described in Note 3 of the 10-K). This is an example of fairly common off-balance-sheet financing.

Other receivables also may exist. Ford Credit is the financial segment of Ford Motor and has substantial financial receivables, both short- and long-term. Ford Credit sells a portion of the receivables to an SPE, where they are securitized (essentially repackaged as note securities).

RESERVE ACCOUNTS

Reserve accounts (contra-assets) exist for most asset categories. These include allowances for doubtful accounts for accounts receivable, reserves for overstated inventory (reduced value, obsolescence, or other measures of impaired value), investment impairments, and so on. Concerns are raised with regard to the relative value of the reserves, changes in reserves (e.g., reduce reserves to increase income in current quarter to meet earnings targets), and the existence of impaired assets that have not been written down.

Levitt (2002) railed against "cookie jar" reserves, essentially excess reserves that can be tapped in "bad years" to smooth earnings. Microsoft was overstating multiple reserve accounts, according to a 2002 SEC Accounting Proceeding, and a cease-and-desist order was issued. Sun Trust Banks restated earnings for 1994–1997, because it overstated its provision for loan losses. Similarly, National City Bancorp (a bank holding company) restated earnings in 1999 after identifying a "special reserve" that reduced loans receivable at subsidiary Diversified Business Credit.

OTHER CURRENT ASSETS

Other current assets generally are combined together in a single line item on the balance sheet and normally described in a separate footnote. Specific items may be important enough to list as separate line items for some companies. The most common are deferred income taxes (those that are current assets) and prepaid expenses. Deferred taxes are described in the income tax footnote and will be discussed in the next chapter. Information on other current assets might be discussed, but as likely as not, it is ignored in the annual report. The usual rationale is lack of materiality. This may indicate a lack of complete disclosure, a concern related to transparency.

ACCOUNTS PAYABLE

The most significant current liability is accounts payable, the accumulated credit balances on purchases from suppliers on short-term credit. The major consideration is the corporation's payment strategy, which might be to pay these liabilities quickly—or not. Delaying payment usually means the conservation of cash, rather than an indicator of high credit risk. Except for discounts for early payment, usually interest is not charged on receivables unless past due. Therefore, the incentive may be to postpone actual payment until the due date. This should be reviewed as part of a reasonable cash management strategy of the firm. However, if the company seems to be having severe operating or credit problems (e.g., bonds are downgraded, especially to a "junk bond" status), then the accounts payable review should be part of an expanded credit risk analysis. Substantial changes in accounts payable also could be a concern.

Apple's accounts payable represented 54.9 percent of current liabilities, with average days payable of 54.5 days $[365/(\$5,742/\frac{1}{2}(\$911 + \$801))]$. This is calculated as sales/average payables; alternatively, an estimate of purchases (cost of goods sold + changes in inventory) can be substituted for sales to calculate days payable. Thus, Apple pays relatively slowly. IBM, on the other hand, had average days payable of 401.5. These substantial differences within the same industry (broadly defined) suggest a more thorough analysis for IBM, including relative liquidity and leverage. IBM has adequate liquidity but relatively high leverage.

OTHER CURRENT LIABILITIES

The major categories include current portions of long-term debt, interest-bearing short-term debt such as commercial paper, deferred tax liabilities, unearned revenues, and other current liabilities. The current portions of long-term debt will be analyzed as part of long-term debt and deferred tax liabilities as part of the tax analysis in the next chapter. Commercial paper is very-short-term borrowing for prime customers.

LONG-TERM ASSETS

Long-term assets are a diverse group; the only feature in common is that they will not be converted to cash within the next year or so. Property, plant, and equipment (PPE, also called fixed assets) historically has been the major category. Others include intangible assets and long-term investments. Industry characteristics and business strategy determine which types of long-term assets will be significant. The major earnings management concerns are listed in Table 4.9.

As with current assets, reserve accounts exist for most long-term assets. The most obvious one is accumulated depreciation of PPE, but others are intangibles and long-term investments. These tend not to be particularly standardized and are subject to income smoothing, sometimes on a large scale. Companies often have considerable flexibility with these accounts. For example, goodwill is no longer amortized but subject to periodic evaluation for the impairment of value. Impairment write-down would be one-time charges that could be substantial. In the first quarter of 2002, AOL Time Warner wrote off $54 billion in goodwill.

Property, Plant, and Equipment (PPE) PPE, also called fixed assets, are the infrastructure assets necessary for manufacturing, maintaining inventory, selling, and administering the company operations. Historically, 90 percent of the assets of the mammoth industrial giants have been PPE. PPE is recorded at acquisition cost and depreciated over

TABLE 4.9	MAJOR EARNINGS MANAGEMENT CONCERNS REGARDING LONG-TERM ASSETS	
Topic	**Concern**	**Detection Strategy**
Property, plant, and equipment	Relative amount and age of fixed assets; possible understatement of depreciation-related expenses; acquisition, disposal, and write-off issues	Ratios, including average age; evaluate note disclosure for reasonableness; evaluate sales of PPE for reported gains and losses
Intangible assets acquired through acquisition	Part of the analysis of business combinations	Complex; see Chapter 9
Intangible assets internally generated	Capitalized costs that are normally expensed; relative spending appropriate to business strategy	Evaluate description and accounting procedures used in notes and MD&A
Long-term investments— debt instruments	How classified, and the impact onrecording gains and losses; when to write-down declining valuations; sales of securities	Evaluate accounting policies; review levels and changes in amount; evaluate gains and losses and when sales are recorded
Long-term investments—equity	Available-for-sale vs. trading categories; sales of securities; potential control issues when ownership approaches 20 percent	Accounting policies; review levels and trends; evaluate gains and losses and when sales are recorded
Long-term investments— equity method	Effective control without majority ownership, resulting in limited financial statement recognition	See Chapter 9, part of acquisition/consolidations analysis
Reserve accounts	Large amounts, suggesting income smoothing, limited disclosure	Evaluate note and MD&A disclosures on reserve accounts
Other long-term assets	High relative magnitude, with limited disclosure	Percentage of "other long-term asset" to total assets; evaluate "other" note disclosure

the estimated useful life of the assets. For a variety of reasons, such as the increased importance of financial and intangible assets, huge levels of PPE are less common. Relatively few companies have PPE greater than 50 percent of total assets.

The magnitude of PPE is important, but more important is the relative age and composition of fixed assets. Despite being a manufacturing company, Apple has PPE of only 9.9 percent of total assets. For 2002 the average age was estimated at 3.7 years (accumulated depreciation/depreciation expense) and the average depreciable life at 9.0 years (ending gross investment/depreciation expense). These were comparable with values for direct competitors Gateway (average age, 2.2 years) and Dell (average age, 2.6 years). Apple's PPE was relatively new, with short-lived assets, mostly equipment, capitalized software, and leasehold improvements. This makes sense, given Apple's strategy of assembling components manufactured by various suppliers, combined with development of unique software. Since 2001, Apple has treated capitalized costs of software as part of PPE.

Primary manufacturing companies and utilities tend to have large fixed-asset bases. Duke Energy was the largest utility in the *Fortune* 500 in 2002. It had net fixed assets of over $28 million, or 58.7 percent of total assets at the end of fiscal year 2001 (acquisition cost was 81.6 percent of total assets). The average age of Duke's PPE was 8.3 years, and the average depreciable life was 29.5 years—a long-lived fixed asset base, but relatively new assets. A utility with an older asset base than Duke's should be less efficient. An older asset base indicates that the company may not be replacing fixed assets on a timely basis. This conserves cash and reduces expenses in the short run, but the strategy has long-term consequences in terms of relative efficiency.

PPE is not the area where aggressive earnings management is expected. The standard accounting is straight-line depreciation for GAAP and accelerated depreciation for tax purposes. The usual question is relative efficiency of the producing asset base (e.g., as measured by average age). However, earnings manipulation has happened in the past. The most egregious example was Waste Management in the 1990s. The company restated earnings in 1997 by $1.4 billion for understating PPE expenses. This was accomplished by inflating the useful lives of fixed assets and overstating their salvage value.

Of some potential concern is the sale of PPE, since the result can be a significant gain or loss. A gain on sale might increase the net income (or other bottom line definition) enough for a company to meet some hurdle (such as a modest net income rather than a loss, income at least as high as the previous year, or meeting analysts' forecasts).

Intangible Assets   Intangible assets lack physical substance. These include goodwill, patents, copyrights, franchises, licenses, brands, and trademarks. Corporations often spend vast sums on research and development, advertising, and other costs that lead to valuable intangible assets. However, these costs are almost always expensed and don't show up on the balance sheet. Generally, intangibles are recorded only when acquired through the purchase method. Acquired patents, copyrights, and so on are recorded at fair value in a purchase acquisition. Goodwill is essentially a "plug figure," the difference between the acquisition cost and the restated value of all assets and liabilities acquired. These are all subject to potential arbitrary valuations and earnings management strategies. A more comprehensive treatment of intangibles is presented in Chapter 9, Business Combinations.

Internal costs associated with intangibles that are normally expensed but instead are capitalized represent an earnings management concern. Generally, these pop up as unique cases. As of 2001, Apple capitalized software development costs (this is allowed by GAAP) as part of PPE rather than other assets. The gross amount for 2002 was $184 million, or 26.6 percent of gross ending investment. This may be considered a modest concern but should be recorded for future reference when reviewing the analyst's perception of the overall management earnings strategy of Apple.

Long-Term Investments   Long-term investments are usually debt and equity financial assets (other assets such as real estate may be included). These investments can be uses of excess cash or stock purchased for influence or control. However, the long-term focus means less liquidity and additional financial risks. Two categories that apply for long-term marketable securities are available-for-sale and held-to-maturity. Valuation issues are fair value versus book value and whether holding gains and losses are recorded. Thus, classification is the first earnings management consideration, especially because the category can be changed. For example, AFLAC, Inc., reclassified debt securities from available-for-sale to held-to-maturity in 1998, and it recorded an unrealized gain of $1.1 billion in the process.

Only held-to-maturity securities (always debt) are recorded at book value (with amortization of premiums and discounts over the life of the debt). However, these securities would be written down if unrealized losses were considered permanent, a judgment call subject to earnings management. Presidential Life had debt investments in increasingly poor prospects (essentially junk bonds), which were not written down to fair value until required by the SEC in 1993. Selling investments is another issue. Companies, of course, have total control over the sale of investments and the timing of the sale. Therefore, planning for sales can be based on whether a gain or a loss is required (treated as part of earnings).

Equity investments are classified as available for sale and therefore recorded at fair value. Unrealized gains and losses are recorded directly to stockholders' equity. Again, selling of securities is another issue, and gains and losses are recorded on the income statement.

Equity investments that result in significant influence or control, usually 20 percent–50 percent ownership, are recorded under the equity method. The purpose is influence or control rather than investment earnings and is considered part of a corporation's acquisition strategy, which is reviewed in Chapter 9.

Apple had $39 million in long-term investments in fiscal year 2002 (versus $2.1 billion in short-term investments). Direct competitor Dell, on the other hand, had $4.4 billion in long-term investments (versus $273 million in short-term investments), a significant item for earnings management analysis. The primary concern is why such a difference exists.

Dell reported the information in Table 4.10 on long-term investments (in millions of dollars) for 2002 (Note 3 on financial instruments).

Realized gains and losses recorded on investments (including impairments) were as shown in Table 4.11 (for three fiscal years, in millions of dollars).

After unrealized gains in 2000 and 2001, Dell recognized net losses of $277 million in 2002. The net amounts were recorded on the income statement, suggesting no obvious earnings manipulation beyond the decisions to dispose of specific investments.

LONG-TERM LIABILITIES

Most long-term liabilities are interest-paying financial instruments, denominated in dollars or foreign currency. In most cases, the initial purpose of issuing debt is to finance ongoing operations or acquisitions. A summary of EMD long-term liability concerns is given in Table 4.12.

TABLE 4.10	DATA ON LONG-TERM INVESTMENTS REPORTED BY DELL FOR 2002		
	Fair Value	Cost	Unrealized Gain
Debt securities			
U.S. corporate and bank debt	$2,393	$2,375	$18
Municipal securities	87	84	3
U.S. government	1,663	1,657	6
International	168	165	3
Total	4,311	4,281	30
Equity securities	335	332	3
Total	4,646	4,613	33
Short-term	273	271	2
Long-term	4,373	4,342	31

TABLE 4.11	DELL'S INVESTMENT GAINS AND LOSSES (MILLIONS OF DOLLARS)		
	2002	2001	2000
Gains	$185	$473	$81
Losses	(462)	(166)	(1)
Net	(277)	307	80

Bonded Debt and Notes The common example of long-term liabilities is corporate bonds, based on a contract to pay semiannual interest at a fixed or variable rate of interest. Categories include debentures (unsecured), callable bonds (can be redeemed or "called" at a future date, based on some terms), and convertible debt (usually convertible to common stock).

Convertibility is an attractive feature to investors, as is callability to the issuer, and these features are reflected in the interest rate and bond price. The interest rate depends on the credit risk of the issuer, with noninvestment grade or junk bonds paying at a much higher rate. Debt instruments are increasingly complex and allow additional alternatives for the issuer and investor. This can mean greater opportunity but also greater credit risk.

Of particular concern is the comprehensive analysis of overall requirements for future interest and principal payments and how the debt structure fits to the overall business strategy of the company. Too much debt means large future cash payments, which reduce liquidity and future operating and financial flexibility. Interest payments also reduce profitability (partially offset by tax deductibility). Complex credit arrangements also can be difficult to fully evaluate.

Apple had long-term debt of $316 million for 2002, not much different from that in the previous two years, plus deferred tax liabilities of $229 million. Total long-term debt, at $545 million, was 24.7 percent of liabilities and 8.7 percent of total assets. The major item was a $300 million note issue in 1994 (listed at the market value of $316 at the end of fiscal year 2002). Apple also had operating lease commitments that totaled $464 million ($83

TABLE 4.12	EMD LONG-TERM LIABILITY CONCERNS

Topic	Concern	Detection Strategy
Bonded debt and notes	Credit risk, associated with magnitude, interest rates, contract terms, and maturity structure	Relative levels, including leverage ratios; interest expense (including the interest coverage ratio); liability notes for description of terms
Warranties	Underestimation of liabilities, which may be large	Look at warranty trends and relate to sales; review notes
Commitments	Commitments with related parties or others that may be large or influence incentives; commitments with potential dire consequences	Review commitment descriptions in notes, proxy statements, and MD&A
Contingencies	Most contingencies are understated or not recorded, a particular concern for some industries	Evaluate contingencies note and MD&A analysis; consider industry factors
Debt retirements	Companies retire debt to increase earnings or use debt defeasance to move debt off-balance-sheet; particularly problematic if declining credit rating results in a substantial gain	Debt retirement disclosures, including extraordinary items, plus note on debt defeasance
Off-balance-sheet obligations	Could represent significant obligations not reported; SPEs may not be recorded but could represent major obligations	Evaluate operating lease note and other commitments; recalculate liabilities if significant; look for evidence of SPEs and evaluate (see Chapter 11)

million for 2003) for facilities and equipment. The company had contingencies for class action lawsuits listed in the notes, which the company stated were without merit; Apple also is subject to European Union proposed regulations on disposal of electrical goods and other legal proceedings.

Consider, as a company with lots of debt, Tyco in fiscal year 2002 (detailed in Appendix 2). Yes, this is the Tyco of former CEO Dennis Kozlowski and 2002 scandal fame. Major accounting problems were associated with questionable accounting practices associated with acquisitions, and the company restated financials back to 1999. Since many of the acquisitions were made with debt, this analysis becomes critical for the evaluations of the earnings management of Tyco and, now, its potential to recover.

Tyco's 2002 balance sheet showed a debt-to-equity ratio of 1.7× ($41,581/$24,791), with total long-term liabilities of $21.9 billion. Much of this debt represented borrowing on lines of credit, short- to long-term notes, and bonded debt, with various terms (e.g., some are convertible), denominated in various currencies. The various terms were summarized in Note 18 to the 2002 10-K. Much of this analysis also involves operations (e.g., interest expense for 2002 was $1.1 billion, when the company had a net loss of $9.4 billion), cash flows (from operations and financing activities—which increased by $2 billion from net proceeds from debt), and the evaluation of business combinations. Tyco will be analyzed further, primarily in Chapter 9 in the section on acquisitions and related activities. Earnings manipulation was present but difficult to identify, given the complexity of the firm's operations.

Warranties   Some long-term liabilities are not denominated in currency, such as warranty obligations. Warranty obligations must be estimated, and these can be understated. Given the litigious environment, future risks can be difficult to evaluate. This is problematic in certain industries such as automobiles and other sophisticated machinery. For example, General Electric underestimated warranty costs for power plant turbines in 1998, which required a later special charge to earnings of $42 million to increase the liability.

Apple's warranty policy (2002 10-K) was as follows: "The Company provides currently for the estimated cost that may be incurred under product warranties at the time related revenue is recognized" (Note 1). Accrued warranty costs were $69 million in 2002 (total accrued expenses were $747 million), or 1.1 percent of total assets. For General Motors, warranties were included with dealer and customer allowances, claims, and discounts. The total amount for 2001 (part of accrued liabilities) was $16.4 billion, 5.1 percent of total assets and 13.0 percent of total automotive liabilities.

Debt Retirements   Corporations can retire long-term debt before the maturity date on the basis of call features or buying back in the open market. This usually occurs when the market value of the bonds declines (when interest rates rise) and the company can "capture" a gain on the retirements. Based on SFAS No. 145 (2002), gains and losses are treated as part of current operations. Companies with declining credit ratings and bond downgradings also find the market value of their debt declining and can record a gain by retiring the debt.

From an analyst's perspective, the "gain" does not represent economic reality (that is, there is no real gain because to replace the debt the firm would have to issue bonds at the new, higher effective interest rate). If significant, current earnings can be restated after deducting the gain on retirement. Note that prior to SFAS No. 145 (i.e., based on SFAS No. 4), gains and losses on debt retirement were recorded as extraordinary items. Since both gains and losses were nonrecurring items, it was more likely that firms would retire low-interest debt (which would rise in value as interest rates increased) and record the loss. As a nonrecurring item, the loss would be considered less important to analysts.

On the other hand, it may make more economic sense to retire high interest-rate bonds and record the loss. Chrysler (now DaimlerChrysler) issued over $1 billion dollars in 12 percent long-term debt in 1990 (a high rate because Chrysler seemed headed toward bankruptcy). As the company recovered, the market value of the debt increased, and Chrysler repurchased about half of the debt in 1996 (recording a pretax loss of $309 million as an extraordinary item) and an additional $300 million in 1998 (with an additional loss of $230 million). The debt was replaced, with substantially lower interest costs. Thus, one-time losses as nonrecurring items offset future lower-interest costs reported as part of continuing operations.

Commitments, Contingencies, and Other Off-Balance-Sheet Debt   Particularly important from an earnings management perspective are liabilities that are not recorded on the balance sheet. These can include commitments, contingencies, and various off-balance-sheet obligations such as operating leases and special purpose entities. Commitments and contingencies are detailed in the notes, and these should be reviewed carefully, particularly considering the characteristics of the industries involved. Chemical, tobacco, and automobile companies are examples of industries where contingencies are likely to be substantial. Generally, companies explain the potential obligations but often understate the potential for future claims.

Chemical company PPG reported the following contingencies in Note 11 (summarized from its 2001 annual report):

> Lawsuits & claims on product liability, contract, patent, environmental, antitrust & other. Lawsuit for fixing prices on auto refinish & glass products; personal injury from exposure to asbestos (about 116,000 asbestos claims pending involving several companies). Company claims a successful defense and no responsibility. Trial court found PPG liable in 2002 in Texas, but PPG will appeal. Lost a lawsuit to Marvin Windows on breach of warranty. PPG will appeal. Environmental contingencies: PPG accrued $29 million in 2001 where liability probable as reserves (total reserves of $94 million). Possible environmental loss contingencies of $200–400 million considered reasonably possible (but unreserved).

Thus, as a typical chemical company, contingencies were widespread. Part of the potential costs was accrued (recognized on the balance sheet with a comparable expense on the income statement), but the total costs could be much higher.

Operating leases are reviewed in a separate note. Again, these tend to be large in certain industries such as airlines (which lease most of their airplanes) and various retail concerns (which often lease retail space). Of particular importance is the relative magnitude of the operating leases and impact on the overall debt structure of the companies. If the magnitude were large (say, equal to or greater than 10 percent of total assets), then restating total liabilities as if the operating leases were capitalized and recalculating leverage ratios would be useful.

As previously mentioned, Apple also had operating lease commitments that totaled $464 million in minimum lease payments for 2002 ($83 million for rent expense in 2003) for facilities and equipment. This was equal to 7.4 percent of total assets. If we assume an arbitrary rule of thumb of 10 percent of total assets, Apple's operating leases are not large enough for further analysis.

Consider Federated Department Stores. Federated reported operating leases of $2,671 million for 2001 (Note 8), compared to total assets of $15,044. On the basis of the arbitrary 10 percent rule, Federated was a concern, with operating leases at 17.8 percent of total assets ($2,671/$15,044). Further analysis is suggested because of the note information. Federated reported total minimum payments of capital leases of $100 million (present value, $57 million). Thus, operating leases were 96.4 percent of total minimum lease payments ($100 + $2,671 = $2,771; $2,671/$2,771). The capital leases were recorded as assets and liabilities of $57 million. The operating leases are not reported on the balance sheet and thus are subject to earnings management. The equivalent amount of operating leases can be added to assets and liabilities to recalculate leverage ratios. If we assume the same relationship of present value to total minimum payments ($57/$100 = 57.0 percent), then the estimated present value of minimum lease payments of operating leases was .57 × $2,671 = $1,522 million. (Note that this value is overstated if operating lease terms are shorter than capital leases.) The adjusted calculations are shown (in millions of dollars) in Table 4.13.

Higher liabilities are recognized, but equity remains unchanged (because leases involves only assets and liabilities). Thus, a high debt-to-equity ratio of 1.7 was made worse (to 2.0×) by this operating lease adjustment.

Other companies have even larger relative amounts. Consider Staples, the office supply retail chain. Staples had operating leases with minimum lease payments of $4,449 million (Note H, 2001 10-K), compared to total assets of $4,093. Thus, the ratio of operating leases to total assets was 108.7 percent, a huge off-balance-sheet amount. Capital leases were only $3.8 million in minimum lease payments. However, Staples did not provide the present value of capital leases to enable further analysis—obvious earnings management, but a complete analysis is not possible.

SPEs are becoming more popular, and because their major purpose is to keep debt off the balance sheet, they are a major concern for earnings management potential. As demonstrated by Enron, these may not be described in detail. This means that it is difficult to properly evaluate the potential risks and overall impact of SPEs. SPEs may be described in footnotes or in MD&A and must be evaluated on the basis of whatever information is presented (more on SPEs in Chapter 11).

If corporations have defined-benefit pension plans and other post-employment benefits, substantial assets and liabilities may exist. These are recorded as a net asset or liability amount (basically a fair value calculation of plan or invested assets, less the GAAP calculation of pension obligations). Pension accounting is complex, particularly if an attempt is made to incorporate economic reality, and the topic is reviewed in some detail in Chapter 10.

STOCKHOLDERS' EQUITY

Equity represents the ownership interests of the corporation, but its complexity has increased, as has its relative significance in evaluations of the stakeholder structure and earnings management potential. Earnings management issues include those in Table 4.14.

Equity is represented by both preferred and common stock. Preferred stock is not common (no pun intended). Since preferred dividends are taxable to the investor receiving the dividends but not a tax-deductible item for the company, preferred stock is less useful than long-term debt. Consequently, the evaluation of equity primarily means the evaluation of common stock (with equity ratios often excluding preferred stock and preferred dividends).

New issues of common stock are of some concern, because this dilutes existing shares of common stock. The new issue must make sense in terms of the business strategy of the

TABLE 4.13	ADJUSTED CALCULATION OF OPERATING LEASES FOR FEDERATED DEPARTMENT STORES (MILLIONS OF DOLLARS)		
	Balance Sheet	Operating Leases	Adjusted
Total liabilities	$9,480	$1,522	$11,002
Total stockholders' equity	5,564	—	5,564
Debt to equity	9,480/5,564 = 1.7×		11,002/5,564 = 2.0×

TABLE 4.14	EARNINGS MANAGEMENT ISSUES CONCERNING EQUITY

Topic	Concern	Detection Strategy
Preferred stock	Unusual characteristics, overall magnitude	Evaluate magnitude as percent of total equity and look for certain characteristics (e.g., convertibility, relative dividends)
Paid-in capital	Impact of new equity issues (especially for companies with credit risk problems), conversion of options, convertible securities	Evaluate statement of stockholders' equity for new issues, redemption of options, and convertibles; evaluate rationale for new issues
Shares outstanding	Shares outstanding particularly important relative to dilution potential	Evaluate number of shares relative to stock options outstanding and other sources of potential dilution; evaluate large changes in shares outstanding
Retained earnings	Indicator of cumulative success net of dividends	Evaluate relative magnitude and relationship to dividend policies
Dividends	Companies may pay out more in dividends than net income	A dividend payout ratio greater than 100 percent is not sustainable
Treasury stock	As a negative equity item (plus the related cash outflow), can be difficult to evaluate; a large balance can significantly reduce equity	Relative magnitude; review statement of stockholders' equity for acquisition scheme; evaluate relative to stock options and maintaining stock price
Other comprehensive income	"Dirty surplus" items can be substantial; large losses may require performance restatements	Evaluate composition and trends over time with use of statement of stockholders' equity

company, relative to future operations, current and future debt levels, stock options, treasury stock, and dividend policy. The key question is: why is a new issue necessary and how does it fit into this comprehensive analysis?

The number of shares outstanding is used for various calculations of market and book value. This is influenced by new common stock issues, stock splits and stock dividends, the purchase of treasury stock, and the use of stock options. The focus is the evaluation of the overall equity strategy of the company.

Treasury stock is the company's outstanding shares that are repurchased in the market. It is usually treated as a separate, "negative equity" item (it reduces the amount of equity) and represents a use of cash. Profitable companies can buy outstanding shares rather than paying dividends. This is mainly used for the payment of future stock options outstanding. Again, the evaluation of treasury stock must be in the context of the overall equity strategy of the firm. Many successful companies in the 1990s bought treasury securities at inflated prices, presumably for future options payouts. The joint impact was a further increase of share prices and no or reduced dividend payment. Then stock prices collapsed. The result has been this expensive treasury stock reducing the equity of a non-dividend-paying company, with reduced operating prospects.

Comprehensive income will be described in more detail in the next chapter. Certain gains and losses are recorded directly to stockholders' equity as "other comprehensive income." These are items related to such categories as marketable securities, pensions, and foreign currency that should tend to "zero out" over time. However, they can be large in any given year, and sometimes large losses can be accumulated. The major concern is relative magnitude. Substantial losses need further analysis.

Apple has a relatively simple equity structure, with four line items: (1) common stock (paid in capital) of $1.8 billion, (2) acquisition-related deferred stock compensation of $–7 million, (3) retained earnings of $2.3 billion, and other comprehensive income of $–49 million, all for a total $4.1 billion, or 65.0 percent of total assets. More details are presented in the statement of stockholders' equity, which reconciles each category by year from 1999.

Consider the information in Table 4.15, from Maytag's 2001 Balance Sheet (in thousands of dollars).

Maytag had $23.5 million in equity, 0.7 percent of total assets, resulting in a debt-to-equity ratio of 133.0×. Essentially, Maytag had no equity, despite paid-in capital of almost $600 million and retained earnings of almost $1.2 billion. The primary problem is the use of treasury stock, which reduced equity by over $1.5 billion, plus an accumulated loss of $186 million in other comprehensive income. The analysis of Maytag's equity, treasury stock, stock options, dividends, and other interrelated factors will be revisited in Chapter 10, in the section on compensation issues. Substantial earnings management issues exist for Maytag.

SUMMARY

This chapter reviewed the major items on the balance sheet and presented an earnings management detection strategy. Level 1 analysis presented an overview approach, using common-size analysis. Level 2 analysis included a review of all major balance sheet categories item by item. Analysis differs by industry and is based on preliminary findings (e.g., relative magnitude of items of potential concern). There were only a few minor concerns about Apple and little need for extensive analysis.

TABLE 4.15	**DATA FROM MAYTAG'S BALANCE SHEETS**		
		2001	**2000**
Shareowners' equity			
Common stock			
Authorized: 200,000,000 shares (par value $1.25)			
Issued: 117,150,593 shares, including shares in treasury		$ 146,438	$ 146,438
Additional paid-in capital		450,683	285,924
Retained earnings		1,164,021	1,171,364
Cost of common stock in treasury (2001: 40,286,575 shares; 2000: 40,910,458 shares)		(1,527,777)	(1,539,163)
Employee stock plans		(23,522)	(31,487)
Accumulated other comprehensive income		(186,297)	(11,400)
Total shareowners' equity		23,546	21,676
Total liabilities and shareowners' equity		$3,156,151	$2,668,924

QUESTIONS

1. SFAS No. 5 defines assets on the basis of probable future economic benefits. Does this definition work well for assets actually presented on the balance sheet? Explain.

2. What are the three categories of marketable securities and how is each accounted for? What are the earnings management implications?

3. What are the alternative ways that inventory can be accounted for? Why are alternatives allowed?

4. Straight-line depreciation is usually used for accounting purposes and accelerated depreciation for tax. Why?

5. Why is the relative age of property, plant, and equipment (PPE) important? How can age be estimated?

6. What is off-balance-sheet reporting? Why is this related to earnings management?

PROBLEMS

Problem 4.1: Quantitative Financial Analysis (Level 1 Analysis)

Given in Table 4.16 is basic information related to the 2002 financial statements for three hotel and resort companies (a service industry). This information will be used in the problems throughout the book. More complete financial information is available in the 2002 10-K reports for the three companies.

The quantitative ratios and other analysis are presented in "Common Financial Ratios" on this book's Web site. For more information on quantitative financial analysis, see Giroux 2003, Chapter 4. Use the information above to complete the following quantitative analysis.

a. Complete these tables to present an abbreviated common-size analysis.

Firms (2002)	Hilton		Marriott		Mandalay	
	$	Common-Size	$	Common-Size	$	Common-Size
Cash + Mkt. Sec.						
Current Assets						
Fixed Assets						
Total Assets						
Current Liability						
Long-term Debt						
Total Liability						
Equity						
Rating						

b. Analyze the common-size information, giving particular attention to potential earnings management concerns.

c. Complete the following financial ratios for 2002, which are presented by major analysis category. Use the information given above.

TABLE 4.16	DATA FROM THE 2002 FINANCIAL STATEMENTS FOR THREE HOTEL/RESORT COMPANIES (MILLIONS OF DOLLARS)

Input (Source Data)		Hilton	Marriott	Mandalay
ASSETS	Cash	$ 54	$ 198	$ 106
	Marketable securities	21	135	—
	A/R, previous year	291	479	78
	A/R, current year	294	524	58
	Prepaid assets	61	300	41
	Inventory, previous year	148	1,161	31
	Inventory, current year	139	633	31
	Current assets	630	1,744	267
	Fixed assets, previous year	3,911	2,460	3,237
	Fixed assets, current year	3,971	2,589	3,050
	Total assets, previous year	8,785	9,107	4,248
	Total assets, current year	8,348	8,296	4,037
LIABILITIES	Current liabilities	575	2,207	309
	Long-term liabilities	6,427	2,516	2,791
	Total liabilities	7,002	4,723	3,100
STOCKHOLDERS' EQUITY	Total equity, previous year	1,783	3,478	1,069
	Total equity, current year	2,053	3,573	941
	Retained earnings	322	1,126	1,374
	MV of equity	4,343	10,521	2,151
CASH FLOW STATEMENT	Cash from operations	675	516	358

Liquidity	Hilton	Marriott	Mandalay
Current Ratio (CA/CL)			
Cash Ratio (Cash + Marketable Securities/CL)			
Cash Flow from Operations Ratio (CFO/CL)			

Leverage	Hilton	Marriott	Mandalay
Total Liabilities/Total Equity			
Total Liabilities (BV)/Equity at Market			
Times Interest Earned (EBIT/Interest Expense)			

d. Analyze the ratios, paying particular attention to earnings management potential.

Problem 4.2: Inventory

As a service company, Hilton is not expected to hold inventories. However, the balance sheet shows inventories of $139 million at the end of 2002. Related information (in millions of dollars) is shown in Table 4.17.

Accounting policies said this about inventories: "Included in inventories at December 31, 2001 and 2002 are unsold intervals at our vacation ownership properties of $132 million and $124 million, respectively. Inventories are valued at the lower of cost or estimated net realizable value.

    a. Calculate the following ratios:

	2001	2002
Inventories/Total Current Assets		
Vacation Ownership Properties/Inventories		
Current Ratio		

    b. Why isn't inventory turnover a useful ratio?

    c. Evaluate the use of inventories by Hilton.

Problem 4.3: Average Age of PPE in the Hotel and Resort Industry

Given in Table 4.18 are 2002 depreciation-related figures for three hotel/resort companies (in millions of dollars).

    a. Calculate the following fixed asset age and useful life ratios:

TABLE 4.17   **INVENTORY AND RELATED INFORMATION FOR HILTON**

	2001	2002
Inventories	$148	$139
Total current assets	996	630
Total current liabilities	902	575

TABLE 4.18   **DEPRECIATION DATA**

	Hilton	Marriott	Mandalay
Accumulated depreciation	$1,318	$ 470	$1,162
Depreciation expense	375	187	216
Ending gross investment	3,971	2,589	3,050

	Hilton	Marriott	Mandalay
Average Age			
Average Age %			
Average Depreciable Life			

    b. Analyze these ratios, focusing particularly on what they mean across the three companies in this industry.

Problem 4.4: Operating Leases in the Hotel and Resort Industry

Given below is lease information for 2002. Calculate minimum lease payments/total assets.

	Minimum Lease Payments (millions of dollars)	Total Assets (millions of dollars)	Minimum Lease Payments/Total Assets
Hilton	$ 37	$8,348	
Marriott	209	8,296	
Mandalay	51	4,037	

    a. Do any of these ratios raise a concern (10 percent or above)?

    b. Calculate debt ratios and recalculate them after adding operating leases for Marriott.

	Balance Sheet	Operating Leases	Adjusted
Total Liabilities	$4,723	$209	
Total Assets	8,296	209	
Total Stockholders' Equity	3,573		
Debt to Equity			
Debt Ratio			

CASES

Case 1: Evaluating the Overall Quality of Apple's Balance Sheet and Earnings Management Potential

The analysis of earnings management considers major concerns (usually treated as red flags) but also an accumulation of minor concerns. A large number of potential problems can indicate overall relatively lower reporting quality. Apple Computer is an example of a successful, high profile high-tech company that has had a somewhat erratic performance over the past decade and seems a good candidate for analysis (refer to Apple's 2002 10-K, www.apple.com).

    a. Overall: Analyze the following balance sheet factors, based on the discussion in this chapter.

Factor	Analysis
Cash Levels	
Liquidity position, based on current assets and liabilities	
Inventory	
Accounts receivable	
Accounting payable	
Other current accounts	
Property, plant, and equipment (PPE)	
Investments	
Intangibles	
Other long-term assets	
Bonded debt	
Commitments and contingencies	
Other long-term liabilities	
Stockholders' equity	
Summary and overall rating	

b. Specific weaknesses and potential concerns: Analyze these potential problems.

Weakness/Concern	Analysis
Does Apple have too much cash?	
Apple has extremely low inventory levels, usually a sign of efficiency. Is Apple's level too low?	
Trade receivables of Ingram Micro 10.8 percent of total receivables	
Treatment of nontrade receivables as other current assets	
Capitalizing software development costs as PPE	
Operating leases of $464 million	
Contingencies from lawsuits and European Union regulations	

Case 2: Leases in the Airline Industry

Given in the table are minimum operating lease payments and total assets for four airlines (in millions of dollars, fiscal year 2001).

a. Calculate the minimum lease payments/total assets. Are these a concern? Explain.

	Minimum Lease Payments	Total Assets	Minimum Lease Payments/Total Assets
American (AMR)	$17,661	$32,841	
United (UAL)	24,538	25,197	
Northwest	8,610	12,955	

b. Calculate in the following table the present value (PV) to total minimum payments for capital leases, and using this percentage, estimate the PV of operating lease payments.

	Capital Lease	Present Value of Capital Leases	PV to Total Capital Lease %	Minimum Operating Lease Payments	Estimated PV of Operating Lease Payments
AMR	$2,557	$1,740		$17,661	
UAL	3,161	2,180		24,538	
Northwest	1,104	586		8,610	

    c. Given the information in the following table, calculate the ratios of debt to equity and adjusted debt to equity (assuming that the present value of minimum lease payment for operating lease is the same as capital leases for each company).

    d. Analyze the impact of operating leases in terms of earnings management.

	AMR	UAL	Northwest
Total Liabilities, Balance Sheet	$27,690	$22,164	$13,386
Total Assets, Balance Sheet	32,841	25,197	12,955
Operating Lease (at Estimated PV)			
Total Liabilities, Adjusted			
Total Assets, Adjusted			
Total Stockholders' Equity	5,373	3,033	−431
Debt-to-Equity Ratio			
Debt to Equity, Adjusted			

Appendix 4.1: Apple Computer Consolidated Balance Sheets

Apple Computer Consolidated Balance Sheets
(in Millions of Dollars, Except Share Amounts)

	September 28, 2002	September 29, 2001
ASSETS		
Current assets		
Cash and cash equivalents	$ 2,252	$ 2,310
Short-term investments	2,085	2,026
Accounts receivable, less allowances		
of $51 and $51, respectively	565	466
Inventories	45	11
Deferred tax assets	166	169
Other current assets	275	161
Total current assets	5,388	5,143
Property, plant, and equipment, net	621	564
Noncurrent debt and equity investments	39	128
Acquired intangible assets	119	76
Other assets	131	110
Total assets	$ 6,298	$ 6,021
LIABILITIES AND SHAREHOLDERS' EQUITY:		
Current liabilities:		
Accounts payable	$ 911	$ 801
Accrued expenses	747	717
Total current liabilities	1,658	1,518
Long-term debt	316	317
Deferred tax liabilities	229	266
Total liabilities	2,203	2,101
Commitments and contingencies		
Shareholders' equity:		
Common stock, no par value;		
900,000,000 shares authorized;		
358,958,989 and 350,921,661 shares		
issued and outstanding, respectively	1,826	1,693
Acquisition-related deferred stock compensation	(7)	(11)
Retained earnings	2,325	2,260
Accumulated other comprehensive income (loss)	(49)	(22)
Total shareholders' equity	4,095	3,920
Total liabilities and shareholders' equity	$ 6,298	$ 6,021

Appendix 4.2: Tyco Long-term Debt

Tyco Long-term Debt
(Fiscal Year End September 30, in Millions of Dollars, Note 18)

	2002	2001
Commercial paper program (2)	$	$ 3,909.5
Euro commercial paper program (2)	—	80.7
Notes payable to Tyco Capital	—	200.0
6.5% public notes due 2001 (3)	—	300.0
6.875% private placement notes due 2002 (4)	—	1,037.2
Variable-rate unsecured bank credit facilities due 2003 (2) (11)	3,855.0	—
Zero coupon convertible debentures with 2003 put Options (5) (11)	1,944.6	2,272.4
6.25% public Dealer Remarketable Securities with 2003 put options (6) (11)	751.9	754.6
Floating rate private placement notes due 2003 (11)	493.8	498.4
4.95% notes due 2003 (11)	565.1	598.0
6.0% notes due 2003	72.7	72.7
Zero coupon convertible senior debentures with 2003 put options (7)	3,519.1	3,499.4
5.875% public notes due 2004	399.1	398.6
4.375% Euro denominated notes due 2004 (8)	486.5	—
6.375% public notes due 2005	747.0	745.9
6.75% notes due 2005	76.7	76.6
6.375% public notes due 2006	993.7	991.9
Variable rate unsecured revolving credit facility due 2006 (2)	2,000.0	—
5.8% public notes due 2006	695.7	694.5
6.125% Euro denominated public notes due 2007	582.4	550.1
6.5% notes due 2007	99.3	99.2
6.125% public notes due 2008	396.6	396.0
8.2% notes due 2008 (10)	388.4	393.4
5.50% Euro denominated notes due 2008 (8)	664.4	—
6.125% public notes due 2009	393.1	386.5
Zero coupon convertible subordinated debentures due 2010	26.3	30.8
6.75% public notes due 2011	992.8	991.9
6.375% public notes due 2011 (9)	1,490.7	—
6.50% British pound denominated public notes due 2011 (8)	285.3	—
7.0% debentures due 2013	86.2	86.1
7.0% public notes due 2028	493.2	492.9
6.875% public notes due 2029	782.5	781.8
3.5% Yen denominated private placement notes due 2030 (10)	—	252.1
6.50% British pound denominated public notes due 2031 (8)	438.9	—
Other (11)	484.8	1,027.8
Total debt	24,205.8	21,619.0
Less current portion	7,719.0	2,023.0
Long-term debt	$ 16,486.8	$ 19,596.0

5

The Income Statement, Part I—Level 1 Analysis

An income statement summarizes the relative success of business performance for a specific period of time, usually annually and quarterly. The annual income statement is comparative, including the current and the two previous years. Basically, the form is sales and other revenue less all expenses (plus and minus gains and losses), to arrive at net income. Net income is then stated on a per-share basis as earnings per share. The format is standardized by GAAP to include several basic components. The income statement for Apple Computer for fiscal year ended September 28, 2002, is presented in Appendix 5.1 as a typical example.

This chapter is Part I on the income statement. It includes an operating overview, an earnings management detection (EMD) strategy, a level 1 analysis, and a thorough review of revenue recognition issues. By far, **revenue recognition** is the most significant area of earnings management concerns, and a long history of fraud and deception is related to revenue issues. The next chapter is Part II of The Income Statement, which includes expenses, nonoperating (called "below the line") issues, net income, earnings per share, and stock market issues.

THE OPERATING ELEMENTS

The financial statement elements associated with the income statements are defined in SFAC No. 6 (para. 25–89) and summarized in Table 5.1.

TABLE 5.1	FINANCIAL ELEMENTS IN INCOME STATEMENTS
Revenues	Inflows or other enhancements of assets of an entity or settlement of its liabilities (or a combination of both) from delivering or producing goods, rendering services, or other activities that constitute the entity's ongoing major or central operations.
Expenses	Outflows or other using up of assets or incurrence of liabilities (or a combination of both) from delivering or producing goods, rendering services, or carrying out other activities that constitute the entity's ongoing major or central operations.
Gains	Increases in equity (net assets) from peripheral or incidental transactions of an entity and from all other transactions and other events and circumstances affecting the entity, except those that result from revenues or investments by owners.
Losses	Decreases in equity (net assets) from peripheral or incidental transactions of an entity and from all other transactions and other events and circumstances affecting the entity, except those that result from expenses or distributions to owners.
Comprehensive income	Change in equity of a business enterprise during a period from transactions and other events and circumstances from nonowner sources, including all changes in equity during a period, except those resulting from investments by owners and distributions to owners.

The major focus on the income statement is the analysis of sales, operating expenses, and earnings, usually defined as net income. **Revenues** and **expenses** are the key operating items, with gains and losses considered peripheral or not directly related to the earnings process. The FASB **conceptual framework** defined comprehensive income but not net income. There has been an ongoing debate since standard setting started on how to define net income; the two camps espouse (1) **current operating performance,** roughly equivalent to income from continuing operations, versus (2) **all-inclusive** or **comprehensive income.** Net income is almost all-inclusive, except that certain gains and losses are recorded directly to stockholders' equity (as "other comprehensive income," also called **"dirty surplus"**).

Revenue includes sales and other revenue items recognized during the fiscal year. A manufacturing company records sales of manufactured products. Other revenue items may include additional services provided and warranty protection. These might be reported separately. Net sales exclude discounts and other adjustments to sales numbers. Cost of revenue is deducted to arrive at gross margin (or gross profit). Cost of revenues for manufacturing sales is cost of goods sold. Other costs associated with sale of services are included in cost of services. Gross margin is an important measure of operating performance, which will be compared over time and to other firms. Service industries sell services rather than products and have no cost of goods sold.

Apple Computer reports sales of $5.7 billion for 2002, up 7.1 percent from 2001. Apple uses the terms *net sales and cost of sales.* Thus, discounts are deducted from and service and related revenues are included in the totals. Cost of sales was $4.1 billion, 72.1 percent of sales. The result was gross profit of $1.6 billion, 27.9 percent of sales, compared to 23.0 percent the previous year.

Operating expenses, including selling, administrative, research and development, and other costs, are then deducted to arrive at operating income. Investment and other income or losses are added to arrive at income before income tax. Note that depreciation and amortization are usually substantial expenses but are usually accumulated as part of cost of sales and other expense items. (Depreciation and amortization totals are found in the statement of cash flows.) Specific items and format vary somewhat from company to company, partially because of industry differences—note that financial intermediaries have quite different formats. Apple had special charges as separate items, an unusual presentation. Apple's operating expenses totaled $1.6 billion, resulting in operating income of a miniscule $17 million or 0.3 percent of sales. However, that's up from a $344 million operating loss the previous year. It's likely that year 2000 operating income of $522 million would be a more typical result—before the tech collapse and minor recession of 2001. Adding other income and expenses, including gains and losses on investments, resulted in income before tax of $87 million, 1.5 percent of sales.

Hilton Hotels, a service company, reported five categories of revenue for 2001: owned hotels, leased hotels, management and franchise fees, other fees and income, and other revenues from managed and franchised properties. Owned hotels revenue was $2.1 billion (53.1 percent of total revenue, $4.0 billion). Operating expenses used essentially the same labels plus depreciation and amortization and corporate expenses as additional line items, with the difference being operating income ($632 million, or 15.8 percent of revenues).

Other operating income and expenses include interest expense, interest and dividend income (these items may be combined), and other gains and losses, to arrive at income before income tax. Provision for income tax (tax expense) is deducted to arrive at **income from continuing operating,** the bottom line number considered **"above the line."** In other words, this is a useful definition of earnings from current operating performance, a potentially useful measure of **earnings power** of the corporation.

Apple had other income and expenses, resulting in a net $70 million "gain," including interest and other income less a loss on noncurrent investments, to arrive at income before tax of $87 million. The provision for income tax (income tax expenses) was deducted to arrive at income from continuing operations, called in this case income before accounting change. Income tax was $22 million, an effective tax rate of 25.3 percent ($22 million/$87 million). Income from continuing operations was $65 million, resulting in a return on sales from continuing operations of 1.1 percent ($65/$5,742).

Hilton had other income and expenses of $382 million, including interest expense of $402 million, plus net loss on asset dispositions of $44 million, less interest and dividend income of $64 million, to arrive at income before tax of $250 million. Provision for income taxes was $77 million, for an effective tax rate of 30.8 percent (below the statutory federal rate of 35 percent). Income from continuing operations was $166 million, for an operating return of 4.2 percent ($166/$3,993).

Various **nonrecurring items** (and sometimes some other unusual items) are deducted from income from continuing operations to arrive at net income, the usual "bottom line" definition associated with the all-inclusive concept of operations. Nonrecurring items should be "unexpected items" and are usually interpreted as a negative signal (likely earnings management). Although these should be rare items, some companies report one or more nonrecurring items almost every year.

Apple reported a small accounting change for 2001 ($12 million) associated with adoption of Staff Accounting Bulletin (SAB) 101 on revenue recognition. Many corporations reported an accounting change based on the SAB, so this is not considered a significant issue (a large amount, on the other hand, would signal relatively aggressive revenue recognition in earlier years—which is discussed later in this chapter). The cumulative effect of the change in accounting principle was a nonrecurring item (essentially not part of continuing operations) from 2001, which was deducted to arrive at net income, the "bottom line." Since there were no nonrecurring items for 2002, net income was $65 million, 1.1 percent return of sales, and better than the $25 million loss from 2001. Hilton had a net income of $166 million (4.2 percent return on sales, down from $272 million in 2000).

Earnings per share (EPS) are calculated both as basic EPS (net income/weighted average number of shares outstanding) and diluted EPS (net income/restated shares outstanding based on potential shares from stock options and other sources). EPS numbers also are calculated before accounting changes, essentially on the basis of income from continuing operations. EPS was $0.18 for Apple, no matter how calculated, much better than the $0.11 loss (basic) or $0.07 loss (diluted) from 2001. Hilton had EPS (both basic and diluted) of $0.45.

Net income (and EPS on a per-share basis) is the most common **"below the line"** definition of earnings. It's an all-inclusive definition of performance (excluding only a small number of gains and losses recorded directly to stockholders' equity as "other comprehensive income" items). For most purposes, net income and EPS are the bottom line measures of most interest, and most performance measures are stated relative to net income (such as return on sales or return on equity) or EPS (price earnings ratios, meeting analysts' forecasts). On the other hand, bonuses or other incentive income may be based on a specific above-the-line measure (which becomes a target for earnings management), and analysts may ignore nonrecurring items and focus most attention on above-the-line performance.

AN EMD INCOME STATEMENT STRATEGY

The EMD strategy for the income statement follows the income statement format, starting at revenue and moving down to net income and EPS. The major focus is on areas of particular concern, especially revenue recognition, expense recognition, and nonrecurring and other unusual items. Traditional quantitative financial analysis techniques include common-size, profitability ratios, turnover ratios as measures of efficiency, and various models that (1) decompose earnings (such as the Du Pont Model), measure financial health (such as Altman's Z-score), and (3) estimate the per-share or firm value (such as the dividend discount model or the earnings growth model). The quantitative EMD perspective follows these traditional techniques.

Because earnings and revenues are central to the relative value of the firm, management success and compensation, and other contractual commitments, significant incentives exist to achieve and maintain excellent earnings performance—that is, manage earnings. Probably the most common strategy is to maintain a near-constant growth rate in earnings (income smoothing). This can be achieved by maintaining high levels of operating performance and efficiency within the context of a viable business strategy. That is a strategy consistent with high-quality earnings. High operating performance is expected to be the most common strategy and discernable, to some extent, in both the qualitative analysis of the MD&A and other sources and the quantitative analysis of the income statement (e.g., profit and performance ratios).

Short-term performance can be managed by (1) adjusting operations (e.g., reduce maintenance, research and development, or employee training) or (2) accounting choices that change numbers rather than actual performance. "Tweaking" accounting numbers to meet quarterly expectations (e.g., sales of investments for gains, adjusting allowance accounts) seems to be common. However, the level of manipulation can increase to the point of fraud or other criminal acts. WorldCom's capitalization of some $9–$10 billion of operating costs seems to be one of the most extreme examples.

In an environment where earnings management incentives exist, how is earnings management detected? The first level of analysis recommended is an income statement overview to determine the reasonableness of the numbers presented, in comparison with previous periods and close competitors. Common-size and percentage changes from previous periods indicate basic relationships and reasonableness of changes over time. The primary focus of analysis is stressing unexpected percentages and relationships. (A more comprehensive analysis of trends and quarterly analysis is presented in Chapter 8.)

The second level of analysis is the detailed evaluation by each income statement category, starting with revenue and working down the income statement. Earnings management is possible in virtually all categories, and certain signs suggest the presence of possible manipulation. Sales and other revenue items are the most likely areas of earnings management and require extensive analysis. However, the various categories of operating expenses have unique features that make them susceptible to manipulation. Nonrecurring items, by definition, should be rare and subject to extreme skepticism by analysts. Successful business strategies are not expected to have a nonrecurring-item component.

EARNINGS MANAGEMENT CONCERNS

Particularly important are situations where earnings management incentives are strong, related to relative earnings performance. Managers may have incentives to "signal" strong performance numbers rather than high-quality earnings. This would seem to be a losing strategy long-term, but the mindset may be entirely short-term. Examples are shown in Table 5.2.

The potential for these problems should be considered in the analysis of the income statement. Reviewing the list, the analyst should consider net income just above zero, slightly above the previous period, or at or slightly above analysts' consensus forecasts as potential concerns. The potential for debt covenant violations should be evaluated from a credit risk perspective, on the basis of standard ratio analysis, consideration of information available on outstanding debt, and external sources like bond ratings. **Big-bath write-offs** should be obvious from evaluating nonrecurring items on the income statement and additional information related to restructuring charges and other unusual circumstances. Political costs are often industry-related, and the business press may be a good indicator of existing political problems.

LEVEL 1 ANALYSIS

A summary of EMD overview concerns (level 1) is shown in Table 5.3.

TABLE 5.2	INCENTIVES FOR EARNINGS MANAGEMENT

Dilemma	Description
Earnings slightly below zero	Reporting a small net loss sends a strong signal of poor performance; better to make at least a small profit
Earnings slightly below the previous period	A small decrease is often viewed as a negative (e.g., the percentage change is negative); strong incentive for "tweaking" earnings
Earnings below consensus analysts' forecasts	Meeting quarterly forecasts considered sacrosanct by many CEOs; large stock price drops often follow missed forecasts (also called a "negative earnings surprise")
Earnings close to violating debt covenants	Violating debt covenants puts the company in technical default on debt, which could lead to bond downgrading and other negative consequences
Matching bonus and other compensation agreements	Managers could be sensitive to the specific bonus and other incentive agreements; how bonuses are constructed (e.g., above the line versus below the line) can be useful for understanding management incentives for earnings management
"Big bath" write-offs	Managers may have incentives to take large losses if current bonuses will be zero; additional losses won't affect current compensation but may boost future compensation; likely to take the form of nonrecurring items.
Political costs	Companies and industries may have incentives to keep earnings low for political reasons: oil companies should be sensitive to big profits for oil interruptions and large price rises in gasoline; Microsoft and others related to antitrust suits; companies attempting to get subsidies or handouts from the government

As with the balance sheet level 1 analysis, this overview is useful to determine obvious red flags and where to spend the most time on level 2 analysis. Generally, revenues are expected to increase each year (there may be seasonal patterns for quarterly analysis), and the gross profit percentage should be relatively constant. That same pattern should exist for income before tax and tax expense. Business cycle factors and unique industry and company characteristics should be investigated.

The existence of nonrecurring items is a particular concern and generally requires extensive analysis from multiple sources (such as specific footnotes and MD&A). Net income can be erratic, because all operating items impact directly on income. However, this is the standard below-the-line figure, often considered the most important single number for analysis. Net losses are particularly problematic and require considerable analysis. Note that losses were common after the 2001 recession.

The most significant earnings management concern involves revenues and how they're recognized. Revenue recognition is based on judgment, which means great potential for manipulation. Any unusual quantitative patterns or qualitative information (e.g., MD&A) that seems suspect should be investigated. Discerning specific instances of earnings management (e.g., specific examples that later prove to be fraudulent) are almost impossible from an external analysis of public data, but determining the potential for earnings management on the basis of these data is more likely.

TABLE 5.3	CONCERNS AND STRATEGIES IN EMD		
Topic	**Concern**	**Detection Strategy**	
Relative amounts of sales and other revenue items	Unusual amounts may indicate problems	Common-size and percentage changes; comparisons over time and to competitors	
Comparison of cost of sales to revenues	Unusual amounts or relationships may suggest problems	Common-size and percent changes, gross margin; changes over time and comparison to competitors	
Amounts of operating expenses	Unusual amounts compared to previous period or level of revenue	Common-size percent changes; comparisons over time to competitors	
Income tax	The rate at the federal level is 35 percent; if the effective rate is analysis; substantially comparisons to competitors	Effective tax ratio and footnote changes over time and different, problems may exist	
Nonrecurring items	Infrequent, unusual, and nonrecurring items should be rare, and their presence is a concern	Existence on income statement and note disclosure; qualitative evaluation of item(s)	
Composition issues	Income statements may not conform to industry standards; important information may be hidden under other revenue, expense, or gains and losses	Incomplete disclosures and reports that are difficult to use raise earnings-quality issues; comparisons to competitors	
Declining or erratic net income	Negative patterns are "bad news" but have been relatively common since the 2001 recession	Standard quantitative analysis; comparisons over time and to competitors; evaluate reasons for this behavior (notes, MD&A) plus analysts' forecasts of future earnings	
Net loss	A net loss should be considered a potential red flag for financial analysis, requiring further investigation	Same as above	

Expense recognition is based on the matching principle to revenue, through both **product** and **period costs.** Cost of goods sold is based on product costs. These are subject to manipulation through a variety of mechanisms, from using reserve accounts against inventory to calculating overhead charges to cost of goods sold. Most of these items would be completely hidden from public documents and can be surmised only by evaluating relative amounts and patterns over time.

Operating expenses are matched, largely as period costs. Some of the same basic techniques can be used for manipulation (such as allowance accounts for receivables and overhead calculations), but additional mechanisms are possible. WorldCom capitalized billions of dollars of operating costs to boost earnings, probably the most blatant recent example of expense manipulation.

A number of earnings management issues are associated with income taxes and the differences between tax and GAAP accounting. A starting point is the effective tax rate of the company, followed by a more detailed analysis of the tax notes and related information. The effective tax rate for most companies usually is approximately the federal tax rate of 35 percent, and rates significantly different from this should be noted as a potential concern. Because corporations also pay state, local, and foreign taxes, a substantially different rate is possible (but must be explained to the satisfaction of the analyst).

The operations of companies are captured in income from continuing operations. The existence of nonrecurring items and other "special items" probably should be listed as a concern for further investigation. With the exception of mandatory accounting changes (these are based on new standards rather than management decisions), these items have the potential for manipulation. Nonrecurring items are often treated differently by financial analysts and in various compensation and debt contracts—which means that incentives may exist for their common use. For example, financial analysts may focus almost exclusively on income from continuing operations (or other above-the-line measures) and pay little attention to nonrecurring items. Various compensation and debt contracts may base contractual terms (e.g., bonus levels for executives, debt covenants) on various above-the-line earnings measures.

The format of the income statement is fairly standard, but alternative presentations exist across industries and companies for a variety of reasons. For example, financial institutions have quite different operations from industrial companies, and financial statement formats follow these differences. Unusual presentations may be used to camouflage information or to provide insufficient data to properly evaluate the company.

Significant bottom line problems should be obvious during the level 1 review. Erratic patterns of net income and other bottom line definitions, and particularly net losses, raise immediate concerns for further investigation. Standard ratio analysis provides considerable detail, and reasons for unexpected performance should be discussed in MD&A and other sources.

LEVEL 1 ANALYSIS FOR APPLE

A simplified common-size analysis for Apple for 2002, with comparisons to the previous years and competitors Dell and Gateway, is shown in Table 5.4.

Revenues were $7,983 million in 2000 and $5,363 million in 2001. Percentage growth from 2000 to 2001 was −32.8 percent [($5,363 − $7,983)/$7,983], and that from 2001 to 2002 was 7.1 percent [($5,742 − $5,363)/$5,363]. The large drop in sales from 2000 to 2001 could be considered a financial analysis red flag. The year 2000 performance numbers are for before the recession of 2001 and probably represent a more typical year for Apple, including the return on sales of almost 10 percent.

The net losses for Apple and Gateway in 2001 indicated the problems this industry has had since the tech bubble exploded. Apple's net income in 2002 was up to 1.1 percent of sales but below the 2000 return on sales of 9.8 percent. Consequently, particular care must be exercised to evaluate operations and the potential return of Apple to previous performance levels. Revenues were down 28.1 percent from 2000 ([$5,742/$7,983]/$7,983). Gross profit was a reasonable 27.9 percent, higher than the previous year and for competitors. Selling, general, and administrative (SG&A) expenses seemed high at 19.3 percent, but dollar amounts are comparable to those for 2001 and 2000. (Apple justified the high SG&A in MD&A analysis as necessary to promote its unique products.) Net income was erratic, with a net loss recorded in 2001, and then rose in 2002 with a small net income (but only a fraction of the 2000 earnings). In summary, the major areas of concern were the level of revenues, SG&A, and erratic net income.

In addition, analysts' earnings forecasts at the start of 2003 (available at www.quicken.com) were as shown in Table 5.5.

Apple is an "average" performer of the three, with earnings growth projections well below Dell's but much better than the dismal performance of Gateway. Assuming the forecasts are reasonably accurate, one can expect Apple to achieve double-digit earnings growth for the foreseeable future, although growth is expected to be only about average for a large industrial company.

REVENUE RECOGNITION

Revenue is recognized when it is (1) realized or realizable and (2) earned. Realizable means assets are received that are convertible into cash. Revenue is earned when exchange transactions (the earnings process) are substantially complete, usually by the time the product is delivered or service rendered.

In a complex business environment, judgment is necessary to determine the appropriate time to recognize revenue. In addition, corporate executives often have earnings management incentives to recognize revenues as soon as possible to increase earnings in the current period. If opportunistic behavior is involved, this is referred to as aggressive revenue.

Revenue recognition is primarily a timing issue. Will specific revenue be recognized this year or sometime in the future? Possible alternatives include recognition when the sale

---

TABLE 5.4   **COMMON-SIZE ANALYSIS FOR APPLE COMPUTER FOR 2002**

	Apple 2002 (Millions of $)	Apple 2002—CS	Apple 2001—CS	Apple 2000—CS	Dell 2002—CS	Gateway 2001—CS
Revenue	$5,742	100.0%	100.0%	100%	100.0%	100.0%
Cost of sales	4,139	72.1	77.0	72.9	82.3	82.9
Gross profit	1,603	27.9	23.0	27.1	17.7	17.1
SG&A	1,111	19.3	21.2	14.6	8.9	33.3
Operating income	17	0.3	−6.4	9.7	5.7	−19.5
Tax expense	22	0.4	−1.0*	13.7	1.6	−4.5*
Nonrecurring items	0	—	0.2†	—	—	−0.4†
Net income	65	1.1	−0.3 (RF)	9.8	4.0	−4.5 (RF)

*Minus signs for tax expense for tax "rebates" (essentially a negative expense).
†Accounting change.
RF = red flag; SG&A = selling, general, and administrative expenses.

TABLE 5.5   **EARNINGS (MILLIONS OF DOLLARS) FORECASTED BY ANALYSTS IN EARLY 2003**

	Actual (EPS)	1 Year Ahead (EPS)	2 Years Ahead (EPS)	5-Year Growth Forecast (%)
Apple	$0.18	$0.23	$0.27	10.3%
Dell	0.48	0.80	0.98	16.8
Gateway	−3.20	−0.72	−0.57	10.5

EPS = earnings per share.

is made, when the product is shipped, when the product is received and accepted by the customer, or when the cash payment is received. Note that there are important exceptions to sales-based revenue, including commodities with liquid markets where revenues can be recognized when production is complete and the use of percentage-of-completion method on long-term construction contracts.

The SEC tightened revenue recognition criteria with Staff Accounting Bulletin (SAB) 101, *Revenue Recognition in Financial Statements* (1999), for fiscal years beginning in 2001. As pointed out in the SAB:

> The accounting literature on revenue recognition includes both broad con-ceptual discussions as well as certain industry-specific guidance. ... The staff believes that revenue generally is realized or realizable and earned when all of the following criteria are met: persuasive evidence of an arrangement exists, delivery has occurred or services have been rendered, the seller's price to the buyer is fixed or determinable, and collectibility is reasonably assured. (Topic 13, A.1.)

Because of SAB 101, recognition policies should be more standardized by industry than in the past—good news for analysts. Many companies included an accounting change in 2001 based on implementing SAB 101. The larger the amount of the accounting change (this can be measured as a percentage of revenues), the more likely the company was using aggressive revenue recognition practices. Revenue recognition issues may be less severe in future years as companies comply with SAB 101 and auditors, regulators, and analysts focus on revenue recognition issues. However, several earnings restatements for 2002 were based on revenue recognition.

Revenue Recognition Concerns   Revenue recognition issues include those listed in Table 5.6. As the list above suggests, the potential for revenue manipulation seems almost unlimited. All of these techniques have been used. Companies, managers, and others have been convicted of fraud for most of them. External detection by evaluating public docu-ments is unlikely, but discovering the potential for revenue manipulation is possible. Although specific detection is not the goal of analysis, these techniques are reviewed in some detail to indicate what the analyst is up against and why these techniques are used and might be relatively common. As discussed in Chapter 1, earnings restatements from 1997 to 2002 occurred for almost 10 percent of listed companies on the three major exchanges, and revenue recognition was the most common category of violations.

The first objective of analysis is to determine the basic recognition policies of the com-pany, which are expected to be conservative. Aggressive policies are a concern, with obvi-ous manipulation implications. Aggressive revenue recognition was central to a number of corporate fraud cases. SeaView Video, for example, recognized revenue after orders were received but before shipment. Less serious, but still a concern, is overly conservative recog-nition for the purpose of income smoothing, with Microsoft being a recent example. Microsoft used various reserve accounts to reduce immediate revenue recognition, estab-lishing "cookie jar reserves," according to the former SEC Chairman Arthur Levitt. A basic technique for evaluating potential manipulation is to evaluate quarterly and annual trends in revenue, relative to accounts receivable and other factors.

Some companies sell products, services, and other items as a package, with service con-tracts over a long-term period. The product should be recognized after shipment and cus-tomer acceptance of the product, while the service revenue should be recognized over the

TABLE 5.6	REVENUE RECOGNITION CONCERNS AND STRATEGIES

Topic	Concern	Detection Strategy
Sales—recognition policies	Aggressive revenue recognition policies, usually blatant manipulation	Review specific revenue recognition policy statements in Note 1 (accounting policies), revenue footnotes and MD&A discussion; compare to competitors
Overly conservative recognition	This seems the antithesis of manipulation, but revenues are still misstated; this is consistent with income smoothing for successful companies	Review recognition policies and review notes and MD&A on recognition and use of reserves
Sales—trends	Changes in sales, especially unexpected increases, and related items such as receivables	Review quarterly and annual changes, including information on specific segments (see Chapter 8)
Combined product and service sales	Revenues on long-term services recognized immediately as revenue rather than over the life of the service contract	Review accounting policies and breakout of revenues for products and services (if available in note disclosure)
Recognizing revenues on service contracts before service is performed	Another form of aggressive recognition, more difficult to justify since SAB 101	Review policy descriptions, notes, and MD&A for evidence
Leases recorded as sales	Long-term leases recorded immediately as revenue rather than recognized over the life of the lease	Evaluate companies that use long-term leases to sell their products; consider accounting policies, specific notes, and unusual sale trends
Sales: installment sales method	Long-term credit terms; immediate recognition as revenue and other problematic procedures	Usually industry-specific (e.g., durable goods, land sales); evaluate sales methods and related notes
Shipping, handling, and other sales-related items	Aggressive policies for shipping and handling charges, insurance, set-up costs. Are these treated as revenue items, and when should they be recorded?	Review policy descriptions and revenue footnotes; compare to how related costs are treated; compare to competitors
Bill-and-hold sales	Product sold with the stipulation that delivery will occur in a later period; could represent blatant manipulation	Difficult to evaluate on basis of annual reports; generally rely on media or SEC coverage
Reporting out-of-period sales	Timing is everything, in this case essentially reporting sales from early the next fiscal year in the current period	Difficult to evaluate on basis of annual reports; rely on external sources and media

(Continued)

TABLE 5.6	REVENUE RECOGNITION CONCERNS AND STRATEGIES (CONTINUED)

Topic	Concern	Detection Strategy
Channel stuffing	Deep discounts to wholesalers to encourage end-of-period sales, another blatant manipulation scheme	Unless specifically stated in the notes or MD&A, can only be detected by auditors, regulators, etc.
Round-trip transaction	Transaction with related parties for the sole purpose of meeting sales and earnings targets	Another method to inflate revenue; unlikely to be detectible; evaluate for fraud environment; review related-party notes
Sales incentives, such as discounts	Given for the sole purpose of boosting end-of-period sales to achieve sales targets	Review accounting policies, MD&A, and notes, but difficult to detect
Disclosure of affiliated and related party sales	Do these, in fact, represent revenues or simply exchanges? Potential for transactions to boost sales, but without economic substance	Review notes on related-party transactions and other disclosures that suggest suspect sales
Prepaid revenue items	Is revenue recognized immediately for multiyear commitments?	Review policy descriptions, MD&A and notes
Long-term construction contracts	Percent-of-completion method allows considerable judgment on estimating revenue; aggressive (early) recognition	Determine which method is used and, if percent-of-completion, review notes and quarterly and annual reporting trends
Other front-end recognition of revenues	Any number of aggressive recognition strategies, before revenue is earned	Review recognition policies and notes for evidence of front-ending
Fraud, including fictitious sales	The most infamous cases of revenue abuse are fraud and other criminal acts	Fraud is usually detected by the auditors, the SEC, or whistle-blowers; evaluate for fraud environment
Back-pocket sales	Fictitious sales recorded only if needed to make earnings targets	Detected only after the fact, usually as the result of a regulatory action or lawsuit

life of the contract. Manipulation is problematic if services and related long-term items are recognized immediately or too early. Somewhat related is the use of lease contracts for products sold (often with a significant training and long-term service component). Revenue recognition should be over the life of the lease. Immediate recognition is manipulation. Xerox did exactly that on the lease-sale of copiers and was forced to restate earnings. Real estate and various durable goods may be sold under long-term installment sales agreements, where revenue may be spread over the payment period when collectibility is uncertain. In these circumstances, early recognition can be considered manipulation.

Different circumstances exist for revenue recognition. As with warranties and service contracts, prepaid items such as magazine subscriptions and insurance policies are deferred and revenue recognized over the prepaid period covered. Engineering and construction companies build major capital and infrastructure projects over several years. How should revenue be recognized in such cases? Two alternatives are allowed: completed contracts (no revenue is recognized until the project is completed) or percentage-of-completion (where revenue is recognized based on the estimated completion of the project). For example, Boeing uses both for aircraft construction. For commercial aircraft, revenues generally are recognized when deliveries are made (completed contracts). For government cost reimbursement contracts, revenue is recognized based on scheduled milestones (percentage-of-completion). Both methods are used for government fixed-price contracts. The completed contracts method is more conservative but usually used only when the percentage-of-completion method is inappropriate.

A number of sales-related issues may be a concern in some industries, such as mail order businesses. Shipping and handling, insurance, and other charges may be included as part of revenue (in which case the actual costs would be picked up in cost of sales). Amazon.com recorded shipping charges as revenues and then recorded shipping and handling expenses to SG&A rather than cost of sales. As of 2001, Amazon has been recording these expenses as cost of sales. How these items are treated can be important to evaluate earnings management and comparability to competitors.

A number of early revenue recognition techniques have interesting names, such as **bill-and-hold, channel stuffing,** and reporting **out-of-period sales.** All are essentially mechanisms to meet sales and earnings targets for the current period, blatant manipulation techniques. Bill-and-hold means a sales agreement has been reached, but goods will not be shipped in the current period. This was one of many techniques used by Sunbeam during the regime of "Chainsaw Al" Dunlap to meet aggressive earnings targets in the mid-1990s. Channel stuffing is the shipment of products at deep discounts to get customers to accept these goods. "Out-of-period sales" is a more generic term to describe all the means to record sales this period, when legitimately the sales should be recognized in another period. All are manipulation methods, and discovery has usually meant earnings restatements and lawsuits charging fraud.

Sales can be made to **affiliated companies** or other **related parties.** These may be legitimate sales but subject to manipulation. Any end-of-period sales to related parties represent likely candidates for manipulation to meet earnings targets. Disclosures of affiliate and related-party sales (note disclosures are required by current GAAP) are a potential concern. An Apple board member, Jerome York, is President and CEO of MicroWarehouse, a marketer of Apple products (3.3 percent of net sales in 2002). Apple also reported a reimbursement agreement with CEO Steve Jobs and a loan to an Apple vice president. These agreements are somewhat disturbing, particularly in the context of the corporate governance environment and motivations.

Another method is the **round-trip transaction,** the simultaneous purchase and sale between colluding companies. Global Crossing and other telecommunications companies practiced this technique, essentially swapping fiber optics capacity in different geographic areas under long-term contracts. Global Crossing immediately recognized the "sale" as revenue and recorded the "purchase" as a capital expenditure.

Fictitious sales are outright fraud and a criminal act. Some of the most infamous accounting scandals included fictitious sales. Examples include Equity Funding and ZZZZ Best. Equity Funding committed massive computer fraud in the 1970s. Bogus insurance policies and related bogus data were entered into the computer system, suggesting a booming company. ZZZZ Best was in the insurance restoration business in the 1980s. However, most of the restoration projects recorded did not exist.

REVENUE REPORTING AT APPLE

For a computer manufacturing company like Apple, key sales events include the initial sale, shipment to the customer, customer billing, receipt and approval of the product by the customer, and cash payment. Apple's revenue recognition policy for product sales (Note 1) was as follows:

> Revenue is recognized when persuasive evidence of an arrangement exists, delivery has occurred, the sales price is fixed or determinable, and collectibility is probable. Product is considered delivered to the customer once it has been shipped, and title and risk of loss have been transferred. For online sales to individuals, for some sales to education customers in the United States, and for certain other sales, the Company defers revenue until product is received by the customer because the Company legally retains a portion of the risk of loss on these sales during transit. For other product sales, these criteria are met by the Company at the time product is shipped. The Company records reductions to revenue for estimated commitments related to price protection and for customer incentive programs, including reseller and end user rebates and other sales programs and volume-based incentives. (Apple 2002 10-K, p. 56)

For services and other revenues the stated policy was:

> Revenue for consulting and implementation services is recognized upon performance and acceptance by the customer. Revenue from extended warranty and support contracts is recognized ratably over the contract period. Amounts billed to customers in excess of revenue recognized on extended warranty and support contracts are recognized as deferred revenue until revenue recognition criteria are met.

> Revenue on arrangements that include multiple elements such as hardware, software, and services is allocated to each element based on vendor specific objective evidence of the fair value of each element. Allocated revenue for each element is recognized when revenue recognition criteria have been met for each element. Vendor specific objective evidence of fair value is generally determined based on the price charged when each element is sold separately. (Apple 2002 10-K, p. 56)

Apple's position of revenue recognition is defensible as realizable and earned (the Conceptual Framework criteria), because the product has been manufactured, the sale has been made, the product has been delivered, and payment is reasonably assured. Revenues from separate services and warranties are deferred until earned—the common practice when payment is received in advance. Although cash is received, revenue has not yet been earned. These are industry standards (both Gateway and Dell have similar policies) and suggest no obvious earnings management from aggressive revenue recognition. The three companies changed revenue recognition policy in 2001 in response to SAB 101. The result was a more standardized policy, which should be relatively universal across most manufacturing industries.

Apple's revenue recognition policy is conservative. It is defensible under the FASB criteria of realizable and earned, is consistent with industry practices, and comes relatively late in the sales event cycle. Analysts associate conservative revenue recognition with higher earnings quality and have more confidence in the earnings numbers. Apple reports relatively little information on revenues; the most detail is actually part of MD&A on net sales by geographic and product segment (see Appendix 5.2). The majority of the sales are in America (53.8 percent), and Macintosh sales represent 54.0 percent of total sales.

OTHER REVENUE REPORTING EXAMPLES

Like Apple, most companies report relatively little information on revenues. General Electric reports more than the norm, largely because it is a conglomerate with diverse operations. Revenues from GE's 2001 income statement are shown in Table 5.7.

With almost $126 billion in revenues from manufacturing, services, and financial services (General Electric Capital Services [GECS]), considerable analysis is possible. Most of the revenue information is stated as segment analysis, both in notes and MD&A. Four segments each had revenues above $10 billion for 2001 (aircraft engines at $11.4, industrial products at $11.6, power systems at $20.2, and GECS at $58.4 before eliminations). NBC came in at a paltry 4.6 percent of revenues. Substantial revenue information by subcategories was presented in MD&A, such as the five categories of GECS revenues.

Hilton Hotels is part of the service industry, with reporting characteristics different from manufacturing companies. The revenue reported by Hilton on the 2001 10-K is shown in Table 5.8 (the same categories were used for operating expenses). Note that 2001 is at the far right.

Revenue recognition policies for each of Hilton's major categories was stated (2001 10-K, pp. 44–45) as follows:

> Revenue is generally recognized as services are performed. Owned and leased hotel revenue represents primarily room rentals and food and beverage sales from owned, majority owned and leased hotels.
>
> Management fees represent fees earned on hotels managed by us, usually under long-term contracts with the hotel owner. Management fees include a base fee, which is generally a percentage of hotel revenue, and an incentive fee, which is generally based on the hotel's profitability. We recognize base fees as revenue when earned in accordance with the terms of the contract. In interim periods we recognize incentive fees that would be due if the contract were terminated at the end of the interim period.Franchise fees represent fees received in connection with the franchise of our brand names, usually under long-term contracts with the hotel owner. Depending on the brand, we charge franchise royalty fees of up to five percent of rooms revenue. We recognize fee revenue as earned, in accordance with FAS 45, "Accounting for Franchise Fee Revenue."

Other fees and income primarily consist of earnings from timeshare operations and equity income from unconsolidated affiliates. Timeshare revenue is generated primarily from the

| TABLE 5.7 | REVENUES (MILLIONS OF DOLLARS) REPORTED ON THE INCOME STATEMENT OF GENERAL ELECTRIC |

Revenues	2001	2000	1999
Sales of goods	$ 52,677	$ 54,828	$ 47,785
Sales of services	18,722	18,126	16,283
Other income	234	436	798
GECS revenues from services	54,280	56,463	46,764
Total revenue	$125,913	$129,853	$111,630

GECS = General Electric Capital Services.

| TABLE 5.8 | REVENUES (MILLIONS OF DOLLARS) REPORTED BY HILTON HOTELS ON THE 2001 10-K |

Revenues	1999	2000	2001
Owned hotels	$1,813	$2,429	$2,122
Leased hotels	26	398	168
Management and franchise fees	120	350	342
Other fees and income	191	274	418
Total revenue	$2,150	$3,451	$3,050

sale of timeshare intervals, financing consumer purchases of timeshare intervals and operating timeshare resorts. We recognize revenue from timeshare sales in accordance with FAS 66, "Accounting for Real Estate Sales." Sales are included in revenue when a minimum of a 10 percent down payment has been received and certain minimum sales thresholds have been attained.

Considerable revenue-related information was presented in MD&A, which should be part of the qualitative analysis. Detailed information is presented for number of hotels and available rooms by type (e.g., owned, leased, franchised) and brand, as well as average occupancy rates. This can be useful to determine if the revenues and changes in revenues seem reasonable. Because of the complexity of Hilton's operations, this is not as easy as it first seems. However, simple calculations may indicate the need for detailed analysis. For example, the number of hotels, at 1,986 in 2001, was up 3.4 percent from 2000. Since revenues dropped 11.6 percent for the year, further analysis seems warranted. (Of course, 2001 was not a good year for the travel industry.)

AGGRESSIVE REVENUE RECOGNITION

Some companies treat revenue recognition aggressively. Revenue recognition is mainly a matter of timing, with the result that revenue is recognized early. This tends to increase current earnings but is shortsighted. Aggressive recognition reduces future recognition and is often a red flag (as an indicator of lower earnings quality) to analysts. Some examples are presented next, based on well-documented cases of restatements of financial data, SEC investigations, and media coverage.

Examples of aggressive revenue recognition are listed in Table 5.9.

The giant telecommunications company Global Crossing sold fiber-optics capacity on its networks using long-term contracts. Global Crossing generally booked the entire contract amount as revenue, although the contracts often ran for twenty years. The company also bought capacity from other carriers but recorded these long-term costs as capital items rather than expenses. Apparently, immediate recognition of revenues on long-term contracts was common in the industry. Despite these aggressive practices, Global lost billions and declared bankruptcy in 2001.

Xerox accelerated revenues from leased copiers and other equipment, especially related to its Mexican operation. Several methods were used. A return on equity allocation method based on fair value was used. As estimated fair value declined, sales revenue was immediately increased. Xerox would sell portfolio streams on leased assets to investors and record revenues immediately (GAO 2002, pp. 225–235).

Microsoft has a history of overly conservative revenue recognition (the concept of "conservative aggressive" revenue recognition seems oxymoronic), in part for "political cost" reasons—an ongoing antitrust case as a monopoly—and to smooth earnings from one quarter to the next. A major tool used by Microsoft was the use of various reserve accounts (called "cookie jar" reserves by Levitt [2002]).

SeaView Video, a maker of underwater video equipment, restated earnings in 2001, in part on the basis of recognition of revenue before items were shipped. Subject to class

TABLE 5.9	EXAMPLES OF AGGRESSIVE REVENUE RECOGNITION
Company	Practice
Global Crossing	Selling or exchanging fiber optics capacity under long-term contracts and recognizing revenue immediately (while capitalizing acquired capacity)
Xerox	Immediately booked revenue from leased contracts on copiers; also inflated reserves, which were drawn down to meet revenue targets
Microsoft	Used various reserve accounts to reduce revenue recognized for income smoothing
SeaView Video	Included revenues and accounts receivable after purchase orders were received but not shipped to customers in time
Critical Path	Back-pocket sales; recognized sales on related-party sales, and recognized revenues prematurely
MicroStrategy	Premature revenue recognition on service contracts and recognized revenues before contracts were signed
Sunbeam	Multiple accounting problems, including bill-and-hold and guaranteed sales transactions
W.R. Grace	A booming health care subsidiary booked part of expanding revenues into reserves in the early 1990s and then released much of the reserves later in the 1990s to show "sustained" earnings growth; subject to SEC enforcement action; restated earnings in 2000

action suits and an SEC investigation, SeaView and the former CFO faced accusations that they:

> misstated the company's sales and revenue figures; improperly recognized revenues; misrepresented the nature and extent of the company's dealer network; falsely touted purported contracts and agreements with large retailers; misrepresented the company's ability to manufacture, or to have manufactured, its products; and misrepresented SeaView's likelihood of achieving certain publicly announced sales targets. (GAO 2002, p. 196)

REVENUE FRAUD

It's difficult to determine when earnings manipulation can be considered fraud, except well after the fact when the companies and/or their executives have been charged with fraud. Revenue-related fraud seems common, in part, because this is the topic that makes the news. Internal and external audits, internal controls, relatively effective corporate governance, regulatory review, and enforcements make fraud difficult in most cases. It usually takes a conspiracy, loose internal controls, and a poor governance environment to even attempt it, let alone get away with it for very long. The following are examples of alleged fraud, based on SEC enforcement actions, lawsuits, and other sources.

Critical Path is an Internet company providing outsource services such as messaging. A new CFO alerted the board of directors about alleged fraud in 2001. The Board formed an investigating committee, with the result that revenues were restated for the third and fourth quarters of 2000 (down $9.7 million each quarter) and for 2001 (down $19.3 million). Alleged violations included back-pocket deals of $4 million (fictitious sales recorded only if needed to meet earnings targets, to be later charged to bad debts reserve), a $7 million sale to a group of big shareholders as resellers (disallowed by auditor PwC because of lack of substance), and recognizing revenue before meeting GAAP criteria. The SEC and United States Attorney investigated and charged several managers with fraudulent acts and insider trading (GAO 2002, pp. 134–143).

MicroStrategy provides business intelligence software (including data mining) to look for trends in raw data. In 2000, the company restated earnings for 1997–1999, resulting in a three-year net income of $18.9 million, becoming a net loss of $36.9 million. Revenue problems involved premature recognition of revenue from software sales, including immediate recognition of long-term license sales, and recognizing revenue on sales that had not been finalized. In a sale to NCR of $27.5 million, the revenue was recognized in the accounting quarter before the contract was signed. Apparently, the rationale was to keep a streak of 15 consecutive revenue growth quarters going. SEC charges of fraud and class action suits followed (GAO 2002, pp. 163–170).

Sunbeam, manufacturing consumer products under its own name as well as Mr. Coffee, Oster, Coleman, and others, had multiple accounting issues, especially from 1996 to 1998. Revenue recognition issues included bill-and-hold sales and sales guarantees. Sunbeam in the late 1990s booked sales that didn't exist for products remaining in the warehouses in order to show rising sales. Class-action lawsuits, SEC investigations, and civil action suits followed, which included auditor Arthur Andersen as a defendant.

EARNINGS RESTATEMENT AND OTHER SOURCES OF MANIPULATION AND FRAUD INFORMATION

The Treadway Commission report, which reviewed alleged fraud of 200 companies from 1987 to 1997 based on SEC enforcement actions, found that over 50 percent of the frauds involved overstating revenues or recording revenues prematurely or fictitiously (SOCO 1999). The GAO report on restatement of financial statements (GAO 2002) showed that 38 percent of the 919 restatements investigated for the period 1997–2002 involved revenue recognition, the most important category by far. Cost- or expense-related issues were second at 16 percent. Many of these restatements were later identified as fraud based on SEC investigations and enforcements actions and various lawsuits. The most common reasons were earlier recognition than allowed by GAAP or recognition of questionable or fictitious revenue.

According to the GAO report, 72 S&P 500 companies restated earnings over the five-year period analyzed. Of these, 31 (43 percent) involved revenue recognition issues. (Note that several restatements included multiple violations.) Table 5.10 summarizes the nature of the revenue recognition issues for these restaters.

The violations ranged from minor to severe. Generally, the minor violations involved restatements based on SAB 101, usually in 2001, or other pronouncements. Other restatements were made in 2002, suggesting that SAB 101 didn't solve all revenue issues. More serious examples include many of the listed concerns, such as round-trip sales (CMS Energy), recognition of vendor rebates (ConAgra), revenue based on sales incentives (Harrah's Entertainment), and bill-and-hold sales (Raytheon). A key question is to what extent the existence of restatements signals an earnings manipulation environment.

MARKET REACTION TO "MANIPULATION ANNOUNCEMENTS"

How are restatements and other indicators of manipulation announced to the public? How do investors react to the "bad news"? The GAO found that for the 689 publicly traded companies (all restaters) analyzed, stock prices fell an average 10 percent, with revenue recognition restatements (involving 39 percent of these companies) associated with higher losses. These figures were based on the three trading days surrounding the public announcements (called a "short window" analysis). The unadjusted market losses totaled about $100 billion, with $56 billion in losses associated with revenue recognition restatements (GAO 2002).

MicroStrategy, a business software company trading on NASDAQ, announced its intention to restate earnings on March 20, 2000. This was based primarily on its immediate revenue recognition of software services and software license sales, rather than over the contract period of the services provided. In addition, MicroStrategy recognized revenue on sales not yet completed prior to the end of periods. On April 13, 2000, the restatements were issued for 1997–1999. Rather than total net income of $19 million, the company reported losses of $37 million; the 1999 loss was $34 million rather than the $13 million net income originally reported. A five-year stock chart (MSTR, compared to Nasdaq) shows the market reaction (Figure 5.1).

TABLE 5.10	REVENUE RECOGNITION FINDINGS	

Corporation	Year	Findings
Aetna	2000	Software system and process errors; duplicate revenue entry
Alcoa	2001	Changed accounting method based on SAB 101
AOL	1997	Reversed $7 million in revenue on long-term contract recognized immediately
Applied Materials	2001	Retroactive restatement based on SAB 101
Avon	2001	Software system and process errors; duplicate revenue entry
Best Buy	1999	Changed accounting method based on SAB 101
Boston Scientific	1998	Business irregularities of Japanese subsidiary
Campbell Soup	2001	Shipping and handling costs reclassified from net sales to cost of sales (based on EITF 00-10)
Centex	2001	Net revenues restated to include freight and delivery costs billed to customers (based on EITF 00-10)
Clorox	2001	Coupon cost included in advertising expense (now deducted from sales)
CMS Energy	2002	Round-trip trades
Computer Associates	2002	Reclassified revenues from SG&A (based on EITF D-103)
ConAgra Foods	2001	Immediate recognition of deferred-delivery sales and vendor rebates and advance vendor rebates (also, related understated bad debts reserve)
Concord Camera	2001	Immediate recognition on shipments to a customer, when payments were expected over an extended period; deferring revenue of $1.7 million resulted in a larger net loss
Delphi Financial	2000	Restated to exclude the effects of a reinsurance contract
Dillard's	2001	Reclassified shipping and handling reimbursements to other income (based on EITF 00-10)
First Data	2001	Restated prior period revenues based on SAB 101
Fortune Brands	2001	Restated net sales for 1998–1999 for billed shipping and handling charges; restatements for 1999–2000 for customer rebates
Gateway	2001	Policy change from recognition when goods shipped until product delivered and accepted, based on SAB 101
Harrah's Entertainment	2001	Recognition of sales incentives and "free products and services" to be delivered in the future—now reported as contra-asset items rather than expenses
Hewlett-Packard	2001	Delayed recognition from date of shipment to date of delivery, plus restatement of costs previously recorded to SG&A and now charged directly against revenue, based on SAB 101
Lucent Technology	2000	Retroactive restatement based on SAB 101
Northrop Grumman	2001	Restated to reflect Aerostructures as a discontinued operation
NVIDIA	2002	Interyear adjustments in the recording of deferred revenues and adjustments in the accrual of certain customer programs
Raytheon	2000	Bill-and-hold sales; ownership passed to buyer but before modifications made and delivery
PNC Financial Services	2002	Sales of residential mortgage banking business

(Continued)

TABLE 5.10	REVENUE RECOGNITION FINDINGS (CONTINUED)	
Corporation	**Year**	**Findings**
TJX	2000	Immediate recognition of layaway sales, now deferred on basis of SAB 101
Tyco	2001	Restated revenues based on SAB 101
Waste Management	1999	Immediate recognition based on landfill assets, now deferred and charged over the life of the assets
Xerox	2002	Immediate recognition associated with bundled leases, to be reallocated to equipment, service, supplies, and financing
Xilinx	1999	Immediate recognition for shipments to international distributors, now deferred until products are sold to end customer

FIGURE 5.1	MARKET REACTION TO INTENDED AND ACTUAL RESTATEMENT OF EARNINGS FOR MICROSTRATEGY (MSTR) (PERCENT CHANGE IN SHARE VALUE)

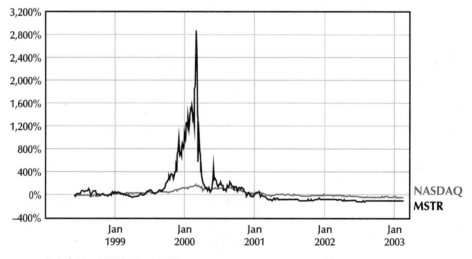

Period: May 4, 1998–May 4, 2003

The reaction was immediate and devastating to the company. From a closing price of $226.75 before the announcement, the stock price fell to $86.75 and continued to fall to $39.06 when the restatements were actually filed. The bottom was $0.47 on July 25, 2000. The stock price has risen since then, closing at $15.10 at the end of 2002. This extreme example indicates the severe effect possible following bad news associated with a high-tech growth company (GAO 2002, pp. 163–170).

SUMMARY

This chapter reviewed the income statement, including an earnings management overview and detailed evaluation of revenue recognition. The operating elements were defined: revenue, expenses, gains, losses, and comprehensive income, followed by a review of the basic format of the income statement. The EMD strategy for the income statement includes both an overview (level 1) analysis and a detailed analysis (level 2) of the major components of the income statement. The basic overview strategy included the importance of earnings benchmarks, including reporting positive net income rather than a loss, beating last year's numbers, and meeting or beating analysts' forecasts.

Level 1 analysis considered a basic income statement overview, including erratic or unusual patterns and composition issues. Level 2 analysis reviewed revenue recognition, the most significant area of potential earnings management. Dozens of techniques have been used to manage revenues, from basic income smoothing techniques to blatant fraud. Attention was paid to aggressive revenue recognition and recent earnings restatements of revenue, including market reaction when restatements are announced.

QUESTIONS

1. Why is the common-size income statement useful for level 1 analysis?
2. What are the basic components of income? What is the "bottom line"?
3. What does "above the line" mean? Why is it important for earnings management analysis?
4. What is revenue recognition and why is aggressive revenue recognition a potential problem in evaluations of earnings quality?
5. What is the difference between round-trip sales, channel stuffing, and bill-and-hold sales? Are these always examples of fraud? Explain.

PROBLEMS

Problem 5.1: Quantitative Financial Analysis (Level 1 Analysis)

Given below is basic information (in millions of dollars) related to the 2002 financial statements for three hotel and resort companies (a service industry). This information will be used in the problems throughout the book. More complete financial information is available in the 2002 10-K reports for the three companies.

Input (Source Data)		Hilton	Marriott	Mandalay
ASSETS	Cash	$ 54	$ 198	$ 106
	Marketable securities	21	135	—
	A/R, previous year	291	479	78
	A/R, current year	294	524	58
	Prepaid assets	61	300	41
	Inventory, previous year	148	1,161	31
	Inventory, current year	139	633	31
	Current assets	630	1,744	267
	Fixed assets, previous year	3,911	2,460	3,237
	Fixed assets, current year	3,971	2,589	3,050
	Total assets, previous year	8,785	9,107	4,248
	Total assets, current year	8,348	8,296	4,037
LIABILITIES	Current liabilities	575	2,207	309

	Long-term liabilities	6,427	2,516	2,791
	Total liabilities	7,002	4,723	3,100
STOCKHOLDERS' EQUITY	Total equity, previous year	1,783	3,478	1,069
	Total equity, current year	2,053	3,573	941
	Retained earnings	322	1,126	1,374
	MV of equity	4,343	10,521	2,151
INCOME STATEMENT	Sales	3,847	8,441	2,462
	Cost of sales	1,563	7,635	1,370
	Gross margin	2,284	806	1,092
	Operating expenses	369	126	86
	SG&A expense	1,312	233	438
	Operating income	603	744	351
	Depreciation and amortization	348	187	216
	Earnings before tax	285	471	93
	Provision for tax (tax expense)	81	32	40
	Interest expense	347	86	230
	Net income	198	277	53

The quantitative ratios and other analysis are presented in "Common Financial Ratios" on this book's Web site. For more information on quantitative financial analysis, see Giroux 2003, Chapter 4. Use the information above to complete the following quantitative analysis.

   a. Common-size analysis: Complete these tables to present an abbreviated common-size analysis.

Firms (2002)	Hilton		Marriott		Mandalay	
	$	Common-Size	$	Common-Size	$	Common-Size
Revenues						
Cost of Revenues						
Gross Profit						
Ops. Inc.						
Net Income						
Rating						

   b. Analyze the common-size information, with particular attention to potential earnings management concerns.

   c. Complete the following financial ratios for 2002, which are presented by major analysis category. Use the information given above.

Activity	Hilton	Marriott	Mandalay
Inventory Turnover (COGS/Avg. Inventory)			
Avg. Number of Days Inventory (365/Inv. Turnover)			
Receivables Turnover (Sales/Avg. AR)			
Working Capital Turnover (Sales/Avg. Working Capital)			
Fixed Assets Turnover (Sales/Avg. Fixed Assets)			
Total Assets Turnover (Sales/Avg. Total Assets)			
Length of Operating Cycle [365((1/Inventory Turnover) + (1/Receivables Turnover))]			

Profit	Hilton	Marriott	Mandalay
Gross Margin (Gross Profit/Sales)			
Return on Sales (Net Income/Sales)			
ROA (Net Income/Avg. Total Assets)			
ROE (Net Income/Avg. Stockholders' Equity)			

ROE = Profit × Activity × Solvency	Hilton	Marriott	Mandalay
= Net Income/Sales			
× Sales/Avg. Total Assets			
= Return on Assets = Net Income/Avg. Total Assets			
× Avg. Total Assets/Avg. Common Equity			
= ROE = Net Income/Avg. Common Equity			

Problem 5.2: Earnings Forecasts

The actual 2002 earnings per share, 2003 EPS forecast (one year ahead), 2004 EPS forecast (two years head), and five-year earnings forecast for the hotel companies are as follows:

	Actual EPS, 2002	1 Year Forecast	2 Year Forecast	5-Year Forecast: % Growth
Hilton	$0.53	$0.41	$0.51	14.3%
Marriott	1.10	1.82	1.82	14.2
Mandalay	1.65	2.29	2.64	14.9

Compare the expected performance of Hilton with its two competitors.

Problem 5.3: Revenue Composition

The revenue categories used by Hilton for the last three years included the following:

	Revenue (Millions of Dollars)		
	2000	2001	2002
Owned hotels	$2,429	$2,122	$2,100
Leased hotels	398	168	111
Management and franchise fees	350	342	329
Other fees and income	274	418	355
Other revenue from managed and franchised properties	945	943	952
Total revenue	$4,396	$3,993	$3,847

a. Calculate the percentage composition of each revenue category by year (essentially a common-size analysis).

Revenue Category	2000	2001	2002
Owned hotels			
Leased hotels			
Management and franchise fees			
Other fees and income			
Other revenue from managed and franchised properties			
Total revenue	100.0%	100.0%	100.0%

b. Which revenue categories are the largest? Has the relative composition changed over the four years? Does this suggest the need for further analysis?

c. Calculate the percentage changes in each of these revenue categories:

Revenue Category	Change %		
	2000–2001	2001–2002	2000–2002
Owned hotels			
Leased hotels			
Management and franchise fees			
Other fees and income			
Other revenue from managed and franchised properties			
Total revenue			

d. Evaluate the percentage changes for the last three years.

CASES

Case 1: Xerox Revenue Recognition Restatements and Market Reaction

Xerox had the following public announcement associated with revenue problems, SEC investigations, and restatements over the past three years:

June 16, 2000	Xerox announced problems with a Mexican subsidiary
June 22, 2000	SEC begins an investigation
April 3, 2001	Xerox announces that it's delaying issuing its 2000 10-K
May 31, 2001	10-K filed, including restatements for 1998 and 1999
April 1, 2002	Settlement with the SEC
April 11, 2002	SEC issues an Accounting and Auditing Enforcement Release against Xerox
June 28, 2002	Restates 1997–2000 reports (and earlier quarterly results from 2002); earnings overstated by $1.4 billion

The following chart shows the performance of Xerox stocks, in comparison with the S&P 500, for the past three years:

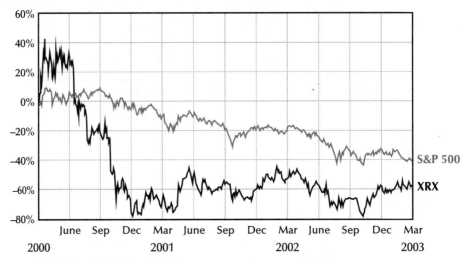

Period: May 3, 2000 – May 3, 2003

a. Analyze the stock price reaction to the public announcement associated with Xerox. Begin with the June 16 announcement and estimate the market reaction percentage.

b. What is the overall investor reaction to Xerox? Explain.

Case 2: Xerox Restatement, Continued

Xerox had the following press release on June 28, 2002:

> Xerox Corporation (NYSE: XRX) announced that it expects to file today the company's 2001 10-K, which includes a restatement for the years 1997 through 2000 as well as adjustments to previously announced 2001 results. The restatement, required under the company's previously announced settlement agreement with the Securities and Exchange Commission, primarily reflects changes to the company's lease accounting under Statement of Financial Accounting Standards No. 13. As a result, adjustments have been made to the timing and allocation of equipment, service, rental and finance revenue streams. Approximately $1.9 billion of revenue that was recognized over past years has been reversed and will be recognized in the company's future results, beginning in 2002. The monetary value of customers' contracts has not changed and there is no impact on the cash that has been received or is contractually due to be received.

> For 1997 through 2001, the company reversed $6.4 billion of previously recorded equipment sale revenue offset by $5.1 billion of revenue that has been recognized and reported during the same period as service, rental, document outsourcing and financing revenues. Revenues for 1997–2001 have been reduced by 2 percent to $91 billion.

The 2001 Revised 10-K had the following reconciliation of revenue:

	2001	2000	1999	1998	1997
Revenue, previously reported	$ 16,502	$ 18,701	$ 19,567	$ 19,593	$ 18,225
Application of SFAS No. 13:					
Revenue allocations in bundled arrangements	65	(78)	(257)	(284)	(87)
Latin America— operating lease accounting	187	(58)	57	(358)	(461)
Other transactions not qualifying as sales-type leases	73	57	(60)	(119)	(152)
Sales of equipment subject to operating leases	197	124	(243)	67	(44)
Subtotal	522	45	(503)	(694)	(744)
Other revenue restatement adjustments:					
Sales of receivables transactions	42	61	(6)	—	—
South Africa deconsolidation	(66)	(72)	(71)	(60)	—
Other revenue items, net	8	16	8	(62)	(24)
Subtotal	(16)	5	(69)	(122)	(24)
Increase (decrease) in total revenue	506	50	(572)	(816)	(768)
Revenues, restated	$ 17,008	$ 18,751	$ 18,995	$ 18,777	$ 17,457

a. Calculate the percentage change in revenue for leases and total for each year [(revised – previous)/previous].

	2001	2000	1999	1998	1997
Leases					
Total					

Pretax earnings were restated as follows:

Pretax Income (Loss), in Millions of Dollars

	2001	2000	1999	1998	1997
Previously reported	$(137)	$(384)	$1,908	$579	$2,005
Restated	365	(367)	1,288	(13)	1,287

b. Calculate the dollar amount and percentage change in pretax earnings:

	2001	2000	1999	1998	1997
Earnings Change					
% Change					

The impact on the 2001 income statement was reported as follows:

**Previously As Reported Adjusted
Year Ended December 31, 2001 (millions of dollars)**

Total revenues	$16,502	$17,008
Sales	8,028	7,443
Service, outsourcing, financing, and rentals	8,474	9,565
Total costs and expenses	16,639	16,643
Net loss	(293)	(71)
Diluted loss per share	$(0.43)	$(0.12)

c. Calculate the changes in these amounts:

	$ Change	% Change
Total revenue		
Sales		
Services, etc.		
Total costs and expenses		
Net loss		

d. Evaluate the specific restatements and magnitude of restatements for Xerox.

Case 3: Investment Income and Loss at Microsoft

Microsoft reported the following investment income information (in millions of dollars) in the 2001 10-K:

	Year Ended June 30 (in Millions)		
	2000	**2001**	**2002**
Dividends	$ 363	$ 377	$ 357
Interest	1,231	1,808	1,762
Net recognized gains/(losses) on investments	1,732	(2,221)	(2,424)
Investment income/(loss)	$3,326	$ (36)	$ (305)

Microsoft went from a large gain of $3.3 billion to a $36 million loss. This had a dramatic effect on the income statement (selectively presented):

	Year Ended June 30		
	2000	**2001**	**2002**
Revenue	$ 22,956	$ 25,296	$ 28,365
Operating income	11,006	11,720	11,910
Losses on equity investees and other	(57)	(159)	(92)
Investment income/(loss)	3,326	(36)	(305)
Income before income taxes	14,275	11,525	11,513
Provision for income taxes	4,854	3,804	3,684
Income before accounting change	9,421	7,721	7,829
Cumulative effect of accounting change (net of income taxes of $185)	–	(375)	–
Net income	$ 9,421	$ 7,346	$ 7,829

a. The result of the investment loss in 2001 and 2002 is that net income was down from 2000 despite increasing operating income. Calculate common-size information below:

	2000	**2001**	**2002**
Revenue			
Operating income			
Investment income (loss)			
Net income			

b. Evaluate the impact of Microsoft's investment income (loss) on overall operating results. Note that Microsoft also reported a $1.2 billion unrealized holding loss (net of taxes of $351 million) in 2001 as part of comprehensive income. How important is this to the evaluation of earnings management?

Appendix 5.1: Apple Computer Consolidated Statements of Operations

Apple Computer Consolidated Statements of Operations
(in Millions, Except Share and per Share Amounts)

	2002	2001	2000
Net sales	$ 5,742	$ 5,363	$ 7,983
Cost of sales	4,139	4,128	5,817
Gross margin	1,603	1,235	2,166
Operating expenses:			
Research and development	446	430	380
Selling, general, and administrative	1,111	1,138	1,166
Special charges:			
Restructuring costs	30	—	8
In-process research and development	1	11	—
Executive bonus	(2)	—	90
Total operating expenses	1,586	1,579	1,644
Operating income (loss)	17	(344)	522
Other income and expense:			
Gains (losses) on noncurrent investments, net	(42)	88	367
Unrealized loss on convertible securities	—	(13)	—
Interest and other income, net	112	217	203
Total other income and expense	70	292	570
Income (loss) before provision for income taxes	87	(52)	1,092
Provision for (benefit from) income taxes	22	(15)	306
Income (loss) before accounting change	65	(37)	786
Cumulative effect of accounting change, net of income taxes of $5	—	12	—
Net income (loss)	$ 65	$ (25)	$ 786
Earnings (loss) per common share before accounting change:			
Basic	$ 0.18	$ (0.11)	$ 2.42
Diluted	$ 0.18	$ (0.11)	$ 2.18
Earnings (loss) per common share:			
Basic	$ 0.18	$ (0.07)	$ 2.42
Diluted	$ 0.18	$ (0.07)	$ 2.18
Shares used in computing earnings (loss) per share (in thousands):			
Basic	355,022	345,613	324,568
Diluted	361,785	345,613	360,324

Appendix 5.2: Net Sales for Apple

Net sales and Macintosh unit sales for geographic segments and by product were as follows (net sales in millions and Macintosh unit sales in thousands):

	2002	Change	2001	Change	2000
Americas net sales	$ 3,088	3%	$ 2,996	(30)%	$ 4,298
Europe net sales	1,251	0%	1,249	(31)%	1,817
Japan net sales	710	0%	713	(47)%	1,345
Retail net sales	283	—	19	—	—
Other segments net sales	410	6%	386	(26)%	523
Total net sales	$ 5,742	7 %	$ 5,363	(33)%	$ 7,983
Americas Macintosh unit sales	1,728	(2)%	1,768	(29)%	2,507
Europe Macintosh unit sales	722	(4)%	754	(32)%	1,110
Japan Macintosh unit sales	386	(2)%	394	(46)%	730
Retail Macintosh unit sales	92	—	7	—	—
Other segments Macintosh unit sales	173	5%	164	(22)%	211
Total Macintosh unit sales	$ 3,101	0%	$ 3,087	(32)%	$ 4,558
Power Macintosh net sales (a)	1,380	(17)%	1,664	(39)%	2,747
PowerBook net sales	831	2%	813	(14)%	948
iMac net sales	1,448	30%	1,117	(53)%	2,381
iBook net sales	875	8%	809	0%	809
Software, service, and other net sales	1,208	26%	960	(13)%	1,098
Total net sales	$ 5,742	7%	$ 5,363	(33)%	$ 7,983
Power Macintosh unit sales (a)	766	(18)%	937	(35)%	1,436
PowerBook unit sales	357	3%	346	(10)%	383
iMac unit sales	1,301	8%	1,208	(45)%	2,194
iBook unit sales	677	14%	596	9%	545
Total Macintosh unit sales	3,101	0%	3,087	(32)%	4,558
Net sales per Macintosh unit sold (b)	$ 1,462		$ 1,426		$ 1,510

The Income Statement, Part II—Expenses, Nonoperating Items

The income statement is of primary concern for earnings management issues, and this chapter continues with an analysis of operating expenses, nonoperating items, bottom line considerations, and market issues. Corporate executives have incentives to target specific earnings levels and a large menu of items to choose from to manage earnings, including any combination of issues.

OPERATING EXPENSES

Expenses are the costs associated with generating revenues. The key concept is the **matching principle.** Operating expenses must be matched to related recognized revenues during the accounting period. **Product costs** are a direct match to specific revenues, especially costs of goods sold related to sales. **Period costs** have no direct cause-and-effect relationship to specific sales but are consumed during the period. Marketing and advertising costs are period costs. As with revenues, timing is critical.

Perhaps the most important accounting topic in matching expenses to revenues is the accrual concept. Accrual accounting rather than the cash basis is used to determine appropriate expense recognition. These are the rules developed through GAAP on how expenses (as well as revenue and other items) are recorded. The costs of fixed assets are allocated to specific time periods using depreciation methods. Other allocation methods are used for long-term amortization of some intangibles. Research and development (R&D) costs, advertising, and human resource costs usually are expensed as incurred. Capitalizing any of these costs raises earnings management concerns.

Companies with a manipulation history are likely to use both revenue and expense recognition strategies simultaneously, such as recognizing revenues early and operating expenses late (a perverse use of the matching principle).

A summary of operating expense concerns is given in Table 6.1.

Cost of sales includes cost of goods sold (COGS) and other direct costs such as shipping and handling, service costs, and so on. Gross margin [(sales − cost of sales)/sales] is a good measure of basic production efficiency. The relationship to sales should be fairly constant (e.g., as measured by gross margin percentages). If gross margins are rising, it suggests that efficiency is improving, whereas declining margins are bad news. Erratic gross margins require further analysis to determine the basic causes. The primary analysis of cost of sales is to compare the dollar amounts and percentages to sales over time and to direct competitors (see Chapter 8). Rite Aid, a drugstore chain, during 1997–1999 made a number of adjustments to COGS to understate COGS and increase earnings. These included recording vendor allowances as reductions to COGS and using other methods to keep costs in inventory rather than COGS. Analysts became aware of this only when Rite Aid restated earnings in 2000.

A tempting target for manipulation, which is simple in execution, is capitalizing operating costs. This process reduces expenses, thereby boosting earnings. WorldCom capitalized almost $10 billion in operating expenses before filing for bankruptcy in 2002. Along with Enron, it was one of the most flagrant examples of recent accounting abuse. The analyst should look for ratios and trends that suggest that operating expenses are out of line with expectations.

As with revenues, reserves associated with expense categories are commonplace and subject to abuse. The most common reserves are allowance for doubtful accounts and inventory reserves (e.g., for future obsolescence and value declines). The theoretical argument of reserve accounts is to ensure that costs are recorded in the correct period. For example, bad debts expensed this year should be based on receivables associated with credit sales this year. Reserves are accounts that promote income smoothing (amounts charged are usually based on long-term averages), but because the amounts are based on judgment, they are subject to considerable abuse. Sunbeam used reserves for product liability and warranty expenses among many techniques to increase earnings, beginning in 1997. Microsoft, on the other hand, was overly conservative and established excess reserves in several categories, essentially an income smoothing strategy. The company also had antitrust problems, and reducing reported earnings had **political cost** implications. The feasibility of evaluating reserves depends on reporting completeness in notes and MD&A.

Selling, general, and administrative (SG&A) expenses are "overhead" items with considerable operating flexibility and potential for manipulation. Lots of unrelated costs can be "dumped" into SG&A, and the process is not standardized. For example, the distinction of how overhead items should be allocated to COGS, SG&A, and other income statement line items is not obvious. Aurora Foods misstated various trade promotion and marketing activities, which understated SG&A and increased earnings to meet earnings targets. AOL capitalized advertising costs as subscription acquisition costs in the mid-1990s; AOL would

| TABLE 6.1 | OPERATING EXPENSE CONCERNS AND STRATEGIES |

Topic	Concern	Detection Strategy
Cost of sales	Measure of operating efficiency, directly related to sales; is it reasonable and reasonably steady over time?	Compare over time and to direct competitors using standard measures (e.g., percent sales, gross margin percent)
Capitalizing operating costs	Generic means of understating current expenses, thus increasing earnings	Compare expense ratios over time and look for unexpected drops; review operating policies and relevant notes
Overstating (or understating) reserves	Reserves can be overstated in "good years," to be reduced in "bad years" to boost income	Review ratio levels over time, with particular concern during down periods
Selling, general, and administrative (SG&A) expenses	"Overhead" measure with considerable flexibility; is the amount reasonable?	Compare over time and to competitors with use of standard measures (e.g., percentof sales, percent change)
Research and development (R&D)	Short-term cuts can improve current earnings but reduce long-term results; capitalizing R&D	Compare current period to earlier periods and as a percent of sales; evaluate with business strategy
Software development costs	Overcapitalizing costs, potential to manipulate costs to meet earnings targets	Review accounting policies and R&D notes on procedures
Depreciation expense	Useful life may be too long and residual value too high; concern with changes in estimates and policy	Review accounting policy and PPE notes; calculate expense ratios and useful life averages and trends
Provision for tax	Deferred tax asset and liability accounts, short- vs. long-term; reasonableness of effective rates; procedures that appear unethical	Start with standard ratio analysis, including effective tax rates and review of tax notes; evaluate specific tax items
Goodwill	Amortizing over too long a period; since 2002, proper valuation and use of write-downs	Calculate amortization rate in years (2001 and before); contemplate valuation and potential write-downs for 2002 and beyond
Interest expense	May be difficult to find and evaluate effectively; high leverage often associated with large interest expense	Review income statement and related notes on interest and debt; calculate interest coverage and other ratios
Other expenses	Various expenses "dumped" into the "other" category; little disclosure if considered immaterial	Evaluate notes on "other assets and expenses" and scour report for additional information

have reported losses if these items were expensed. The SEC objected and required AOL to reverse the practice.

R&D costs are expensed as incurred according to GAAP, with a few exceptions. Because of immediate expensing, companies can reduce expenses by reducing R&D, which boosts short-term performance but probably is detrimental in the long-term. Like other operating costs, these can be capitalized—a clear GAAP violation. Some R&D costs can be legitimately capitalized, such as software development costs (once technological feasibility has occurred; SFAS No. 86). In part on the basis of determining feasibility, companies capitalize between zero (Microsoft) and close to 100 percent of all development costs. The amortization period can vary from eighteen months or so to about five years. The capitalization alternative and differences in relative amounts capitalized and amortization periods make comparability difficult. This represents another earnings management opportunity. To make comparisons, software development expense can be reestimated by adding back the amount capitalized, less the estimated annual amortization of development costs, adjusted for income tax.

Depreciation is one of the most accepted accrual principles in accounting, involving the allocation of expenses by formula. Alternative techniques exist, usually between straight-line and various accelerated methods, and estimated useful lives and residual values are subject to judgment. Waste Management misstated depreciation expenses in the mid-1990s, associated with lengthening the estimated useful lives of landfill assets and vehicle, equipment, and container salvage value assumptions.

Tax is a major expense category. Tax accounting includes the potential to manage both the provision for tax (tax expense based on GAAP and reported in the income statement) and the amount of tax paid to the federal government. Tax policies can be aggressive and appear unethical, such as moving the home office to a tax haven such as Bermuda. SeaView Video misstated deferred tax assets related to tax operating loss carry-forwards.

Goodwill is a major asset category of corporations making acquisitions under the purchase method. Until 2001, goodwill was amortized over a maximum of forty years. Companies used vastly different amortization periods, resulting in a lack of comparability. As of 2002, goodwill is no longer amortized but is subject to testing for valuation. Based on certain tests, write-downs should be made. In the first quarter of 2002, AOL Time Warner wrote off over $50 billion in goodwill associated with lost market valuation (more on goodwill and related issues in Chapter 9).

Interest expense is a basic cost of corporate borrowing and may be listed as a separate line item on the income statement. Alternatively, it can be combined with interest income and other accounts or captured as part of other income and expense. The evaluation of interest expense and the cost of borrowing depend on the available disclosure. The evaluation of interest expense is especially important for high-leverage, high-credit-risk companies.

Other expense (or other income and expenses) can include any number of unrelated operating items. The ability to analyze these depends on the level of disclosure presented.

EXPENSE RECOGNITION AT APPLE

The major expense and related items on Apple's income statement were cost of sales (72.1 percent of net sales for 2002); R&D (7.8 percent); selling, general and administrative expense (19.3 percent); and special charges (0.5 percent); gains and losses on investments (0.7 percent); net interest income (−2.0 percent; that is, income increasing); and income tax

(0.4 percent). Most were similar to the previous year. The exceptions were gross margin (27.9 percent in 2002 versus 23.0 in 2001), gains and losses on investments, special charges, interest income and tax expense, which all changed considerably over the three year period. Special charges would be the most concern, although the magnitudes are relatively small.

Standard quantitative analysis of performance and operating efficiency (turnover) and profit models such as the Du Pont Model are the next step (see Giroux 2003 or another financial analysis textbook for a thorough analytical review). The primary concern is unusual results requiring further analysis. Apple's performance was poor the last two years, producing a small net loss in 2001 and a small profit in 2002.

Note 1 included accounting policies used for shipping costs (part of cost of sales), warranty expense (estimated based on timing of revenue recognition), R&D (expensed as incurred), and advertising (expensed as incurred). R&D for 2002 was $446 million (8 percent of net sales), up from $430 million in 2001. Development costs of some software (e.g., Mac OS X) were capitalized, totaling about $25 million in 2002 (less than 6 percent of R&D expense for the year). Beginning in 2001, Apple recorded capitalized development costs as part of property, plant, and equipment (PPE; prior to that it was recorded as another asset). The amount capitalized as "internal-use software" was $184 million, or 17.4 percent of PPE (note that part of this amount would have been based on acquisitions rather than internal R&D). Assuming an amortization period of four years (Apple's policy is to amortize over three to five years), the annual amortization would be $46 million, or greater than the amount capitalized in 2002. Capitalizing software development costs varies across the industry; consequently, relatively small capitalization charges would not be a major issue.

SG&A expense at $1.1 billion was 19.3 percent of sales, rather high for "overhead" but down slightly from the previous year (21.2 percent for 2001). MD&A emphasized the importance of marketing to maintain the competitive position of Apple products. Interest and other income (Note 3) included interest income, interest expense, foreign currency gains, net discounts on foreign exchange instruments, and other items. The largest item was interest income at $118 million; all were relatively small amounts.

Special charges were detailed in Note 5. For fiscal year 2002, restructuring charges totaled $30 million to eliminate certain activities, resulting in the reduction of 600 jobs. A bonus of $90 million (primarily for the cost of an airplane) was made to the CEO. In-process R&D from acquisition also was charged off (see Chapter 9). Income tax included federal, state, and foreign, with an effective rate of 25.3 percent ($22/$87). This included a large deferred amount associated with federal taxes of $28 million based on operating loss carry-forwards.

In summary, Apple's expensing strategy appeared generally conservative, with a few minor issues. These included SG&A (expense marketing costs), capitalizing software development costs, and special charges.

AGGRESSIVE EXPENSE RECOGNITION

As with revenue, expense recognition can be used to manipulate earnings to meet management incentives. Virtually all expense categories have been used for this purpose, and several examples will highlight the most blatant examples. The GAO's analysis of restatements of financial statements showed that 16 percent of the 919 restatements analyzed from 1997 to 2002 were cost- or expense-related. Examples of aggressive recognition are shown in Table 6.2.

TABLE 6.2	EXAMPLES OF AGGRESSIVE EXPENSE RECOGNITION
Company	**Practice**
Sunbeam	Various costs and allowances not accrued, including allowances on sales returns, advertising, reserves for product liabilities and warranty expense
Rite Aid	Adjustments to cost of goods sold and inventory to reduce COGS; capitalizing maintenance and repair costs of plant and equipment; misapplication of accruals associated with compensation items
Aurora Foods	Misstated marketing expenses to meet earnings targets
Waste Management	A complex scheme of "fraudulent accounting" to meet targeted earnings, including depreciation expense, misstating useful lives of plant and equipment and salvage value, capitalization of interest on landfill construction projects, write-downs of reserves for litigation, insurance, and environmental costs

Sunbeam, mentioned under revenue recognition, also used a variety of cost-related manipulations. Al Dunlop took over in the middle of 1996 and inflated reserves that year to boost future earnings. In addition to the revenue side, cost manipulation included costs and accruals that were misstated or not recorded, including sales returns, advertising, warranty expenses, and product liability reserves. Some operating costs were charged to restructuring or asset impairment (for which reserves were established in 1996). Sunbeam restated earnings in 1998 (for fiscal years 1998–1998), resulting in a stock price drop from a high of $52 to under $10 by July 1998. The company declared bankruptcy in 2001, to reemerge as American Household at the end of 2002.

Rite Aid, a retail drugstore chain with about 3,400 drugstores, recorded many cost-related manipulations, especially in 1997–1998. These included misstated cost of goods sold (e.g., unearned vendor allowances recorded as a reduction in COGS, failure to write-down slow-moving and obsolete inventory); failure to expense stock appreciation rights; capitalizing maintenance costs and repairs to property, plant, and equipment; misstating lease obligations; failing to expense costs of store closures; and failure to recognize compensation costs such as vacation pay and incentive compensation. Rite Aid restated in 1999 for fiscal years 1997–1998. The SEC required further restatements, and auditor KPMG resigned late in 1999. A class action lawsuit charged the company, directors, executives, and auditor KPMG with false and misleading statements, and the SEC began a formal investigation (settled in 2002), charging the company with financial fraud.

Aurora Foods produced such well-known brands as Duncan Hines, Mrs. Butterworth's, Log Cabin, Van de Kamp's, and Aunt Jemima, with about $1 billion in sales. The company misstated expenses, liabilities, and assets. As stated by the GAO (2002, p. 130):

> Aurora was not accurately reporting trade marketing expense, which is the
> expense Aurora incurs to induce grocery stores to purchase its products.
> Instead of properly booking the expense [managers] allegedly tried to conceal
> it from the auditors by directing division level officers and employees to
> make false entries in various accounts on the company's books. The effect
> was to falsely and substantially inflate the Aurora's financial results. ... The
> object of the scheme was to conceal from the investing public the fact that
> the company had not met its earnings targets from quarter to quarter.

In 2000, the company restated earnings for fiscal years 1998 to 1999. The U.S. Attorney filed charges in 2001. Various managers were convicted of accounting fraud, and the CFO was sentenced to almost five years in jail. Class-action lawsuits followed, which were settled out of court.

Waste Management (WM) provided waste management services, the result of several business combinations, and had a long history of earnings manipulation (primarily 1992–1997). The most blatant expense misstatement was the manipulation of depreciation expense and other accounts associated with property, plant, and equipment. The main techniques were (1) to lengthen the useful lives and overstate the salvage value of vehicles, containers, and equipment and (2) to incorrectly calculate interest capitalization on land-fill construction projects. SEC charges stated: "defendants' improper accounting practices were centralized at corporate headquarters. … They monitored the company's actual operating results and compared them to the quarterly targets set in the budget" (GAO 2002, p. 221). WM restated in 1998 (for fiscal years 1992–1997), for a total of $1.3 billion in overstated earnings. WM settled a stockholder lawsuit in 2001, and the SEC filed suit against several managers and auditor Arthur Andersen.

According to the GAO (2002) report, eleven S&P 500 companies (15.3 percent of 72 restaters) restated earnings based on expense or cost issues. These were as shown in Table 6.3.

TABLE 6.3	FINDINGS CONCERNING RESTATED EARNINGS	
Corporation	**Year**	**Findings**
Andrews Corp.	2001	Orders, sales, and cost of sales restated to include freight costs billed to customers (based on EITF 00-10)
AOL	2001	Restated to include the operations of Netscape for all periods presented (merger used pooling-of-interests method)
Avon	2000	Restated to reflect shipping and handling fees as revenues (based on EITF 00-10); all prior-period EPS data restated (based on SFAS No. 128)
Boise Cascade	2000	Restated to increase both sales and expenses (based on EITF 00-10)
Health Management	1997	Accounting irregularities to understate allowances for doubtful accounts; overstated inventories
JDS Uniphase	2001	Executive compensation recorded as acquisition costs rather than compensation expense
McDonald's	1998	Number of common shares and per-common-share amounts restated to give retroactive effect of stock split
NVIDIA	2002	Inter-year adjustments in recording certain manufacturing costs; timing of inventory write-downs, timing of recording accruals
Unisys	1999	Impairment charges classified as "other expense" and product warranty costs as one-time charges
Williams	1999	Alternative inventory methods (changed to all conform to average-cost or market if lower)
Xerox	2001, 2002	Charge-offs of uncollectible long-term receivables and other contracts; error in interest expense calculation (from interest swap)

NONRECURRING ITEMS AND OTHER UNUSUAL ITEMS

Revenues, cost of goods sold, and most period costs are recurring items that are included in the calculation of income from continuing operations ("above the line" earnings). These are items that are consistent with the concept of **current operating performance.** Nonrecurring items are gains and losses that are unusual and expected to occur infrequently (part of "below the line" earnings). Because of these characteristics, they don't provide much information to analysts about normal operations. However, they may indicate changes in business strategy (such as discontinued operations associated with a separate industrial segment), and they can be problematic and likely candidates for red flags.

Particular issues with nonrecurring items include timing and classification. Since companies have wide latitude for most of these items, the question is why a particular period was chosen. Depending on the circumstance, many of these items can be recorded as part of continuing operations, a special or unusual item, or a specific type of nonrecurring item. Analyst issues to consider include likely income smoothing issues, the potential for "big bath" write-offs, and how "good news" or "bad news" is reported (e.g., "buried," separate line item, "above or below the line"). Concerns related to nonrecurring and related items are summarized in Table 6.4.

Other unusual or infrequent items (which might be considered "below the line" items, no matter where they are actually recorded) may be of concern and may show up in various places on the income statement or notes. Examples are given in Table 6.5.

Nonrecurring items include extraordinary items, discontinued operations, and accounting changes. These are reported separately after continuing operations, net of tax. Firms also must report earnings-per-share amounts separately for these items. According to APB Opinion 30 (1973), extraordinary items are unusual in nature and infrequent in occurrence. They are recorded only if material in amount. Examples could be unexpected weather damage such as flood or tornado, where these are unusual or expropriation of assets by foreign governments. Under SFAS No. 4 (1975), gains and losses on debt retirement (buying the debt obligations in the market) were treated as extraordinary items.

TABLE 6.4	CONCERNS RELATED TO NONRECURRING AND RELATED ITEMS	
Category	Description	Concern
Extraordinary items	Unusual in nature and infrequent in occurrence	It is bad luck or real manipulation?
Discontinued operations	The discontinuance or sale of a business component can be recorded as a discontinued operation	Either a gain or loss can be recorded; company has flexibility on how and when to record these items. Is there a good reason for the discontinuance? What is the impact on business strategy?
Accounting change	Various changes include accounting estimate, accounting principle, or reporting entity; change in principle can be mandatory (usually based on a new pronouncement) or discretionary (where alternatives are allowed by GAAP)	Discretionary accounting changes are a concern. Why was the change necessary? Earnings manipulation is a likely explanation; relative magnitude important.

TABLE 6.5	**EXAMPLES OF UNUSUAL AND INFREQUENT ITEMS THAT MAY APPEAR ON THE INCOME STATEMENT OR IN THE NOTES**

Category	Description	Concern
Restructuring charge	Some operations are restructured; usually associated with layoffs and inventory write-offs.	Potential to reclassify operating activity to nonrecurring items; likely impact on business strategy.
Special charges	Term lacks specificity; could be for restructuring or any number of other items, such as marketing.	Same as above; operations potentially treated as nonrecurring. What is impact on business strategy?
Other unusual or special items	These can be virtually any write-off, from PPE write-down or abandonment to inventory or investments.	Many of these are seemingly part of operations, and the use of a separate charge, especially as a nonrecurring item, suggests manipulation.

This was changed by SFAS No. 145 (2002), which now requires treatment as part of continuing operations.

The discontinuance or sale of a business component can be recorded as a discontinued operation under SFAS No. 144. A business component is defined as having separate identifiable operations, assets, and cash flows. Operating income is reported from the discontinued operations and any gains or losses on sales reported separately (net of tax). Once a firm formally decides to dispose of a component (measurement date), the operations are segregated, and the details are usually reported in a separate note.

Accounting changes can be changes in principle or changes in estimate. Principle changes can be: (1) mandatory, based on the requirements of new pronouncements, or (2) voluntary (discretionary), changing from one allowable alternative to another (such as from LIFO to FIFO inventory). Cumulative prior-period earnings changes on voluntary accounting changes usually are reported as separate line items net of tax (plus additional footnote disclosure). However, several exceptions to this are identified in APB Opinion 20, such as changes from LIFO to other inventory methods (which require retroactive restatement). Changes in estimate would include changing the useful life or residual value of property, plant, and equipment (remember Waste Management) or bad debts percentage on receivables. A change in estimate is for the current period forward (i.e., no adjustments are made for prior periods). There can also be a change in reporting entity associated with a business combination (see Chapter 9).

The "other" category, which includes restructuring, special charges, and other unusual or infrequent items, can be particularly problematic. They typically have characteristics of both current operations and "abnormal" circumstances. Generally, they're treated as part of continuing operations, often "buried" and occasionally recorded as a separate line item on the income statement if material. Losses are more likely to be recorded as separate items to emphasize that they are not really "current operations." Where these items actually show up and how they're disclosed is largely based on management judgment. Thus, the potential for manipulation is high.

The use of the various nonrecurring items and other "special" charges should be rare, but 57 percent of New York Stock Exchange and American Stock Exchange firms reported at least one in 1998 (up from 44 percent in 1989). The majority of these were "special or unusual items" (49 percent of the firms reported at least one of these in 1998), compared to 12 percent for extraordinary items and 10 percent for discontinued operations (Revsine et al., 2002). This is not good news for the analyst, because of the manipulation potential and the difficulty of evaluating these items.

Apple, Dell, and Gateway all reported a change in accounting principle for fiscal year 2001 to adopt SAB 101 on revenue recognition (a mandatory change based on the cumulative effect). This was common across a large number of companies and not a concern, because it was a mandatory change and the amounts were small. The amount was a gain of $12 million for Apple (0.2 percent of revenue for 2001). If this accounting change had been large and negative, it would suggest the company had been recognizing revenues aggressively prior to conforming to SAB 101. The amount of the accounting change was a loss of $444 million (net of tax) for General Electric in 2001, but this was still less than 1 percent of revenues.

Examples of nonrecurring items worth analyzing in some detail are shown in Table 6.6.

Goodyear changed accounting principles for inventory valuation from LIFO to FIFO in the fourth quarter 2000, citing a better match of revenues to expenses. This would seem normal enough, except that net income after the change for 2000 was $40.3 million (a poor 0.3 percent return on sales). Instead of a loss of $4.1 million, the accounting change conveniently increased net income by $44.4 million. Thus, it seems an example of blatant manipulation to ensure a positive net income. Particularly irksome is that this was explained in Note 7 on inventory, rather than on the income statement—where no accounting change was required.

Du Pont recorded income from discontinued operations for 1997 and 1998, a gain on disposal of discontinued business in 1999 and 1998, and an extraordinary loss from early extinguishments of debt in 1998, all net of tax. These were described in more detail in Notes 9 and 10 of the 2000 annual report. The discontinued operation was the divestiture of Conoco. What makes this especially problematic is that nonrecurring item amounts were larger than income from continuing operations (ICO). In 1999, ICO was $219 million, but net income was $7,690 million, thanks to the $7.5 billion gain on disposal. Net income showed healthy annual gains from 1997 ($2,407 million) through 1998 ($4,480 million) to 1999. But how useful is this big rise in earnings when analyzing Du Pont? ICO dropped from 1997 ($1,432) to 1999 ($219 million). Du Pont's return on sales for 1999 was a healthy 28.6 percent ($7,690/$26,918), but when ICO is substituted for net income the

TABLE 6.6	NONRECURRING ITEMS WORTH ANALYSIS
Company	**Occurrence**
Goodyear	Change in accounting principle from LIFO to FIFO in 2000
Du Pont	Disposed of Conoco in 1999 and Du Pont Pharmaceuticals in 2001
TWA	Recorded losses for discontinued operations during period when substantial operating losses were generated, a "big bath" write-off
AOL Time Warner	Wrote off $54 billion in goodwill as a nonrecurring item in 2002, a really *big* "big bath" write-off
Sunbeam	Special charges recorded for restructuring, marketing, and other items after new CEO was hired in 1996; related reserves later used to boost earnings in future years
Sun Trust Banks	Extraordinary gain on sale of credit card portfolio in 1999

return on sales was only 0.8 percent. Du Pont's ICO increased from $219 million in 1999 to $2,314 million in 2000. However, net income for 2000 also was $2,314 million, because no nonrecurring items were recorded. Consequently, for 1997 to 2000, ICO increased by $2,095 million (957 percent), but net income decreased by $5,376 million (70 percent).

In 2001, Du Pont sold Du Pont Pharmaceuticals to Bristol-Myers Squibb for a total price of $7.8 billion, booking a $6.1 billion pretax gain. Du Pont treated this sale as part of continuing operations (the after-tax gain on the sale was $3.9 billion), rather than a non-recurring item. The result was 2001 net income of $4.3 billion, rather than a miniscule income of $0.4 billion (before the gain). This transaction seems similar to the earlier Conoco sale, but it was treated in a different manner. This appears to be aggressive earnings management, and the financial analyst has to determine how to treat these sales and what further analysis is needed. At a minimum, performance measures should be made both before and after the sale.

Nonrecurring items require additional analysis, because they are unexpected and don't contribute to the understanding of normal operations. Some of these items may represent bad luck (e.g., caused by unexpected weather), while others may be problematic. Nonrecurring items may relate to troubled companies and poor management decisions in earlier periods. In most cases, the analyst should consider the possibility of earnings management. For example, management may have "big bath" incentives to write off large amounts of losses in poor performing periods when cash bonuses are not expected anyway. For example, TWA reported an operating loss for 1999 of $92.7 million. TWA then reported nonrecurring write-offs for discontinued European operations, leasehold improvements, special charges, and other items to arrive at a net loss of $353 million for the year. By taking large write-offs, earnings in future periods should be higher than without the write-offs. In the case of TWA, the write-offs were ineffective, because the company filed for Chapter 11 bankruptcy in January 2001.

The largest nonrecurring item ever was AOL Time Warner's write-off of goodwill, based on the FASB's new pronouncement on intangibles, SFAS No. 142. AOL Time Warner wrote off $54.2 billion in the March 2002 quarter, turning a small loss of $1 million (income before the accounting change on the income statement) to a $54.2 billion net loss (roughly the gross domestic product of New Zealand). Consequently, equity fell from $157 billion to $98 billion. Was this a "big bath" write-off based on earnings management incentives or a required adjustment based on the application of a new pronouncement? Both chief architects of the mergers (Gerald Levin and Steven Case) resigned, so whatever the reason for the write-off, the merger hasn't worked well.

Al Dunlap had a reputation for restructuring companies and turning them around, partly through slashing expenditures and employees (figuratively—he just fired them). He took over Sunbeam in 1996 and almost immediately recorded a massive restructuring as a special charge of some $340 million. He established corresponding reserves as the credit. These reserves were later released to increase earnings in 1997 and later. This was part of the pattern of massive earnings manipulation across the company. The later profitability was wiped out by restatements mandated by the SEC, not to mention extensive legal actions by regulators and investors.

Extraordinary items appear to be recorded more often than expected, and most of the items seem "ordinary," that is, far from the unusual and infrequent requirements of GAAP. An example is Sun Trust Bank's extraordinary gain of $203 million (net of tax) for the sales of its consumer credit card portfolio to MBNA American Bank. This transaction increased net income 15 percent but seemed an ordinary business transaction.

It may be useful to conduct a quantitative analysis of nonrecurring items and other unusual items. A first step would be to calculate the ratio of the individual item and totals by net income and sales. Further analysis would depend on the individual items under analysis, the relative magnitude, and the likely manipulation potential. For example, nonrecurring items for the Du Pont example above are shown in Table 6.7.

Financial statement numbers included those given in Table 6.8.

Du Pont ratios are given in Table 6.9.

The impact of the special/nonrecurring items was substantial, roughly 25 percent of revenues in both years. Consequently, they dominate performance measures. For 1999, it's obvious that operating performance was poor; ICO/Revenues is less than 1 percent. However, when the focus is on net income (which includes the huge gain on sale of Conoco), then performance is excellent, with a return on sales of 27.6 percent. The sale of Du Pont Pharmaceuticals seems virtually the same as that of Conoco, except it was considered part of operating income. Without this item, operating performance again would be poor. This gives the appearance of manipulation, with the presumption that sales of major segments were timed to offset poor performance. The alternative explanation is a major shift in business strategy, which also has merit as an explanation for both discontinued operations.

TABLE 6.7 DU PONT NONRECURRING ITEMS

2001 Accounting change in 2001 (adapting to SAB 101 on revenue recognition); sale of Du Pont Pharmaceuticals, part of continuing operations

1999 Discontinued operations in 1999, sale of Conoco

TABLE 6.8 FIGURES FROM DU PONT'S FINANCIAL STATEMENTS (MILLIONS OF DOLLARS)

Variable	2001	1999
Revenues	$ 25,370	$ 27,892
Du Pont Pharmaceuticals	6,136*	
Income from continuing operations (ICO)	6,844	219
Discontinued operations (sale of Conoco)		7,471
Accounting change	11	
Net income (NI)	4,339	7,690

*Part of continuing operations (therefore, before tax).

TABLE 6.9 FINANCIAL RATIOS FOR DU PONT

Item	Ratio 2001	1999
ICO/Revenues	27.0%	0.8%
NI/Revenues	17.1	27.6
Special/Nonrecurring items/Revenues	24.2	26.8

ICO = income from continuing operations; NI = net income.

NET INCOME AND EARNINGS PER SHARE

Net income usually is considered the "bottom line," the most appropriate measure of profitability. Net income is a relatively complete measure of all business activity (close to all-inclusive), because it includes nonrecurring items in addition to normal operating income. However, not all gains and losses are included in net income; a number of items are recorded directly to the balance sheet, resulting in the "dirty surplus" previously mentioned. SFAS No. 130 requires the presentation of comprehensive income to include net income plus all other gains and losses reported directly to stockholders' equity.

A major issue with net income is the emphasis given to this number by analysts, compensation contracts, and other purposes. Meeting earnings targets specified in terms of net income or earnings per share suggests the potential for earnings management in some set of revenue or expense categories. Of course, this is accomplished through all the categories above to arrive at net income. (Additional bottom line analysis will be presented in the next chapter.)

Earnings per share (EPS) is net income (and other bottom line measures) presented in two formats: (1) basic (net income – preferred dividends)/weighted average number of common shares outstanding and (2) diluted, which adjusts for the potential for additional shares associated with stock options, convertible securities, and related factors. Diluted EPS is expected to be the same or lower than basic EPS. If companies have nonrecurring items, EPS will be stated both before and after these items.

EPS should be evaluated for the impact of changes in the number of shares outstanding. Thus, a growing net income could be a flat EPS if number of shares increases (that is, if net income increases 10 percent and the number of the shares also increases 10 percent, there is no growth in EPS). The company can issue new equity securities, issue substantial amounts of stock options, or have lots of convertible securities likely to be converted. All of these dilute earnings—bad news for existing stockholders. On the other hand, **treasury stock** essentially reduces dilution. These represent manipulation opportunities and will be discussed in more detail in Chapter 10.

Market Value Considerations Net income, EPS, and other performance measures are expected to be closely related to stock price and other market indicators. Market analysts typically forecast EPS quarterly, annually, and for longer periods (five-year forecasts are the most common). Consequently, EPS numbers typically are considered the most significant financial information to both executives and investors. This works if these bottom line numbers represent economic reality. Then, calculations of **price earnings** (PE) ratios, price earnings to growth (**PEG**), **market-to-book,** and a host of other calculations are vital to valuing stocks.

Since the point of this chapter is to highlight earnings management techniques, which essentially involves misstating the current bottom line numbers, these numbers may not be accurate in the presence of substantial manipulation. What happens then? The market is expected to "discount" the value of the stock, which results in a lower PE ratio (i.e., associated with a lower stock price than expected, given the EPS). This is a difficult process to evaluate, since the "discounting mechanism" cannot be observed. However, the analyst can be on top of the process by a thorough analysis of earnings management potential and by knowing how to reevaluate or restate earnings net of earnings management. This will be a primary focus in Section 3 of this book, on special topics.

Consider the stock charts of Apple (AAPL), in comparison with Dell, Gateway (GTW), and the NASDAQ average for the past one year and five years (as of the start of 2003), as shown in Figure 6.1.

The stock price history of Apple compared to competitors and relevant market averages should make sense relative to the financial information evaluated, especially earnings analysis. Over the last year, Apple's stock price dropped about 30 percent after rising about 20 percent at the start of the year. This performance was roughly comparable to NASDAQ.

FIGURE 6.1	STOCK PERFORMANCE OF APPLE COMPUTER (AAPL), DELL, GATEWAY (GTW), AND THE NASDAQ AVERAGE

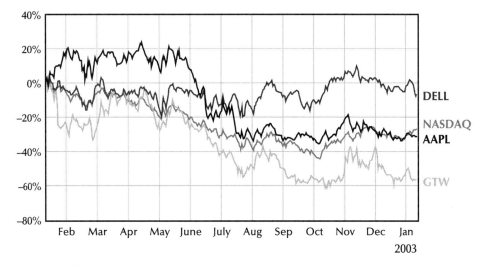

Period: January 14, 2002–January 14, 2003

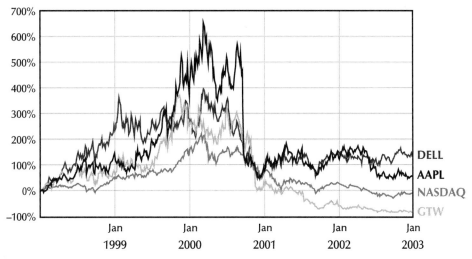

Period: January 14, 1998–January 14, 2003

Apple outperformed Gateway but underperformed Dell. This is probably consistent with the relatively mediocre performance for Apple and comparable to the entire tech sector for the period. Over five years, the stock price actually ended up about 50 percent, but after a large price run up to the middle of 2000 and then a collapse in price after the middle of that year. Determining the specific price drop over a short period requires further investigation (see Chapter 11).

CREDIT RISK ISSUES

Credit risk is the probability a company will default on debt or declare bankruptcy. Credit risk rises when companies have high debt levels, hefty interest payments on long-term debt, and deteriorating performance. As credit risk rises, companies have increasing incentives to manipulate earnings and to recognize outstanding debt. Early signals of potential problems are recurring losses, "big bath" write-offs, and restructuring. More serious signals include troubled debt restructuring (including restating debt terms or replacing debt with equity), bond rating downgradings (especially from investment grade to non–investment grade or junk status), and going-concern audit qualifications. A Moody's bond rating below Baa is considered a below-investment grade or junk rating.

Bankruptcy rates have been on the rise, especially among large, well-recognized corporations, as stated in a recent *Fortune* article (Charan & Useem, 2002):

> How many more must fall? Each month seems to bring the sound of another giant crashing to earth. Enron. WorldCom. Global Crossing. Kmart. Polaroid. Arthur Andersen. Xerox. Qwest. They fall singly. They fall in groups. They fall with the heavy thud of employees laid off, families hurt, shareholders furious. How many? Too many; 257 public companies with $258 billion in assets declared bankruptcy last year, shattering the previous year's record of 176 companies and $95 billion. This year is on pace, with 67 companies going bust during the first quarter. And not just any companies. Big, important, FORTUNE 500 companies that aren't supposed to collapse.

Several multivariate models have been developed to predict bankruptcy. Primarily, a sample of bankrupt firms is matched to a comparable sample of nonbankrupt firms and a set of ratios used to correctly classify firms as bankrupt or nonbankrupt. The best known of these models was developed by Altman (1968) to predict failure of manufacturing firms. A more recent **Altman Z-score** model can be applied to a broader range of firms, including service firms (Altman, 1983):

$$6.56 \times \text{(working capital/total assets)}$$
$$+ 3.26 \times \text{(retained earnings/total assets)}$$
$$+ 6.72 \times \text{(EBIT/total assets)}$$
$$+ 1.05 \times \text{(book value of equity/book value of debt)}$$

Under this model the Z-score cutoffs are as follows:

<1.1	bankrupt
1.10–2.6	gray area
>2.6	healthy

This Z-score model can be used as a general indicator of financial health. A Z-score below 1.1 doesn't mean the company will go bankrupt, but it is a red flag and suggests the need for further analysis of credit risk.

The Z-score calculations for the personal computer (PC) companies are tabulated (calculations shown for Apple) in Table 6.10.

Apple had a large Z-score and was rated a healthy 7.15, substantially above the cutoff of 2.6. The only negative was a small EBIT amount. Gateway had a large EBIT loss. Despite that, Gateway still was categorized in the gray area, although the score was below Dell's. The company compensated with substantial working capital and a relatively good leverage ratio. Dell had relatively low scores for all four areas, although its consistent strong performance suggests no real concern. From a credit risk perspective, Gateway is a concern.

As demonstrated by Dell, Altman's method isn't foolproof, but it still is a good quantitative starting point for evaluating credit risk. The most significant perspective is the incentive structure for earnings management. The weaker the company is in terms of credit risk, the greater the incentives are to manipulate both earnings and the recognition of debt on the balance sheet.

SUMMARY

This chapter continued analysis of the income statement, including operating expenses, nonrecurring items, net income, and EPS, and the importance of credit risk issues. Expenses are matched to revenues and an integral part of a potential manipulation strategy. Paralleling revenues, this includes aggressive long-term expense avoidance (e.g., capitalizing operating expense categories) and techniques to "tweak" quarterly earnings (such as modifying reserve accounts). Nonrecurring items can be used to move losses "below the line." The ultimate test is the overall impact of earnings management on net income and EPS, standard bottom-line measures. Finally, credit risk considerations are important, especially for companies with deteriorating performance and high debt loads.

QUESTIONS

1. Explain how the matching principle works and its relationship to revenue recognition.
2. What is "dirty surplus"? What's the difference between net income and comprehensive income, and what are the implications to earnings management?

TABLE 6.10	Z-SCORE FIGURES FOR PERSONAL COMPUTER COMPANIES		
	Apple	**Dell**	**Gateway**
Working Capital	$[(5,388 - 1,658)/6,298] \times 6.56 = 3.885$	0.174	2.146
Retained Earnings	$(2,325/6,298) \times 3.26 = 1,204$	0.329	0.672
EBIT	$[(87 + 16)/6,298] \times 6.72 = 0.110$	0.874	−2.884 (RF)
Equity/Debt	$(4,095/2,203) \times 1.05 = 1.952$	0.506	1.337
Z-score	7.15	1.880	1.270
Category	Healthy	Gray area	Gray area

RF = red flag (need for further analysis).

3. What are nonrecurring items and why are they potential red flags?
4. Why is credit risk an important consideration for earnings management?
5. Why do some companies capitalize software development costs, while others expense the costs? Is this an important consideration for earnings management?
6. Is Altman's Z-score a good measure of credit risk? Is other information available to do a more thorough analysis? Explain.

PROBLEMS

Problem 6.1: Income Tax Allocation in the Hotel and Resort Industry

Given below is the 2002 income tax-related information for three companies in the hotel/resort industry.

	Hilton	Marriott	Mandalay
Pretax income	$285	$471	$93
Income tax expense	81	32	40
Taxes payable	149	107	41

a. Calculate the reported effective tax rate and taxes payable rate for these companies.

	Hilton	Marriott	Mandalay
Reported effective tax rate			
Taxes payable rate			

b. Analyze these ratios for each company. Do earnings management concerns exist for unexpected ratios?

Problem 6.2: Revenue and Operating Income Analysis for Hilton

The segment reporting note reports revenue and operating income in a different format than the income statement, but with the same total amounts, as follows:

	2000	2001	2002
Revenues			
Hotel ownership	$2,930	$2,388	$2,270
Managing and Franchising	1,295	1,285	1,281
Timeshare	171	320	296
Total Revenue	4,396	3,993	3,847
Operating Income			
Hotel Ownership	716	470	412
Managing and Franchising	302	290	278
Timeshare	30	86	73
Corporate and Other Expenses	(218)	(214)	(160)
Total Operating Income	830	632	603

a. Calculate the operating return (operating income/revenues) for each segment:

	2000	2001	2002
Hotel ownership			
Managing and franchising			
Timeshare			
Total			

b. Evaluate the operating return for each segment over the three years.

c. Calculate the percentage changes in operating return over the period.

	2000–2001	2001–2002	2000–2002
Hotel ownership			
Managing and franchising			
Timeshare			
Total			

d. Evaluate the percentage change over the period.

Problem 6.3: Calculating Z-Scores in the Hotel and Resort Industry

Below are the financial numbers for three companies needed to calculate Altman's Z-score (1983) for 2002 (in millions of dollars):

	Hilton	Marriott	Mandalay
Total current assets	$ 630	$1,744	$ 267
Total current liabilities	575	2,207	309
Total assets	8,348	8,296	4,037
Retained earnings	322	1,126	1,374
Earnings before tax	285	471	93
Interest expense	347	86	230
Total stockholders' equity	2,053	3,573	941
Total liabilities	7,002	4,723	3,100

a. Calculate Altman's Z-score for each company and rate each company's status as failing, healthy, or indeterminate.

	Hilton	Marriott	Mandalay
$6.56 \times$ working capital/total assets			
$3.26 \times$ retained earnings/total assets			
$6.72 \times$ EBIT/total assets			
$1.05 \times$ BV of equity/BV of debt			
= Z-score			
Category			

b. Bond ratings for the companies are as follows:

	Hilton	Marriott	Mandalay
Moody's	Ba1	Baa2	Ba1
Standard & Poor's	BBB–	BBB+	BB+

c. Evaluate the credit worthiness of these companies, using Altman's Z-score, bond ratings, and previous financial analysis.

Problem 6.4: Interest Expense

Hilton has some problems with credit risk and has a relatively high interest expense and debt load. The following information summarizes the related information (in millions of dollars).

	2000	2001	2002
Interest Expense	$ 469	$ 368	$ 347
Revenues	4,396	3,993	3,847
Earnings before Income Tax	479	250	285
Long-term Debt (+ Current Portion)	5,716	5,315	4,565
Total Assets	9,140	8,785	8,348

a. Calculate the following ratios:

	2000	2001	2002
Interest Expense/Revenues			
Interest Expense/Earnings before Income Tax			
Interest Expense/Long-term Debt			
Interest Expense/Total Assets			
Long-term Debt/Total Assets			

b. Evaluate the long-term debt and interest expense policies of Hilton.

CASES

Case 1: Evaluating the Overall Quality of Apple's Income and Earnings Management Potential

The analysis of earnings management considers major concerns (usually treated as red flags), but also the accumulation of a large number of minor concerns. A large number of potential problems can indicate overall relatively lower reporting quality. Apple Computer is an example of a successful, high profile, high-tech company that has had a somewhat erratic performance over the last decade and seems a good candidate for analysis. (Refer to Apple's 2002 10-K, www.apple.com.)

a. Overall: Analyze the following income statement factors for Apple:

Factor	Analysis
Revenue recognition policies	
Net sales	
Cost of sales and gross margin	
Research and development	
SG&A	
Special charges	
Operating income	
Gains and losses on investments	
Loss on convertible securities	
Interest and other income	
Provision for income tax	
Accounting change	
Net income	
Earnings per share	

b. Specific Weaknesses and Potential Concerns. Analyze these potential problems for Apple.

Weakness/Concern	Analysis
Small operating income, despite high gross margin	
Capitalization of software development costs	
SG&A percent much larger than Dell's	
Restructuring charges	
Executive bonus	
Net income small after loss in previous year	
Drop in stock price	

Case 2: Evaluating the Credit Risk of Airlines—Calculating Z-Scores in the Airline Industry

Below are the financial numbers for three companies needed to calculate Altman's Z-score (1983) for 2001 (in millions of dollars):

	AMR	UAL	Northwest
Total current assets	$ 6,540	$ 5,086	$ 3,790
Total current liabilities	7,512	8,066	4,146
Total assets	32,841	25,197	12,955
Retained earnings	538	−199	−518
Earnings before tax	−2,756	−3,357	−670
Interest expense	4,188	525	369
Total stockholders' equity	5,373	3,033	−204
Total liabilities	27,468	22,164	13,159

a. Calculate Altman's Z-score for each company and rate each company's status as failing, healthy, or indeterminate.

	AMR	UAL	Northwest
6.56 × working capital/total assets			
3.26 × retained earnings/total assets			
6.72 × EBIT/total assets			
1.05 × BV of equity/BV of debt			
= Z-score			
Category			

New bond ratings for the companies, from Moody's, were as follows:

AMR	UAL	Northwest
Downgraded to B3 on February 10, 2003	Downgraded to Caa3 on August 15, 2002	Downgraded to B1 on December 21, 2001

b. Evaluate the credit-worthiness of these companies, using Altman's Z-score, bond ratings, and previous financial analysis, and rate the companies on a 1–10 scale.

c. Case 2 in Chapter 4 indicated the use of operating leases by these airlines to manipulate recorded debt levels. The suggestion was that manipulating both earnings and debt levels is common in companies with deteriorating credit risk. Does that apply to this industry? Explain.

CHAPTER 7

Cash Flows and Alternative Definitions of the Bottom Line

The balance sheet and income statement depend on accrual accounting to measure financial position and operating performance. Additional information can be evaluated based on cash flows, because SFAS No. 95 requires the statement of cash flows. The cash flow statement is comparative, with the current year compared to the two previous years. Essentially this is information restated from a different perspective—cash. The statement provides additional information on the liquidity of the company and its ability to finance operations and growth from internal funds. It can highlight certain problems such as lagging cash collections or the relative need for operating capital.

Cash from operations is an alternative definition of performance, one of many that can be used rather than net income. More important for earnings management, comparisons across measures may signal potential problems. These measures include gross profit, operating profit, **Earnings Before Interest and Taxes (EBIT)**, **Earnings Before Interest, Taxes, Depreciation, and Amortization (EBITDA)**, **income from continuing operations, comprehensive income,** and various *pro forma* **earnings** measures. These run the gamut from definitions of **current operating performance** to **all-inclusive** earnings. The alternatives provide additional information on the overall performance and can be better measures than net income in some circumstances.

The concept of current operating performance is **sustainable earnings,** to discern the continuing trend in earnings potential. Measuring earnings quality depends on correctly stating sustainable earnings. The alternative definitions, from gross margin or operating income to income from continuing operations, are first attempts at capturing a measure of sustainable earnings. Because of earnings management and other factors, capturing sustainable earnings is difficult. Hopefully, adjusting one or more measures is a better measure of real economic performance (essentially, attempting to back out of the earnings management techniques).

The all-inclusive concept is a major focus of the FASB's Conceptual Framework, with its definition of comprehensive income. Net income is almost all-inclusive, because it includes nonrecurring and various "special items." This captures all performance-related (including peripheral transactions and events) factors, assuming that an all-factor model is the best bottom line measure. As part of the analysis process, the alternative measures can be directly compared.

THE STATEMENT OF CASH FLOWS

The statement of cash flows evaluates cash receipts (inflows) and cash payments (outflows) in three categories: operating, investing, and financing activities. The focus of cash flows from operations (CFO) is cash effects of all transaction related to income. The indirect method, which is used by most companies, starts with net income and then adds back noncash items such as depreciation and amortization as well as changes in noncash current items. Most often, CFO is positive, because net income is normally positive and noncash expenses such as depreciation increase CFO. Cash flows from investing (CFI) include capital expenditures and investments. Generally, CFI is negative because investments are uses of cash. Cash flow from financing (CFF) includes the acquisition or disposal of equity or debt and the payment of dividends. Then cash is reconciled from the beginning balance to the ending balance. Apple's Statement of Cash Flows for fiscal year 2002 is presented as Appendix 7.1.

ANALYSIS USING THE CASH FLOW STATEMENT

Apple's 2002 Statement of Cash Flows (indirect method) included the information shown in Table 7.1.

This results in a minor decrease in cash for the year of about $58 million, leaving a balance of $2.25 billion. CFO measures cash from operating activities, beginning with net income ($65 million) and adding back noncash operating and other items. Thus, CFO for Apple ends up 37 percent higher than net income [($89 − $65)/$65]; these are

TABLE 7.1	STATEMENT OF CASH FLOWS FOR APPLE COMPUTER, 2002
Cash Flows	**Millions of Dollars**
From operating activities	$ 89
From investing activities	−252
From financing activities	105
Net increase in cash	$ −58

small numbers, given the more than $2 billion in cash. Positive CFOs are expected in most cases. One exception may be rapidly growing companies, where negative CFOs are common. In most other cases, this would be a red flag. CFI represents cash used to acquire fixed assets and other investments. Consequently, a negative CFI, which is the case for Apple, is expected. The biggest factors are the purchase of property, plant, and equipment, a net increase in investments, and acquisitions. Cash flow from financing (CFF) includes cash related to capital structure, both debt and equity. CFF is usually positive, which it is for Dell because of the issuance of new common stock. The net cash flow numbers for Apple are tiny in relation to the size of the company and its cash balance.

Lucent Technologies showed a 2000 net income of $1,219 million, reduced by a loss from discontinued operations of $214 million and down from 1999 net income of $4,789 million. But CFO suggested even more problems. Despite income from continuing operations of almost $1.7 billion, CFO was a negative $703 million. This was largely due to increases in accounts receivable of $1.6 billion and inventory of $2.2 billion. This is a potential red flag. Increases in accounts receivable suggest that the company was easing credit standards to customers to increase sales, with expected future increases in bad debts. Inventory increases may relate to slow-selling or obsolete items. Lucent's problems have continued, with a net loss of $16.2 billion in 2001 and $11.8 billion in 2002.

Free cash flow (FCF) is a measure of cash available for discretionary uses after required cash outlays. Although there are several potential calculations, the basic concept is cash from operations less capital expenditures required to maintain existing productive capacity. This can be estimated as cash from operations less cash from investments (CFO − CFI). Apple's FCF, based on this measure, is $−163 million ($89 − $252). Alternatively, FCF can be measured as CFO-capital expenditures. Under this calculation, Apple's FCF is $−85 million ($89 − $174). Thus, Apple did not generate enough operating cash to maintain and expand operating capacity. Since Apple's FCF for the previous two years was positive under either definition, this is probably not a concern. In the previous year, FCF was $1,077 million as CFO − CFI (CFI was positive because of sales and maturities of investments), but it was $−47 million as CFO − capital expenditures.

The results for Lucent Technologies were more serious for 2000. FCF was $−703 to $1,559 = $−2,262 million based on CFO − CFI, a negative amount almost triple the net income. FCF based on CFO − capital expenditures was $−703 to $1,915 = $−2,618 million. This further highlights Lucent's operating problems. In 2002, FCF was $1 million, with a negative CFO of $756 million, offset by CFI of $757 (largely because of sales of investments and disposal of a business).

CFO/Total Liabilities measures the company's ability to cover debt with current operating cash flows. The higher the ratio, the better. The 2000 calculation for Lucent was $−703/$22,620 = −3.1 percent, extremely low (−12.0 percent in 2002). By comparison, Apple's ratio for 2002 was $89/$2,203 = 4.0 percent, a possible concern. However, because the ratios were higher in the previous two years, it's likely a short-term problem.

CFO per share can be compared to earnings per share and current stock price. Apple had 351 million shares outstanding at the end of fiscal year 2002, resulting in a CFO per share of $89/$351 = $0.25. This compares to a basic EPS of $0.18. Given Apple's 1/15/03 stock price of $14.43, price to CFO per share was $14.43/$0.25 = 57.7, versus a PE of 80.2.

Gateway is an interesting comparison to Apple and Dell. Its performance has been seemingly catastrophic, but the company has maintained a high cash balance. Consider the summary in Table 7.2 of performance and cash flows for the three competitors in 2002 (2001 for Gateway).

TABLE 7.2	PERFORMANCE AND CASH FLOWS FOR PERSONAL COMPUTER MANUFACTURERS (MILLIONS OF DOLLARS)		
	Gateway 2001	Apple 2002	Dell 2002
Net income	$–1,034	$ 65	$ 1,246
Cash and marketable securities	1,166	4,337	3,914
Cash from operations	–270	89	3,797
Cash from investing	109	–252	–2,260
Cash from financing	405	105	–2,702
Net increase in cash	247	–58	–1,269

Despite losing a billion dollars, Gateway actually increased cash by $247 million and had almost $1.2 billion in cash at year-end. By comparison, both Apple and Dell were profitable, but cash actually decreased for the year. Both still had lots of cash and cash equivalents. Gateway had a current ratio of almost 1.9× and a cash ratio of 1.0×. Based on cash, Gateway seemed a successful company. Despite hemorrhaging money from operations, the company increased liquidity. Major items from the cash flow statement to explain this include the sale of financial receivables of over half a billion dollars and the issuance of new equity and notes payable ($200 million each). This is certainly cash management; it's not clear how long Gateway can keep selling receivables and issuing stock and notes to maintain cash levels.

EARNINGS MANAGEMENT CONSIDERATIONS

According to economic theory, the purpose of corporate finance is to generate future cash flows. The economic focus on performance is cash. Accounting numbers are considered an artifact based on accrual accounting primarily under a historical cost model. Accruals can be manipulated (a major focus of this book), but so can cash flows in the short run. Whatever cash can be collected, from whatever source, less whatever bills are paid, determines cash position. Therefore, why cash flow analysis? The answer is that analyzing cash, particularly from the cash flow statement, provides additional information. Thus, CFO should roughly parallel net income, and when the trends between these two numbers change over time, then earnings manipulation is a possibility.

Specific cash flow concerns include those listed in Table 7.3.

CFO is often considered the most important single measure from the cash flow statement, primarily as an alternative performance measure that may be less subject to manipulation than net income. A number of accounting and finance studies have compared the usefulness of CFO relative to net income on stock prices. Generally, net income is considered a better measure relative to stock price, although cash flow performance is directly related to stock price changes. (See, for example, Watts and Zimmerman, 1986, Chapter 12.)

Because of the importance and focus on CFO, it should be compared to net income and also directly evaluated for earnings management potential. The analysis should include evaluating changing trends over time, evaluating the composition in terms of (1) operating accounts and (2) other current items. A number of specific items are problematic and should be reviewed. The framework of CFO (indirect method) is to start with net income, add or subtract noncash operating adjustments, beginning with depreciation and amortization, and then add or subtract the changes in balances of the other current asset

TABLE 7.3	CASH FLOW CONCERNS AND DETECTION STRATEGIES	
Topic	**Concern**	**Detection Strategy**
Relationship of CFO and net income	CFO should be positive and larger than net income; if not, why?	Compare income and CFO amounts; look for unexpected balances
Changing trends in CFO relative to net income	The basic relationship should be fairly constant; a concern exists if CFO is declining relative to net income	Look at quarterly and annual trends and calculate ratios comparisons and percentage changes over time (see Chapter 8)
Composition of CFO, from both operations and changes in other current items	Certain operating items may suggest earnings management; large changes in other current items may be suspect	Evaluate each line item for several years to determine trends
Trading marketable securities	Nonfinancial companies that treat marketable securities as trading are possibly manipulating CFO	Review accounting policies of marketable securities and statement composition
Taxes paid	Taxes paid are CFO items that can differ substantially from the tax expense	Review tax notes in addition to statement composition
Stock options	Can impact CFO, different accounting for tax and GAAP	Part of stock option analysis (see Chapter 10)
Nonrecurring items and special charges	These items are subject to alternative reporting in the statement and are difficult to evaluate	Evaluate cash flows as part of analysis of nonrecurring items
Composition of CFI	Normally negative (use of cash), but composition can be used to smooth earnings	Evaluate composition trends and how cash is invested
Composition of CFF	A useful analysis of long-term financing and relationship between debt and equity	Evaluate composition relative to balance sheet amounts and changes in these amounts, relative to optimum levels
Relative cash balances	Consider cash balance amounts compared to the sources and uses	Companies have different cash strategies, but certain activities suggest manipulation, such as funding negative operations by issuing new equity
Companies with negative working capital and low cash balances	Why do liquidity problems seem to exist, particularly for companies that have good credit and viable operations?	Analyze relative working capital and cash percentages and review trends in these balance sheet accounts and cash flow statement; evaluate MD&A

and liability accounts. Wide swings in these accounts may suggest earnings management toward some CFO target.

Pulte Homes is the largest homebuilder in the United States. The company and the industry have been successful, even in the recent downturn. This is unusual for a durable goods manufacturer, but the industry was aided by low mortgage rates. Because this is still unexpected, net income should be compared to CFO (see Appendix 7.2). Although net income was over $300 million, CFO was a negative $419 million. CFO for the previous two years also was substantially below net income. The major items were increases in inventories ($648 million) and residential mortgage loans ($157 million). (Note that mortgages are assets for Pulte.) These were offset by proceeds from borrowing of almost $1 billion (CFF). Inventory included houses (at $876 million in 2001, up from $546 million) and land ($2,958 million, up from $1,351 million). Mortgages were $432 million, up from $259 million. Because the primary business is the sale of residential houses and mortgaging these houses, the increases are a major concern. It suggests the potential of a stalling market and accumulation of inventory difficult to sell. With a debt-to-equity ratio of about 1.5×, leverage also was a concern. Competitors had similar results. Horton had positive net income at $192 million but a CFO of $–108 million. Centex had a CFO well below net income. Inventory levels were the primary reasons.

Short-term marketable securities held by nonfinancial companies are investments expected to earn a return on excess cash holdings. Therefore, they should be categorized as available-for-sale or held-to-maturity, which are investment items on the cash flow statement. Trading securities are part of CFO (they are common operating items of financial institutions). For a nonfinancial firm, the acquisition of trading securities reduces CFO, and selling them increases CFO. These would be considered as unusual items and to represent potential manipulation of the CFO balance.

Tax accounting is difficult, in part because it involves federal, state, local, and foreign taxes and in part because tax accounting differs from GAAP. Consequently, there are complex rules for reporting the differences, e.g., the use of deferred tax asset and liability accounts. The difference between the cash paid and the tax expense has a direct impact on the cash flow statement. All income tax items are treated as CFO items, including gains and losses on nonoperating items. The gains and losses associated with discontinued items, net of their tax effects, could be eliminated from CFO, such as the gain on sale of Conoco by Du Pont in 1999, and perhaps for some extraordinary items that better fit financing or investing.

The composition of both CFI and CFF should be evaluated, especially for the net change in cash. CFI represents investments, especially the net acquisition of property, plant, and equipment. Thus, this category generally is a use of cash (that is, negative). However, included in CFI are investments, acquisitions and divestitures of other firms, and other items that may swamp the investment in fixed assets. CFF includes long-term financing items such as debt and equity. Therefore, it tends to be a source of cash. Large debt or equity acquisition should be evaluated with some skepticism. The rationale for these items should be evaluated in the context of the business strategy of the firm and potential cash management.

Related to the evaluation of the cash flow statement are the relative cash balance and liquidity characteristics of the firm. Some firms have large amounts of cash and maintain high liquidity levels, such as the PC companies analyzed. However, others maintain low levels of both, and some firms have negative working capital. The firms with low cash and liquidity levels should be evaluated more carefully, especially to determine why low cash/liquidity is maintained. Apparent liquidity problems may be associated with poor operating performance, with build-up in other accounts such as inventory or receivables (which would maintain working capital but decrease cash), with long-term financing or equity issues (e.g., paying out more cash dividends that net income, acquiring treasury stock), or with other factors. The reasons should make financing and business strategy sense (e.g., some companies prefer low receivables and inventories and postpone paying accounts payable) or be considered a red flag. It should be noted that some analysts think low current ratios are a good thing.

Manipulation and fraud problems are almost always stated in terms of operating (income statement) or financial position (balance sheet) accounts. Information from the cash flow statement is supplementary relative to the balance sheet and income statement. However, certain cash flow relationships suggest earnings management concerns, such as comparing net income to CFO and the interrelationships of operations, investing, and financing.

Xerox was working on a negative cash balance in 1999. According to the GAO (2002, pp. 234–235),

> Unable to generate cash, Xerox management instructed its largest operating units to explore the possibility of engaging in factoring transactions with local banks. These transactions materially affected Xerox's 1999 operating cash flows but these transactions were not disclosed in its 1999 financial statements. In some of the factoring transactions involved buy-back agreements in which Xerox would reacquire the receivables after the end of the year. By accounting for these transactions as true sales, Xerox violated GAAP. Not only did Xerox fail to disclose the agreements, it failed to reverse them in the next year.

This is typical of manipulation issues. The impact and analysis of cash flows are secondary to balance sheet and income statement concerns. However, the cash flow analysis adds additional evidence to earnings management concerns.

ALTERNATIVE BOTTOM LINE NUMBERS

The bottom line is the most important single number evaluated by analysts of commercial firms. The purpose of corporations is to make money—the more the better (profit maximization, according to economists). However, there is no universal agreement on a single bottom line number. Net income is the most common and the most used, but several additional measures can be used in lieu of or in addition to net income. These include operating income, EBIT and EBITDA, income from continuing operations both before and after tax, net income adjusted for various things (such as dividends or eliminating certain nonrecurring or special charges), comprehensive income, and any number of *pro forma* calculations of earnings.

Each measure provides a different perspective and may suggest important information on potential earnings management. Corporations have considerable flexibility in the treatment of gains and losses, and these can be used for certain manipulation strategies. Focusing on these other measures may provide significant information on earnings management concerns and suggest areas for further analysis. A summary of bottom-line concerns is shown in Table 7.4.

GROSS PROFIT AND OPERATING INCOME

Gross profit or gross margin is sales less cost of goods sold (COGS) for a manufacturing company and sales less cost of sales for a service company (terminology will differ from company to company). COGS/cost of sales has a direct relationship to sales, and this relationship normally is fairly constant. This relationship can be measured by gross margin (or gross margin percentage, gross profit/sales). If this margin is rising, it may signal increased

TABLE 7.4	BOTTOM-LINE CONCERNS AND DETECTION STRATEGIES	
Measure	**Concern**	**Detection Strategy**
Gross Margin (GM) and Operating Margin (OM)	Declining or erratic GM and OM, suggesting serious problems with basic operations	Calculate GM percent and OM percent for several periods and in comparison with competitors
EBIT and EBITDA	Large differences, suggesting big expenses associated with interest expense, taxes, depreciation, or amortization	Calculate and evaluate component parts; compare across periods and to competitors
Income from Continuing Operations (ICO) vs. Net Income (NI)	ICO substantially different from NI, because of nonrecurring items and related earnings manipulation potential	Compare and calculate alternative return ratios
Net Income vs. Comprehensive Income	Other comprehensive income items represent large losses, especially if these continue year after year	Compare and calculate alternative return ratios; evaluate each comprehensive income item

efficiency and be a strong signal of future performance. On the other hand, a declining or erratic margin may indicate any number of problems. Gross margin should be discussed in detail in MD&A, especially if the percentage is changing. Erratic or negative performance that is not thoroughly explained is a major concern.

Consider the gross margins for Apple and competitors, shown in Table 7.5.

Apple's 2002 gross margin is a solid 30.0 percent, up from 24.9 percent, while Dell's and Gateway's gross margins were much lower and declined from the previous year. This seems to be good news for Apple in a struggling industry. The major questions are (1) Is it too good, possibly because of earnings management, and (2) Does the percentage represent improved efficiency rather than earnings management, and is it sustainable?

Operating income is sales minus operating expenses, which include cost of sales; selling, general, and administrative expenses (SG&A), and other operating costs, which for these companies include research and development (R&D) and special charges. Operating income does not include interest expense or taxes.

Operating income for the PC companies is shown in Table 7.6.

Despite the excellent gross margin, Apple had a poor operating margin (operating income/sales), at 0.8 percent. It was an improvement from the previous year and better than Gateway's but not Dell's. Operating income was only $46 million, in part because of relatively high SG&A, at $1.1 billion.

TABLE 7.5	GROSS MARGINS (MILLIONS OF DOLLARS) FOR APPLE COMPUTER AND COMPETITORS					
	Apple 2002	**Apple 2001**	**Dell 2002**	**Dell 2001**	**Gateway 2001**	**Gateway 2000**
Sales	$5,742	$5,363	$31,168	$31,888	$6,080	$9,601
COGS	4,021	4,026	25,661	25,445	5,241	7,542
Gross Profit	1,721	1,337	5,507	6,443	838	2,059
Gross Margin, %	30.0%	24.9%	17.7%	20.2%	13.8%	21.4%

| TABLE 7.6 | OPERATING INCOME (MILLIONS OF DOLLARS) FOR THE PERSONAL COMPUTER COMPANIES |

	Apple 2002	Apple 2001	Dell 2002	Dell 2001	Gateway 2001	Gateway 2000
Sales	$5,742	$5,363	$31,168	$31,888	$ 6,080	$9,601
Operating Expenses	5,696	5,696	29,379	29,225	7,264	9,090
Operating Income	46	−333	1,789	2,663	−1,184	511
Operating Margin, %	0.8%	−6.2%	5.7%	8.4%	−19.5%	5.3%

EBIT AND EBITDA

Two measures of current operating performance are (1) earnings before interest and taxes (EBIT) and (2) earnings before interest, taxes, depreciation, and amortization (EBITDA). EBIT (also called operating earnings) excludes the impact of interest and taxes from earnings and can be used as an indicator of a firm's ability to service its debt. EBITDA (also called cash earnings) somewhat resembles cash flows from operations and can be used for an alternative analysis of cash flows. Depreciation and amortization are noncash expenses and major expense categories at many large corporations.

Consider the PC companies' data for the 2002 fiscal year (2001 for Gateway, in millions of dollars), as shown in Table 7.7.

EBIT for Apple for 2002 was $98 million (65 + 22 + 11), $33 million (50.8 percent) above income from continuing operations (also net income because Apple had no nonrecurring items). EBITDA for Apple was $216 million (65 + 22 + 11 + 118), $151 million (232.3 percent) above income from continuing operations. Thus, earnings were much higher using these numbers. It's the same story for Dell. Gateway had losses from continuing operations, and income tax was a "negative expense." Consequently, EBIT was roughly the same as income from continuing operations (because interest expense basically offset income tax). EBITDA for Gateway was $−812 million, a somewhat smaller loss than continuing operations.

A key question is whether these are useful numbers to evaluate earnings. They provide some information on operating cash flows and capital structure. These numbers will differ substantially from net income when (1) there are large nonrecurring items, (2) capital structure includes substantial interest-paying debt, and (3) the firm has a large fixed assets and intangible asset base, subject to depreciation and amortization.

| TABLE 7.7 | OPERATIONS-RELATED DATA |

	Apple	Dell	Gateway
Income from Continuing Operations	$ 65	$1,246	$−1,014
Provision for Income Tax	22	485	−278
Interest Expense	11	29	294
Depreciation and Amortization	118	239	186
EBIT	98	1,760	−998
EBITDA	216	1,999	−812

Particularly when EBIT and EBITDA differ substantially from net income, profitability ratios should be recalculated using EBIT and EBITDA. Alternative calculations for Apple for 2002 are shown in Table 7.8.

Apple's ratios for EBIT are 51 percent higher than net income and 232 percent higher for EBITDA. The EBIT and EBITDA numbers are sometimes presented as *pro forma* earnings, because they are accepted as useful earnings numbers and can boost operating results considerably.

INCOME FROM CONTINUING OPERATIONS

Income from continuing operations (ICO) is the bottom line for current operations. This may be considered a better measure than net income, because it excludes all nonrecurring items. The argument is that nonrecurring items are erratic, should be rare, and provide no information about that fundamental performance of a corporation. It follows from this argument that nonrecurring items should be analyzed separately, especially for earnings manipulation potential (such as the analysis of Du Pont sales of Conoco and Du Pont Pharmaceuticals in Chapter 6). ICO for the three PC companies is the same as net income, because none has nonrecurring items for the current year.

NET INCOME VERSUS COMPREHENSIVE INCOME

Net income is a relatively complete measure, because it includes nonrecurring items and other unusual items in addition to normal operating income. However, not all gains and losses are included in net income, because a number of items are recorded directly to the balance sheet, resulting in the "dirty surplus" previously mentioned. SFAS No. 130 requires the presentation of comprehensive income to include net income plus all other gains and losses reported directly to stockholders' equity.

The advantage of comprehensive income is that it includes absolutely all revenues, expenses, gains, and losses, consistent with the all-inclusive concept of earnings. A rationale for other comprehensive income is that these tend to be items that zero out over time (e.g., foreign currency fluctuates with the changing value of the dollar), which may or may not be true in particular cases. Of particular concern is the potential to eliminate important, although unrealized, gains and losses (particularly losses) from the income statement.

Apple's fiscal year 2002 net income was $65 million. To arrive at comprehensive income, Apple has three other comprehensive income items listed in the statement of shareholders' equity: a foreign currency translation gain of $5 million, a $15 million unrealized loss on derivatives, and a $17 million unrealized loss on investments, to arrive at comprehensive income of $38 million (58.5 percent of net income). These adjustments (marketable securities, derivatives, and foreign currency) probably are the most common categories of "dirty surplus." Other items that may be reported in comprehensive income include minimum pension liability adjustments.

TABLE 7.8	**ALTERNATIVE CALCULATIONS FOR APPLE COMPUTER FOR 2002**		
	Using Net Income	**Using EBIT**	**Using EBITDA**
Return on Sales	1.1%	1.7%	3.8%
Return on Average Equity	1.6	2.4	5.4

In 2001, Maytag had a relatively poor year, recording net income of $47.7 million (a return on sales of 1.1 percent), compared to $201.0 million in 2000 and $328.5 in 1999. However, other comprehensive income was a negative $178.1 million for the year, primarily related to pension liability adjustments. Thus, comprehensive income for the year (net income plus other comprehensive income) resulted in a comprehensive loss of $130.4 million. On this basis, Maytag had a disastrous year rather than a poor but profitable year. Given that the company had a very small total equity position and still paid cash dividends of over $55 million for the year, a possible red flag seems justified.

Thus, analysts have several measures of profitability, from earnings before interest and taxes (EBIT) to other measures of continuing operations (before nonrecurring items), net income, or comprehensive income. All measures provide information and should be evaluated thoroughly. Net income is the most common measure. Comprehensive income considers all potential components. Operating income ignores unusual items, which may best represent long-run earnings potential. Income from continuing operations may include some unusual items such as special charges but usually is a reasonable measure of earnings potential. Of course, all measures are subject to earnings management.

PRO FORMA EARNINGS

In addition to these accepted bottom-line measures (all part of GAAP), companies and analysts can restate earnings in various ways to emphasize certain features or components. *Pro forma* earnings are restated earnings, based on another perspective or based on future forecasts. When management prepares *pro forma* statements, the usual point is to put the company in a better light than under GAAP.

When PETCO announced first quarter 2002 financial results, the company reported: "*pro forma* earnings increased three-fold to $0.15 per diluted share." Unfortunately, based on GAAP the company had a net loss of $29.7 million ($–0.57 a share). Earnings included an extraordinary loss, restructuring costs, and legal and financing fees. If these were excluded, then the *pro forma* earnings were $8.7 million, or $0.15 a share. PETCO must present financial statements on a GAAP basis, but it can explain a GAAP loss as positive earnings if certain information is ignored. It's up to the analysts and investors to determine if the restated, *pro forma* information is useful.

Amazon.com is one of the amazing dot-com companies of the 1990s that seemed to do everything right in the new Internet world, except make money. With the ability to generate losses without fail from quarter to quarter, Amazon also provided substantial *pro forma* earnings information, excluding such items as stock-based compensation, amortization of intangibles, and restructuring charges. The rationale was "we use this *pro forma* measure internally to evaluate our performance and believe it may be useful" (2001 10-K, p. 32). For 2001, the information included (in thousands) that shown in Table 7.9.

TABLE 7.9	INFORMATION REPORT FOR 2001 BY AMAZON.COM	
	Pro forma	**GAAP**
Income from operations	$–45,002	$–412,257
Net income	–157,031	–567,277
Basic EPS	–0.43	–1.53

The tables in the 10-K presented considerably more information, including the last three years of operations and a breakout by quarter. The losses are much smaller, but the usefulness of the *pro forma* analysis is problematic. It's non-GAAP and not comparable to any other company.

S&P'S CORE EARNINGS

Unlike management-generated *pro forma* earnings, earnings often are restated by analysts to make them reflect economic reality. Because of earnings management incentives and flexible GAAP, the claim is made that reported income numbers based on GAAP are exaggerated. In May 2002, Standard & Poor's (S&P) introduced its own measure to standardize income, called Core Earnings, "to return transparency and consistency to corporate reporting" (S&P, Press Release, May 14, 2002). It includes certain expenses that are often not reported on the income statement and excludes certain income that it does not consider part of ongoing operations, generally reporting a lower earnings number than net income.

S&P's Core Earnings measure focuses on ongoing operations. Its report on this concept, entitled *Measures of Corporate Earnings,* presents a table on what is included and excluded (Table 7.10).

In summary, major differences from net income are as follows: employee stock options are treated as an expense, pension asset investment gains are not part of income, and various gains and losses are excluded. A *Business Week* article (May 27, 2002, p. 37) recalculated earnings per share for General Electric (Table 7.11), comparing reported 2001 EPS at $1.42 to Core Earnings.

Thus, per-share core earnings were $0.31, or 21.8 percent lower than GAAP EPS. S&P's core earnings is a reasonable bottom line measure and is expected to be more conservative than net income (that is, lower) in most cases. What's not clear is if this is a better bottom line measure. In any case, it may be worth the effort to calculate this as a comparative measure.

TABLE 7.10	**INCOME AND EXPENSES INVOLVED IN REPORT OF CORE EARNINGS, ACCORDING TO S&P**
Included in Core Earnings	**Excluded from Core Earnings**
Employee stock option grant expense	Goodwill impairment charges
Restructuring charges from ongoing operations	Gains/losses from asset sales
Write-downs of depreciable or amortizable operating assets	Pension gains
Pension costs	Unrealized gains/losses from hedging activities
Purchased R&D expenses	Merger/acquisition-related expenses
	Litigation or insurance settlements and proceeds

TABLE 7.11	RECALCULATED EARNINGS PER SHARE FOR GENERAL ELECTRIC
GE's 2001 EPS	$1.42
Changes from asset sales	−.06
Stock options expense	−.04
Pension gain	−.19
Other adjustments	−.02
GE's Core Earnings	$1.11

SUMMARY

This chapter reviewed cash and the cash flow statements and the importance of evaluating alternative bottom line measures. The cash flow statement separates cash by operations, investments, and financing. Cash flows from operations are particularly important for earnings management evaluation, as an additional approach to considering decisions that impact on both operations and cash flows. Free cash flows is a measure of internally generated cash available to fund additional activities. Earnings management issues focus on numbers and relationships that are unexpected, such as negative CFO when net income is positive.

Alternative bottom line numbers can be used to emphasize various aspects of ongoing operations and provide additional perspective on operating activities and earnings management strategy. Current operating performance can be emphasized using gross profit, EBIT and EBITDA, and income from continuing operations. An all-inclusive perspective is emphasized using net income and comprehensive income. Companies also can present *pro forma* income, usually a non-GAAP perspective, to show better earnings than under GAAP.

QUESTIONS

1. How is the statement of cash flows useful for understanding both liquidity and performance?
2. If cash from operations is substantially less than net income, does this suggest an earnings management concern? What if free cash flows are negative? Explain.
3. Are earnings per share more useful than net income as a measure of profit? How useful and reliable are EPS forecasts?
4. There are many possible definitions of the bottom line, including EBIT and EBITDA, income from continuing operations, net income, and comprehensive income. Is this complexity needed? Do the alternatives make detecting earnings management more difficult or provide additional useful information? Explain.
5. What are *pro forma* earnings and *pro forma* statements? Are they useful or reliable? Do they represent additional earnings management concerns? Explain.

PROBLEMS

Problem 7.1: Cash Flow Analysis

The following information is for fiscal year 2002 (millions of dollars).

	Hilton	Marriott	Mandalay
Cash flow from operations (CFO)	$ 675	$ 516	$ 358
Cash Flows from investments (CFI)	(189)	317	(160)
Cash flows from financing (CFF)	(467)	(1,447)	(198)
Total Liabilities	7,002	4,723	3,100
Number of Shares Outstanding	376.0	235.9	72.8
Net Income	198	277	53
Basic earnings per share (EPS)	0.53	1.15	0.73
Stock Price, 4/01/03	$11.55	$31.29	$26.70

    a. Calculate the following:

	Hilton	Marriott	Mandalay
Free Cash Flows (FCF)			
CFO/Total Liabilities			
CFO per Share			
Price/CFO per Share			
PE (Price/EPS)			

    b. Analyze cash flows for Hilton in comparison with Marriott and Mandalay.

Problem 7.2: Cash from Operations (CFO) Summary for Hilton

The following table summarizes CFO (millions of dollars) for Hilton for the last three years.

	2000	2001	2002
Net income	$272	$166	$198
Depreciation and amortization	382	391	348
Other operating adjustments	(24)	54	44
Changes in working capital components	(41)	(26)	85
Cash from operations	589	585	675

    a. If CFO = 100 percent, complete a common-size analysis for CFO components.

	2000	2001	2002
Net income			
Depreciation and amortization			
Other operating expenses			
Changes in working capital components			
Cash from operations	100.0%	100.0%	100.0%

b. Evaluate the CFO trends from 2000 to 2002.

Problem 7.3: EBIT and EBITDA

Given below are summary earnings numbers (millions of dollars) for the three hotel and resort companies for 2002.

	Hilton	Marriott	Mandalay
Net Income	$198	$277	$ 53
Income from Continuing Operations	285	471	93
Provision for Income Tax	81	32	40
Interest Expense	347	86	230
Depreciation and Amortization	348	187	216

a. Based on this information, calculate EBIT and EBITDA and the percentage change over net income for EBIT [(Net Income – EBIT)/Net Income] and EBITDA [(Net Income – EBITDA)/Net Income].

	Hilton	Marriott	Mandalay
EBIT			
EBIT % change from Net Income			
EBITDA			
EBITDA % change from Net Income			

b. Calculate alternative profitability ratios.

	Hilton	Marriott	Mandalay
Return on Sales			
Return on Total Assets			
Return on Equity			

	Hilton	Marriott	Mandalay
Sales	$3,847	$8,441	$2,462
Average Total Assets	8,567	8,702	4,143
Average Equity	1,918	3,526	1,005

c. Based on the information in the table on the previous page, evaluate the usefulness of EBIT and EBITDA as alternative earnings numbers.

Problem 7.4: Reconciling Bottom Line Numbers for Hilton

Hilton's MD&A for 2002 included the following alternative performance and EBITDA-to-net-income reconciliation:

	2001	2002	% Change
Revenues	$3,993	$3,847	
Operating income	632	603	
Net income	166	198	
EPS basic	0.45	0.53	
EBITDA	$1,072	$990	
Operating interest and dividend income	(15)	(9)	
Depreciation and amortization	(415)	(375)	
Other items	(10)	(3)	
Operating income	632	603	
Interest and dividend income	64	43	
Interest expense	(402)	347	
Provision for income tax	(77)	(81)	
Other items	(51)	(20)	
Net income	166	198	

a. Calculate the percentage change for these items for the year.
b. Hilton had other comprehensive income items that totaled $(11) for 2001 and $(6) for 2002.
c. Evaluate the alternative bottom line measure and the reconciliation of EBITDA to net income for Hilton.

CASES

Case 1: Evaluating Overall Quality of Apple's Cash Flows and Earnings Management Potential

The analysis of earnings management considers major concerns (usually treated as red flags) but also the accumulation of a large number of minor concerns. A large number of potential problems can indicate overall relatively lower reporting quality. Apple Computer is an example of a successful, high profile, high-tech company that has had a somewhat erratic performance over the last decade and seems a good candidate for analysis. (Refer to Apple's 2002 10-K, www.apple.com.)

a.   Overall. Analyze the following statement of cash flow factors for Apple for 2002:

Factor	Analysis
Relationship of CFO to net income	
Composition of CFO, adjustments	
Composition of CFO, changes in other current accounts	
Free cash flows	
Composition of CFI	
Composition of CFF	
Comparison to beginning and ending cash balances	

b.   *Specific Weaknesses and Potential Concerns.* Analyze these potential problems for Apple.

Weakness/Concern	Analysis
Provision for deferred tax	
Gains/losses on investments	
Net negative changes in other current accounts	
Sale of common stock	

Case 2: Evaluating the Alternative Bottom Line Measures Associated with Apple's Income and Cash Flows and Earnings Management Potential

The analysis of earnings management considers major concerns (usually treated as red flags) but also the accumulation of a large number of minor concerns. A large number of potential problems can indicate overall relatively lower reporting quality. Apple Computer is an example of a successful, high profile, high-tech company that has had a somewhat erratic performance over the last decade and seems a good candidate for analysis. (Refer to Apple's 2002 10-K, www.apple.com.)

a.   Overall: Analyze the following alternative bottom line measures (the percentage to sales is given in columns 2 and 3 for 2002 and 2001, respectively):

Measure	2002	2001	Analysis
Gross margin	27.9%	23.0%	
Operating margin	0.3	–6.4	
EBIT	1.7	–0.7	
EBITDA	3.8	1.2	
Income from continuing operations (after tax)	1.1	–0.7	
Cash from operations	1.5	3.4	
Net income	1.1	–0.5	
Comprehensive income	0.7	–4.5	

b. Compare the measures in terms of measuring sustainable earnings and earnings management potential. What adjustment to any of these should be included to correct for the impact of potential earnings management?

Case 3: Alternative Bottom Line Ratios for Du Pont

Given below is summary information from Du Pont's income statement for the last three years (in millions of dollars).

	2001	2000	1999
Sales	$24,726	$26,268	$26,918
Income from Continuing Operations (ICO)	4,328	2,314	219
Gain from Disposal of Discontinued Business (sale of Conoco)			7,471
Net Income (NI)	4,339	2,314	7,690
Translation Adjustment	–19	–38	172
Minimum Pension Liability Adjustment	–16	4	76
Unrealized Gains on Marketable Securities	–24	–21	51
Comprehensive Income (CI)	4,254	2,259	7,989

a. Calculate return on sales using (1) income from continuing operations (ICO/sales); (2) net income (NI/sales); and (3) comprehensive income (CI/sales).

	2001	2000	1999
ICO/Sales			
NI/Sales			
CI/Sales			

b. In 2001, Du Pont sold Du Pont Pharmaceuticals for a gain of $6,136 million ($3,866 million, net of tax). This was recorded as a separate line item as part of continuing operations. How does this affect the analysis? (Note: consider recalculating profit, excluding this transaction.) Is this an example of earnings management? Explain.

Case 4: Comprehensive Income

Given are summaries of comprehensive income tables for three chemical companies for 2001 (in millions of dollars):

	Du Pont	Dow	PPG
Net income	$4,339	$–385	$ 387
Unrealized gains and losses—marketable securities	–24	27	10
Foreign currency translation gains and losses	–38	–148	–131
Pension liability adjustment	–16	–21	–20
Other	6	–45	–51
Comprehensive income	4,254	–572	238
Comprehensive income/net income			

Calculate comprehensive income as a percent of net income (comprehensive income/net income) for these companies. Is earnings management a concern for any of these companies? Explain.

Appendix 7.1: Apple Computer Statement of Cash Flows

Apple Computer Consolidated Statements of Cash Flows
(in Millions of Dollars)

Three fiscal years ended September 28, 2002	2002	2001	2000
Cash and cash equivalents, beginning of the year	$2,310	$1,191	$1,326
Operating:			
Net income (loss)	65	(25)	786
Cumulative effect of accounting change, net of taxes	—	(12)	—
Adjustments to reconcile net income to cash generated by operating activities:			
Depreciation and amortization	118	102	84
Provision for deferred income taxes	(34)	(36)	163
Loss on disposition of property, plant, and equipment	7	9	10
(Gains) losses on investments, net	35	(88)	(367)
Unrealized loss on convertible securities	—	13	—
Purchased in-process research and development	1	11	—
Changes in operating assets and liabilities:			
Accounts receivable	(99)	487	(272)
Inventories	(34)	22	(13)
Other current assets	(114)	106	(37)
Other assets	(11)	12	20
Accounts payable	110	(356)	318
Other current liabilities	45	(60)	176
Cash generated by operating activities	89	185	868
Investing:			
Purchase of short-term investments	(4,144)	(4,268)	(4,267)
Proceeds from maturities of short-term investments	2,846	4,811	3,075
Proceeds from sales of short-term investments	1,254	278	256
Purchases of long-term investments	—	(1)	(232)
Purchase of property, plant, and equipment	(174)	(232)	(142)
Proceeds from sales of equity investments	25	340	372
Cash used for business acquisitions	(52)	—	—
Other	(7)	(36)	(34)
Cash generated by (used for) investing activities	(252)	892	(972)

Apple Computer Consolidated Statements of Cash Flows (Continued)
(in Millions of Dollars)

Three fiscal years ended September 28, 2002	2002	2001	2000
Financing:			
Proceeds from issuance of common stock	105	42	85
Cash used for repurchase of common stock	—	—	(116)
Cash generated by (used for) financing activities	105	42	(31)
Increase (decrease) in cash and cash equivalents	(58)	1,119	(135)
Cash and cash equivalents, end of the year	$2,252	$2,310	$1,191
Supplemental cash flow disclosures:			
Cash paid during the year for interest	$ 20	$ 20	$ 20
Cash paid for income taxes, net	$ 11	$ 42	$ 47
Noncash transactions:			
Issuance of common stock for conversion of Series A preferred stock	$ —	$ 76	$ 74
Issuance of common stock in connection with acquisition	$ —	$ 66	$ —

Appendix 7.2: Pulte Homes, Inc., Consolidated Statements of Cash Flows, for the Years Ended December 31, 2001, 2000, and 1999 ($000s Omitted)

Pulte Homes, Inc., Consolidated Statements of Cash Flows
($000s Omitted)

For the years ended December 31	2001	2000	1999
Cash flows from operating activities:			
Net income	$301,393	$188,513	$178,165
Adjustments to reconcile net income to net cash flows provided by (used in) operating activities:			
Amortization, depreciation and other	32,876	14,230	13,497
Deferred income taxes	(8,176)	652	23,161
Gain on sale of securities	—	—	(1,664)
Increase (decrease) in cash, excluding effects of acquired entities, due to:			
Inventories	(648,266)	(210,025)	(258,196)
Residential mortgage loans available-for-sale	(157,124)	(41,177)	16,912
Other assets	10,808	(14,141)	(60,559)
Accounts payable and accrued liabilities	5,022	77,034	101,245
Income taxes	44,671	8,236	2,552
Net cash provided by (used in) operating activities	(418,796)	23,322	15,113

CHAPTER 8

Evaluating Trends, Norms, and Quarterly Data

Traditional quantitative financial analysis includes the most recent year or two, which is considered the most relevant. However, significant long-term trends may exist and be crucial to a complete financial analysis. Therefore, additional quantitative analysis is suggested for at least the previous five years. In addition, financial data are available on a quarterly basis, which becomes the most recent information available on performance and other aspects of financial conditions. Although quarterly data are limited, a quarterly quantitative analysis is essential. The evaluation of multiperiod data is called time series **analysis** or **trend analysis.**

This analysis can include comparisons to competitors, industry averages, market averages, or other measures of normal or expected results (norms). Any combination of comparisons can be potentially useful, although comparisons with direct competitors are the most likely to be fruitful. Direct competitors are most likely to have financial characteristics in common, and deviations relative to them are important. The example used again is Apple, with Dell and Gateway, the direct competitors, used to evaluate possible norms.

There are quantitative methods for evaluating earnings management potential by focusing on unexpected trends or changes in ratios. The point is not to prove manipulation but rather to suggest potential concerns. It's basically up to corporate insiders, auditors, and regulators to determine the existence of blatant manipulation. Generally, after a thorough analysis of the most recent financial statement information, additional time series analysis will focus on more limited data but analyzed over an extended time period. Red flag items are most likely to be the focus of multiperiod analysis.

TREND ANALYSIS

Several techniques can be used to evaluate data over several periods to determine longer-term trends. These are widely used for annual data, although they are equally applicable to quarterly data as well. Three techniques will be reviewed, using Apple and personal computer (PC) competitors as examples: common-size, growth analysis, and base year analysis. Common-size highlights changing percentages over time by category. Growth analysis focuses on percentage changes by category (this is also called horizontal common-size analysis). Base-year analysis highlights changes relative to a base year for comparison, somewhat similar to the consumer price level and other indexes.

COMMON-SIZE ANALYSIS

The only difference in this analysis is to expand common-size to more periods, usually five to ten or more years. The longer the period of analysis, the more likely it is that very long-term relationships will be determined. On the other hand, the competitive environment, the business strategy, and even the structure of operations change fairly rapidly. In this context, analyzing decade-old data may be considered futile. No matter how long the period under study, the most recent data must be considered the most relevant.

Consider abbreviated income statement numbers for the last six years for the three PC competitors, shown in Table 8.1.

It should be noted that these are the same fiscal years, except that Gateway's fiscal year ends December 31, Dell's about January 30, and Apple's on September 30. The analysis can be abbreviated or quite comprehensive. Abbreviated statements are used just to show the fundamental techniques employed. Note that with different year-ends, the data differ by several months. Consequently, the analysis should be supplemented with quarterly data review for greater chronological comparability.

Based on these numbers, common-size statements are as shown in Table 8.2.

The expected common-size pattern for performance is a relatively constant gross margin and net income (return on sales). Better yet, if both are rising, increased operating efficiency is suggested. That's not the pattern for any of these companies, although Dell comes the closest. The preferred trends exist from 1997 to 1999, but performance fell off beginning in 2000. This is explainable, given the recession and the big hit to the high-tech companies. Both Apple and Gateway exhibit erratic performance. Apple had net losses in 1997 and 2001, and both gross margin and net income percentages bounced around over the period of analysis.

The negative return on sales for Apple in 2001 and small return in 2002 suggest the potential for earnings management, to keep the loss small in 2001 and to increase performance in 2002 at least enough to be profitable in 2002. Because of the erratic performance numbers, understanding Apple's operations over this period is important. Why did Apple have such erratic performance, especially in the late 1990s, when tech

| TABLE 8.1 | INCOME STATEMENT DATA (MILLIONS OF DOLLARS) |

	Apple					
	1997	1998	1999	2000	2001	2002
Revenues	$7,081	$5,941	$6,134	$7,983	$5,363	$5,742
Gross Profit	1,368	1,479	1,781	2,166	1,235	1,603
Net Income	−1,045	309	601	786	−25	65

	Dell					
	1997	1998	1999	2000	2001	2002
Revenues	$7,759	$12,327	$18,243	$25,265	$31,888	$31,168
Gross Profit	1,666	2,722	4,106	5,218	6,443	5,746
Net Income	518	944	1,460	1,666	2,177	1,246

	Gateway					
	1996	1997	1998	1999	2000	2001
Revenues	$5,035	$6,294	$7,468	$8,646	$9,601	$6,079
Gross Profit	936	1,077	1,546	1,900	2,059	1,038
Net Income	251	110	346	428	241	−1,034

| TABLE 8.2 | COMMON-SIZE STATEMENTS (MILLIONS OF DOLLARS) |

	Apple					
	1997	1998	1999	2000	2001	2002
Revenues	100.0%	100.0%	100.0%	100.0%	100.0%	100.0%
Gross Margin	19.3	24.9	29.0	27.1	23.0	27.9
Net Income	−14.8	5.2	9.8	9.8	−4.7	1.1

	Dell					
	1997	1998	1999	2000	2001	2002
Revenues	100.0%	100.0%	100.0%	100.0%	100.0%	100.0%
Gross Margin	21.5	22.1	22.5	20.3	20.2	18.4
Net Income	6.7	7.7	8.0	6.6	6.8	4.0

	Gateway					
	1996	1997	1998	1999	2000	2001
Revenues	100.0%	100.0%	100.0%	100.0%	100.0%	100.0%
Gross Margin	18.6	17.1	20.7	22.0	21.4	17.1
Net Income	5.0	1.7	4.6	5.0	2.5	−17.0

spending was booming? The evaluation of earnings management is tied to the analysis of operating performance. The analysis of Gateway focuses on predicting the ability of the company to avoid bankruptcy.

A similar analysis is used for an abbreviated balance sheet analysis for these firms (Table 8.3).

A common-size balance sheet analysis includes the data shown in Table 8.4.

The balance sheet analysis for the PC companies indicates some common characteristics across this industry. All have high cash levels, have high current assets and liabilities, and appear to have relatively low equity because of the high current liability levels. Apple has high cash levels, and with the exception of 2000, the cash levels tended to increase. Current liability levels trended down and equity levels trended up. These roughly paralleled

TABLE 8.3 **ABBREVIATED BALANCE SHEET DATA (MILLIONS OF DOLLARS)**

Apple						
	1997	**1998**	**1999**	**2000**	**2001**	**2002**
Cash	$1,459	$2,300	$3,226	$1,191	$4,336	$4,337
Current Assets	3,424	3,698	4,285	5,427	5,143	5,388
Total Assets	4,289	4,289	5,161	6,803	6,021	6,298
Current Liabilities	1,818	1,520	1,549	1,933	1,518	1,658
Total Liabilities	3,033	2,647	2,057	2,696	2,101	2,203
Equity	1,222	1,642	3,104	4,107	3,920	4,095

Dell						
	1997	**1998**	**1999**	**2000**	**2001**	**2002**
Cash	$1,352	$1,844	$2,649	$ 3,809	$ 5,438	$ 3,914
Current Assets	2,747	3,912	5,807	7,681	9,491	7,877
Total Assets	2,993	4,268	6,877	11,471	13,435	13,535
Current Liabilities	1,658	2,697	3,685	5,192	6,543	7,519
Total Liabilities	1,908	2,975	4,556	6,163	7,813	8,841
Equity	806	1,293	2,321	5,308	5,622	4,694

Gateway						
	1996	**1997**	**1998**	**1999**	**2000**	**2001**
Cash	$ 516	$ 632	$1,328	$1,336	$ 614	$1,166
Current Assets	1,318	1,545	2,228	2,697	2,267	2,123
Total Assets	1,673	2,039	2,890	3,955	4,181	2,987
Current Liabilities	800	1,004	1,430	1,810	1,659	1,146
Total Liabilities	858	1,109	1,546	1,938	1,800	1,422
Equity	816	930	1,344	2,017	2,380	1,565

TABLE 8.4 COMMON-SIZE BALANCE SHEET ANALYSIS (MILLIONS OF DOLLARS)

Apple

	1997	1998	1999	2000	2001	2002
Cash	23.4%	53.6%	62.5%	17.5%	72.0%	68.9%
Current Assets	79.8	86.2	83.0	79.8	85.4	85.6
Total Assets	100.0	100.0	100.0	100.0	100.0	100.0
Current Liabilities	42.4	35.4	30.0	28.4	25.2	26.3
Total Liabilities	70.7	61.7	39.9	39.6	34.9	35.0
Equity	28.0	38.3	60.1	60.4	65.1	65.0

Dell

	1997	1998	1999	2000	2001	2002
Cash	45.2%	43.2%	38.5%	33.2%	40.5%	28.9%
Current Assets	91.8	91.7	84.4	67.0	70.6	58.2
Total Assets	100.0	100.0	100.0	100.0	100.0	100.0
Current Liabilities	55.4	63.2	53.6	45.3	48.7	55.6
Total Liabilities	63.7	69.7	66.2	53.7	58.2	65.3
Equity	26.9	30.3	33.8	46.3	41.8	34.7

Gateway

	1996	1997	1998	1999	2000	2001
Cash	30.8%	31.0%	46.0%	33.8%	14.7%	39.0%
Current Assets	78.8	75.8	77.1	68.2	54.2	71.1
Total Assets	100.0	100.0	100.0	100.0	100.0	100.0
Current Liabilities	47.8	49.2	49.5	45.8	39.7	38.4
Total Liabilities	51.3	54.4	53.5	49.0	43.1	47.6
Equity	48.8	45.6	46.5	51.0	56.9	52.4

those of Dell and Gateway, suggesting no obvious earnings management concerns. The relative low level of cash for Apple in 2000 should be explained, however.

GROWTH ANALYSIS

Growth analysis considers growth rates in dollars and growth rate percentages, especially for operations. An understanding of the relationship of earnings to revenues and expenses also is important, because they are indicators of sustainability of earnings growth rates. Balance sheet changes and growth rates are important for credit decisions and provide information on sustainability of operating performance and indicators of future problems and risk. Accounts receivable growth may indicate the potential for aggressive revenue recognition. Increasing leverage suggests rising credit risk and potential problems if economic conditions worsen.

There are several techniques to analyze growth rates. First, as with the common-size analysis, the relevant numbers can be presented in a table. Alternatively, information can be presented as graphs or bar charts. This is largely a matter of preference. However, annual or quarterly data are relatively more useful in tabular form, whereas stock prices, which change daily, are usually presented in graph form. Growth rates can also be stated as annual changes for some period, such as five or ten years.

The annual performance growth percentages can be calculated, as shown in Table 8.5.

The desired result of growth analysis is an upward "straight line" of performance; e.g., revenues and net income increase about 10 percent each year. That would be one definition of high earnings quality (assuming no evidence of earnings management). Apple's 1997–1998 revenue growth rate was a poor –16.1 percent ($5,941 – $7,081) / $7,081 [(more recent – previous)/previous], one of many concerns for Apple associated with changing performance levels. All three companies had evident problems over the last six years, particularly with poor performance in the more recent years relative to earlier years. As demonstrated with common-size analysis, Apple's performance was erratic across the entire period. This suggests a concern for earnings management incentives but provides no obvious signals. Apple's recurring performance problems indicate that other structural problems may be present. Thus, Apple's future success would seem to depend more on restructuring and the viability of the current business strategy for long-term success.

It should be pointed out that acquisitions and divestitures influence trend analysis. For example, Apple acquired a number of relatively small high-tech companies over the trend

---

TABLE 8.5 | **ANNUAL GROWTH PERCENTAGES**

	Apple					
	1997–1998	1998–1999	1999–2000	2000–2001	2001–2002	Total, 1997–2002
Revenues	–16.1%	3.2%	30.1%	–32.8%	7.1%	–18.9%
Gross Profit	8.1	20.4	26.3	–40.6	29.8	17.2
Net Income	NM	94.5	30.8	–103.2	NM	NM

	Dell					
	1997–1998	1998–1999	1999–2000	2000–2001	2001–2002	Total, 1997–2002
Revenues	58.9%	48.0%	38.5%	26.2%	–2.3%	301.7%
Gross Profit	63.4	50.8	27.1	23.5	–10.8	244.9
Net Income	82.2	54.7	14.1	30.7	–42.8	140.5

	Gateway					
	1996–1997	1997–1998	1998–1999	1999–2000	2000–2001	Total, 1996–2001
Revenues	25.0%	18.7%	15.8%	11.0%	–36.7%	20.7%
Gross Profit	15.1	43.5	22.9	8.4	–49.6	10.9
Net Income	–56.2	214.5	23.7	–43.7	–528.6	–512.4

NM = not meaningful.

analysis period. Consequently, part of Apple's growth, such as it is, can be attributed to these acquisitions. On the other hand, Du Pont divested two large holdings over the same time period, Conoco in 1999 and Du Pont Pharmaceutical in 2001. Consequently, Du Pont sales appear to have declined partly based on this "downsizing."

Growth analysis for balance sheet items usually is less informative (with some striking exceptions). Consider the analysis for Apple shown in Table 8.6.

The same calculations are made to determine percentage change: [(later − earlier)/earlier]. The focus is on unusual percentage changes in any account or combination of accounts. Analysis is usually made with consideration to dollar amounts and common-size simultaneously. This analysis suggests some important trends at Apple. The company was growing as measured by total assets (by almost 50 percent over the six years), with cash growing four times as fast. Simultaneously, liabilities declined on a percentage basis, offset by an increase in equity. Thus, standard liquidity and leverage measures improved over the period. Negative trends on the asset side should be investigated, particularly in 2001. Although cash increased substantially, current assets, total assets, and equity declined. Apple lost money in 2002, suggesting that both balance sheet and income statement analysis should be done simultaneously.

BASE YEAR ANALYSIS

A variation to the growth analysis is to use the earliest year (or another year) as the base year, thus creating an index. The base year growth analysis for the PC companies is presented in Table 8.7. The base year numbers are set equal to 100 and the remaining numbers are calculated relative to that base. Thus, Dell's 1997 revenues of $7,759 million are set equal to 100. The revenue index for 1998 is calculated as $12,327/$7,759 = 1.5887 (stated as 158.9). Dell's 2002 net income was $1,246/$518 = 2.4054 (240.5). A limitation is that the base year must be positive to be calculated meaningfully. (Note that if the base year number is abnormally large or small, the analysis is much less meaningful.) Apple had net losses in 1997. Therefore, 1998 is set as the base year for Apple's performance analysis.

Although the same performance numbers were used, the base year analysis has a slightly different perspective than growth analysis, and either or both can be evaluated. For the analysis of Apple, it's another way to indicate erratic performance. The tremendous operating growth of Dell is highlighted, with 2002 revenues four times those of 1997—a growth of 300 percent. Net income was more modest, at 240.5. Note that the declines from

TABLE 8.6   ANNUAL GROWTH PERCENTAGES FOR BALANCE SHEET ITEMS

	Apple					
	1997–1998	1998–1999	1999–2000	2000–2001	2001–2002	Total, 1997–2002
Cash & MS	57.6%	40.3%	−63.1%	264.1%	0.0%	197.3%
Current Assets	8.0	15.9	26.7	−5.2	4.8	57.4
Total Assets	1.3	20.3	31.8	−11.5	4.6	48.8
Current Liabilities	−16.4	1.9	24.8	−21.5	9.2	−8.8
Total Liabilities	−12.7	−22.3	31.1	−22.1	4.9	−27.4
Total Equity	36.8	89.0	32.3	−4.6	4.5	241.3

MS = marketable securities.

| TABLE 8.7 | BASE YEAR GROWTH ANALYSIS |

Apple

	1997	1998	1999	2000	2001	2002
Revenues	119.2	100.0	103.2	134.4	90.3	96.7
Gross Profit	92.5	100.0	120.4	191.7	236.7	211.1
Net Income	NM	100.0	194.5	254.4	−8.1	132.0

Dell

	1997	1998	1999	2000	2001	2002
Revenues	100.0	158.9	235.1	325.6	411.0	401.7
Gross Profit	100.0	163.4	246.5	313.2	386.7	344.9
Net Income	100.0	182.2	281.9	321.6	420.3	240.5

Gateway

	1996	1997	1998	1999	2000	2001
Revenues	100.0	125.0	148.3	171.7	190.7	120.7
Gross Profit	100.0	115.1	165.2	203.0	220.0	110.9
Net Income	100.0	43.8	137.8	170.5	96.0	−412.0 RF

NM = not meaningful.

2001 to 2002 seem minor without minus signs. The performance problems of Gateway are highlighted: Gateway was down in 2001 and the 2000 drop in net income was also obvious. Apple's revenues declined over the six years and never recovered to its 1996 level. Apple's poor performance in 2001 is emphasized. The long-term perspective of trend analysis is particularly useful in cyclical industries and companies with periodic problems.

The balance sheet also can be evaluated with use of base years. Such an analysis of Apple is shown in Table 8.8.

The interpretation of the data doesn't differ much from growth analysis, but the emphasis is relative to the base year. With the assumption that the base year represents fairly normal results, it can be easier to interpret trends. (If the base year is unusual, the

| TABLE 8.8 | BASE YEAR ANALYSIS OF APPLE'S BALANCE SHEET (% GROWTH) |

Apple

	1997	1998	1999	2000	2001	2002
Cash & MS	100.0	157.6	221.1	81.6	297.2	297.3
Current Assets	100.0	108.0	125.1	158.5	150.2	157.4
Total Assets	100.0	101.3	121.9	160.7	142.2	148.8
Current Liabilities	100.0	83.6	85.2	106.3	83.5	91.2
Total Liabilities	100.0	87.3	67.8	88.9	69.3	72.6
Total Equity	100.0	136.8	258.7	342.3	326.7	341.3

MS = marketable securities.

analysis tends to be futile.) In this case, base year analysis emphasizes the move from debt to equity and the increase in cash over time.

PROBLEMS WITH TREND ANALYSIS

The direct evaluation of annual trend data is not as straightforward as presented above, because several factors distort the ability to compare financial numbers over time. First, economic, competitive, and other environmental considerations are dynamic and constantly changing. Second, accounting standards change over time, and many of these changes make comparisons more difficult. Third, business acquisitions and divestitures may completely distort multiyear comparisons before and after the acquisition or divestiture dates.

Economic and other environmental factors may be estimated and appropriate adjustments made to restate the analysis. For example, the numbers can be deflated by the consumer price index or other measure of inflation. Performance numbers also can be discounted based on interest rate (e.g., based on average interest rates by year of analysis). Some accounting standards may require retroactive disclosures in the notes, which can be used for adjustment purposes. Otherwise, the impact may be estimated and performance numbers restated (if possible). Acquisitions and related issues are very difficult to evaluate over time, except for the short period of time when basic performance numbers are restated (more on acquisition issues in the next chapter).

Like the rest of the tech sector and PC companies in particular, Apple was hit hard by the recession of 2001 and when the tech bubble burst in early 2000. Performance numbers reflect the downturn. Consequently, the trend analysis must be based on how well Apple has handled the crisis and how well it is expected to perform in the future. Unfortunately, the analysis above indicates that Apple had problems before the tech bubble, especially the net loss in 1997, when Dell was doing well (Gateway also had some problems in 1997). Since 2000, Apple has performed reasonably well, given the recession, and both gross margin and net income improved in 2002.

Apple has a history of acquiring relatively small high-tech firms or patent and other technology rights, such as for Emagic GmbH, and assets of Zayante, Prismo Graphics, and Silicon Grail—these were all in 2002. Although each was immaterial to the financial picture of Apple, there is a cumulative affect. Part of the trend analysis is to evaluate the impact of acquisitions and divestitures as a whole, which will be described in Chapter 9.

QUARTERLY ANALYSIS

Financial statements are prepared quarterly. The information is less complete than annual reports, and there are seasonality problems associated with quarterly information (e.g., a large percentage of retail sales occur around Christmas). However, for most of the year, this is the most up-to-date information and a necessary part of financial analysis. Changes in performance trends and other important signals may be discerned first in the analysis of quarterly data. Particularly important are comparisons of (1) the current quarter to the previous quarter and (2) the current quarter to the same quarter a year ago.

The same analytical techniques as above are used for quarterly data. Abbreviated income statement data for the most recent five quarters for the PC companies (from www.hoovers.com) are shown in Table 8.9.

| TABLE 8.9 | QUARTERLY ANALYSIS (MILLIONS OF DOLLARS, FOR QUARTERS ENDING ON INDICATED DATES) |

Apple					
	Sept. 2002	June 2002	March 2002	Dec. 2001	Sept. 2001
Revenue	$1,443	$1,429	$1,495	$1,375	$1,450
Gross Profit	414	419	438	450	467
Operating Income	−15	13	28	20	53
Net Income	−45	32	40	38	66

Dell					
	Oct. 2002	July 2002	April 2002	Jan. 2002	Oct. 2001
Revenue	$9,144	$8,459	$8,066	$8,061	$7,468
Gross Profit	1,716	1,567	1,442	1,470	1,373
Operating Income	758	677	590	594	544
Net Income	561	501	457	456	429

Gateway					
	Sept. 2002	June 2002	March 2002	Dec. 2001	Sept. 2001
Revenue	$1,118	$1,005	$992	$1,135	$1,410
Gross Profit	212	178	163	282	165
Operating Income	−81	−94	−213	0.7	−555
Net Income	−47	−59	−123	9	−520

COMMON-SIZE ANALYSIS

Given the financial data for the three PC companies, the common-size statements are as shown in Table 8.10.

The common-size analysis for Apple indicates several poor trends. The gross profit percentage declined over the five quarters, from 32.2 percent to 28.7 percent by the September 2002 quarter. The negative trends continued for both operating income and net income. Net income (return on sales) declined from a reasonable 4.6 percent to a loss of 3.1 percent. Dell, on the other hand, showed positive trends on most dimensions, especially net income (return on sales), rising from 5.7 percent to 6.1 percent. Gateway seemed a complete disaster, with substantial losses. The only "good news" for Gateway was the small net income for the December 2002 quarter and that return on sales was less negative in September 2002 than in the previous two quarters.

GROWTH ANALYSIS

Growth analysis (Table 8.11) really emphasizes negative changes, and even small changes are highlighted.

| TABLE 8.10 | COMMON-SIZE ANALYSIS FOR QUARTERS ENDING ON INDICATED DATES |

	Apple				
	Sept. 2002	June 2002	March 2002	Dec. 2002	Sept. 2001
Revenue	100.0%	100.0%	100.0%	100.0%	100.0%
Gross Profit	28.7	29.3	29.3	32.7	32.2
Operating Income	−1.0	0.9	1.9	1.5	3.7
Net Income	−3.1	2.2	2.7	2.8	4.6

	Dell				
	Oct. 2002	July 2002	April 2002	Jan. 2002	Oct. 2001
Revenue	100.0%	100.0%	100.0%	100.0%	100.0%
Gross Profit	18.8	18.5	17.9	18.2	18.4
Operating Income	8.3	8.0	7.3	7.4	7.3
Net Income	6.1	5.9	5.7	5.7	5.7

	Apple				
	Sept. 2002	June 2002	March 2002	Dec. 2002	Sept. 2001
Revenue	100.0%	100.0%	100.0%	100.0%	100.0%
Gross Profit	19.0	17.7	16.4	24.8	11.7
Operating Income	−7.2	−9.4	−21.5	0.1	−39.4
Net Income	−4.2	−5.9	−12.4	0.8	−36.9

Apple's performance seems particularly bad, with significant negative numbers on all measures. Revenues were relatively constant for the year but rose and fell from quarter to quarter. Gross profit was consistently negative, suggesting Apple was not controlling cost of production. Operating income and net income were negative in all but one quarter, and the losses in the September 2002 quarter resulted in huge negative changes for the quarter and in comparison with the September 2001 quarter. Note that large changes may result with a low base for the denominator, such as Gateway's operating income for December 2002, which was only $0.7 million.

Dell looked good in comparison, although the number bounced around a bit. But overall, Dell showed increases in all performance measures for the year—the only one in this industry. With consistent losses evident, the growth analysis for Gateway lent little additional insight.

BASE QUARTER ANALYSIS

Base year analysis (Table 8.12) emphasizes changes relative to the base period and, in that sense, is particularly useful to evaluate trends. This assumes that the base period is "normal," and comparisons from this base add insight.

Note that the losses for Gateway in September 2001 make this analysis meaningless (except that losses occur in almost all recent quarters for Gateway). The comparison of

TABLE 8.11	GROWTH ANALYSIS: PERCENTAGE CHANGE FROM QUARTER ENDING ON INDICATED DATE

	Apple				
	Sept. 2002	June 2002	March 2002	Dec. 2001	Sept. 2001*
Revenue	1.0%	−4.4%	8.7%	−5.2%	0.5%
Gross Profit	−1.2	−4.3	−2.7	−3.6	−11.3
Operating Income	−215.4	−53.6	40.0	−62.3	−128.3
Net Income	−240.6	−20.0	5.3	−42.4	−168.2

	Dell				
	Oct. 2002	July 2002	April 2002	Jan. 2002	Oct. 2001*
Revenue	8.1%	4.9%	0.1%	7.9%	22.4%
Gross Profit	9.5	8.7	−1.9	7.1	25.0
Operating Income	12.0	14.7	−0.7	9.2	39.3
Net Income	12.0	9.6	0.2	6.3	30.8

	Gateway				
	Sept. 2002	June 2002	March 2002	Dec. 2001	Sept. 2001*
Revenue	11.2%	1.3%	−12.6%	−19.5%	−20.7%
Gross Profit	19.1	9.2	−42.2	70.9	28.5
Operating Income	NM	NM	−30,528.6	NM	NM
Net Income	NM	NM	−1,466.7	NM	NM

*Percentage change from same quarter one year ago [(Sept. 2002 − Sept. 2001)/Sept. 2001].
NM = not meaningful.

revenue across the PC companies suggests the utility of this analysis. The sales growth of Dell is emphasized in comparison with the flat sales of Apple and loss of sales for Gateway.

The above quarterly comparison is abbreviated. A thorough quarterly analysis could extend back two or three (or more) years to better understand the seasonal and cyclical relationships in operations and include more operating categories, as well as a balance sheet and cash flow analysis. Changing trends in operations and other accounts need to be discovered as quickly as possible to make correct decisions, and this determination is best made with quarterly analysis.

Although the separate analyses are somewhat redundant, they all add some insight. To a large extent, the specific methods used depend on preference and the specific purpose of the analysis. A brilliant analyst probably can interpret the important relationships by looking at a table of the raw dollar amounts. Until brilliance is achieved, calculating some percentages is a reasonable alternative.

PROBLEMS WITH QUARTERLY ANALYSIS

Quarterly disclosure provides the most current information on corporate performance (for the first three quarters of the fiscal year). Analyst's forecasts are focused on quarterly earnings, and therefore quarterly earnings and actual EPS at the earnings announcement

TABLE 8.12	**BASE QUARTER ANALYSIS, WITH QUARTERS ENDING ON INDICATED DATES**				

Apple

	Sept. 2002	June 2002	March 2002	Dec. 2001	Sept. 2001
Revenue	99.5	98.6	103.1	94.8	100.0
Gross Profit	88.7	89.7	93.8	96.4	100.0
Operating Income	−28.3	24.5	52.8	37.7	100.0
Net Income	−68.2	48.5	60.6	57.6	100.0

Dell

	Oct. 2002	July 2002	April 2002	Jan. 2002	Oct. 2001
Revenue	122.4	113.3	108.0	107.9	100.0
Gross Profit	125.0	114.1	105.0	107.1	100.0
Operating Income	139.3	124.4	108.5	109.2	100.0
Net Income	130.8	116.8	106.5	106.3	100.0

Gateway

	Sept. 2002	June 2002	March 2002	Dec. 2001	Sept. 2001
Revenue	79.3	71.3	70.4	80.5	100.0
Gross Profit	128.5	107.9	98.8	170.9	100.0
Operating Income	NM	NM	NM	NM	100.0
Net Income	NM	NM	NM	NM	100.0

NM = not meaningful.

date are major events. That makes this information, especially the announced EPS, particularly important. However, there are some problems. First, the quarterly 10-Q disclosures are incomplete and much less detailed than the 10-K. Second, quarterly information is unaudited, although auditors review quarterly. Both factors make earnings manipulation easier during the first three quarters—nobody externally is checking the figures in detail. And the manipulations can be reversed before the books are closed for the fiscal year end.

Despite the relative weaknesses of quarterly reporting, many earnings management issues are best analyzed on a quarterly basis. This is particularly true because many manipulation strategies are based on meeting quarterly investor and analyst expectations. In part because of the lack of disclosure and less audit focus, managers may feel more confident that deceptive practices more than likely will work. Since the primary purpose of earnings management detection is to signal potential manipulation rather than pinpoint specific fraudulent acts, the more current but limited data provide useful evidence.

USING MULTIPERIOD ANALYSIS TO DETECT EARNINGS MANAGEMENT

The basic methods described above can be used to track any specific financial statement item or combination of items that can be interrelated in explaining possible earnings management. Many concerns discussed in previous chapters indicated that multiperiod analysis is a viable technique to evaluate manipulation potential. A key perspective is to determine when disclosure seems suspect and subject to further multiperiod analysis.

BALANCE SHEET ISSUES

Following up on Chapter 4 earnings management concerns, additional information can be provided on certain issues by using time series analysis. Common concerns and specific suggestions on quantitative techniques are summarized in Table 8.13.

Some balance sheet-related issues require multiperiod analysis to suggest earnings management potential, by year and/or quarter. The same basic quantitative procedures are used as described earlier in this chapter. As demonstrated with the PC companies, multi-period numbers can fluctuate dramatically and may be difficult to evaluate. However, some trends signal possible problems that have earnings manipulation potential.

TABLE 8.13 | **QUANTITATIVE ANALYSIS OF EARNINGS MANAGEMENT CONCERNS**

Topic	Concern	Quantitative Analysis
Low cash and low or negative working capital	Lack of liquidity, especially declining values; high credit risk	Cash and current ratios over several years or quarters; evaluate liquidity and overall credit risk
Cash burn rate	Cash reserves are used up before success (earnings) is achieved.	Specific metrics to forecast number of months of "survival;" evaluate MD&A on business strategy
Relationship of receivables and inventories to sales	Potential for aggressive revenue recognition signaled by rising receivables; obsolescence of inventory not recognized; LIFO liquidation	Time series of relative magnitudes, sales growth compared to changes in receivables and inventory
Property, plant, and equipment (PPE)	Rising average age resulting from not investing in new PPE	Calculate changes in PPE and average age percentage over time
Warranties	Understated warranty obligations; warranty reserves used to smooth income	Trend analysis of warranty levels/changes and change in warranties to sales
Operating lease levels	Large off-balance-sheet obligations growing over time	Time series of operating lease levels/changes and ratio to total liabilities
Long-term debt levels	Rise in interest-paying obligations; leverage problems and related credit risk	Long-term debt levels, changes in debt levels, long-term debt-to-equity ratios, interest coverage
Other assets and liabilities	Many items can be "buried" in this category with little or no disclosure	Big jumps, quarterly or annually, suggest that manipulation is possible; evaluate note disclosure
Treasury stock	Aggressive acquisition of Treasury stock, with rapidly declining equity; executive compensation issues	Treasury stock magnitude to equity, changes over time, fit to business strategy; evaluate executive compensation incentives

LIFO = last in, first out; MD&A = management discussion and analysis.

Cash levels and working capital are fundamental cash management considerations. Relative cash and working capital (or other definitions of liquidity) can vary substantially by company and industry. The PC companies have high cash levels (including short-term marketable securities) and working capital, but these are exceptional. Some companies maintain very low cash levels (a negative cash balance is rare) and negative working capital. Trend analysis can provide more information on the potential long-term liquidity problems (e.g., default on liabilities as they come due) versus a temporary issue or a low-balance cash management strategy.

Boeing had negative working capital and a low cash balance at the end of 2001. To further analyze basic liquidity trends, financial data are summarized in Table 8.14 for the previous six years for Boeing.

The trend analysis shows that liquidity problems started in 2000, with much lower cash ratios (cash included short-term marketable securities) and negative working capital (measures as a current ratio below one). Prior to 2000, cash ratios were much higher and working capital was positive. Generally, these liquidity ratios have been declining. A quarterly analysis (Table 8.15) can be used to update Boeing's liquidity crisis.

The quarterly update indicates that the cash position was substantially improved by September 2002, but working capital was still negative. This can be considered a red flag requiring further analysis and signaling possible credit risk problems.

The **cash burn** rate represents a metric to evaluate a start-up company before profitability is achieved. It has been particularly popular for evaluating dot-coms and other new high-tech companies. It is a measure of cash available to fund operations, capital expenditures, and research and development (R&D) on a monthly basis, assuming no injection of cash is made from debt or equity. It can be estimated from the cash flow statement as negative CFO (plus capital expenditures and R&D, if applicable), divided by number of months (12 for the annual report, three for the quarterly report). Note that it is assumed that CFO is negative. EBITDA (also assumed to be negative) divided by number of months can be used as an alternative

TABLE 8.14   BOEING'S FINANCIAL DATA FOR SIX YEARS (MILLIONS OF DOLLARS)

	2001	2000	1999	1998	1997	1996
Cash	$ 633	$ 1,010	$ 3,454	$ 2,462	$ 5,149	$ 6,352
Current assets	16,206	16,513	15,712	16,610	19,263	20,509
Current liabilities	20,486	18,927	13,656	13,774	14,152	12,726
Cash ratio	3.1%	5.3%	25.3%	17.9%	36.4%	49.9%
Current ratio	79.1%	87.2%	115.1%	120.6%	136.1%	161.2%

TABLE 8.15   QUARTERLY ANALYSIS FOR BOEING

	Sept. 2002	June 2002	March 2002	Dec. 2001	Sept. 2001
Cash	$ 1,702	$ 816	$ 643	$ 633	$ 633
Current assets	16,611	15,760	16,073	16,206	15,921
Current liabilities	19,024	19,139	19,215	20,486	20,201
Cash ratio	8.9%	4.3%	3.3%	3.1%	3.1%
Current ratio	87.3%	82.3%	83.6%	79.1%	78.8%

measure. Months-to-burnout then is cash (including cash equivalents and short-term marketable securities)/cash burn rate (see Revsine 2002, pp. 904–907.) For Amazon.com, according to the 2002 10-K, the cash burn rate is as follows: (CFO of negative $120 million + Capital Expenditures of $50 million) = $170 million/12 = $15.2 million per month. Cash is $997 million; therefore, months-to-burnout is: $997/$15.2 = 66 months. If the number is low, the quarterly trends become very important.

Aggressive revenue recognition is considered the most pervasive earnings manipulation issue, and evaluating accounts receivable and inventory trends is a likely way to uncover manipulation potential. One way a company can increase sales is to lower credit standards for customers and sell products to credit customers with a higher bad debts potential. The result should be rising receivables and lower receivables turnover ratios, because high credit risk customers tend to pay later if at all. A multiperiod quarterly analysis for two or more years is likely to indicate the change in credit policies as (1) a rising receivables to sales percentage and (2) a lower receivables turnover (which can also be stated as average days receivables outstanding). Note that companies can camouflage this by factoring the receivables or "selling" them to a special purpose entity (SPE; more on this in Chapter 11).

Aggressive inventory accounting can include a number of options. A company can avoid writing down obsolescent or slow-moving inventory items. The signal should be rising inventory levels. A twist on this is accumulating problem inventory over an extended period and then writing the full amount off as a single special charge, which may be considered a nonrecurring item by analysts. Cisco did exactly this, with a $2.5 billion write-off in 2001. A different problem is LIFO liquidations, when inventory prices have increased over time. With rising prices, inventory amounts are understated (but cost of goods sold normally matches sales reasonably well). Under LIFO liquidation, inventory levels are reduced to the "old" inventory levels, on the books at much lower values. Thus, during this period of LIFO liquidation, cost of goods sold (COGS) can be much lower—resulting in higher gross margins for at least a brief period and low inventory levels. LIFO liquidation may be disclosed in the notes.

Inventory turnover (cost of goods sold/average inventory) and receivables turnover (sales/average receivables) are standard efficiency measures that also can be used to signal possible manipulation if these ratios are rising or falling. They can be stated in days by dividing the ratios into 365, which can be easier to analyze. In addition, the days' inventory in stock and the days' receivables outstanding can be added together to estimate the length of the operating cycle. Again, from an earnings management perspective, it is the changes from quarter to quarter that are important.

To evaluate both accounts receivable and inventory earnings management detection, consider Boeing's liquidity problems identified above and shown in Table 8.16.

The inventory trends indicate that inventory levels were generally falling (a sign of increased efficiency), with days' inventory in stock declining from 114 days in 1996 to 52 days in 2001. Receivables are more problematic. Receivables levels increased over the period, suggesting possible easing of credit terms to increase sales. The receivables in days ratio is a bit more difficult. Days fell from almost 36 days in 1996 to almost 24 days in 1998 but rose to over 46 days in 2000—again, a sign of possible credit easing. However, receivables in days fell in 2001.

To include more recent data, the receivables-in-days figure was calculated for the most recent quarters (91-day quarters are assumed), as shown in Table 8.17.

TABLE 8.16	BOEING'S LIQUIDITY PROBLEMS					
	2001	**2000**	**1999**	**1998**	**1997**	**1996**
Cost of sales	$48,778	$43,712	$51,320	$50,492	$40,644	$29,383
Receivables	5,156	5,519	3,453	3,288	3,121	2,870
Inventory	6,920	6,852	6,539	8,584	8,867	9,151
Receivables turnover*	9.5	7.9	14.9	15.4	13.0	10.2
Receivables in days	38.4 days	46.2 days	24.5 days	23.7 days	28.1 days	35.8 days
Inventory turnover†	7.0	6.4	7.8	5.9	4.6	3.2
Inventory in days	52.1 days	57.0 days	46.8 days	61.9 days	79.3 days	114.1 days

*In this example, stated as cost of sales/receivables (because cost of goods sold was not available).
†In this example, stated as cost of sales/inventory.

TABLE 8.17	BOEING'S RECEIVABLES IN DAYS		
	Sept. 2002	**June 2002**	**March 2002**
Receivables in days	37.9 days	45.5 days	37.9 days

The receivables-in-days ratio is comparable to 2001 results (with the June quarter higher). This indicates a loss of collection efficiency, which can be explained as an earnings management technique to allow lower-quality buyers or simply the result of poor economic conditions. Most likely, the results can be explained based on economic conditions, and this would be considered only a minor concern.

An industrial company with a large investment in property, plant, and equipment (PPE) must continually update and expand this fixed asset base to maintain operating efficiency. If capital expenditures are used to maintain the base, the level of net PPE and average age of fixed assets (estimated as accumulated depreciation/depreciation expense) should stay relatively constant. If the asset base is expanding, net PPE will increase and average age decline. The concern is if PPE is not being maintained, in which case the net PPE balance will decline and average age rise. The result is probable reduced efficiency of production and the inability to stay competitive in the long run.

Ford's net PPE in the automotive sector fell from $27.0 billion in 2000 to $24.3 billion in 2001, suggesting that continued improvements were not being made. A trend analysis for the last six years is summarized in Table 8.18.

The trend analysis suggests that Ford was expanding PPE through 1999, when gross PPE was almost $61 billion. Since 2000, gross and net PPE have declined. Simultaneously, the average age percentage (accumulated depreciation/gross PPE), which declined from 1996 to 1999, rose in both 2000 and 2001. In 2001, Ford's infrastructure was more than half depreciated at 53.1 percent, up from 45.8 percent in 1999. (Note that average age is misstated because of the impairment charges in 2000 and 2001; thus, the average age percentage is a better measure.) This suggests an operating earnings management decision to cut back capital expenditures, which may have negative longer-term implications for manufacturing efficiency.

Warranties are usually offered on most industrial goods, from alarm clocks to turbine engines. The actual cost is unknown, but it usually is estimated based on past experience. The periodic expense (based on a percentage of sales) is offset to a warranty liability

TABLE 8.18	PROPERTY, PLANT, AND EQUIPMENT TREND ANALYSIS OF FORD (MILLIONS OF DOLLARS)					
	2001	**2000**	**1999**	**1998**	**1997**	**1996**
Gross PPE*	$51,833	$51,302	$60,748	$56,043	$53,083	$51,698
Accumulated Depreciation	27,510	24,327	27,832	26,840	26,004	26,176
Net PPE	24,323	26,975	32,916	29,203	27,079	25,552
Depreciation Expense	5,300†	3,507†	3,262	2,804	2,759	2,644
Average Age	5.2 years	6.9 years	8.5 years	9.6 years	9.4 years	9.9 years
Average Age %	53.1%	47.4%	45.8%	47.9%	49.0%	50.6%

*Excludes special tools.
†Includes impairment charges of $3.6 billion in 2001 and $866 million in 2000.

reserve. Over time, this number can be way off (and subject to revision). In addition, the periodic expense can be dramatically misstated for earnings manipulation purposes. The potential for manipulation can be estimated by analyzing warranty reserve balances (as well as annual warranty expenses and any related write-downs or write-ups), focusing on changes in the balance and relationship to sales levels. A large reduction in the reserve balance and warranty expense suggests manipulation. Unfortunately, complete information on warranties often is not available.

Operating leases were previously discussed as a problem area for analyzing certain industries. When operating leases are associated with long-term assets (common for airlines and retail chains) and equivalent to a large percentage of total liabilities, further analysis should include a longer-term trend analysis to discern patterns in magnitude and also the relative leverage levels of the companies.

Other assets and liabilities (either current or noncurrent) can hide operating-related items, reserves, prepaid items, deferred taxes, and so on. The use of "other" simplifies the balance sheet, but the composition should be explained in some detail in one or more notes. Particularly if these items are (1) large (e.g., as a percentage of total assets), (2) not explained in the notes, or (3) changing substantially from the previous year, a trend analysis of several years can be useful. This gives additional perspective on whether this seems to be a dumping ground for manipulation. In 2002, Apple had $275 million in other current assets (4.4 percent of total assets) and $131 million in other assets (2.1 percent of total assets), for a combined 6.5 percent of total assets. Of more concern is that other current assets increased 70.8 percent from the previous year, and no note disclosure explained the composition of these categories (presumably considered immaterial items). This probably is not a red flag, but a trend analysis for the last few years may be considered.

A trend analysis of long-term debt levels should be conducted for companies with high leverage. The relative levels of long-term debt to equity over time are particularly important, because they indicate relative trends. Where long-term debt levels are rising without a corresponding increase in equity, credit risk increases. Particularly important would be the composition of debt and factors associated with the rising debt load.

Maytag was previously noted for red flags for extremely high leverage, caused largely by the aggressive acquisition of treasury stock. With accumulated treasury stock valued at $1.5 billion (over 40 million shares), Maytag had a debt-to-equity ratio of 130.5× (i.e., equity is less than 1 percent of total assets). A long-term analysis is warranted and is summarized in Table 8.19.

TABLE 8.19	LONG-TERM ANALYSIS OF MAYTAG'S TREASURY STOCK (MILLIONS OF DOLLARS)				
	2001	2000	1999	1998	1997
Treasury Stock	$1,528	$1,539	$1,191	$ 806	$ 508
Equity	24	22	427	508	616
Total Liabilities	3,133	2,647	2,209	2,081	1,898
Treasury Stock/Equity	63.7%	70.0%	2.8%	1.6%	82.5%
Debt to Equity	130.5%	120.3%	5.2%	4.1%	3.1%

The trends are straightforward and disturbing. Treasury stock and liabilities were rising, while equity was falling. The problem has been developing over an extended period, apparently with no attempt by management to think through the problems of increasing treasury stock to the point of wiping out equity. The debt-to-equity ratio emphasizes the problem, rising from a somewhat high 3.1 in 1997 to over 130 in 2001. Return on equity may be high, but how does the company survive any major financial problems without an equity cushion?

INCOME STATEMENT ISSUES

A summary of income statement–related issues is shown in Table 8.20.

Income statement trends are a crucial extension of performance analysis and attempting to determine earnings management potential. Detailed operating information is normally available on a quarterly basis and this analysis is particularly important to spotting new trends. Unexpected changes in operating performance should be explained, because the likelihood of manipulation increases with unexpected changes, particularly negative and erratic performance. The basic trend analysis of performance numbers was presented above.

Sales to affiliates and related parties are problematic, because these are not arms-length transactions. Consequently, it is difficult to determine if they are true financial transactions or used entirely to boost sales and earnings numbers. If the information is available, it is useful to analyze the total transaction amounts and changes by period and to calculate the ratio of affiliated and related-party sales to total sales. The existence of these transactions should be explained in either or both the notes and management discussion and analysis (MD&A).

Selling, general, and administrative (SG&A) expenses are a measure of marketing costs and overhead. Of particular concern are the changes from period to period and the relationship to sales. A particular concern is if SG&A is growing, particularly as a percentage of sales, and if the percentages are above industry norms. Consider Apple's SG&A as a percentage of revenues for the last five quarters, compared to the same information for Dell and Gateway, as shown in Table 8.21.

Apple spent between 25 percent and 30 percent of revenues each quarter, compared to a consistent 10 percent for Dell. Gateway's SG&A was erratic, but the general level was similar to Apple's and much higher than Dell's. From an operating or earnings management perspective, the reasons for this disparity are not obvious. Given the relatively poor performance of Apple (and worse for Gateway), why isn't this category of spending being reduced? Note that Apple reviewed the rationale for high SG&A levels extensively in MD&A.

Research and development (R&D) is a major expense category for Apple and, to a lesser extent, for Dell. Because all R&D costs are expensed (with the possible exception of

TABLE 8.20	INCOME STATEMENT-RELATED ISSUES

Topic	Concern	Quantitative Analysis
Trends in sales, gross margins and operating margins	Erratic relationships, suggesting lack of control over operating costs	Trend analysis as above
Disclosure of affiliated and related-party sales	Potential for transactions to boost sales, but without economic substance	Time series of amounts of disclosed (potential problems) and percent to total sales; evaluate related-party notes
Selling, general, and administrative (SG&A) expenses	High and rising "overhead"	Time series of SG&A amounts, percent changes and percent to sales; evaluate to business strategy
Research and development	Big drops in R&D or erratic R&D spending, suggesting operating manipulation to meet earnings targets	Trend analysis of R&D, amounts and percent to COGS; evaluate in relation to business strategy
Effective tax rates	Declining or rising effective rates, suggesting changing tax strategies, possibly part of a manipulation scheme	Trend analysis of effective tax and tax paid rates; review in relation to operating factors and business strategy
Recurring special charges	If special charges are recorded year after year, manipulation is suspected	Look for special charges as separate line items and/or note disclosure; if recurring, conduct a trend analysis of magnitude and as a percent of sales and operating income
Nonrecurring items	If these are frequent, manipulation is suspected	Evaluate individually plus trend analysis of magnitude and percent of sales and operating income
Net income	Erratic patterns or downward trends, suggesting increased motivation for manipulation	Trend analysis as above
Alternative bottom line numbers	Unusual or unexpected patterns	Extension of trend analysis as above
Stock price to EPS relationships	Declining price earnings (PE) ratios may indicate declining earnings quality	Quarterly analysis of stock price on earnings announcement date/actual EPS
Earnings "surprise"	Negative earnings surprise; meeting analysts' rating "too good," suggesting manipulation to meet these targets	Quarterly and trend analysis of actual EPS compared to consensus EPS analyst's forecast before announcement date; evaluate stock price reaction

TABLE 8.21	ANALYSIS OF SG&A AS A PERCENTAGE OF REVENUES OVER FIVE QUARTERS

	Sept. 2002	June 2002	March 2002	Dec. 2001	Sept. 2001
Apple	27.4%	26.5%	25.5%	29.2%	26.5%
Dell*	9.9	9.9	9.9	10.2	10.3
Gateway	22.2	24.1	34.1	21.1	47.9

*Dell's most recent quarter is October 2002.

software development costs), an operating earnings management decision may be to reduce or eliminate R&D in tough times. In the case of Apple, the amount of R&D capitalized as software development costs also may be an earnings management decision. Therefore, evaluating the long-term R&D trends can be important. R&D expenses and R&D as a percentage of revenues are given for Apple and Dell in Table 8.22.

After declining R&D spending in the late 1990s, Apple substantially increased in R&D in 2001 and 2002. This was by design according to the MD&A, in an attempt to increase the level of innovation and thus the strength of the company's products. Despite the poor current performance, a case can be made for stressing R&D spending. Dell, by comparison, maintains a stable 1.5 percent of revenues on R&D—product innovation is not a strength of Dell (but is consistent with the "Wintel" strategy).

Changing tax strategies may be best assessed with a time series analysis. If effective tax rates change substantially, it may be the result of a changing earnings management focus. The provisions for tax and effective tax rates for Apple were as shown in Table 8.23.

The effective tax rate was erratic, especially in 1999 and 2000. This probably relates to loss-carry-forwards from the earlier loss years. The 2002 and 2000 results are roughly as expected, somewhat below the federal statutory rate of 35 percent.

Both Apple and Dell record special charges as operating expenses on the income statement. Since by definition these should be unusual, further analysis over time is warranted. The amounts of special changes and percentages in relation to operating expenses are as shown in Table 8.24.

This is an area of concern for Apple, with special charges in each of the last six years. Generally, the special charges were for restructuring costs (e.g., reducing staff and facilities). The large amounts in 2000 (6 percent of operating expenses) and 1997 (over 27 percent of operating expenses) need further analysis. In 2000, $90 million represented the purchase of an airplane for CEO Steve Jobs, called an executive bonus. This specific item is a concern under the general category of corporate governance. The major item in 1997 was a $375 million write-off of in-process R&D, a topic which will be discussed in the next chapter. The remaining charges related to restructuring and restating the terms of a licensing agreement.

TABLE 8.22	R&D EXPENSES (MILLIONS OF DOLLARS) AND AS A PERCENTAGE OF REVENUES					
	2002	2001	2000	1999	1998	1997
Apple R&D	$446	$430	$380	$314	$303	$485
Apple R&D %	7.8%	8.0%	4.8%	5.1%	5.1%	6.8%
Dell R&D	$452	$482	$374	$272	$204	$126
Dell R&D %	1.5%	1.5%	1.5%	1.5%	1.7%	1.6%

TABLE 8.23	APPLE'S PROVISIONS FOR TAX (MILLIONS OF DOLLARS) AND EFFECTIVE TAX RATES					
	2002	2001	2000	1999	1998	1997
Provision for tax	$22	$–15	$306	$75	$20	—
Effective tax rate	25.3%	NM	28.0%	11.1%	6.1%	NM

NM = not meaningful; Apple had a net loss that year.

TABLE 8.24	AMOUNTS OF SPECIAL CHARGES (MILLIONS OF DOLLARS) AND PERCENTAGE OF OPERATING EXPENSES					
	2002	**2001**	**2000**	**1999**	**1998**	**1997**
Special Charges, Apple	$ 29	$ 11	$ 98	$27	$7	$667
% of Operating Expenses, Apple	1.8%	0.7%	6.0%	2.0%	0.6%	27.4%
Special Charges, Dell	$484	$105	$194	0	0	0
% of Operating Expenses, Dell	13.0%	2.8%	6.6%	—	—	—

This category is an earnings management concern for Apple. Special charges also were large at Dell for the last three years, primarily restructuring costs.

The presence of nonrecurring items suggests earnings management, because they should be rare events. When they show up, especially if regularly, they should be analyzed separately and in as much detail as possible. The major consideration is, what is the manipulation potential? When one or more nonrecurring items are found in the most recent income statement, a long-term hunt for further examples is suggested. Apple and the other PC companies each had an accounting change in 2001 associated with adopting SAB 101 on revenue recognition, a required change in accounting principle. Because these were required and included small adjustments (large adjustments would have suggested aggressive revenue recognition before adopting SAB 101), no further analysis is necessary.

The 2001 income statement of Maytag indicated changes in accounting principle, extraordinary items, and discontinued operations during the three years presented. Therefore, additional analysis is warranted. An analysis of 1996 to 2001 for Maytag is shown in Table 8.25.

Maytag had nonrecurring items in each of the last six years, including all three major categories. All items were losses, but by a significant amount only in 2001 (when earnings dropped over 70 percent). The extraordinary losses were retirement of indebtedness, required by SFAS No. 4. The discontinued operations were related to losses on a joint venture in China and its Blodgett subsidiary. The company also recorded special charges in 2000 and 2001, as well as a restructuring charge in 1996, as part of operating expenses. In summary, the use of these items suggests the potential for earnings manipulation.

Net income is the standard bottom line, but several alternatives exist for a variety of purposes. It can be useful to calculate performance ratios (e.g., as a percentage of sales) and

TABLE 8.25	ANALYSIS OF MAYTAG'S NON-RECURRING ITEMS (MILLIONS OF DOLLARS)					
	2001	**2000**	**1999**	**1998**	**1997**	**1996**
Income from continuing operations	$167,538	$216,367	$328,582	$286,510	$183,490	$137,977
Discontinued operations	−110,904	−15,400	−54	—	—	—
Extraordinary Items	−5,171	—	—	−5,900	−3,200	−1,548
Accounting change	−3,727	—	—	—	—	—
Net income	$ 47,736	$200,967	$328,528	$280,610	$180,290	$136,429
NI/ICO	28.3%	92.9%	100.0%	97.9%	98.3%	98.9%

NI = net income; ICO = income from continuing operations.

changes using alternative definitions for several quarters (e.g., a couple of years) or several years on the basis of annual data. The relative trends can be important to imply the existence of manipulation. The basic trend analyses for Apple and competitors have been shown earlier in the chapter.

A table of alternative performance numbers and ratio analysis can be presented on a time series basis. Performance numbers for Apple are shown in Table 8.26.

The financial numbers are not positive, with erratic and somewhat declining sales and erratic profitability numbers throughout. The loss years of 2001 and 1997 have few redeeming qualities, and 2002 is positive only because sales and gross profit are better than in 2001.

These numbers can be converted to a common-size analysis, shown in Table 8.27.

The erratic nature of Apple's performance is reinforced by the common-size analysis. No specific signals of earnings manipulation are obvious; however, the unusual pattern may suggest that executives have incentives to manage the financial numbers. Further analysis could include changes in each category and various additional performance ratios.

A market analysis can be a time series extension of income statement analysis, with a particular focus on quarterly EPS. The relationship of EPS to both analysts' consensus forecasts and stock price is particularly useful. The difference between actual EPS and the analysts' consensus forecasts, an "earnings surprise," is particularly important because this is

TABLE 8.26 — TIME SERIES ANALYSIS OF THE PERFORMANCE OF APPLE (MILLIONS OF DOLLARS)

	2002	2001	2000	1999	1998	1997
Sales	$5,742	$5,363	$7,983	$6,134	$5,941	$7,081
Gross Profit	1,603	1,235	2,166	1,696	1,479	1,368
Operating Profit	17	−344	522	359	261	−1,070
EBIT	98	−36	1,113	723	391	−974
EBITDA	216	66	1,197	808	502	−856
Income from Continuing Operations	65	−37	786	601	309	−1,045
Net Income	65	−25	786	601	309	−1,045
Comprehensive Income	38	−291	924	746	307	−1,067

TABLE 8.27 — COMMON-SIZE ANALYSIS OF APPLE

	2002	2001	2000	1999	1998	1997
Sales	100.0%	100.0%	100.0%	100.0%	100.0%	100.0%
Gross Profit	27.9	23.0	27.1	27.6	24.9	19.3
Operating Margin	0.3	−6.4	6.5	5.9	4.4	−15.1
EBIT	1.7	−0.7	13.9	11.8	6.6	−13.8
EBITDA	3.8	1.2	15.0	13.2	8.4	−12.1
Income from Continuing Operations	1.1	−0.7	9.8	9.8	5.2	−14.8
Net Income	1.1	−0.5	9.8	9.8	5.2	−14.8
Comprehensive Income	0.7	−5.4	11.6	12.2	5.2	−15.1

often considered the most important earnings target that companies are expected to meet. Problematic are "misses," when actual EPS is below forecasts (which usually results in a fall in stock price on the earnings announcement date).

Some companies have a record of meeting or exceeding consensus analysts' forecasts quarter after quarter. The question is whether this suggests strong earnings quality or continuous manipulation to meet these targets. The patterns in earnings surprise are particularly important to attempt to get an idea of the relationship and the likelihood that corporations are likely managing earnings to meet these expectations.

Apple had the quarterly actual and forecast EPS shown in Table 8.28 for the last four quarters, including earnings announcement dates.

Apple had two "earnings surprise" periods, for March 2002 (positive) and September 2002 (negative). Although it was only a penny in each case, a stock price change is possible around the announcement dates. To check this, both a stock chart and stock prices for a three-day window (including the day before and the day after the announcement date) are presented in Figure 8.1 and Table 8.29.

Apple's stock performance was dismal for the last year but only slightly worse than NASDAQ. The three-day window provides limited evidence of a price effect associated with earnings surprise. On April 17, the "good news" earnings surprise was associated with a jump in stock price of $0.37 to 26.11, as expected; however, the price declined the next day. The October 16 "bad news" announcement resulted in the expected price decline of

TABLE 8.28	**QUARTERLY EPS FOR APPLE**			
	March 2002	**June 2002**	**Sept. 2002**	**Dec. 2003**
EPS Actual	$0.11	$0.09	$0.02	$0.03
EPS Forecast	0.10	0.09	0.03	0.03
Announcement Date	April 17, 2002	July 16, 2002	Oct. 16, 2002	Jan. 15, 2003

FIGURE 8.1	**STOCK CHART FOR APPLE, COMPARED TO NASDAQ**

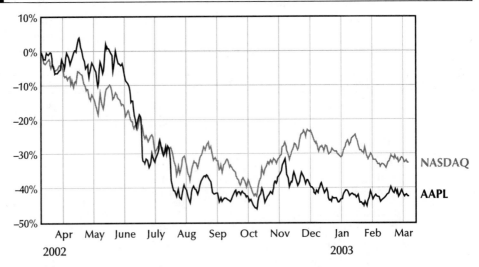

Period: March 11, 2002–March 9, 2003

TABLE 8.29	VALUE OF APPLE STOCK IN RELATION TO ANNOUNCEMENT OF EARNINGS			
	March 2002	June 2002	Sept. 2002	Dec. 2003
Day Before	25.74	18.23	15.16	14.61
Announcement Date	26.11	17.86	14.56	14.43
Day After	25.41	15.63	14.11	14.62

$0.60 to 14.56 and a further decline the next day. Overall, these are minor events in a poor year for Apple and most of the rest of the tech sector. However, the price drop associated with "bad news" indicates why executives focus on meeting analysts' expectations.

CASH FLOW ISSUES

Potential cash flow issues include those listed in Table 8.30.

Particularly important are CFO trends over time, especially as related to net income. If the current CFO numbers are disturbing, it's useful to extend the analysis to several years to discern longer-term patterns. Part of the analysis is the comparison to cash flows from investing and financing activities. These are related, because the company is expected to maintain a relatively stable cash balance. Particularly disturbing is a negative CFO (especially if net income is positive) offset by rising long-term borrowing. As an extension of evaluating PPE, the level of capital expenditures over time should be evaluated.

Cash flow results for Apple are shown in Table 8.31.

TABLE 8.30	POTENTIAL CASH FLOW ISSUES		
Topic	Concern	Quantitative Analysis	
Cash flows from operations (CFO) trends	Declining CFO (especially relative to net income) increases manipulation potential	Time series of CFO levels, CFO changes, and CFO/NI	
Relationships of CFO, CFI, CFF, and comparisons to cash balances	"Poor relationships," such as long-term borrowing to compensate for low or negative CFO	Trend analysis of amounts, percent age changes, and percent comparisons to CFO, NI, or cash balances	
Capital expenditures	Low levels indicate potential for not updating PPE	Time series of capital expenditures, changes in levels, and comparison to average age of PPE	

TABLE 8.31	CASH FLOW FOR APPLE (MILLIONS OF DOLLARS)					
	2002	2001	2000	1999	1998	1997
Net Income	$ 65	$ −37	$ 786	$ 601	$ 309	$−1,045
Cash from Operations	89	185	868	798	775	154
Cash from Investing	−252	−892	−972	−964	−543	−499
Capital Expenditures	−174	−232	−142	−24	43	−6
Cash from Financing	105	42	−31	11	19	23
Ending Cash Balance	2,252	2,310	1,191	1,326	1,481	1,230

Comparative data for cash flow analysis are somewhat more difficult to assess because of the need for a viable scale. Any of the above numbers can be positive or negative, as well as small or big. Changes over the period also can be calculated. Apple maintained high cash levels (the lowest level was $1.2 billion in 2000), primarily from operations (which was always positive despite two net losses). Cash from operations was higher than net income every year. Cash from investing was primarily related to marketable securities, although the company increased capital expenditures in the last three years.

SUMMARY

The chapter expanded the specific evaluation of financial statements by considering trend analysis. The analysis of trends can be done on a quarterly or annual basis, and results may be compared to those for direct competitors or "norms." Specific quantitative techniques include common-size analysis, growth analysis, and base analysis. Virtually any category of financial statement items can be evaluated for earnings management on the basis of trend analysis. A common approach includes a detailed trend analysis based on concerns found in reviewing the current accounting period, such as low working capital, unusual relationships of receivables or inventories, or earnings surprises.

QUESTIONS

1. Why would a growth or base year analysis be useful for evaluating performance and detecting earnings management?
2. Assume that basic performance data for the last six years are somewhat erratic. What does the analyst do then?
3. Is limited annual performance data for the last six years enough, or should a thorough financial analysis be conducted for, say, the last 20 years? How much data are enough?
4. Is quarterly data useful? Explain.
5. Since quarterly data are unaudited, what additional earnings management concerns are present?
6. Would erratic revenue growth be expected on a quarterly basis? Erratic relative expenses? Explain.

PROBLEMS

Problem 8.1: Trend Analysis

Given are abbreviated performance numbers for the last six years for three hotel companies.

| | Hilton | | | | | |
	1997	1998	1999	2000	2001	2002
Revenue	$1,475	$1,769	$1,959	$3,177	$2,632	$3,847
Gross Profit	395	464	567	1,008	686	2,284
Net Income	250	297	174	272	166	198

	Marriott					
	1997	**1998**	**1999**	**2000**	**2001**	**2002**
Revenue	$10,172	$12,034	$8,739	$10,017	$10,152	$8,441
Gross Profit	452	569	992	1,117	918	806
Net Income	306	335	400	479	236	277

	Mandalay*					
	1997	**1998**	**1999**	**2000**	**2001**	**2002**
Revenue	$1,355	$1,480	$2,051	$2,524	$2,462	$2,343
Gross Profit	271	275	898	1,133	1,092	—
Net Income	90	85	42	120	53	116

*Fiscal year ending January (fiscal years are 1/31/1998 to 1/31/2003).

a. Calculate common-size statements for these three companies.

Hilton						
	1997	**1998**	**1999**	**2000**	**2001**	**2002**
Revenue						
Gross Profit						
Net Income						
Marriott						
	1997	**1998**	**1999**	**2000**	**2001**	**2002**
Revenue						
Gross Profit						
Net Income						
Mandalay*						
	1997	**1998**	**1999**	**2000**	**2001**	**2002**
Revenue						
Gross Profit						
Net Income						

*Fiscal year ending January (fiscal years are 1/31/1998 to 1/31/2003).

b. Calculate the growth analysis for the three hotel companies.

Hilton						
	1997–1998	**1998–1999**	**1999–2000**	**2000–2001**	**2001–2002**	**1997–2002**
Revenue						
Gross Profit						
Net Income						
Marriott						
	1997–1998	**1998–1999**	**1999–2000**	**2000–2001**	**2001–2002**	**1997–2002**
Revenue						
Gross Profit						
Net Income						
Mandalay*						
	1997–1998	**1998–1999**	**1999–2000**	**2000–2001**	**2001–2002**	**1997–2002**
Revenue						
Gross Profit						
Net Income						

*Fiscal year ending January (fiscal years are 1/31/1998 to 1/31/2003).

c. Calculate the base-year analysis for the three hotel companies.

Hilton (%)						
	1997	**1998**	**1999**	**2000**	**2001**	**2002**
Revenue	100					
Gross Profit	100					
Net Income	100					
Marriott (%)						
	1997	**1998**	**1999**	**2000**	**2001**	**2002**
Revenue	100					
Gross Profit	100					
Net Income	100					
Mandalay (%)*						
	1997	**1998**	**1999**	**2000**	**2001**	**2002**
Revenue	100					
Gross Profit	100					
Net Income	100					

*Fiscal year ending January (fiscal years are 1/31/1998 to 1/31/2003).

d. Evaluate the trend analysis information, paying particular attention to the earnings management potential.

Problem 8.2: Quarterly Analysis

Given below is basic information related to the fourth quarter, 2002, financial statements (compared to the previous quarter and the same quarter one year previously) for three hotel and resort companies. Additional information is available in the 2002 10-Q reports for the three companies (and summarized at Hoover's—www.hoovers.com).

Hilton								
Quarterly Analysis	4th Quarter, 2002	4th Quarter, 2002	3rd Quarter, 2002	3rd Quarter, 2002	4th Quarter, 2001	4th Quarter, 2001	% Change from previous quarter	% Change from same quarter, 1 year ago
	$ Millions	Common-Size	$ Millions	Common-Size	$ Millions	Common-Size	Compared to 3rd Quarter	Compared to 4th Quarter
Revenue	$957		$934		$887			
Gross Margin	551		545		502			
SG&A Expenses	324		322		320			
Net Income	40		48		4			

Marriott								
Quarterly Analysis	4th Quarter, 2002	4th Quarter, 2002	3rd Quarter, 2002	3rd Quarter, 2002	4th Quarter, 2001	4th Quarter, 2001	% Change from previous quarter	% Change from same quarter, 1 year ago
	$ Millions	Common-Size	$ Millions	Common-Size	$ Millions	Common-Size	Compared to 3rd Quarter	Compared to 4th Quarter
Revenue	$1,037		$2,454		$2,139			
Gross Margin	163		111		(228)			
SG&A Expenses	49		25		37			
Net Income	(37)		103		(116)			

							% Change from previous quarter	% Change from same quarter, 1 year ago
Quarterly Analysis	4th Quarter, 2002	4th Quarter, 2002	3rd Quarter, 2002	3rd Quarter, 2002	4th Quarter, 2001	4th Quarter, 2001		
	$ Millions	Common-Size	$ Millions	Common-Size	$ Millions	Common-Size	Compared to 3rd Quarter	Compared to 4th Quarter
Revenue	$542		$503		$629			
Gross Margin			164		279			
SG&A Expenses			126		112			
Net Income	4		33		(48)			

(Table titled "Mandalay")

a. Complete the common-size analysis and determine the percent changes.

b. Analyze the information presented, paying particular attention to the earnings management potential.

CASES

Case 1: Trend Analysis Issues for Apple

Evaluate the concerns and earnings management potential for Apple based on trend analysis, using both annual and quarterly data.

Concern	Analysis
Erratic revenues and gross margin, annual and quarterly	
Net income and other performance measures (especially 1997 and 2000)	
High levels of SG&A	
R&D levels	
Special charges	
Alternative bottom-line measures	
Cash levels compared to other assets	
Rising equity levels	

Case 2: Quarterly Analysis of Boeing's Liquidity, Leverage Performance, and Related Considerations

The following quarterly information summarizes quarterly balance sheet and income statement information for Boeing (in millions of dollars).

Balance Sheet

	Dec. 2002	Sept. 2002	June 2002	March 2002	Dec. 2001
Cash	$ 2,333	$ 1,702	$ 816	$ 643	$ 633
Inventory	6,184	5,902	5,446	6,084	6,920
Receivables	5,007	5,207	5,713	5,696	5,156
Current assets	16,855	16,611	15,760	16,073	16,206
Total assets	53,342	48,320	47,228	46,551	48,343
Current liabilities	19,810	19,024	19,139	19,215	20,486
Liabilities	44,646	37,417	36,826	36,798	37,518
Equity	840	839	839	839	838

Income Statement

	Dec. 2002	Sept. 2002	June 2002	March 2002	Dec. 2001
Revenue	$13,701	$12,690	$13,857	$13,821	$15,702
Gross Profit	2,835	2,019	2,653	2,572	3,029
Operating Income	1,166	566	1,203	1,015	1,058
Net Income	590	372	779	−1,249	100

a. Calculate the following liquidity and leverage ratios:

	Dec. 2002	Sept. 2002	June 2002	March 2002	Dec. 2001
Cash Ratio					
Current Ratio					
Debt-to-Equity					
Debt Ratio					

Based on these ratios, is there evidence of liquidity or leverage problems? Explain. Are these potential problems interrelated? Explain.

b. Calculate the following performance ratios:

	Dec. 2002	Sept. 2002	June 2002	March 2002	Dec. 2001
Gross Margin					
Operating Margin					
Return on Sales					
Return on Assets*					
Return on Equity*					

*Most recent four quarters.

Based on these ratios, evaluate the relative performance of Boeing.

c. Calculate these ratios/relationships:

	Dec. 2002	Sept. 2002	June 2002	March 2002	Dec. 2001
Inventory/Sales					
Receivables/Sales					
Change in Inventory/ Change in Sales					
Change in Receivables/ Change in Sales					

Is there any evidence that inventory or receivables changes are unusual in relation to sales or changes in sales? Explain.

d. Summarize the relationships and findings in liquidity, leverage, performance, and credit risk of Boeing, based on a quarterly trend analysis.

CHAPTER 9

Business Combinations and Related Issues

America has a long history of business combination and related activities. American industry is Big Business primarily as a result of this acquisition activity over the last century and a half. There are significant public policy issues associated with business combinations, such as the elimination of competition and thus potential antitrust violations. Of more concern to the analyst are a host of problems inherent in evaluating the financial consequences of these transactions. A merger involves more than just adding the accounts of the two old companies together to create a new company. The opportunities for earnings management are magnified substantially, and the ability to effectively evaluate existing manipulation is severely reduced.

Because most large companies have acquired companies in the recent (and distant) past, how are the acquisitions accounted for? How does this impact the financial analysis? This chapter looks at the accounting for business combinations, considers the accounting for some recent acquisitions, and develops financial analysis techniques to enable a better understanding of merger issues. As with many accounting issues, earnings management incentives are extensive and difficult to analyze.

BACKGROUND

There is nothing new about business combinations. Railroads and telegraph companies, high-tech in mid-nineteenth century America, were combining by 1850. This merger boom slowed down in depressions but never stopped. The story of big business is as much the story of acquisitions as innovation and individual entrepreneurship. After the Civil War, John D. Rockefeller was particularly gifted at gobbling up all oil refining competitors. His company, Standard Oil, invented the trust and later used the holding company to control most of the oil refining capacity. Other business tycoons were paying attention and combined everything from sugar to meatpacking and from matches to steel.

Most acquisitions were **horizontal mergers,** in which companies bought out or offered partnerships to direct competitors. Rockefeller, for example, became the largest refiner in Cleveland and negotiated railroad rebates that reduced his costs relative to competitors'. He then attempted to acquire the other thirty or so Cleveland refiners (with either cash or ownership interests). Those who didn't agree were driven out of business by his cutthroat competition. Eventually, Standard Oil had a national 90 percent market share. Rockefeller's stated purpose was to maintain reasonable prices and ensure consistent quality of kerosene and other oil products. Others saw him as a ruthless robber baron.

By 1902, J. P. Morgan, the most powerful banker in America, acquired Carnegie Steel and most of the rest of the industry to form U.S. Steel, the first billion-dollar corporation in the United States—formed basically as a series of horizontal and vertical mergers on a vast scale. The financial reporting and auditing of U.S. Steel were excellent by the standards of the time but involved "watering the stock" by overvaluing assets (that is, not based on historical cost and not necessarily based on reasonable current value calculations) and by using various practices now illegal. The potential for misleading reporting has been a continual problem for business combinations.

Mergers can be used to (1) increase economies of scale and reduce competition (horizontal mergers such as Standard Oil), (2) expand activities into related areas (**vertical mergers**), or (3) diversify (**conglomerate mergers**). Rockefeller, Carnegie, and other businessmen of the late nineteenth century moved from horizontal mergers to eliminate competitors to vertical mergers to obtain raw materials, ensure distribution channels, and reduce overall costs.

Henry Ford was the premier entrepreneur in the first half of the twentieth century. He introduced the moving assembly line (although meat packers used similar methods long before) and the cheap, standardized Model T a century ago. Ford grew using retained earnings and then used a vertical merger strategy to acquire related firms: parts suppliers, ships and railroads for distribution, mines, and basic metal manufacturers. Ford owned most business components of auto manufacturing, from mines to transportation to dealerships.

The strategies for conglomerate mergers developed during the 1950s. The advantages for diversification are well known. In theory, a manager can run a company in any industry effectively. The practice of owning a "portfolio" of unrelated businesses became particularly popular in the 1960s. James Ling took Ling Electronic public in 1955 and bought Temco and Chance Vought to form Ling-Temco-Vought (LTV). Ling formed a holding company and proceeded to build an empire across multiple industries with borrowed money. Major acquisitions included Braniff Airlines, Wilson Sporting Goods, National Car Rental, and Jones and Laughlin Steel. The acquisitions brought in additional revenues, and the "magic of accounting" resulted in increasing earnings recognized. (GAAP had little to say about accounting for business combinations at the time.) Other well-known conglomerates active in this period included Litton, ITT, and Gulf+Western.

Difficult economic times (e.g., recessions and the "stagflation" of the 1970s and early 1980s) and the problems of controlling the complex and diverse empire led to huge losses, massive sell-offs of segments, and bankruptcy in 1986. LTV would emerge from bankruptcy primarily as a steel company. There is less enthusiasm for the concept of conglomerate management (Tyco was the latest example of a conglomerate going belly up), but conglomerates exist and many are successful. General Electric is one of the largest and most successful companies in the United States, and it is a conglomerate.

Acquisitions are every bit as common today as 50 or 100 years ago. According to Henry (2002), mergers worth almost $4 trillion were completed between 1998 and 2000. These included some megamergers (p. 64), listed in Table 9.1.

These are the mergers where the acquisition was valued at over $50 billion, based on market value, when announced. For size and impact, current mergers match any period in American history. The effects on concentration and business strategies across industries are enormous. Given the leeway in accounting practices, the earnings management potential also is enormous.

ACCOUNTING ISSUES

Accounting for acquisitions has been a continuing problem for standard-setters. The basic methods prior to SFAS Nos. 141 and 142 were (1) pooling of interests and (2) the purchase method. Both methods rely on valuations of existing assets and liabilities rather than valuing the earnings capacity of the acquired firm. Conceptually, pooling of interests assumes a combination of two "near-equal" firms by exchanging stock. Accounting was essentially "adding up" the combined book value. Under the purchase method, one firm acquires another, often for cash. The acquiring firm records the assets and liabilities of the acquired company at fair values. The difference between the acquisition price and the revalued net assets is goodwill—this is the only circumstance where a corporation records goodwill.

Historically, both methods were allowed, with few limitations. Pooling concepts were initially developed in the 1930s but seldom used prior to 1950. The method came to be accepted for most acquisitions by common stock, and by 1970 over 80 percent of mergers involved pooling. The APB issued Opinion No. 16 in 1970, primarily to limit the use of pooling. Twelve criteria had to be met before pooling of interests was allowed. If an acquiring

TABLE 9.1	MEGA-MERGERS, 1998–2000			
Buyer	**Target**	**Year**	**Value (Billions)**	**Premium (%)**
America Online	Time Warner	2000	$165.9	55.8%
Pfizer	Warner-Lambert	1999	93.9	29.7
Exxon	Mobil	1998	77.2	34.7
Travelers Group	Citicorp	1998	70.0	10.4
SBC Communications	Ameritech	1998	61.4	23.1
Nations Bank	Bank America	1998	59.3	48.4
AT&T	Media One Group	1999	55.8	24.3
Bell Atlantic	GTE	1998	52.8	3.8

firm wanted to use pooling of interests, all twelve criteria had to be met; otherwise, the purchase method was required.

Assume that Octopus, Inc., acquires Guppy Company. Guppy has the balance sheet information summarized in Table 9.2.

In the first scenario Guppy is acquired for common stock with a fair value of $30 million, and the twelve criteria for pooling of interests are met. (Note that this was recorded before SFAS No. 142 went into effect.) The simplified journal entry is shown in Table 9.3.

Thus, the acquisition is recorded at book value. The economic substance of the transaction (i.e., Guppy effectively cost Octopus $30 million in stock) is ignored.

Alternatively, assume that Guppy is acquired for cash of $30 million, and therefore the purchase method was used. The simplified journal entry is shown in Table 9.4.

In this case, all assets and liabilities are recorded at fair value, including new intangible assets of patents and goodwill. Guppy is recorded at its economic cost of $30 million. Goodwill is created as an intangible asset and is a plug figure to balance debits and credits ($30 million – $18.1 million). Essentially, it is the difference between the acquisition cost

TABLE 9.2	SUMMARY OF BALANCE SHEET INFORMATION (MILLIONS OF DOLLARS) FOR "GUPPY COMPANY"	
	Book Value	Fair Value
Accounts Receivable, net	$1.1	$1.0
Inventory	2.9	3.5
Fixed Assets, net	8.0	10.6
Patents	0.0	5.0
Liabilities	(2.0)	(2.0)
Net Assets	10.0	18.1

TABLE 9.3	SIMPLIFIED JOURNAL ENTRY USING POOLING OF INTEREST METHOD (MILLIONS OF DOLLARS)	
Accounts Receivable, net	$1.1	
Inventory	2.9	
Fixed Assets, net	8.0	
Liabilities		2.0
Equity		10.0

TABLE 9.4	SIMPLIFIED JOURNAL ENTRY USING PURCHASE METHOD (MILLIONS OF DOLLARS)	
Accounts Receivable, net	1.0	
Inventory	3.5	
Fixed Assets, net	10.6	
Patents	5.0	
Goodwill	11.9	
Liabilities		2.0
Cash		30.0

and fair value of net assets. Prior to SFAS No. 142, goodwill was to be amortized over a period of 40 years or less.

Income tax consequences of business combinations are complicated. To the stockholders of the acquired firm, most pooling-of-interests acquisitions were nontaxable. The stockholders would exchange shares of stock. To the same stockholders of the acquired firm, the purchase method is taxable when cash is involved. The stockholders must recognize gains and losses on the sale (generally taxable at capital gains rates).

SFAS NUMBERS 141 AND 142

The FASB passed SFAS No. 141, *Business Combinations,* and SFAS. No. 142, *Goodwill and Other Intangible Assets,* in June 2001. The major change is that the purchase method is required for all business combinations. The effective date is July 1, 2001. Since that date, all business combinations are to use the purchase method. A primary reason for the new standards was the lack of comparability between purchase and pooling. As stated in paragraph B29, the purchase method

> generally accounts for transactions in which assets are acquired and liabilities
> are assumed or incurred, and it therefore produces information that is com-
> parable to other accounting information. ... [U]sers of financial statements
> are better able to assess the initial costs of the investments made and the sub-
> sequent performance of those investments and compare them with the per-
> formance of other entities.

Paragraph 37 of SFAS No. 141 states the valuation bases for assets and liabilities (for example, marketable securities at fair value, raw materials at current replacement costs, and plant and equipment at current replacement cost, for similar capacity). Intangible assets that meet the separability criteria (e.g., patents) are recognized separately from goodwill. Examples are listed in paragraph A14 of the document.

Under SFAS No. 142, goodwill and some other intangibles are no longer amortized. Instead, goodwill is tested for impairment at least annually. Examples of impairment events (paragraph 28 of the document) include adverse legal factors, unanticipated competition, and a loss of key personnel. An impairment loss is recognized if the carrying value is not recoverable and its carrying value exceeds its fair value. The second step is to measure the amount of the impairment loss. The impairment testing began for fiscal year 2002 in most cases. Thus, impairment write-offs can be expected, and they might be big.

AOL Time Warner recorded a $54 billion loss for first quarter 2002. The write-off of goodwill turned a $1 million operating loss to a net loss of $54,240 million. Because the loss was noncash, cash from operations was $1.8 billion on the cash flow statement. However, stockholders' equity declined from $208.6 billion to $160.4 billion, a loss of $48.2 billion or 23.1 percent. As stated in footnote 3,

> Upon adoption of FAS 142 in the first quarter of 2002, AOL Time Warner
> recorded a one-time, noncash charge of approximately $54 billion to reduce
> the carrying value of its goodwill. ... The amount of the impairment prima-
> rily reflects the decline in the Company's stock price since the Merger was
> announced and valued for accounting purposes in January 2000.

AOL charged the impairment against specific segments, including cable for $23 billion and networks for $13 billion.

The elimination of the pooling-of-interest method makes financial analysis of business combinations somewhat easier, because all mergers now use the same method. However, the impairment charges to goodwill under SFAS No. 142 are problematic. It's not at all clear how fair value of goodwill can be determined or under what circumstances goodwill should be written off. The AOL Time Warner write-off suggests a "big-bath" earnings management strategy in a money-losing quarter (although AOL's loss was small, at only $1 million). Further write-offs are likely from any number of firms. From an analyst's perspective, these will be hard to predict and may be difficult to evaluate, even after the fact.

EARNINGS MANAGEMENT ISSUES AT ACQUISITION DATE

A business combination is consummated on a specific date, usually during the middle of the fiscal year of both companies (and they may have different year-end dates). On that date, the acquired company is essentially consolidated into the parent. There are key questions on recognition strategies and the specific amounts that are recorded. Ultimately, the acquired company has to be recorded at acquisition price (the purchase method must be used). Valuing assets is not an exact science, and considerable leeway is allowed. Auditors are not experts and may rely on appraisal and other experts. Even so, flexibility is substantial.

Alternative price allocation strategies exist; this is one example of earnings management. Consider three different allocation strategies. Under the first strategy, allocate as much of the value to depreciable or amortizable assets as possible. Restate PPE and intangibles such as patents to the highest possible values. The results will be (1) lower future net income because of increased expenses and (2) lower future tax expense because depreciation and amortization are tax-deductible. This makes the most economic sense, because it saves cash (less is paid to the IRS). An alternative strategy is to allocate as much as possible to **in-process research and development** (IPRD). Because the R&D results have not been finalized, valuing IPRD is particularly difficult. IPRD has to be written-off immediately after the acquisition, potentially representing a big loss. However, it is a nonoperating item and may be ignored by analysts. The third strategy is to allocate as much as possible to goodwill. Under SFAS No. 142, goodwill is not expensed, and this method should yield the highest earnings after the acquisition. The downsides of this strategy are the lack of depreciable/amortizable assets as well as the potential for write-downs of goodwill in future years, such as the case for AOL Time Warner.

Evaluating acquisition allocation strategies is dependent on the corporate disclosures for the acquisition year, which may be less than thorough. Apple disclosed three acquisitions for fiscal year 2002 (Note 4): Emagic, Space Technologies, and Power School. As required, the purchase method was used, and the allocation of fair values to agree with the "market price" actually paid is summarized in Table 9.5.

The total acquisition cost was $107 million, with $68 million (63.6 percent) allocated to goodwill. In-process R&D of $11.3 million was recognized and written off as special charges (categorized as operating expenses). Thus, the earnings management strategy seems to be to allocate as much as possible of the cost to goodwill, reducing expenses in future years (assuming no goodwill write-offs will occur). Apple's 2002 balance sheet showed $119 in acquired intangible assets, 1.9 percent of total assets. Capitalizing goodwill fits with Apple's erratic performance problems—it doesn't need higher operating expenses.

If specific acquisitions are considered immaterial, virtually no disclosures may be included. The conglomerate Tyco made a vast number of relatively small acquisitions under Dennis Kowzlowski. As reported by Maremont (2002) in the *Wall Street Journal*,

TABLE 9.5	ALLOCATION OF VALUES FOR APPLE'S ACQUISITIONS (MILLIONS OF DOLLARS)			
	Emagic	Space Technologies	Power School	Total
Net tangible assets	$ 2.3	$–0.7	$ 0.2	$ 1.8
Acquired technology	3.8			3.8
Trade name	0.8			0.8
Other intangible assets		5.9	2.6	8.5
In-process R&D	0.5		10.8	11.3
Deferred stock compensation			12.8	12.8
Goodwill	18.6	9.7	39.7	68.0
Total	26.0	14.9	66.1	107.0

Tyco spent some $8 billion on over 700 acquisitions over a three-year period and disclosed not a one. Tyco spent some $4 billion in cash and increased debt over $3 billion. These were signals for analysts to puzzle over. Individually, each deal was miniscule, but the totals added up to real money. A key question for the CFO (Mark Swartz at the time) and auditor (PricewaterhouseCoopers for Tyco) was: What is the reporting responsibility under GAAP? Somewhat like Enron, the disclosure decisions were based on the individual acquisitions, which were allowable under GAAP, but the net effect was deceptive.

AN EMD ACQUISITION DETECTION STRATEGY

Acquisitions can represent legitimate and viable transactions that fit into the business strategy of the corporation. However, many of the recent acquisitions have been less than satisfactory, and several have proven to be real disasters. Key questions are whether these were based on business strategy considerations or the increased potential for earnings manipulation. Beyond the operating characteristics, acquisitions are expensive to consummate and subject to considerable accounting choice and therefore to earnings management. This is an area for skepticism, and the analyst should make considerable effort to consider the earnings management signals from acquisitions and the accounting decisions reported. Lack of disclosure also is a potential concern.

An earnings management detection strategy for business combinations is summarized in Table 9.6.

ACCOUNTING ISSUES AND DISCLOSURES AROUND THE ACQUISITION DATE

An interesting manipulation technique, called "spring loading," is to notify the acquired company to modify accounting policies before the acquisition and make various write-offs and adjustments, with the intent of improving the perceived performance of the parent immediately after the acquisition. Apparently, Tyco specialized in this activity. (Tyco's counter-argument was that the restructuring of acquisitions resulted in big losses.)

In 2001, Tyco acquired CIT Group, a financial services company renamed Tyco Capital. Before the acquisition date, CIT disposed of $5 billion in poorly performing loans,

| TABLE 9.6 | EARNINGS MANAGEMENT DETECTION STRATEGY FOR BUSINESS COMBINATIONS |

At Acquisition Announcement Date

Topic	Concern	Detection Strategy
Existence of acquisitions	Does the specific acquisition make sense based on the business strategy of the acquirer?	Evaluate the acquisition target and review MD&A other sources on relevant business strategy.
Prices paid	Acquisitions often are made at an excessive premium, which can be the first sign of future failure.	Evaluate the stock price reaction to the press release on the acquisition decision. Was the price reaction for the acquiring firm negative?
Consider longer-term acquisition strategy	What are the recent acquisition (and divestiture) trends? Are there disasters in the making?	Review all acquisitions for the last five or so years and consider the business strategy implications and relative success.
Quantity and magnitude of acquisitions	If these are common (and especially if large), it suggests increased earnings management potential.	Review acquisitions and calculate frequency and amounts involved, market reactions, and evidence of later problems (including divestitures).

After Acquisition Date

Topic	Concern	Detection Strategy
How were asset values allocated?	Allocation decisions signal earnings management strategies.	Determine allocation percentages to specific categories (listed below).
Depreciable/amortizable assets	These will increase future operating expenses but are tax deductible. Do these seem to be inflated or too small?	Calculate percent to total acquisition costs; compare to typical percentages for the company and industry.
In-process R&D	Must be written off. Does the amount seem reasonable?	Same as above.
Goodwill	No longer amortized but subject to write-offs. Can be overstated to reduce future expenses associated with the acquisition.	Same as above.

made downward adjustments of $221.6 million, increased the credit-loss provisions, and took a $54 million charge to acquisition costs (apparently "pushed down" from Tyco). Revenues for CIT were extremely low and dramatically increased after the deal. The result, according to Symonds (2002), was a net loss reported by CIT just before the acquisition date. After the acquisition, CIT reported net income of $71.2 million. That increased Tyco's earnings for the September 2001 quarter, but luck ran out. Tyco Capital had extreme problems with credit, because it was now tied to Tyco. Ultimately, this new business segment was sold as an initial public offering in 2002. Tyco recorded this as a discontinued operation (recording an after-tax loss of $6.3 billion). For the year ended September 30, 2002,

Tyco had a total net loss of $9.4 billion. CEO Kozlowski and CFO Swartz resigned and shortly thereafter were indicted for a number of illegal acts.

The information for CIT and Tyco was available only because CIT continued to file reports to the SEC for the first few months after the merger. This was necessary to maintain a high credit standing with the debt markets. In most cases, the analyst must rely on the quarterly reports of the two companies just before the acquisition date and then on reports for the parent company for the quarter after the acquisition. The target firm has "disappeared" from the financial statements, with only the limited note disclosure provided. Beyond that, it's speculation how the before-and-after statements line up.

ISSUES AFTER THE ACQUISITION

After the acquisition, the marriage begins. The usual rationale for the merger is economies of scale and restructuring to increase efficiencies. Specific decisions on acquisition issues also are made. The major issues are (1) write-offs based on the acquisition, (2) the nature of the restructuring in progress, (3) in-process research and development, and (4) goodwill. The major problem for the external analyst is to understand what the corporation did and why. The earnings management potential is substantial: What's capitalized or expensed, how are charges against earnings made, and how is the profitability from the acquisition firm incorporated?

Acquisitions are expensive (and a major revenue source to investment bankers, attorneys, and accountants who set them up). What to do with these costs? They could be capitalized, expensed as operating or nonoperating items, or (as in the case at Tyco) "pushed down" to the acquisition. These would seem to be operating expenses and highlighted as such, but try to find the disclosure. No definitive answer is possible in most cases, beyond speculating on the basis of the limited information from before-and-after financial statements and note disclosure.

The concept of restructuring typically is stressed in the acquisition decision, and many companies with a history of acquisitions quickly restructure the new subsidiaries. General Electric perhaps has gobbled up more firms than anyone else, but it seems to do it very successfully. The GE team seems fairly ruthless in sliming down acquisitions with substantial layoffs and other cost cutting. The financial results make the GE strategy seem successful, but the direct impact of earnings management is difficult to detect.

In-process research and development is fairly straightforward. The acquiring firm will write off the amount recognized in the acquisition. However, earnings management issues are present. The value of IPRD is difficult to determine, because at the development stage the potential value is—what? Consequently, a case can be made that the value is near zero or worth millions. "Near zero" is a swell answer to limit the write-off cost. "Millions" works if a big write-off is desired. This can be recorded as a nonoperating expense and justified specifically as an acquisition cost. Lucent acquired Octel in 1997 and Yurie in 1999. Both were billion-dollar acquisitions, and large amounts were recorded as IPRD and expensed as nonoperating costs. This "saved" later amortization expenses, which would have been recognized as operating expenses.

The nature of earnings management issues for goodwill changed substantially with SFAS No. 142. Prior to 142, goodwill was capitalized (under the purchase method) and then amortized over a maximum forty years. The key strategies were (1) how much to allocate to goodwill, which was a tax-deductible expense (since 1993), and (2) what amortization period to use. A long amortization period reduced the annual expense but meant that large goodwill balances would stay on the books.

Consider the goodwill and amortization strategies of competing hotel and resort companies (fiscal year 2001), outlined in Table 9.7.

The goodwill strategies differ between Hilton and Mandalay. Hilton has substantial goodwill and wrote off only 6 percent in 2001, suggesting an amortization period of about twenty years. One result of the low amortization rate was greater than $1 billion dollars in goodwill, equal to almost 15 percent of total assets. Thus, goodwill was a major asset category. A major reason seems to be to maintain a low impact on income; however, even the small allocation percentage represented almost half of net income. Mandalay amortized more than a quarter of outstanding goodwill in 2001, which had a substantial effect on earnings at 22.6 percent. The big write-offs resulted in relatively little goodwill on the balance sheet.

Since 2002, goodwill has not been expensed. Instead, goodwill is tested for impairment at least annually based on criteria specified in SFAS No. 142. Now the earnings management strategy involves deciding under what circumstances an impairment loss should be taken and how much. If a loss cannot be avoided, key issues are timing and amount. AOL Time Warner, as described earlier, used the "big bath" option. Big bath seems the most likely strategy for most prospective goodwill write-offs, that is, big one-time charges.

IMPACT ON FINANCIAL STATEMENTS AND RATIOS

When an acquisition is made, the acquiring company is expanded in size and operations. How this affects specific balance sheet and income statement items as well as cash flows depends on the specific characteristics of the agreement: the exchange of voting common stock versus cash, debt instruments, or a combination of these, and prior to SFAS No.141, whether it was accounted for as a pooling or purchase.

Under pooling of interests, financial statements were combined at book value. Balance sheet ratios changed only to the extent that the acquisition had a different asset and liability mix than the acquiring firm. The income statement showed "excess" growth solely because of the added operations of the acquired firm, but ratios differed only to the extent that the acquisition had different operating characteristics and efficiency. Equity was increased by the book value of the acquisition's net assets (although the composition of stockholders' equity would change).

TABLE 9.7 **GOODWILL AND AMORTIZATION STRATEGIES (MILLIONS OF DOLLARS)**

	Goodwill	Amortization	Total Assets	Net Income
Hilton	$1,273	$77	$8,785	$166
Mandalay	45	12	4,037	53

	Amortization/Goodwill	Amortization/Net Income	Goodwill/Total Assets
Hilton	6.0%	46.4%	14.5%
Mandalay	26.7%	22.6%	1.1%

The circumstances under the purchase method are more complex and variable. When the acquisition is cash (some or all the cash involved may be borrowed), the net asset (equity) position does not go up. Acquired assets (and liabilities) are recorded at fair values, which are offset by the cash paid. Balance sheet totals rise only to the extent that external financing is used, either debt or equity. But asset and liability composition can change substantially. Patents, goodwill, and other intangibles are recorded (internally generated intangibles usually are expensed). Cash ratios will drop for the acquiring firm (unless the acquisition was funded by new debt or equity), with liquidity ratios partially offset by the working capital position (at fair value) of the acquisition. Fixed assets and intangibles can rise substantially because fair values are used and goodwill recognized. Liabilities rise because of the acquisition's obligations and any debt used to finance the acquisition. Equity is unchanged in a cash or debt transaction. Consequently, leverage ratios can rise, often substantially.

The income statement of the combined firm includes the acquisition's operations only after the effective date of the merger. Revenues rise because of the acquired firm's operations. Several negative results occur. Operating expenses usually are relatively larger because of write-ups of inventory to fair value at the acquisition (particularly if the acquired firms used LIFO), higher depreciation, and other allocations because fixed and other assets generally are written up, plus the potential write-down of goodwill and other intangibles. Also, if the cash paid is from borrowed funds, additional interest expense is recorded. Investing, banking, and other transaction costs are substantial. Consequently, profitability and activity ratios can suffer. That is, earnings for the combined entity should be higher because of the acquired firm's operations, but performance ratios may decline because of increased expenses.

Under the purchase method, there are substantial cash flow effects. The acquisition price paid in cash (less preacquisition cash held by the acquired firm) is recorded as cash used for investing (if there was any borrowing, cash received is recorded as cash flows from financing). Requirements of SFAS No. 95 on the cash flow statement are relatively complex on acquisitions (and beyond the scope of this book).

The impact on financial statements is considerably different if equity is exchanged under the purchase method. Assets and liabilities are restated to fair value, and equity used also is recorded at fair value (unlike pooling of interests). Liquidity usually would be higher because cash is not used. Inventory is generally restated upward. PPE, intangibles, and other items are recorded the same whether cash or equity is used under the purchase method. Leverage ratios are lower when equity is used. (Note that the acquirer assumes the debt of the acquisition.) There should be little difference in the income statement under the circumstances of the alternative purchase method. Interest expense would be higher if borrowed cash is used rather than equity, but equity dilution occurs when stock is used.

ACQUISITION DISASTERS

A relatively high proportion of acquisitions—perhaps two out of three—turn out to be mistakes. The rationale for merger usually sounds great. As stated by Henry (2002, p. 60),

The spring of 1998 was a fast and furious time for dealmakers. ... These deals were solid undertakings—purchases of long-established companies with proven business models, tangible assets, and thousands of workers. ... On April 6, Travelers Group announced a $70 billion merger with Citigroup ... The next day, insurer Conseco announced it was paying $7.1 billion and a huge 86 percent premium to buy mobile-home lender Green Tree Financial. The following Monday, Bank One offered $28.8 billion for First Chicago, and NationsBank bid $509.3 billion for BankAmerica. Three weeks later, Germany's Daimler Benz snapped up Chrysler for $38.6 billion.

Business Week analyzed 302 big mergers from mid-1995 to mid-2001, which included a monster deal: AOL's acquisition of Time Warner for $166 billion. A key point was that about two thirds were losing deals. Four major reasons were suggested: overpaying by offering a big premium over market value, inflating the possible cost savings and synergies, delayed integration of operations, and cutting costs beyond reason and damaging operations and customer relations (Henry 2002, p. 64).

Then there were mergers that were complete disasters. Perhaps the biggest disaster, because of the fraud involved, was the acquisition of CUC (formerly Comp-U-Card) by HFS to form Cendant in 1997. Unfortunately for HFS CEO Henry Silverman and HFS investors, CUC had been reporting fraudulent earnings for years. CUC sold consumer products using long credit terms. To meet analysts' expectations, long-term revenues (which should have been deferred) often were recognized immediately, and related marketing and other costs were capitalized. Some "other revenues" were entirely fictitious. The fraud scheme was initially developed in the early 1980s, essentially a "menu" of revenue, cost, reserves, and write-offs specifically to meet earnings targets (see Schilit 2002, pp. 3–9).

Acquisitions became necessary to keep up the gimmicks, because of the new fraud opportunities. With acquisitions, large reserves could be created with charges lost in the shuffle, through a combination of "spring-loading" results to the acquisition before the merger and netting costs to the balance sheet in the consolidation. The reserves would then be used to increase earnings after the acquisitions, by charging expenses against the reserves. The HFS acquisition was big and made essential to CUC when the schemes were falling apart—the real losses were increasingly hard to camouflage. The fraud was reported shortly after the merger, and financials were restated. Restatements for 1995–1997 reduced net income by $440 million, including a net loss of $217.2 million in 1997 instead of the $55.4 million gain initially reported. Investor suits against Cendant and auditor Ernst & Young followed, as did criminal indictments against several former CUC executives.

MARKET REACTION TO ACQUISITION ANNOUNCEMENTS

Why are corporations difficult to analyze after acquisitions? When a company is announced as being acquired, the stock price can rise substantially, because the acquiring company usually pays a premium price relative to the current stock price of the acquired firm. The stock price of the acquiring company can rise or fall. How does the merger fit the business strategy of the acquiring company? How does this merger affect the existing portfolio of the investor? How do mergers affect analysts' buy and sell recommendations? Analysts working for investment bankers, consulting firms, or large companies that regularly acquire firms can become experts in mergers—by helping to develop investment strategies, recommending merger targets, or designing strategies to avoid being acquired.

An acquiring firm typically pays a substantial premium over current stock price to complete a merger. This is needed to persuade the target company's board of directors (presumably on the basis of stockholder interests) to accept the offer and to fend off other potential acquiring firms. This market premium can top 50 percent of current price (Henry [2002] reported a 36 percent average premium in the *Business Week* analysis), resulting in an immediate market reaction for both acquiring and target firms. Almost always, the stock price of the target approaches the announced acquisition price (discounted by the probability the combination will ultimately be completed). The price of the acquiring firm can go up or down, depending on how investors view the benefits of the acquisition relative to the premium paid.

Consider the announcement of the AOL acquisition of Time Warner on January 10, 2000. A stock chart is presented for both firms in Figure 9.1 (Time Warner's ticker was TWX).

Time Warner received an immediate 30 percent rise in price, as expected because of the relative premium to be paid. The early view of AOL was somewhat mixed, but skeptical (note the stock price was dropping before January 10). The price went down slowly, and by the middle of February it had dropped 40 percent. AOL was a high-tech communications company. Time Warner was a large, multifaceted communications company considered "old economy." An interesting point is that Time Warner was a much bigger company on virtually any measure except market value (market capitalization) at the time.

Analysts debated whether this was an appropriate move for AOL. Was it (1) a brilliant vertical acquisition to combine old and new economy advantages or (2) an albatross that would drag AOL down to the low performance associated with old economy firms and added complexity of a diverse empire beyond the scope of AOL expertise? The stock

FIGURE 9.1 | **STOCK CHART FOR THE AOL ACQUISITION OF TIME WARNER**

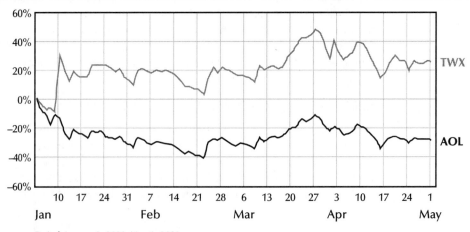

Period: January 3, 2000–May 1, 2000

price results suggest the latter view prevailed for the first three months after the announcement. The potential for the tech bubble to burst and for AOL devastation apparently didn't occur to anyone.

The AOL website (www.aoltimewarner.com) called itself the "first fully integrated media and communications company in the Internet age." The effective date of the merger was January 11, 2001, almost exactly 1 year after the announcement of the merger. A year-to-date stock chart for the first six months indicated the initial market perspective of the merger (Figure 9.2).

The combined company had a substantial price rise for most of January and was up about 50 percent for the period (through the end of May 2001). Because high tech was down (e.g., NASDAQ was down about 15 percent year-to-date, while the DJIA was essentially even), AOL's claims seemed correct so far.

The stock chart for the last 24 months (ending in January 2003) shows a different perspective (Figure 9.3).

Both the Dow and NASDAQ were down, but AOL dropped over 70 percent to less than 12. This was reflected in the goodwill write-off of $54 billion in the first quarter of 2002 and the net loss of $99 billion for the year—both are records (and no other companies are close). Consequently, perspective can change from the initial announcement to early results, relative to a longer-term period. The merger was a disaster, the largest in history according to both earnings losses and market value decline.

REGULATORY ISSUES

Mergers by big business can have a major impact on economic activity. One aspect is increasing market share and reduced competition, which can involve potential antitrust violations. Declining competition also may reduce innovation. Therefore, the Department

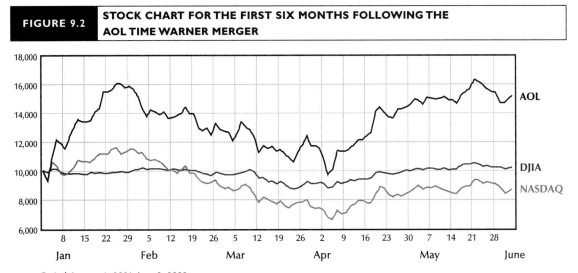

| FIGURE 9.2 | STOCK CHART FOR THE FIRST SIX MONTHS FOLLOWING THE AOL TIME WARNER MERGER |

Period: January 1, 2001–June 3, 2000

FIGURE 9.3	STOCK CHART SHOWING LONGER-TERM RESULTS OF AOL TIME WARNER MERGER

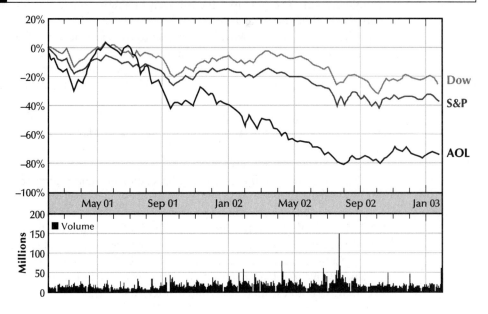

of Justice, the Federal Trade Commission, and other federal regulators review mergers by major corporations. The regulators may disallow the merger or require certain structural changes (e.g., selling off certain market segments) to meet antitrust criteria.

The investor and analyst must evaluate antitrust and other legal characteristics of merger activity beyond the standard financial analysis. What is the probability that the merger will be denied? Will major restructuring or business segment sell-offs be required that make the merger less attractive? How should the investor react to these projections? How will mergers impact the competitiveness of the industry? These are issues that can be answered only on a case-by-case basis. The analysis is most critical for horizontal mergers and in industries that are highly regulated, where antitrust and other regulatory violations are most likely.

OWNERSHIP SHORT OF CONTROL

Corporations can invest in other companies without 100 percent ownership. For accounting purposes, control means greater than 50 percent common stock ownership, which also means consolidation. Investments that are less than 50 percent dramatically change the accounting characteristics and, therefore, the earnings management strategies. Three categories of ownership are particularly important from an accounting perspective: (1) equity investments, (2) the **equity method,** and (3) **joint ventures.** Equity investments that are acquisitions of less than 20 percent of outstanding shares presume no significant control, and these shares are treated as marketable securities (covered in Chapter 4). The remaining two categories are reviewed in some detail.

There are unique earnings management techniques that companies seem to employ when using the equity method and joint ventures. Consolidation is avoided, and there is potential for various off-balance-sheet accounting and other factors that impact on the earnings management evaluation. Issues and concerns are summarized in Table 9.8.

TABLE 9.8	**EARNINGS MANAGEMENT DETECTION STRATEGIES FOR THE EQUITY METHOD AND JOINT VENTURES**	
Topic	**Concern**	**Detection Strategy**
Use of the equity method	Is the equity method used only for earnings management purposes?	Evaluate the use of the equity method and how it fits in the business strategy
How were these investments established?	Particular concern with former subsidiaries that were spun off and the equity method adopted; this signals earnings management	Review the history of specific investments under the equity method, usually presented in the notes, MD&A, or both; sometimes it is necessary to refer to earlier years' reports
Evaluate former low-performing subsidiaries	Low performing subsidiaries from earlier years that are spun off suggest earnings management	Same as above
Evaluate accounting procedures associated with former subsidiaries	Former subs may include substantial debt from the parent; gains from the transaction also may be recorded; both signal earnings management	Same as above plus evaluation of relative balance sheet composition of parent and investment before and after the spin-off; evaluate the income statement of parent
Are joint ventures used?	Existence suggests earnings management potential	Disclosure in note and/or MD&A
Do the JVs make economic sense?	The concern is about use of earnings management versus reasonable business strategy decisions	Evaluate JV descriptions in notes to MD&A and other sources
Financing arrangements	The JV can be used for financing, in which case it suggests a form of off-balance-sheet accounting	Evaluate the descriptions and partners of the specific JVs; evaluate financial impact on the basis of note disclosures
Use of equity method by JV	JVs usually use the equity method and are subject to the same earnings management concerns	See analysis above for equity method
Specific JV agreements	Be on the lookout for earnings management concerns	Evaluate note and MD&A discussions of specific JVs
Potential political risks of JV	Various risks possible, especially related to foreign JVs, including foreign governments	Same as above; consider political problems with JVs with foreign governments

JV = joint venture.

EQUITY METHOD

The equity method generally can be used when the corporate investor owns between 20 percent and 50 percent of outstanding common shares. The rationale is that the investor has significant influence but not control. The equity method avoids **consolidation.** Under this method, the acquisition is recorded at cost (purchase price) as an investment at the purchase date. The parent company's share of net income is recorded as income and an increase in investment. Cash dividend payments are recorded as an increase in cash and a decrease in investment. Thus, consolidation is avoided. This can result in some interesting earnings management opportunities for the parent.

Coca-Cola Company is the world leader in soft drinks. Despite having over $20 billion in revenue and $11 billion in equity, Coca-Cola does no bottling. This is left to "bottling partners" around the world. What Coke does is sell the concentrate at a high margin to the bottlers, and the bottlers' margins are much lower. The bottlers can be (1) independent, (2) an investment of Coca-Cola, using the equity method, or (3) subsidiaries, in which Coca-Cola has a controlling interest and full consolidation is used. Investments in the independent bottlers (that is, Coca-Cola has less than 20 percent of the equity) are marketable securities recorded at fair value, and gains and losses are recorded as other comprehensive income (available for sale). In terms of book value, about a third of the bottlers are recorded as marketable securities and two thirds are recorded under the equity method. Currently, none of the bottlers is consolidated.

Coca-Cola uses the equity method for the major bottling affiliates. The equity investments for 2001 are shown in Table 9.9.

In addition to the $5.1 billion in investments using the equity method (22.9 percent of total assets), an additional $2.8 billion in investments were treated as marketable securities. The fair value of the affiliates recorded by the equity method was $3.3 billion higher than recorded on the balance sheet.

The fair value of Coca-Cola Enterprises (CCE) was $3.2 billion, making it the largest bottling company in the world. Coca-Cola owned 38 percent of CCE, plenty for effective control. CCE was created as a 1986 spin-off from Coca-Cola. Bottling has a much lower profit margin, and CCE has a massive amount of debt, which is no longer on the books of Coca-Cola. At the end of 2001, Coca-Cola had a debt-to-equity ratio of 97.2 percent, while CCE's debt to equity was 7.4 percent. For the same year, Coca-Cola had net income of almost $4 billion (a return on sales of 19.8 percent), while CCE had a net loss of $321 million, 38 percent of which was included in Coca-Cola's net income. Consequently, the

TABLE 9.9	COCA-COLA'S EQUITY METHOD INVESTMENTS (MILLIONS OF DOLLARS)	
	2001	**2000**
Coca-Cola Enterprises	$ 788	$ 707
Coca-Cola Amatil Limited	432	617
Coca-Cola HBC	791	758
Other	3,117	3,164
Total	5,128	5,246

combination of the bottling spin-off and use of the equity method was great for Coca-Cola—and a significant example of earnings management.

White (2003) lists three distortions associated with the equity method, all of which have earnings management implications: (1) profitability measures are overstated, (2) liabilities are hidden, and (3) considerable information is lost on the underlying contracts (p. 478). The proportionate share of income is included, but most of the assets are excluded; therefore, return on assets is overstated. Because income is reported net, revenues and expenses of the affiliate are excluded and return on sales is overstated. Affiliate liabilities are excluded (another possible form of off-balance-sheet accounting), understating leverage. Information loss includes the lack of information on assets, liabilities, commitments, and contingencies of the affiliate.

JOINT VENTURES

Joint ventures (JVs) are contractual arrangements with other corporations to form a separate legal entity, usually a corporation or partnership. The JV could be central to the operation of the parent, represent a financial arrangement, or virtually anything else. The JV would keep its own accounting records, and each partner would record its proportionate share. If the ownership is between 20 percent and 50 percent (the usual arrangement), the equity method is used for accounting. Consequently, the same earnings management issues exist as discussed above.

What is potentially different about a JV is the unique contractual arrangements that may be involved. Virtually anything that can be thought up as a partnership can be contracted as a JV. Examples include major global operations in the primary business of the company, financial agreements, and supplier/customer arrangements. JVs are common in oil and gas, particularly the global integrated corporations, as well as banking and financial organizations.

Chevron and Texaco merged in 2001 to become the second largest energy company in the world, behind Exxon Mobil. ChevronTexaco (CVX) had revenues of $106 billion in 2001 and total assets of $77 billion. CVX has ownership interests in over 1,000 companies in 180 countries, many of which are joint ventures. In fact, the initial two companies had a joint venture in Caltex before the merger (so Caltex is now a wholly owned subsidiary). Chevron Phillips is a Houston-based chemical company that's a JV with Phillips Petroleum. CVX has a 26.5 percent interest (called a strategic alliance) in Dynegy. Various JVs exist for exploring, drilling, and refining around the world. Long-term relationships exist with various Middle East countries; newer JVs include Kazakhstan (1993).

The joint ventures can be defended as risk-sharing relationships. JVs with countries can have significant political implications and corresponding risks. Risk sharing may include operating risks, financial risks, political risks, and other legal risks that may be global in scale. Simultaneously, accounting issues can cloud the risk-reward relationships.

Other joint venture examples are shown in Table 9.10.

Because JVs are normally accounted for under the equity method, the same earnings management concerns exist as with the other equity method examples. Particular concerns involve off-balance-sheet financing and potential outstanding commitments and contingencies. Additional concerns would be JV-specific, that is, depending on the nature of the specific JV terms.

TABLE 9.10	EXAMPLES OF JOINT VENTURES
Du Pont	Du Pont has several affiliates, in which Du Pont owns 50 percent as a JV. The emphasis is on foreign operations, such as Du Pont Elastomers LLC, Du Pont. Teijin Films, Du Pont Sabanci Polyester, and Du Pont Sabanai International.
Georgia Pacific	GP has a 50 percent partnership with Metropolitan Life, where the G/M JV owns the GP headquarters building in Atlanta, financed by the mortgage from MET.
Micron	Micron has JVs with Asian chip producers, essentially to supply chips to Micron with take-or-pay agreements.
Hilton	Hilton has a number of hotel JVs associated with the operations of hotel properties, including Hilton HHonors Worldwide and Hilton Reservations Worldwide. Both represent 50 percent ownership with Hilton Group plc.

DIVESTITURES

The other side of combining is divesting, potentially part of a successful business strategy or a change in strategies. Also, parts of a major acquisition may be divested. Various methods exist to divest, from selling a subsidiary to another corporation, to a **spin-off,** to establishing a JV from a wholly owned subsidiary. However, substantial earnings management concerns exist with each **divestiture.** The specific accounting arrangements and requirements are particularly important for further analysis.

Earnings management concerns associated with divestitures include those shown in Table 9.11.

The most famous divestiture was the 1984 agreement to break up American Telephone and Telegraph (AT&T). This was the result of an agreement with the Justice Department after a decade-long antitrust case. As AT&T put it:

> The United States woke up on January 1, 1984, to discover that its telephones worked just as they had the day before. But AT&T started today a new company. Of the $149.5 billion in assets it had the day before, it retained $34 billion. Gone even was the famous Bell Logo (www.att.com).

AT&T has been in the acquisition and divestiture business ever since, trying to figure out how to compete in a newly competitive business. Thus, an evaluation of earnings management by AT&T should begin with the year 1984 or earlier.

In 1995, AT&T announced that it was separating into three public companies: AT&T as a communications service company, a computer company (NCR—from an earlier acquisition), and a systems and equipment company (Lucent Technologies). In April 1996, AT&T sold 112 million shares of Lucent as an initial public offering (the proceeds increased paid-in capital). Later in the year, the remaining shares were spun off to AT&T shareholders as well as the NCR spin-off. These spin-offs decreased stockholders' equity by $2.2 billion. AT&T also sold the remaining shares of AT&T Capital for $1.8 billion, resulting in a gain on discontinued operations of $162 million. For 1996, total liabilities decreased by almost $10 billion, while equity increased by over $3 billion. Prior to the spin-offs, these discontinued operations had been losing money ($4.3 billion in 1995 before tax).

In 2000, another restructuring followed, including divestitures of AT&T Wireless and AT&T Broadband (AT&T Broadband was created from the acquisition of Tele-Communications by merger in 1999). The AT&T Wireless spin-off occurred in 2001, and

TABLE 9.11	EARNINGS MANAGEMENT CONCERNS ASSOCIATED WITH DIVESTITURES		
Topic	**Concern**		**Detection Strategy**
Are they common?	Divestitures should be rare events, and their presence usually is a negative signal		Evaluate note and MD&A for the existence of divestitures for the last two to five years
Why are the divestitures made?	Divestitures may signal poor operating choices and prior bad acquisition or operating decisions		Evaluate each divestiture and how it fits into the business strategy of the company
How is the divestiture recorded?	Evaluate composition of the divestiture and how gains and losses are recorded elimination of problem subs, reduction of debt, and gains and losses are potential concerns		Evaluate based on note and financial statement information; compare balance sheet before and after divestiture
What is the impact on earnings in the year of divestiture?	Discontinued operations or part of operations; both have concerns, especially related to whether a gain or loss is recorded		Same as above
What is the impact of debt levels?	Divestiture could be an earnings management technique to decrease debt loads		Evaluate relative debt positions before and after divestiture

AT&T Broadband merged with Comcast in 2002 (as AT&T Comcast, another spin-off, with AT&T stockholders receiving a proportionate share). AT&T set up AT&T Wireless as a **tracking stock** and then spun off the remaining shares to AT&T stockholders in 2001. AT&T wrote up the net assets of AT&T Wireless to fair value and recorded a tax-free gain of $13.5 billion. This was recorded as a gain from discontinued operations (plus an additional income from discontinued operations of $150 million). This was great timing, because the company had a loss from continuing operations of $6.8 billion. Thanks largely to this spin-off, AT&T recorded net income of $7.0 billion for 2001, compared to net income of $4.7 billion in 2000.

As described in Chapter 6, Du Pont divested Conoco in 1999 and Du Pont Pharmaceuticals in 2001. Conoco was recorded as discontinued operations, while Du Pont Pharmaceuticals was part of continuing operations. Of additional concern was that both divestitures were made in down years, with the gains reported substantially increasing net income for both years.

SEGMENT REPORTING

Large corporations have complex operations, often operate in several industry segments, and often have foreign subsidiaries. These are combined in the financial statements, but SFAS Nos. 14 and 131 require additional disclosure. According to SFAS No. 131, reportable segments are components that have 10 percent of any of three characteristics: total revenues, combined operating profits, and combined identifiable assets. Disclosure requirements include sales, operating profit, and identifiable assets. Foreign operations also require disclosure, on the basis of the 10 percent criteria for sales or identifiable assets. Companies have substantial leeway in defining segments. For example, Disney's baseball and hockey teams are included in Parks and Recreation; PepsiCo defines operating segments as Pepsi, Frito Lay, etc., while Coca-Cola defines only geographic segments, as North America, Asia, and so on.

Additional information on business combination may be available from segment reporting. That assumes that the acquisition represents a complete business segment with separate disclosures. If this is the case, a measure of the relative success of acquisition is possible. Whether based on acquisitions or not, the success of the company depends on the success of the major reporting subsidiaries. Of particular concern to the analysis is the segment's relative performance and how this may fit into the overall business strategy. For example, new segments may perform poorly, but poor performance should not go on indefinitely. Poorly performing segments also may be likely candidates for future divestiture.

Earnings management concerns include those shown in Table 9.12.

Apple provides geographic segment information, but not by specific industrial products or services. (Sales data by specific product are available in MD&A-related information, but operating profit that would provide useful comparisons by product is not.) Geographic information for 2002 is summarized (from Note 11) in Table 9.13.

Geographic segment ratios for Apple are shown in Table 9.14.

Considerable variability existed by geographic segment. Unlike its competitors, the American market had the lowest operating return on sales, while Japan and "other" had the largest, at 19.7 percent and 21.5 percent, respectively. "US, Retail" represented sales at

---

TABLE 9.12 | **EARNINGS MANAGEMENT CONCERNS RELATED TO SEGMENT REPORTING**

Topic	Concern	Detection Strategy
Full disclosure issues	Limited information is presented and important information is camouflaged or not disclosed	Evaluate note disclosure and MD&A relative to financial statements
Relative performance	If performance information is available, industry and geographic segments can be compared; disclosure of poor performing segment is crucial	Ratio analysis of performance and activity, based on disclosure; evaluate based on information available; review MD&A to evaluate the fit to the business strategy
Segments related to specific acquisitions	If a specific segment represents a direct acquisition, additional analysis of effectiveness is possible; a concern is evidence of poor acquisition strategies	Review segment relative to earlier information, specifically on the original acquisition
Financial operation risks	Risk potential may be a concern for some segments, especially related to certain foreign operations; consider earnings management implications	Calculate return efficiency ratios; evaluate based on note MD&A disclosure

Apple stores, with negative results. Efficiency varied, with asset turnover from 2 percent to 14 percent.

Industrial segment reporting for AT&T for 2001 is shown in Table 9.15.

While Consumer Services showed good profitability, both Business Services and AT&T Broadband recorded operating losses. AT&T Broadband also had operating losses in 1999 and 2000. The Broadband subsidiary was based on the Tele-Communications acquisition in 1999, and its performance suggests that this was a disaster. This poor performance also seems to be the rationale for the AT&T Broadband spin-off of 2001.

Segment reporting can be difficult to evaluate because presentation and disclosure levels can vary substantially from one company to another and operations can vary by both operating and geographic segment. Because SFAS 131 allows considerable reporting flexibility, information may be difficult to compare across companies.

Segment reporting represents additional information that can be useful for evaluating earnings management. It is particularly useful to highlight segment problems, which could relate to earnings management decisions. Thus, the information from AT&T reinforces the interpretation of the AT&T Broadband spin-off as eliminating a money-losing subsidiary.

TABLE 9.13   GEOGRAPHIC INFORMATION FOR APPLE, 2002 (MILLIONS OF DOLLARS)

	Americas	US, Retail	Europe	Japan	Other
Net Sales	$3,088	$283	$1,251	$710	$410
Operating Income	280	−22	122	140	88
Segment Assets	395	141	165	50	67

TABLE 9.14   APPLE'S GEOGRAPHIC SEGMENT RATIOS

	Americas	US, Retail	Europe	Japan	Other
Operating Income/Net Sales	9.1%	−7.8%	9.8%	19.7%	21.5%
Net Sales/Identifiable Assets	7.8%	2.0%	7.6%	14.2%	6.1%

TABLE 9.15   INDUSTRIAL SEGMENT REPORTING BY AT&T, 2001 (MILLIONS OF DOLLARS AND %)

	Business Services	Consumer Services	Broadband
Net Sales	$28,024	$15,079	$ 9,799
Operating Income	−2,154	4,875	−3,215
Segment Assets	40,339	2,141	103,060
Operating Income/Net Sales	−7.7%	32.3%	−32.8%
Net Sales/Identifiable Assets	69.5%	7.0%	9.5%

SUMMARY

This chapter reviewed accounting characteristics and earnings management concerns associated with business combinations, investments with less than majority ownership, divestitures, and segment reporting. These are complex, interrelated areas with significant accounting issues and considerable potential for earnings manipulation. Business combinations now require the purchase method, and goodwill is no longer amortized. This has changed accounting strategies in terms of valuing acquisition assets and liabilities, especially those with expense and related tax issues. Parent companies can maintain control without majority ownership, which changes accounting requirements and leads to additional earnings management issues. The equity method, including the use of joint ventures, allows off-balance-sheet reporting and can be a mechanism to "de-emphasize" money-losing subsidiaries. Divestitures should be rare and typically should be viewed skeptically by analysts. Segment reporting provides limited information on subsidiary performance, and the degree of usefulness depends on disclosures presented.

QUESTIONS

1. Why are acquisitions common today? Are there particular earnings management issues with companies that consistently acquire other companies? Explain.

2. Why is the purchase method the only accounting procedure now used for acquisitions? Explain.

3. What is goodwill? Why is it a difficult issue for analysts?

4. What earnings management issues exist at the acquisition date and that fiscal year?

5. Under what circumstances is an acquisition desirable to (1) the potential acquirer and (2) the target firm? Why are some acquisitions disasters?

6. Why is the equity method often used rather than consolidation, when the parent has effective control? What are the associated earnings management concerns?

PROBLEMS

Problem 9.1: Goodwill for Hilton

Given is information on goodwill, amortization, and relative size presented earlier in the chapter (in millions of dollars) for 2001:

	Goodwill	Amortization	Total Assets	Net Income
Hilton	$1,273	$77	$8,785	$166

	Amortization /Goodwill	Amortization /Net Income	Goodwill /Total Assets
Hilton	6.0%	46.4%	14.5%

Given is the 2002 information on goodwill for Hilton:

	Goodwill	Total Assets	Net Income
Hilton	1,273	8,348	198

a. Calculate the following ratios for 2002:

	Amortization "Savings"*/Goodwill	Goodwill/Total Assets
Hilton		

*Use 2001 amortization/net income rate times 2002 goodwill.

Hilton reported the following goodwill analysis in the 2002 Annual Report (in millions of dollars):

	2000	2001	2002
Net Income	$272	$166	$198
Goodwill, net of tax	49	49	0
Net Income, Adjusted	321	215	198

b. Evaluate the impact of the new policy of not amortizing goodwill, by comparing the results for 2002 to results for 2000–2001.

Problem 9.2: Segment Reporting by Hilton

a. Hilton reported the following information on industry segments for 2002 (in millions of dollars).

	Revenues	Operating Income	Assets
Hotel Ownership	$2,270	$412	$5,278
Managing and Franchising	1,281	278	2,114
Timeshare	296	73	257

b. Calculate (1) operating income/revenues and (2) revenues/assets

	Operating Income/Revenue	Revenues/Assets
Hotel Ownership		
Managing and Franchising		
Timeshare		

c. Evaluate the industry segment information for Hilton.

Problem 9.3: Segment Reporting by Marriott

Marriott reported the following information on industry segments for 2002 (in millions of dollars).

	Revenues	Operating Income	Assets
Full-Service Lodging	$5,474	$397	$3,423
Select-Service Lodging	967	130	771
Extended-Service Lodging	600	(3)	274
Time Share	1,207	183	2,225
Synthetic Fuel	193	(134)	59

a. Calculate (1) operating income/revenues and (2) revenues/assets.

	Operating Income/Revenue	Revenues/Assets
Full-Service Lodging		
Select-Service Lodging		
Extended-Service Lodging		
Time Share		
Senior Living		
Distribution Services		

b. Evaluate the industry segment information for Marriott.

CASES

Case 1: Evaluating the Use of Business Combination, Divestitures, and Related Issues at Apple Computer

Analyze the following factors and concerns:

Factor	Analysis
Acquisitions in 2002	
Asset allocation decisions associated with acquisitions	
Use of goodwill	
Use of IPRD	
Segment reporting, especially lack of industry segments	

Case 2: Acquisitions by WorldCom

Consider these excerpts from a recent *Fortune* article (Charan and Useem, 2002)

> WorldCom founder Bernard Ebbers liked to eat. He ate MCI. He ate MFS and its UUNet subsidiary. He tried to eat Sprint. Wall Street helped him wash it all down with cheap capital and a buoyant stock price. Pretty soon WorldCom was tipping the scales at $39 billion in revenues. But there was a problem: Ebbers didn't know how to digest the things he ate. A born dealmaker, he seemed to care more about snaring new acquisitions than about making the existing ones—all 75 of them—work together. At least Ebbers was up front about it: "Our goal is not to capture market share or be global," he told a reporter in 1997. "Our goal is to be the no. 1 stock on Wall Street."

a. Calculate common-size (CS) amounts for WorldCom's abbreviated balance sheet information (in millions of dollars):

	2001 ($)	2001 (CS)	2000 ($)	2000 (CS)
Total current assets	$ 9,205		$ 9,755	
Property, plant, and equipment	38,809		37,423	
Goodwill, other intangibles	50,537		46,594	
Other assets	5,363		5,131	
Total assets	103,914		98,903	
Total current liabilities	9,210		17,613	
Long-term liabilities	34,680		22,431	
Northwest	57,930		55,409	

WorldCom had revenues of $35.2 billion in 2001 (down from $39.1 billion in 2000) and net income of $1.4 billion (down from $4.1 billion). Moody's rated senior debt at A3 and S&P at BBB+. Given that WorldCom had equity of $58 billion, is there any evidence that WorldCom was a problem company?

    b. WorldCom reported the following major acquisitions in its 2001 10-K:

Intermedia	On July 1, 2001, we acquired Intermedia Communications, for approximately $5.8 billion, including assumed long-term debt, pursuant to the merger of a wholly owned subsidiary with and into Intermedia, with Intermedia continuing as the surviving corporation and as a subsidiary of WorldCom.
Skytel Communications	On October 1, 1999, we acquired SkyTel Communications, Inc., pursuant to the merger of SkyTel with and into a wholly owned subsidiary of WorldCom.
MCI	On September 14, 1998, we acquired MCI Communications Corporation for approximately $40 billion, pursuant to the merger of MCI with and into a wholly owned subsidiary of WorldCom. Upon consummation of the MCI merger, the wholly owned subsidiary was renamed MCI Communications Corporation.
Embratel	On August 4, 1998, MCI acquired a 51.79 percent voting interest and a 19.26 percent economic interest in Embratel Participacoes S.A., Brazil's facilities-based national and international communications provider.
Compuserve	On January 31, 1998, WorldCom acquired CompuServe Corporation for approximately $1.3 billion, pursuant to the merger of a wholly owned subsidiary of WorldCom, with and into CompuServe.
Brooks Fiber Properties	On January 29, 1998, WorldCom acquired Brooks Fiber Properties, Inc., pursuant to the merger of a wholly owned subsidiary of WorldCom, with and into Brooks Fiber Properties.

These are only a fraction of the total number of acquisitions made by WorldCom. Given the amount of goodwill reported by WorldCom, analyze the likely valuation strategy used by WorldCom for the acquisitions. Is this a serious problem, and does it suggest a likely manipulation strategy? Explain.

    c. WorldCom reported the following in its July 22, 2002, 8-K filing: "On July 21, 2002, WorldCom, Inc. (the "Company") and certain of its direct and indirect U.S. subsidiaries (collectively, the "Debtors") filed voluntary petitions for relief under Chapter 11 of Title 11 of the United States Code (the "Bankruptcy Code") in the United States Bankruptcy Court for the Southern District of New York (the "Bankruptcy Court") (Case No. 02-13533)."

Should investors and analysts have been able to predict this bankruptcy of WorldCom on the basis of available public information? Explain.

    d. WorldCom issued the following statement in its 8-K filing of January 30, 2003:

As described in the Operating Report, the Company previously announced restatements of earnings affecting 1999, 2000, 2001 and first quarter 2002. In June 2002, Arthur Andersen LLP ("Andersen"), the Company's previous external auditors, advised the Company that Andersen's audit report on the Company's financial statements for 2001 and Andersen's review of the Company's financial statements for first quarter 2002 could not be relied upon. The Company's new external auditors, KPMG LLP ("KPMG"), are undertaking a comprehensive audit of the Company's financial statements for 2000, 2001 and 2002.

A Special Investigative Committee of the Company's Board of Directors is overseeing an independent investigation of these matters, led by William R. McLucas, former Director of the Division of Enforcement for the Securities and Exchange Commission ("SEC") and a partner with the law firm of Wilmer, Cutler & Pickering. The Company's accounting practices also are under investigation by the SEC, by the U.S. Attorney's Office for the Southern District of New York, and by the Examiner appointed by the Bankruptcy Court, Richard Thornburgh, former Attorney General of the United States. On November 26, 2002, the Company consented to the entry of a permanent injunction that will resolve claims brought in a civil lawsuit by the SEC regarding the Company's past accounting practices. The injunction imposes certain ongoing obligations on the Company and permits the SEC to seek a monetary penalty in the future.

The Company has terminated or accepted the resignations of various financial and accounting personnel, including its chief financial officer and its corporate controller, and is continuing its internal financial investigation. Investors and creditors should be aware that additional amounts of improperly reported pre-tax earnings may be discovered and announced. Until the Company has completed its internal review and KPMG is able to complete an audit of 2000, 2001 and 2002, the total impact on previously reported financial statements cannot be known. The Company intends to continue to announce unaudited changes to previously reported financial statements if it discovers additional issues.

Analyze this statement and evaluate the accounting and auditing environment and related ethical standards associated with business combinations and other accounting issues.

CHAPTER 10

Corporate Governance, Compensation, and Other Employee Issues

The corporate governance environment signals the likely potential for earnings management and related practices not in the interests of investors. As documented in Chapter 1, severe manipulation and fraud have been associated with loose governance and executive incentive structures conducive to opportunistic behavior. Compensation issues are important as part of the qualitative analysis to determine if the incentive structure makes earnings manipulation more likely. In addition to base salary and bonuses, compensation issues include stock options, pensions, and other post-employment benefits. These have earnings management potential and present additional problems for evaluating economic reality.

THE CORPORATE GOVERNANCE ENVIRONMENT

Historically, boards of directors were made up of corporate executives, investment bankers, major suppliers or customers, relatives, and other persons representing interlocking interests. The interests of insiders were promoted, with investor interests secondary. Of course, stock exchanges and bankers were subject to little regulation, audits were not required, and no accounting standards existed. As expected, corporate abuse, fraud, and financial collapse were common. With each round of financial fiascos, new rules and regulations were instituted.

The most extensive reforms came as a result of the market collapse of 1929 and the subsequent Great Depression of the 1930s. Federal and state laws provided much of the legal framework for reform. The New York Stock Exchange and other formal financial markets instituted new registration, financial reporting, and auditing regulations. New accounting and auditing standard-setters were established in the private sector. The regulations have expanded ever since.

Despite expanding regulatory requirements, executives and others had little trouble circumventing the regulations. It took the market collapse of 2000 and the recession of 2001 to reveal the extent of the interrelated problems. Regulations intensified at all levels in the early twenty-first century, and the debate continues on how extensive reform needs to be. From the earnings management perspective of major corporations, the environment for abuse starts at the top, the board of directors. The members of the board and the existing corporate governance structure are significant signals of the potential for earnings manipulation and opportunistic behavior. Thanks in part to beefed-up regulatory requirements, the current governance structure is more likely to limit further abuses. The problem is that incentives for abuse have not changed much.

Evaluating the corporate governance environment is a qualitative analysis, based on a review of the proxy statement, annual report, corporate Web site, and other sources. The topic is complex and involves many interrelated aspects. Six areas related to corporate governance are particularly important: (1) the CEO and board of directors, (2) executive compensation, (3) auditing, (4) related-party transactions, (5) insider trading, (6) investment banking relationships, and (7) evidence of past abuse.

THE CEO AND BOARD OF DIRECTORS

The board of directors is responsible for the overall business strategy, long-range planning, hiring and determining compensation terms of executives, and oversight, including audit overviews. The chief executive officer (CEO) and other senior executives are normally responsible for day-to-day operations and developing plans and strategies for board approval. The professional responsibilities of these leaders are extensive, and they are rewarded with substantial compensation. How they function is central to the overall operations and future of the corporation, as well as the establishment of the earnings management environment of the firm.

Particular earnings management concerns associated directly with the board and CEO and detection strategies are shown in Table 10.1.

The current operating success of a major corporation rests squarely on the CEO and his or her executive team. The focus is on real economic performance, based on the execution of a successful business strategy. In addition, the CEO is central to the basic earnings management environment of the firm. The key issue is whether the company is run solely for the best interests of the investors on the basis of economic reality. Executive compensation may or may not be based exclusively on investor interests.

Concerns relate to the history of the CEO (or whatever title is used). The corporate founder usually has substantial control, because that person developed the company from scratch and picked the executive team and board members. The earnings management environment might be suspect, dependent on the management style, personal ethics, and other characteristics of the founder. After the founder leaves, the CEO is more likely to be a professional manager and to have relatively less control than the board. The competence of the individual is subject to evaluation, as is the potential for manipulation.

	EARNINGS MANAGEMENT CONCERNS ASSOCIATED WITH CEO AND
TABLE 10.1	**BOARD OF DIRECTORS**

Topic	Concern	Detection Strategy
Role of the CEO	Strong CEO with little or no control by the board; alternatively, weak CEO or poor fit to the job	Review proxy statements and other sources on biographical data on the CEO; the business media may have insight on the CEO
Composition of the board	Too many company executives, major customers or suppliers, friends or relatives of the CEO	Same as above, with particular attention to direct connections to the company
Committees of the board	Few committees exist beyond minimum requirement; obvious lack of competence or independence of committee members	Review proxy statement and other sources, specifically on board committees and specific members on the committees
Compensation of board members	Overly generous compensation, which may make them less objective on possible earnings management issues; compensation not tied to performance; board members not putting in an adequate amount of time and effort	Review proxy statement disclosures on board compensation, specific responsibilities of the directors, number of meetings attended

The board of directors has substantial control (limited to some extent by founders and other strong CEOs). Thus, the composition of the board, the number of board members, and the board's committee structure are major signals of the manipulation potential. Key factors could be the relative indifference of the board, its ability or willingness to stand up to a strong CEO, and possible collusion of board members in questionable acts. An ideal board comprises primarily outsiders, who are picked for competence rather than because they are friends of the CEO. Deviations signal potential earnings management problems. The number of board members, the relative split between internal (company executives and directors with direct connections to the firm) and external members, background and training, performance requirements, and compensation are issues to review.

The existence of board committees is important to the specific performance of the board. Many of the crucial board functions are directed to specific committees. All major corporations now are required to have an audit committee and a compensation committee, and firms may have additional committees as well. Committee structure and composition should be reviewed to ensure independence and relative competence. The number of meetings held by the specific committees during the year gives some indication of the relative seriousness of the committee members.

Compensation packages differ substantially from one company to another. Compensation can include cash payments, bonuses, ownership interests in various forms, stock options, and various perquisites. The compensation package should be commensurate with the responsibilities and time commitments required. The specific composition of the package also may be an indicator of the expected behavior of the board.

Detailed information on the board of directors, senior executives, auditing, and executive compensation for Apple Computer is available in both the proxy statement and the 10-K. The proxy statement is issued to stockholders to provide information for voting on directors and other important issues at the annual meeting. The analysis below is based on Apple's 2002 proxy statement (issued for the April 2002 annual meeting), which was updated by information in the 2002 10-K (for year-end September 30, 2002).

Steve Jobs, original cofounder of Apple, is CEO and a director. As a founder, he is in a unique position of control and has been highly visible in the high-tech and business community. He takes $1 (not a typo, only one buck) as base salary but has substantial stock options and has received bonuses and other perks. Given the composition of the board, Jobs seems firmly in charge—great news for Steve Jobs fans but a concern in terms of earnings management considerations.

According to the proxy statement, Apple had only six directors, all corporate CEOs (Larry Ellison of Oracle resigned in September 2002, leaving only five). This small a board is very unusual (GE, for example, has 16 board members), as was pointed out as a concern by Levitt (2002), mainly because of possible independence issues. Board member Jerome York is CEO of Micro Warehouse, a major customer of Apple and not independent according to SEC and NASDAQ rules. In addition, director Millard Drexler is CEO of Gap; Steve Jobs was a director of Gap until he resigned in September 2002 (a problem of interlocking directors). Director William Campbell is chairman of Intuit, another high-tech company.

The stockholders elect all board members annually at the stockholders' meeting. At the 2002 meeting, only six people were on the ballot, and the mission was to pick the top six contenders—a Hobson's choice (that is, no choice at all). These six were the sitting directors. The board established a nominating committee in August 2001 to nominate new members of the board. Presumably, the committee will be more active in future years.

Apple no longer pays cash compensation to directors. Instead, stock options are granted annually (initially, 30,000 shares to each new director), and these vest in installments. Thus, their long-run compensation is tied directly to stock price performance. This seems reasonable, but it increases incentives to keep the stock price moving higher. In summary, Steve Jobs as CEO and the board composition raise some concerns on the earnings management environment for Apple.

EXECUTIVE COMPENSATION

The board of directors must have a compensation committee. The board determines executive compensation and generally approves employee compensation and benefits. The compensation agreements for senior executives are summarized in the annual proxy statement (and this information occasionally is found in the annual report). Employee compensation and benefits are summarized in the notes to the annual financial statement. Detailed notes usually are presented for pension plans and other post-employment benefits, stock options, and other compensation agreements. The qualitative analysis focuses primarily on the executive compensation packages.

Executive compensation has four basic components: (1) base salary; (2) bonuses, which are usually based on current earnings performance; (3) stock options (with restricted stock and stock appreciation rights ownership-based alternatives); and (4) various perquisites. Base salary is normally limited to $1 million because of IRS regulations on deductibility; however, performance-based salary, including bonuses, is effectively unlimited. Base salary usually is not an earnings management concern.

Bonuses can be important, because executives subject to large bonuses have increased incentives to meet bonus targets. Bonus targets typically are based on a specific definition of earnings, which means that executives would tend to focus on that specific target. Consequently, if the target is based on some definition of income from current operations (**above the line**), earnings management strategies are expected to dump losses as nonrecurring items (**below the line**). Stock options became more popular in the 1990s and with the booming stock market became a huge source of wealth to many executives. Consequently, the executive mindset seemed to focus on whatever it took to ensure that stock prices continued to ratchet up. Perquisites vary substantially, and their evaluation must be done on a case-by-case basis.

Executive compensation-related concerns include those listed in Table 10.2.

Apple's proxy statement (2002, pp. 4, 7, 8) defined the role of the compensation committee in some detail. The explanation of the role of the committee is fairly standard and is quoted in some detail in Table 10.3.

Prior to August 2001, the entire board served as the "compensation committee." The creation of a separate compensation committee and relatively formal policies represents a substantial improvement in terms of the corporate governance environment, as does having independent board members on the committee.

Of particular interest is the compensation of CEO Steve Jobs, described in the 2002 proxy statement as follows (p. 8):

> In December 1999, in recognition of Mr. Jobs' outstanding performance over the previous two and a half years, the Board awarded Mr. Jobs a special executive bonus in the form of a Gulfstream V airplane. The Board delivered the plane to Mr. Jobs during fiscal year 2001. Accordingly, the amounts paid during fiscal year 2001 towards the purchase of the plane and the tax assistance associated with the transfer of the plane were reported as income to Mr. Jobs. Mr. Jobs will continue to receive a salary of $1 per year for the services he performs as the Company's Chief Executive Officer.

TABLE 10.2	EXECUTIVE COMPENSATION-RELATED CONCERNS	
Topic	**Concern**	**Detection Strategy**
Composition of the compensation committee	Insiders included on the committee, suggesting lack of independence	Review proxy statement on the members of the compensation committee
Functions and authority of the committee	Lack of authority to adjust compensation to focus on executive performance	Review committee authority and specific decisions made
Specific compensation packages	Actual compensation paid does not match actual firm performance	Review annual compensation packages for each executive and correlate to basic performance indicators (those listed, if available)
Poorly performing companies	Overcompensation of executives based on actual performance	Same as above
Companies with previous abuse	Particular concern that compensation packages changed to increase compensation rather than match compensation with economic performance	Same as above plus history of abuses and actions company took to correct them

| TABLE I0.3 | THE ROLE OF APPLE'S COMMITTEE, AS QUOTED FROM THE 2002 PROXY STATEMENT |

Role	Description
Responsibility of the committee	The Compensation Committee is primarily responsible for reviewing the compensation arrangements for the Company's executive officers and for administering the Company's stock option plans. The Compensation Committee was re-established in August 2001 and, as a result, had an opportunity to meet and/or take action by written consent [only] once before the end of fiscal year 2001. Members of the Compensation Committee are Messrs. Campbell, Levinson and York.
Overview	The Committee reviews and approves the base salaries, bonuses, stock options and other compensation of the executive officers and management-level employees of the Company and administers the Company's stock option plans.
Performance	The Company's executive compensation program focuses on Company performance, individual performance and increases in stockholder value over time as determinants of executive pay levels. These principles are intended to motivate executive officers to improve the financial position of the Company, to hold executives accountable for the performance of the organizations for which they are responsible, to attract key executives into the service of the Company, and to create value for the Company's shareholders. The compensation for executive officers is based on two elements: cash compensation and equity-based compensation.
Cash compensation	The Company reviews executive compensation surveys in both the computer industry and general industry to ensure that the total cash compensation provided to executive officers and senior management remains at competitive levels so that the Company can continue to attract and retain management personnel with the talents and skills required to meet the challenges of a highly competitive industry. The compensation of executive officers is reviewed annually.
Bonuses	For fiscal year 2001, employees at the level of director and above were eligible for cash bonuses. Bonus payouts are dependent upon the Company achieving specific revenue and profit targets in conjunction with certain specified performance goals for individual business divisions. Several divisions achieved the metrics specified in the Bonus Plan and payments were made hereunder.
Equity-based compensation	In fiscal year 2001, the cornerstone of the Company's executive compensation program was equity-based compensation, principally in the form of stock options. Equity awards are typically based on industry surveys, market conditions, each officer's individual performance and achievements, future responsibility and promotion, the number of unvested options held by each individual at the time of grant and the number of above market options held by the individual. During fiscal year 2001, all of the Company's executive officers, excluding Mr. Jobs, received stock option grants under the 1998 Plan. The options granted under the 1998 Plan were at an exercise price equal to the fair market value of the Common Stock on the date of grant.

Since substantially all of Mr. Jobs; existing options are significantly underwater [worthless], in October 2001 the Compensation Committee recommended and the Board approved granting Mr. Jobs options to purchase 7,500,000 shares under the 1998 Plan in order to provide him with an incentive to continue to serve as the Company's CEO and maximize shareholder value. The options were granted at an exercise price per share of $18.30, which is equal to the fair market value of the Common Stock on the date of grant. 25% of the options were vested as of the date of grant and the remainder vest in three equal annual installments, commencing on the first anniversary of the date of grant.

The airplane is an unusual perk (accounted for as a special charge in 1999). The additional stock options could be considered excessive, again a problem in evaluating the compensation of a founder. The 2002 compensation for the senior executives is summarized by major category (from the 2002 10-K) in Table 10.4.

The bonus and "other" for Jobs was for "tax assistance" and other payments in 2001 related to the purchase of an airplane in 1999; "other" was matching contributions to 401(k) plans for the other executives. Performance for 2002 was relatively poor, so lack of bonus payments was not unexpected. The unusual compensation was for the CEO, beginning with the lack of a base salary, but a big bonus, new stock options, and "tax assistance." This was approved by the compensation committee, but the analyst should be skeptical of the corporate governance environment.

AUDITING

Corporations have both external audits and internal audit departments, which are the responsibility of the audit committee. Given the recent corporate scandals and the perceived deficiencies of external auditors, this oversight function is vital. Audit committees are now required by the major stock exchanges.

Potential concerns associated with the audit function include those in Table 10.5.

The role of the audit committee should be described in detail in the proxy statement, including the members, the role of the committee, analysis of the selection process of the external auditor, how the auditor is to be evaluated, and fees paid to the auditor. The auditor's report or opinion is presented in the financial statement section of the annual report. The content indicates whether there is an unqualified ("clean") opinion or if specific problems exist. Almost all opinions are unqualified ("the statements present fairly the financial position and results of operations … in accordance with GAAP"). A qualified or other opinion is a potential red flag. The date of the opinion indicates when the audit was completed; a relatively early date suggests a relatively problem-free audit. The corporation has 90 days to issue the 10-K from the end of the fiscal year, and auditor's reports coming close to or exceeding the 90 days may be a red flag.

Apple's audit committee responsibilities as stated in the 2002 proxy statement (pp. 7, 13, 14, 27, 28) are shown in Table 10.6.

TABLE 10.4	COMPENSATION FOR SENIOR APPLE EXECUTIVES IN 2002			
Executive	Base Salary ($)	Bonus ($)	Stock Options (Shares)	Other ($)
Steve Jobs	$ 1	$2,268,698	7,500,000	$1,302,795
Fred Anderson	656,631	0	0	11,000
Timothy Cook	563,829	0	0	8,025
Jonathan Rubinstein	452,588	0	0	9,996
Avadis Tevanian	492,212	0	0	10,700

TABLE 10.5	**CONCERNS ASSOCIATED WITH THE AUDIT FUNCTION**	
Topic	Concern	Detection Strategy
Composition of audit committee	"Insider directors" on the committee; potential lack of competence	Review proxy statement description on the audit committee
Audit procurement	Poor audit procurement practices; lack of disclosure on procurement practices	Same as above
Nonaudit services	Fees for nonaudit services excessive; potential for lack of auditor independence	Evaluate audit and nonaudit fees from the proxy statement for reasonableness
Audit opinion	Qualified opinion, indicating dispute with auditor; late audit report date	Review auditor's opinion in the annual report; determine number of days from end of fiscal year to audit report date
Auditor oversight	Committee oversight inadequate	Proxy statement should indicate due diligence, including number of meetings and discussions with auditors

The composition of the audit committee is of particular interest. Jerome York, as CEO of MicroWarehouse, is not independent. However, as a former CFO, he's the only member with the required background to effectively evaluate audit details. A February 2002 amendment to the written charter banned certain consulting services. More companies are adopting similar rules to ensure auditor independence.

The board appointed KPMG (a Big 4 firm) as auditor for fiscal year 2002 (a reappointment from 2001). This required a vote of the stockholders (Proposal 3 in the proxy statement). The specific criteria and auditor procurement procedures were not stated in the proxy statement. Fees charged by KPMG for 2001 (in millions) included those in Table 10.7.

Of the total $17.9 million charged by KPMG, 90 percent represented nonaudit services. When the audit fee represents only a small share of total revenue to the audit firm, the question of auditor independence arises. The audit charter now bans the auditor from performing information technology services, which represented 72.6 percent of fees (although most of that went to KPMG Consulting, now a separate firm).

The auditor's opinion was presented in the 2002 10-K. It was an unqualified opinion, indicating no major accounting or auditing problems ("the financial statements present fairly … in accordance with GAAP"). The report was dated October 15, 2002, only two weeks after the fiscal year end of September 30, 2002. Again, this suggests a relatively smooth audit process.

RELATED-PARTY TRANSACTIONS

Related-party transactions involve buying, selling, and other transactions with officers, directors, partners, employees, family members, and so on. Current accounting and auditing standards require the disclosure of these related-party transactions (only if material) but no more. These are not illegal or necessarily a violation of any kind. However, they signal potential earnings management issues. Thus, the perspective is qualitative—with a focus on corporate governance.

TABLE 10.6	APPLE'S DESCRIPTION OF AUDIT COMMITTEE

Role	Description
Responsibilities	The Audit Committee is primarily responsible for assisting the Board in fulfilling its oversight responsibility by reviewing the financial information that will be provided to shareholders and others, reviewing the services performed by the Company's independent auditors and internal audit department, evaluating the Company's accounting policies and its system of internal controls that management and the Board have established, and reviewing significant financial transactions.
Members	The Audit & Finance Committee (the "Audit Committee") is comprised of three members: Messrs. York, Campbell and Levinson. Both Mr. Campbell and Dr. Levinson are independent directors under the NASDAQ audit committee structure and membership requirements. Because of Mr. York's affiliation with MicroWarehouse, (see "Certain Relationships and Related Transactions"), he is deemed to be a "non-independent" director. As permitted under the NASDAQ audit committee structure and membership requirements, the Board carefully considered Mr. York's affiliation with MicroWarehouse as well as his accounting and financial expertise and determined that it is in the best interest of the Company and its shareholders that he continue to serve as a member of the Audit Committee.
Meetings	The Audit Committee met eight times during fiscal year 2001. It is required by charter to meet at least four times a year and review the status of the audit at least quarterly with the auditor.
Written charter	The Audit Committee operates under a written charter adopted and recently amended by the Board, which is included in the proxy statement as Appendix A.
Procedures	In fulfilling its oversight responsibility of reviewing the services performed by the Company's independent auditors, the Audit Committee carefully reviews the policies and procedures for the engagement of the independent auditor, including the scope of the audit, audit fees, auditor independence matters and the extent to which the independent auditor may be retained to perform non-audit-related services. The Audit Committee considered the independent auditors' provision of nonaudit services in 2001 and determined that the provision of those services is compatible with and does not impair the auditors' independence.
Nonaudit services	In February 2002, the Company adopted a new auditor independence policy that bans its auditors from performing nonfinancial consulting services, such as information technology consulting and internal audit services. The Company will continue to use its auditors to perform financial consulting in such areas as audits of statutory filings of foreign subsidiaries, 401(k) audits, SEC registrations, and tax compliance and planning. The new auditor policy mandates that an annual budget for both audit and nonaudit services be approved by the Audit Committee in advance, and that the Audit Committee be provided with quarterly reporting on actual spending. The policy also mandates that no auditor engagements for nonaudit services may be entered into without the express approval of the Director of Technical Accounting and the Chief Financial Officer.

TABLE 10.7	FEES (IN MILLIONS) CHARGED TO APPLE BY KPMG FOR 2001

Audit Fee	Information Technology	Tax Services	Financial Assurance	Other	Total
$1.8	$13.0*	$1.7	$0.7	$0.7	$17.9

*Included $10.5 million to KPMG Consulting, which was spun off in 2001.

The disclosure of related-party transactions is expected as a separate note in the financial reporting section and part of MD&A. Three related-party items were listed in Apple's 2002 10-K (item 13), as shown in Table 10.8.

These related-party issues could be viewed as part of normal operations and of no additional significance. Alternatively, they could be viewed as a signal of a permissive environment. There are plenty of examples of real manipulation with use of related-party transactions. One of the blatant examples was the use of special-purpose entities at Enron, when the partner providing the required equity was CFO Andrew Fastow or other Enron executives (more on this in Chapter 11). Adelphia concealed "rampant self-dealing by the Regas family, including the undisclosed use of corporate funds for Regas family stock purchases and the acquisition of

TABLE 10.8	RELATED-PARTY ITEMS LISTED IN APPLE'S 2002 10-K

Role	Description
Relocation loan	In connection with a relocation assistance package, the Company loaned Mr. Johnson (Senior Vice President, Retail) $1,500,000 for the purchase of his principal residence. The loan is secured by a deed of trust and is due and payable in May 2004. Under the terms of the loan, Mr. Johnson agreed that should he exercise any of his stock options prior to the due date of the loan, that he would pay the Company an amount equal to the lesser of (1) an amount equal to 50 percent of the total net gain realized from the exercise of the options; or (2) $375,000 multiplied by the number of years between the exercise date and the date of the loan. The largest amount of the indebtedness outstanding on this loan during fiscal year 2002 was $1,500,000.
Nonindependent board member	Mr. Jerome York, a member of the Board of the Directors of the Company, is a member of an investment group that purchased MicroWarehouse, Inc. (*MicroWarehouse*) in January 2000. He also serves as its Chairman, President, and Chief Executive Officer. MicroWarehouse is a multi-billion-dollar specialty catalog and online retailer and direct marketer of computer products, including products made by the Company, through its MacWarehouse catalogue. During fiscal year 2002, MicroWarehouse accounted for 3.3 percent of the Company's net sales. The Company also purchases products from MicroWarehouse for its own internal use.
Reimbursement for CEO	In March 2002, the Company entered into a Reimbursement Agreement with its Chief Executive Officer, Mr. Steven P. Jobs, for the reimbursement of expenses incurred by Mr. Jobs in the operation of his private plane when used for Apple business. The Reimbursement Agreement is effective for expenses incurred by Mr. Jobs for Apple business purposes since he took delivery of the plane in May 2001. During 2002, the Company recognized a total of $1,168,000 in expenses pursuant to this reimbursement agreement related to expenses incurred by Mr. Jobs during 2001 and 2002.

luxury condominiums" (GAO 2002, p. 122). Adelphia also concealed $2.3 billion in bank debt by shifting it to an unconsolidated affiliate.

INSIDER TRADING

Directors and managers buy and sell the stock of their company on a somewhat regular basis. This is an important component of **insider trading.** This is partially based on the use of stock options (more on that later in this chapter). Insider trading becomes illegal when someone (in addition to corporate directors or employees, it can include investment bankers, analysts, friends, and relatives) uses insider (nonpublic) information for personal gain. However, it's difficult to prove. As stated by Levitt (2002, p. 91):

> The Supreme Court had ruled, in a 1983 case called *Dirks v. SEC* [stock analyst Raymond Dirks passed on non-public information on fraud at Equity Funding to clients], that to bring insider-trading charges, the SEC must prove that the company insider providing the information acted in breach of a fiduciary duty by receiving a personal benefit. Examples of such a benefit might include cash payments or reputational gain. This was a high hurdle.

If a CEO tips friends and family to a pending merger and they trade on that information, that's insider trading. Former Imclone CEO Samuel Waksal was found guilty of exactly that.

Corporations are subject to two filings to the SEC on insider trading (from www.sec.gov), as shown in Table 10.9.

Of particular concern for evaluating the corporate governance environment is the potential for these executive insiders to profit from insider information. Purchases and sales don't prove illegal acts but provide potential signals of executive reaction to new events. Form 4 and Form 144 information is available by company on several financial Web sites (and these are more convenient than going directly to the SEC Web page). For example, MSN Money (moneycentral.msn.com) has both disclosures available by company. Form 144 indicates the intention to sell, and Form 4 represents the actual purchases and sales. Form 4 must be disclosed to the SEC by the tenth of the month following the actual trade. Note that this is not particularly current information.

The insider trading information was pulled for calendar year 2002 for Apple with use of MSN Money. The only transaction involving directors was the purchase of 50,000 shares by Arthur Levinson in August 2002. However, lots of sales (and no purchases) were made by senior executives during the year, as illustrated in Table 10.10.

TABLE 10.9	SEC-REQUIRED FILINGS RELATED TO INSIDER TRADING
Form 144	This form must be filed as notice of the proposed sale of restricted securities or securities held by an affiliate of the issuer in reliance on Rule 144 when the amount to be sold during any three-month period exceeds 500 shares or units or has an aggregate sales price in excess of $10,000.
Form 4	Every director, officer or owner of more than ten percent of a class of equity securities registered under Section 12 of the '34 Act must file with the Commission a statement of ownership regarding such security. The initial filing is on Form 3 and changes are reported on Form 4. The Annual Statement of beneficial ownership of securities is on Form 5. The forms contain information on the reporting person's relationship to the company and on purchases and sales of such equity securities.

TABLE 10.10	SALES BY APPLE SENIOR EXECUTIVES IN 2002 (NUMBER OF SHARES)			
Name	Month	Planned Sale (Form 144)	Transaction (Form 4)	
Avadis Tevanian (SVP)	May	87,920	87,920	
Peter Oppenheimer (SVP)	May	227,500	227,500	
Fred Anderson (CFO)	May	380,332	380,332	
Nancy Heinen (SVP)	May	75,000	75,000	
Sina Tamaddon (SVP)	May	250,000	—	
Timothy Cook (EVP)	May	302,500	127,500	
Fred Anderson (CFO)	April	472,500	200,000	
Nancy Heinen (SVP)	April	125,000	125,000	
Timothy Cook	April	397,500	—	

CFO = chief financial officer; EVP = executive vice president; SVP = senior vice president.

Substantial insider selling occurred in April and May 2002. Note, however, that not all planned sales were actually consummated.

Additional useful information includes the relative performance of Apple for the year, including performance and stock price. Quarterly revenues and earnings during calendar year 2002 are reviewed in Table 10.11.

Net income was modestly profitable early but turned negative in the second half of the calendar year. With the insider sales in April and May, the evidence is disturbing rather than compelling. The stock chart for the twelve months ended in early February 2003 (compared to NASDAQ and S&P 500) is shown in Figure 10.1.

The stock price started downward about the time of the insider sales. However, both the S&P 500 and NASDAQ also dropped at the same time. It could be argued that the sales represented the executives' views of the market rather than trading on specific insider knowledge.

INVESTMENT BANKING RELATIONSHIPS

Commercial banks service the cash and short-term financing needs of corporations. Investment banks initiate new public offerings of equity and debt securities, provide advice, fund acquisitions and divestitures, and offer a plethora of complex financial instruments, from leases to derivatives and special purpose entities. Other financial intermediaries offer insurance, broker services, and various financial services. The giant integrated banks offer all these services (thanks largely to huge merger deals). These are the one-stop-shopping sources for major corporations.

These services are extremely profitable, and the "full service" opportunities increase conflict of interest incentives across services. Thus, the lawsuits (and scandals described in Chapter 2) against Citigroup, Merrill Lynch, and other major investment banks for deceptive

TABLE 10.11	QUARTERLY REVENUES AND EARNINGS, APPLE, 2002 (MILLIONS OF DOLLARS)			
	December	September	June	March
Revenue	$1,472	$1,443	$1,429	$1,495
Net Income	–8	–45	32	40

FIGURE 10.1 **APPLE'S STOCK PERFORMANCE AFTER NEWS OF INSIDER SALES**

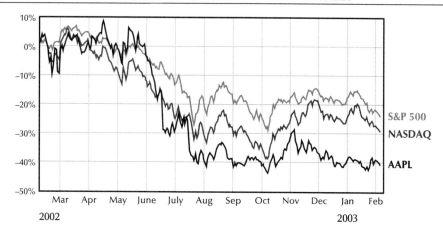

Period: February 8, 2002–February 8, 2003

practices resulted in fines approaching $2 billion. However, the incentives remain, and it's not obvious that the bankers are repentant.

Various questionable banking practices have been around for more than a century. Some are still legal. A recent *Business Week* article entitled "Tech's Kickback Culture" (Himelstein and Elgin 2003) noted that the tech bubble was fueled partly by an investor love fest for **initial public offerings** (IPOs). The tech companies often passed out pre-IPO stock grants or stock options to various decision-makers:

> The booming stock market had minted a new currency: a plethora of pre-ferred and friends-family shares from hundreds of high-tech initial public offerings. Much of the industry was lavishing this new payola on the top brass of customers, partners, and suppliers alike—dividing the loyalties of execs between their companies and their personal portfolios (Himelstein and Elgin 2003, p. 74).

Investment bankers have been involved in this same action and for the same basic reasons:

> During the boom, Wall Street firms allocated coveted IPO shares to the private accounts of CEOs such as Ford Motor Co.'s William Clay Ford and WorldCom Inc.'s Bernard J. Ebbers, allegedly to win future banking business. The influence-peddling spread beyond customers and suppliers—even reaching so-called independent research houses that write industry reports and market forecasts (Himmelstein and Elgin 2003, p. 74).

Giving gifts and granting stocks on a favored basis is not illegal (why not is unclear); but it signals a potential manipulation environment. Some high-tech companies have maintained employee investment policies that limit or prohibit this type of activity, including Dell, IBM, and Microsoft.

Investigating a corporation's investment banking relationships and the impact on the earnings management environment is easier said than done. Even companies with extensive deals can minimize the available disclosure, such as Enron with special-purpose entities and Tyco with acquisitions. Companies disclose commercial banking relationships, but investment banking disclosures typically are limited to specific new equity and debt issues. Disclosures may imply extensive and expensive relationships, but the impact on corporate governance can be difficult to evaluate.

Apple disclosed relatively little related to potential investment banking relations in the 2002 10-K. Five areas of disclosure were those in Table 10.12.

In summary, there is little evidence that investment banking relationships are extensive or would likely cause governance concerns at Apple. Note that the lack of evidence may be attributed to limited disclosure.

EVIDENCE OF PAST ABUSE AND ONGOING PROBLEMS

Thanks to the extensive regulatory environment and active business media, evidence of previous abuse and ongoing problems often can be found (and may be extensive). Many of the firms with the most blatant abuse are now bankrupt, but most of them are still around and are likely claiming to have mended their ways. Some have been embarrassed by one-time problems, but others are serial offenders.

There is no single source of past earnings management abuse. The evidence takes several forms, and some skill is required to track down the necessary information. Basic categories of possible abuse are shown in Table 10.13.

Prior to the mid-1990s, earnings restatements were rare events. A recent GAO report (2002) documents a sharply rising percentage since 1997. From 1997 to 2002, over 900 restatements were reported from almost 850 companies. Included were 80 restatements by S&P 500 firms. Consequently, it's now clear that major companies are likely to engage in earnings management abuse. The GAO report lists the 919 restatements by year (pp. 88–112). Consequently, a good starting point is to see if the company being evaluated is on this list. In addition, computer searches on "earnings restatements" or similar terminology should pick up more recent examples. Many of the companies discussed are on this list, including AOL (1997), Waste Management (1997, 1999), Sunbeam (1998), Rite Aid (1999), Lucent (2000), Enron (2001), Gateway (2001), Tyco (2001), Xerox (2001, 2002), Aldelphia (2002), Du Pont (2002), Reliant Energy (2002), and WorldCom (2002).

The Division of Corporation Finance of the SEC conducts desk reviews of SEC filings, currently with a major emphasis on 10-Ks. Questions by the SEC staff usually are handled by comment letters (which may be available through the Freedom of Information Act). Investigations and actions against wrongdoers are the responsibility of the Division of Enforcement.

The SEC has four categories of Enforcement Actions (see www.sec.gov), shown in Table 10.14.

TABLE 10.12	FIVE AREAS OF INVESTMENT BANKING DISCLOSURE BY APPLE IN THE 2002 10-K
New securities	Last debt issue was for $300 million in 1994; issued $150 million of convertible preferred stock to Microsoft in 1997
Acquisitions and derivatives	Fairly active in small acquisitions (see Chapter 9)
Derivatives	Used for hedging interest rates and foreign currency (see Chapter 11)
SPEs	None reported
Financial commitments	Operating leases, total minimum lease payments of $464 million

TABLE 10.13	BASIC CATEGORIES OF POSSIBLE EARNINGS MANAGEMENT ABUSE
Category	**Discussion**
Earnings restatements	When companies restate financial statements, it's a likely sign of manipulation.
SEC enforcement actions	The Division of Enforcement has several categories of enforcement actions, partly based on accounting problems.
SEC 8-K filings	Report material events or corporate changes of importance to investors; key events include auditor resignations and firings.
Bankruptcy filings	The company has failed and stockholders lose their investment; it's too late to take action by this time. Note that bankruptcy requires an 8-K filing.
Bond rating downgrading	Downgrading is associated with increased credit risk and other problems and is a major concern if the ratings go from an investment grade to a junk rating.
Business media	Documentation of problems often is reported, usually after the evidence has appeared elsewhere (e.g., earnings restatements).
Press releases	The company may disclose the discovery of past wrong-doings, such as findings from auditors, whistle-blowers, or other sources.

TABLE 10.14	THE FOUR CATEGORIES OF ENFORCEMENT ACTIONS BY THE SEC
Federal Court Actions	Litigation releases concerning civil lawsuits brought by the Commission in federal court.
Administrative Proceedings	Orders and related materials released by the Commission when administrative proceedings are instituted and/or settled.
Administrative Law Judges' Decisions	Opinions issued by Administrative Law Judges in contested administrative proceedings.
Commission Opinions	Opinions issued by the Commission on appeal of Initial Decisions or disciplinary decisions issued by self-regulatory organizations (e.g., NYSE or NASD).

The enforcement actions are listed by category on the SEC Web page. Of particular importance are the Accounting and Auditing Enforcement Releases (AAERs), which are mainly litigation releases (based on Federal Court Actions) and administrative proceedings (listed at www.sec.gov/divisions/enforce/friactions.shtml). Included here for 2002 are familiar names such as Adelphia, Dynegy, Xerox, WorldCom, and Rite Aid.

Apple had thirteen 8-K filings for the last five years (essentially from 1998 to 2002, based on a Lexis/Nexis search), none of which was serious. For example, 8-Ks reported that Apple changed its fiscal year end in 1998 and announced a half-billion-dollar stock repurchase program in 1999. On the other hand, Xerox reported 116 8-K filings for the last five years, many of which were serious. A December 2002 filing reported as follows:

> Registrant reported today that it has discovered an error in the calculation of its non-cash interest expense related to a debt instrument and associated interest rate swap agreements. The error, which was identified by Registrant and occurred with the adoption of Financial Accounting Standard No. 133 in January 2001, resulted in an after-tax understatement of interest expense of

approximately $5 million to $6 million or less than 1 cent per share in each of the four quarters of 2001 and for the first three quarters of 2002. To adjust for these items, Registrant will restate its 2001 financial statements and revise 2002 quarterly financial information. The restated financial statements are expected to be filed next month.

Web site searches can be useful for company press releases, media stories, bond rating downgrades, and related newsworthy information. The corporation's Web page is a good starting place for press releases and other company-specific news. "Company Capsule" at Hoover's Web page (www.hoovers.com) lists company press releases and stories mentioning the listed company. The bond rating agencies list their new bond-rating decisions and have complete corporate information on a subscriber-only basis.

Apple's recent press releases include earnings announcements (e.g., first quarter 2003 on January 15, 2003, posting a net loss of $8 million) and new product information. A September 20, 2002, press release announced the resignation of Larry Ellison from Apple's board of directors, a factor to consider when evaluating the corporate governance environment. Hoover's listed 166 stories mentioning Apple (for roughly the last three months), including several commenting on the first-quarter loss.

CORPORATE GOVERNANCE AT APPLE

Apple doesn't get particularly good marks for corporate governance. Potential problem areas were the cofounder serving as CEO, the composition of the board of directors (a non-independent member and an interlocking directorate), executive compensation of senior executives (especially stock options and perks for Steve Jobs), the composition of the audit committee (a nonindependent member), nonaudit fees paid to auditor KPMG (only 10 percent of total fees were for the audit), related-party transactions (three separate instances), and insider trading before reporting net losses and before the stock price declines of Apple. These raise concerns. However, considerable improvements were noted. The committee structure of the board of directors recently adopted more formal structures that were in line with NASDAQ requirements. These improvements should continue and be watched closely. The new nominating committee should suggest new independent board members, for example.

STOCK OPTIONS

Corporations often grant managers, directors, and employees stock options. Options permit the holder to purchase stock at a set price (the exercise price) over some fixed time period. The most common price is the closing market price of the stock at the issue date. At that price (or higher), the company is not required to record compensation expense, based on APB Opinion No. 25. However, expensing options would decrease net income and increase the volatility of earnings (because the expense is based on changes in fair value associated with the changing stock price).

After a lengthy and politically charged process, FASB issued SFAS No. 123 in 1995, which allows companies to either expense the estimated cost of stock options or use complex options-pricing models (such as the Black-Scholes model) to estimate the value of options and provide *pro forma* disclosures in the notes. Most companies use note disclosure rather than expensing options, although some companies such as General Electric are switching to expensing options. SFAS No. 123 requires considerable disclosure when options are not expensed. This information can be used to reevaluate the impact of options and normalize earnings by restating net income on a *pro forma* basis and recalculating performance and market ratios on that basis. On the balance sheet, the primary impact is classification between paid-in capital and retained earnings (e.g., when treating options as an expense, retained earnings are reduced).

When executives or employees exercise stock options, which are classified as nonqualified stock options for tax purposes, the employee pays cash to the company equal to the exercise (or strike) price determined at the date of grant. The company records this transaction as an increase in paid-in capital (with some details on the statement of stockholders' equity). In addition, the difference between the market price and exercise price (essentially the "profit" from holding the options) represents a tax benefit to the company (that is, it's a tax-deductible item) and a tax liability to the employees. When companies use the disclosure method (that is, they use APB Opinion No. 25 and don't expense the options), the tax gain should be reported directly to stockholders' equity rather than on the income statement. The tax benefit potentially could have a large impact on cash from operations. For example, Oracle's tax benefit for 2000 of $1.2 billion was more than half of cash from operations. In summary, the use of APB Opinion No. 25 for stock options can keep significant items off the financial statement, thus creating considerable earnings management concerns. Fortunately, disclosures are extensive enough to conduct considerable analysis and restate various financial statement components.

Stock options became a popular form of management and employee compensation in the 1990s, widely used by high-tech companies. With the stock market crash beginning in early 2000, the price of stocks and therefore the value of options dropped precipitously and often became worthless (the term "underwater" was widely used).

Why would executives, directors, and employees prefer stock options rather than higher salaries or cash bonuses? The advantage of the options is the one-direction participation in the success of the company. As the stock price increases, the value of the options rises. If the stock price plummets, the employee does not exercise the options. Stocks of high-tech companies have a history of substantial price increases (also many failures), so options have the potential to generate substantial wealth. Real tax advantages also exist for both the company and recipients.

Why would a corporation want to use options? First, as long as the exercise price is the market price or higher at issue date, no compensation expense needs to be recorded when using the APB Opinion No 25 method. In terms of the income statement, it can be a zero cost form of management compensation. Second, it should make the incentives of the managers identical to the owners of the company. Because the benefit of options is future ownership and managers increase the value of the options by increasing the value (i.e., stock price) of the company, management incentives parallel owner incentives. Firms can recruit successful and high-priced executives and retain existing managers and employees by issuing stock options liberally. This can be a useful "low-compensation" strategy for high-tech start-ups. Finally, the tax deductibility of exercised nonqualified options is beneficial.

THE COST OF STOCK OPTIONS

What is the downside to stock options? There are real costs, which can be recognized. The impact of stock options that are issued and exercised is the increase in number of shares outstanding, resulting in stock dilution. The earnings of the company have to be spread over more shares, decreasing EPS. The impact of future dilution is estimated by using diluted

EPS. If this has a potentially large impact on future EPS, it can represent a potential red flag. Because no compensation expense is recorded in most cases, the use of stock options can be considered a form of earnings management.

Apple summarized its stock option plans (and related incentives) in Notes 8 and 9 for fiscal year 2002. Separate plans exist for directors, executives, and employees. According to the notes, stock options are generally issued at fair market value (or above), become exercisable over four years, and expire ten years from the grant date. At the beginning of the 2002 fiscal year, 97 million option shares were outstanding. During the year, six million shares were exercised, five million canceled, and an additional 23 million shares granted, resulting in 109 million options outstanding at year-end (with an average exercise price of $27.18). Table 10.15 considers stock options outstanding at the end of the fiscal year relative to shares outstanding (in millions) for the PC competitors.

Apple's number of stock options outstanding was considerably higher than their competitors'. Assuming that an options-to-shares outstanding ratio greater than 10 percent is significant, stock option dilution is a concern to all three companies—but by far the biggest concern with Apple. At a current stock price (January 31, 2002, closing price) of 14.36, most options were "underwater." Of the 109 million options outstanding, only 22 million have an exercise price of $17.31 or lower (weighted average price for this group was $12.74—Note 8). Consequently, assuming only these would be likely to be exercised, then the dilution potential is only 6.1 percent (22/359).

Because of the potential dilution, *pro forma* calculations of the expense impact of stock options are important. The necessary information is available from Note 9, which compares Net Income–Reported to Net Income–*Pro forma*, which includes the estimated stock options expense as if included in income. Apple's *pro forma* calculations are compared with those for PC competitors Dell and Gateway in Table 10.16.

The *pro forma* difference was devastating to Apple's performance for 2002, changing a small net income to a much larger net loss. The difference also was substantial for Dell.

TABLE 10.15 | **STOCK OPTIONS AND SHARES OUTSTANDING FOR 2002**

	Stock Options Outstanding (Millions)	Shares Outstanding (Millions)	Options to Shares Outstanding
Apple	109	359	30.4%
Dell	350	2,654	13.2
Gateway	64	324	19.8

TABLE 10.16 | **EXPENSE IMPACT OF STOCK OPTIONS (MILLIONS OF DOLLARS)**

	Apple	Dell	Gateway
Net Income–Reported	$ 65	$1,246	$–1,034
Net Income–Pro Forma	–164	282	–1,106
Difference	229	964	72
% Difference	352.3%	77.4%	7.0%

Because Apple used the disclosure method (options were not expensed), the tax benefit from employees exercising options was recorded directly to paid-in capital (reported on the statement of shareholders' equity). Apple's tax benefit for 2002 was $28 million, compared to $7 million in 2001 and $110 million in 2000. Because Apple's cash from operations was $89 million, the tax benefit was equivalent to 31.5 percent ($28/$89) of CFO. In summary, the real economic impact of stock options for Apple was substantial and requires analysis to unravel.

ALTERNATIVES TO STOCK OPTIONS

There are a number of alternatives to stock options to reward executives (and sometimes employees), associated with the increase in share price. These include **restricted stock, phantom stock,** and **stock appreciations rights** (SARs). They tend to be more flexible than stock options, but the benefits (usually increases in fair value) are usually treated as compensation expenses by the corporations.

Restricted stock is a grant of stock to an employee in which the employee's rights to the shares are limited until the shares vest and are no longer subject to the restrictions. Typically, the employee may not sell or transfer the shares of stock until they vest, at which point the employee has full ownership of the stock. The restrictions usually involve working for a certain number of years or until specific performance goals have been met. Awards provide service or performance targets for employees to achieve before actually receiving shares or having the right to acquire shares. Unlike stock options or stock appreciation rights, restricted stock retains some value for employees even if the price goes down.

Phantom stock is a promise to pay a bonus in the form of the equivalent of either the value of company shares or the increase in that value over a period of time. It is taxed as ordinary income at the time it is received. SARs are similar to phantom stock, except they provide the right to the monetary equivalent of the increase in the value of a specified number of shares over a specified period of time. As with phantom stock, this is usually paid in cash but could be paid in shares. SARs can be granted in tandem with stock options to help finance the purchase of the options and pay taxes due when the options are exercised. SARs and phantom stock are designed to provide employees with the economic benefits of stock ownership without any actual transfer of stock occurring.

Given the increased flexibility associated with restricted stock, phantom stock, and SARs, they are expected to become increasingly common. Stock options are less popular with stockholders, who have seen bloated compensation paid to inept executives and the corresponding dilution of outstanding shares. Because these alternatives require the recognition of compensation expense, the awards should be more modest that stock options. Assuming that the FASB will require the expensing of options in the near future, then restricted stock and the other alternatives should become even more popular, because they can be tailored to individual needs without having the current disadvantage of being expensed.

Earnings management concerns will continue with restricted stock, phantom stock, and SARs. Of most concern are the relative level of compensation to senior executives and the specific terms of compensation agreements. The actual and potential rewards should be commensurate with actual performance and should provide appropriate incentives to managers. This requires the qualitative evaluation of disclosures in the proxy statements and 10-K.

THE RELATIONSHIP OF STOCK OPTIONS TO TREASURY STOCK AND DIVIDENDS

As discussed in Chapter 4, there can be a significant relationship between options, treasury stock, and dividends. Historically, companies have paid out a large percentage of net income as cash dividends. As companies used stock options, they became less likely to issue dividends and more likely to buy back outstanding shares and use the accumulated **treasury stock** when employees exercise options. Consequently, these should be evaluated together. In terms of cash flows, the use of stock options can be considered to have "inverse incentives"; that is, to focus on option incentives by purchasing treasury stock and limiting or avoiding the payment of cash dividends. This is a beneficial strategy for executives (especially for those who don't actually own much stock) but is potentially detrimental to any investors who prefer dividends.

The practice of buying back outstanding stock has a number of potential earnings management problems and can have a dramatic effect on the financial position of corporations. Acquiring treasury stock can be problematic because (1) acquisition reduces both cash and stockholders' equity. If substantial, this can have a sizable effect on standard quantitative financial analysis. (2) It can be used as a rationale for not paying dividends. The argument is that this is the best use of available cash and investors can "cash in" their shares if they disagree. (3) Large purchases can be used to prop up share prices (potentially when executives are selling their own shares, perhaps by exercising and cashing out their options).

Although Apple has a substantial cash balance ($2.3 billion, or 35.8 percent of total assets), the company pays no cash dividends. Apple has a stock repurchase plan initiated in 1999 (Note 7) and purchased 2.55 million shares for $116 million in 2000. No transactions were made in 2002, but the repurchase plan indicates the potential to acquire over six million shares. Normally, this would be recorded as treasury stock; however, Apple nets the purchases against paid-in capital (recorded as "common stock repurchased" in the statement of shareholders' equity). Simultaneously, Apple records the exercise of stock options as "common stock issued under stock option and purchase plan." Over the last three years (2000–2002), exercised stock options have been much larger than stock repurchased, meaning that the difference represented as "authorized but unissued shares" became "issued and outstanding." This disclosure makes it difficult to identify the repurchased stock, because it is not listed on the balance sheet. On the other hand, the amount involved is relatively small (2.55 million shares actually purchased), or less than 1 percent of outstanding shares.

An extreme case is Maytag, previously discussed in Chapter 4. At the end of 2001, options outstanding were 1.4 million, or 1.9 percent of outstanding shares. *Pro forma* net income was $39.2 million, compared to net income of $47.7 million, a reduction of $8.6 million or 17.9 percent—so far, a limited concern with *pro forma* net income. But accumulated treasury stock was 40.3 million shares, at a total cost of $1.5 billion. This was the major item that resulted in stockholders' equity of only $23.5 million. When compared to total liabilities of $3.1 billion, Maytag had a debt-to-equity ratio of over 130×. In other words, Maytag has almost no equity (less than 1 percent of total assets). On top of that, Maytag paid out $55.1 million in dividends (a dividend payout of 1.2 percent—dividends were greater than net income). Treasury stock was rising at a good clip over the previous three years, and it seems difficult to explain why, except Maytag's actions to maintain stock price. (Case 2 reviews Maytag in more detail.)

STOCK OPTION CONCERNS AND EARNINGS MANAGEMENT DETECTION STRATEGY

Based on the previous analysis, earnings management concerns and detection strategies are summarized as shown in Table 10.17.

Calculating dilution potential and option expense was just described and represents the most obvious direct impact of stock option use. After the burst of the tech bubble in early 2000, large numbers of outstanding options were quickly underwater (stock price below exercise price). That's the risk of options. Note that equity investors face the market risk of declining share price all the time. Investors are not sympathetic with management's loss. The managers have lost nothing except the potential for the vast rewards of stock price gains, while the investors' losses are real. Revaluing options (actually, reissuing new options to replace "underwater options") essentially rewards executives for the past lousy performance; that is, they can now make money as stock prices rise from the new lows. A similar executive focus also can be detected with the relative amounts of options to executives and directors rather than employees. Presumably, stock options can represent important incentives to long-term (and relatively poorly paid) employees. Not everyone believes that huge option rewards should be necessary to executives already paid million-dollar salaries and bonuses.

The relationship of stock options with treasury stock and dividend policy can be an important one and possibly suggests the emphasis on long-term executive compensation to the detriment of investors. This is partly based on relative philosophy. Historically, corporate success has been measured in terms of dividend payments. The big tax bite notwithstanding, using cash for treasury stock can be a smoke screen for maintaining stock prices

TABLE 10.17 | **EARNINGS MANAGEMENT CONCERNS INVOLVING STOCK OPTIONS**

Topic	Concern	Detection Strategy
Dilution	Substantial dilution potential (perhaps equal to 10 percent or more of outstanding shares)	Outstanding options at year-end (note disclosure) divided by shares outstanding at year-end
Option Expense	Substantial percent of net income (perhaps 10 percent or more)	Note disclosure on pro forma net income; calculate percent impact
Revaluing (or Reissuing) Options	"Underwater options" revalued regularly	Revaluations announced in option note; check for rationale and frequency
Relative Focus on Executives vs. Employees	Options too generous to executives and directors, while stingy with employees	Evaluate options policy in notes and MD&A; consider relative magnitudes compared to competitors
Use of Treasury Stock	Treasury stock as a poor use of cash plus reducing equity; used as a rationale for not paying dividends	Evaluate treasury stock magnitudes on balance sheet and changes on statement of stockholders' equity, plus note or MD&A disclosure
Dividend Policy	Policy promotes executive compensation to the detriment of investors	Quarterly dividends stated; calculate dividend payout relative to options and use of treasury stock

(advantage to options holders) rather than paying dividends. The most common arguments for buying treasury stock are (1) it's the best use of available cash and (2) the acquisition, given the current stock price when acquired, was a real bargain. For companies with a history of stock purchases during the stock price bubble of the late 1990s, these arguments are less than compelling, because inflated values of stock repurchased are recorded as negative equity.

PENSION AND OTHER POST-EMPLOYMENT BENEFITS

Pensions provide accumulated retirement resources. Larger employers generally provide some form of pension benefit. The two major categories are (1) **defined contribution plans** and (2) **defined benefit plans.** Firms with defined benefit plans and a large labor force have substantial obligations, which may or may not be fully funded. GAAP for defined benefit plans are complex and currently based on SFAS Nos. 87 and 132. Many corporations also have committed themselves to obligations for benefits to employees that have retired early or have left the firm for other reasons (called **other post-employment benefits,** or OPEB). SFAS No. 106 requires these commitments to be recognized as liabilities, and the accounting is similar to that of defined benefit pension plans.

PENSION PLANS

A pension is a long-term contract to provide retirement benefits to employees. Under a defined contribution plan, the employer makes periodic cash payments, usually based on a percentage of salary and often allowing or requiring employee matching. The funds are invested and the accumulated total investments plus portfolio earnings represents the retirement "fund," usually under the direction of the employees. The employer does not promise a specific level of future benefits. Defined benefit plans specify the retirement benefits the employee will receive. The most common plans are "pay-related" and determined primarily on some definition of "final salary" and length of service.

Assume that the defined benefit plan at Grumpy Gary's Gizmos provides a 2 percent of final salary retirement benefit for each year of service. Foreman Mitty Smitty retires after 30 years, making a final salary of $60,000; therefore, his annual retirement benefit is $0.02 \times 30 \times \$60,000$, or $36,000. The employer manages (directly or indirectly) the retirement fund, makes cash payments to provide pension assets that are invested in securities portfolios, gives cash payments to retirees, and handles all pension-related calculations and journal entries. Thus, the employer specifies the commitments and bears all the risk associated with meeting the pension obligations. Management of the pension plan must comply with federal law, based primarily on the Employee Retirement Income Security Act of 1974 (ERISA).

The incentives to offer pension plans are substantial. Pension contributions (both employer and employee) are income tax-exempt to the employees, and earnings on invested pension assets are deferred until the employee retires (and then only the employee is taxed, based on the pension annuities received by the employee—usually at a lower tax rate than when the employee was working). The pension can be considered part of the employee compensation package and may make employees more loyal to the company. In a defined benefit plan, dual incentives can exist. The company may feel paternalistic for employees' retirement and thus guarantee retirement benefits. Also, pension accounting for a defined benefit plan allows considerable judgment, and there is substantial room for earnings management. GAAP requires considerable income smoothing for defined benefit plans.

DEFINED CONTRIBUTION PLANS

Defined contribution plans are based on employers' cash contributions, usually a percentage of employee salary and often tied to employee contributions. The employee typically has investment portfolio options and generally has "ownership" of the portfolio after some vesting period. The company essentially has no additional obligations after the cash contributions are made.

Apple has a defined contribution plan complying with Section 401(k) of the Internal Revenue Code, a 401(k) plan, common in high-tech industries. This "employee savings plan" was described in Note 8 of the 10-K:

> The Company has an employee savings plan (the Savings Plan) qualifying as a deferred salary arrangement under Section 401(k) of the Internal Revenue Code. Under the Savings Plan, participating U.S. employees may defer a portion of their pre-tax earnings, up to the Internal Revenue Service annual contribution limit ($11,000 for calendar year 2002). The Company matches 50% to 100% of each employee's contributions, depending on length of service, up to a maximum 6% of the employee's earnings. The Company's matching contributions to the Savings Plan were approximately $19 million, $17 million, and $16 million in 2002, 2001, and 2000, respectively.

Both Dell and Gateway have similar 401(k) plans. Further analysis of pension plans for earnings management concerns is unnecessary for these companies.

DEFINED BENEFIT PLANS

In a defined benefit plan, the employer has an obligation for benefits to be paid to employees and invests in plan assets to meet these future obligations. Because the commitments are long-term and obligations recognized have to be estimated on the basis of many assumptions, pension accounting is quite complex. This section will review only highlights and focus on basic investor concerns. The pension accounting of General Electric will be used as a typical presentation. Accounting procedures are based on SFAS No. 87, with additional disclosure requirements from SFAS No. 132. See White et al. (2003, Chapter 12) for a more detailed analysis of defined benefit plans.

The plan assets of a defined benefit plan represent the fair value of the investment portfolio used to fund current and future retirement benefits, made up primarily of stocks, bonds, and other earning assets. The end-of-period plan assets essentially include the fair value of the plan assets at the start of the period, plus the return on plan assets, cash contributions from the employer and employees, less retirement payments during the period.

GE's presentation of plan assets (presented in Note 6) for 2001 is shown in Table 10.18.

Perhaps the most important actuarial calculation is the projected benefit obligation (PBO). PBO is the present value of amounts the employer expects to pay retired employees, based on employee service to date and expected future salary at retirement (as adjusted by various actuarial assumption, including average retirement age, mortality rates after retirement, number of employers staying to retirement, and so on). The GAAP calculations of obligations are based largely on PBO. GE's PBO calculation for 2001 is shown in Table 10.19.

Definitions of key items of PBO are provided in Table 10.20.

TABLE 10.18	BENEFIT PLAN ASSETS AT GENERAL ELECTRIC, 2001

	Fair Value of Assets (Millions of Dollars)	
	2001	**2000**
Balance at January 1	$ 49,757	$ 50,243
Actual return on plan assets	(2,876)	1,287
Employer contributions	75	85
Participant contributions	141	140
Benefits paid	(2,091)	(1,998)
Balance at December 31	$ 45,006	$ 49,757

TABLE 10.19	PBO CALCULATION FOR GENERAL ELECTRIC FOR 2001

	2001	**2000**
Balance at January 1	$ 28,535	$ 25,522
Service cost for benefits earned*	884	780
Interest cost on benefit obligation	2,065	1,966
Participant contributions	141	140
Plan amendments	–	1,155
Actuarial loss†	889	970
Benefits paid	(2,091)	(1,998)
Balance at December 31	$ 30,423	$ 28,535

*Net of participant contributions.
†Principally associated with discount rate changes.

TABLE 10.20	PROJECTED BENEFIT OBLIGATION (PBO) DEFINITIONS

Item	Definition	Discussion
Service Cost	Actuarial present value of benefits earned during the period	Importance of discount rate to determine PV plus other assumptions
Interest Cost	Increase in future pension payments, based on the interest owed on benefit obligation	Calculated as beginning PBO multiplied by the discount rate
Actuarial Loss	Changes in actuarial assumptions (can be net gain or loss)	Loss increases PBO
Benefits Paid	Actual cash retirement benefits paid	Reduces PBO, a cash outflow for the plan

GE's PBO increased almost $2 billion. Typical of most long-standing pension plans, interest cost was the major item increasing PBO. Both interest cost and service cost are sensitive to the discount rate. A higher discount rate reduces service cost but increases interest cost. The net effect of a higher discount rate is usually a net decrease in PBO (that is, the impact on service costs usually is greater than on interest cost).

The funded status of the pension plan is the fair value of plan assets less the PBO. The funded status of GE (from the note disclosures presented above, in millions) is

$45,006 – $30,423 = $14,583. GE's plan is overfunded. White et al. (2003, p. 412) refers to funded status as the "pension plan's economic position." However, funded status is not the amount actually recorded on the balance sheet. Recording funded status would result in volatility in the balance sheet amount, primarily because the fair value of plan assets can fluctuate widely from year to year—especially from stock market gyrations.

GAAP require that various smoothing devices be introduced to limit the fluctuations (extremely annoying to earnings management analysis; these require additional analytical tests). GE's calculations, which include all the smoothing components, are shown in Table 10.21.

GE starts with funded status, as described above. To that are added adjustments, defined in Table 10.22.

The impact of the adjustments is a decrease in net pension assets by $2,168 million ($14,583 – $12,415), plus a separate liability of $1,325 million. As defined in Note 6:

> The GE Supplementary Pension Plan is a pay-as-you-go plan providing supplementary retirement benefits primarily to higher-level, longer-service U.S. employees.

TABLE 10.21 PENSION FUNDING STATUS, GENERAL ELECTRIC (MILLIONS OF DOLLARS)

	Prepaid Pension Asset/(Liability) December 31	
	2001	**2000**
Funded status*	$ 14,583	$ 21,222
Unrecognized prior service cost	1,373	1,617
Unrecognized net actuarial gain	(3,541)	(12,594)
Net asset recognized	$ 12,415	$ 10,245
Amounts recorded in the Statement of Financial Position:		
Prepaid pension asset	$ 13,740	$ 11,377
Supplementary Pension Plan liability	(1,325)	(1,132)
Net asset recognized	$ 12,415	$ 10,245

*Fair value of assets less PBO, as shown in the preceding tables.

TABLE 10.22 ADJUSTMENTS TO GENERAL ELECTRIC'S PENSION FUNDING STATUS

Item	Definition	Discussion
Unrecognized prior service cost	The impact of plan amendments, usually increasing pension cost	Amortized over the average remaining employee service life
Unrecognized net actuarial gain	Reestimates of PBO based on restated estimates	Usually amortized over the average remaining employee service life
Prepaid pension asset	The net amount actually recorded on the balance sheet	The item is treated as part of "all other assets" (Note 17)
Supplementary Pension Plan liability	A separate liability unique to GE	Reported separately as part of "other liabilities"

Of particular concern are the underfunded plans, which represent a liability to the corporation—but this is not a problem at GE.

Now the income statement—where the real smoothing occurs. Each year the employer recognizes the net expense (pension cost), which includes annual service cost and interest cost (roughly the increase in the projected benefit obligation) plus or minus other adjustments. Essentially, the entry is a debit to pension expense and a credit to pension liability. However, one of the adjustments is to record the expected return on plan assets (note this is an "estimated return," not actual). This expected return can be large. It is always a positive, because real world year-to-year investment experience is not recorded. The result for GE is a "negative expense"; that is, the net effect is an increase in earnings. The reconciliation for GE for 2001, compared to the two previous years, is shown in Table 10.23.

For 2001, GE had a "net cost reduction" or "pension income" of $1.48 billion (note that this includes other post-employment benefits); in other words, GE's pension (and OPEB) plans increased earnings by almost $1.5 billion in 2001.

Definitions of key pension cost items are given in Table 10.24.

The disclosure for GE is "backward" in the sense that the result is "pension income," really a negative pension cost. The reason for that is the $4.3 billion recognized as expected return on plan assets, which is greater than the accumulated pension expenses. The major expense categories are interest cost ($2.1 billion) and service cost ($0.9 billion). The net pension income is $2.1 billion. Retiree benefit plan cost of $615 million is deducted, but this represents other post-employment benefits (discussed in the next section).

In summary, the key points for GE are that (1) the company is substantially overfunded, by $12.4 billion in terms of the amount that actually is recorded on the balance sheet; (2) the actual return on plan assets was a loss of almost $2.9 billion, a potential red flag; and (3) the company reported a negative pension cost, actually increasing net income. Further analysis is necessary to evaluate the earnings management potential and possible restatement of earnings to better understand economic reality.

Thanks largely to the rapid stock price increases in the 1990s, most defined benefit plans were overfunded by the end of the decade. However, the market collapse beginning early in 2000 changed performance results, and more firms have been moving into

---

| TABLE 10.23 | NET EFFECT OF PENSION PLAN (IN MILLIONS OF DOLLARS) |

| | Effect on Operations | | |
	2001	2000	1999
Expected return on plan assets	$ 4,327	$ 3,754	$ 3,407
Service cost for benefits earned*	(884)	(780)	(693)
Interest cost on benefit obligation	(2,065)	(1,966)	(1,804)
Prior service cost	(244)	(237)	(151)
SFAS 87 transition gain	–	154	154
Net actuarial gain recognized	961	819	467
Income from pensions	2,095	1,744	1,380
Retiree benefit plans cost (Note 5)	(615)	(478)	(318)
Net cost reductions from postretirement benefit plans	$ 1,480	$ 1,266	$ 1,062

*Net of participant contributions.

TABLE 10.24	KEY PENSION COST ITEMS

Item	Definition	Discussion
Expected return on plan assets	Expected long-term rate of return multiplied by the operating fair value of plan assets at the beginning of the year	Estimated (to smooth out volatility of actual return) rather than actual return
Service cost for benefits earned	Actuarial present value of benefits earned during the period	Importance of discount rate to determine PV plus other assumptions
Interest cost on benefit obligation	Increase in future pension payments (benefit obligation)	Calculated as beginning PBO, multiplied by the discount rate
Prior service cost	Prior service cost (based on plan amendments) amortization for the current period	Another adjustment "smoothed" over remaining employee service life
SFAS 87 transition gain	Technical adjustment based on the initial transition to SFAS 87 requirements and amortized	Same as above
Net actuarial gain recognized	Changes in actuarial assumptions (can be net gain or loss)	Gain reduces pension cost
Income from pensions (usually pension expense)	The pension cost (the net pension expense) recorded on the income statement	"Negative" pension cost for GE, increasing net income

negative territory. In addition, there are a host of earnings management issues that require additional analysis.

Earnings Management Concerns and a Detection Strategy for Defined Benefit Plans

Pension accounting for defined benefit plans has an "off-balance-sheet" focus, and much of the important information is not disclosed directly on the financial statements. Most of the significant issues can be analyzed based on extensive note disclosure. Accounting procedures are based on a substantial set of assumptions, primarily (1) actuarial rate assumptions and (2) GAAP requirements for smoothing procedures that incorporate a number of undisclosed assumptions. Given this structure, there are a number of specific concerns as well as procedures to better understand the real impact of defined benefit pension plans.

Key earnings management concerns include those listed in Table 10.25.

Some of these concerns are obvious from the previous discussion of GE; others need further explanation. Each will be discussed and examples included.

GE's pension plan was substantially overfunded for 2001, by $14.6 billion in terms of "real economic position" and by $12.4 billion based on reported funding level. However, other companies have substantial underfunding positions or face underfunding if the stock market continues to decline. General Motors (GM) recorded the information shown in Table 10.26 in the 2001 annual report (Note 14).

On the basis of funded status (economic position), GM was underfunded by $12.7 billion, a significant red flag. However, according to the reported funding level (net amount

TABLE 10.25	KEY EARNINGS MANAGEMENT CONCERNS POSED BY BENEFIT PLANS

Topic	Concern	Detection Strategy
Economic position	Pension plan "real" underfunding (based on funded status)	Calculate as fair value of plan assets less PBO (stated as funded status in notes)
Reported funding level	"Reported" pension plan underfunding	Note disclosure that records a net pension liability
Pension expense	"Negative" pension expense (increases earnings)	Note disclosure showing "net pension income"; evaluate expected return on plan assets; consider restating earnings net of expected return on plan assets
Expected return on plan assets compared to actual return	Actual return substantially lower than expected return	Compare based on note disclosure; consider restating earnings based on the difference
Actuarial assumptions	Aggressive assumptions for discount rate, expected return on plan assets, and rate of compensation increases	Compare disclosed rates to competitors and over time
Actuarial assumption trends	Changes in rates used may suggest earnings management	Same as above
Cash flows	Large employer contributions and potential for future contributions; large impact on cash from operations	Note disclosure on employer contributions; evaluate pension cost relative to net income
Investing in company stock	Pension plan has large holdings in company stock	Percentage stated in note should be reasonable for a diversified portfolio

TABLE 10.26	PENSION PLAN FUNDING AT GM IN 2001 (MILLIONS OF DOLLARS)

	US	Non-US	Total
Fair value of pension assets	$67,322	$6,340	$73,662
PBO	76,383	9,950	86,333
Funded status	–9,061	–3,610	–12,671 (RF)
Net amount recognized	19,320	–1,008	18,312

RF = red flag (needs further analysis).

recognized), GM was overfunded by $18.3 billion. The major items for the U.S. amount recognized were unrecognized actuarial losses and prior service costs, which totaled $28 billion. In other words, because of the "smoothing" requirements of SFAS No. 87, these losses/costs were not yet recognized. Consequently, net liabilities are substantially understated based on economic reality.

Pension expense for General Electric was actually "pension income," an earnings-increasing amount of $2.1 billion. This pension income is based on an expected return on plan assets of $4.3 billion. GE's net income for 2001 was $13.7 billion. Consequently, if the $4.3 billion less an assumed tax rate of 35 percent ($2.8 billion) were deducted from net income, net income would be reduced to $10.9 billion (a reduction of 20.4 percent).

Even more disturbing in terms of economic reality was the actual return on plan assets, a loss of $2.9 billion ($7.2 billion less than the expected rate of return). An alternative calculation (which reports actual or "real world" investment gains and losses) would be a restated net income number of $13.7 billion less $4.7 billion ($7.2 billion net of an assumed 35 percent tax rate), resulting in a restated net income of $9.0 billion (down 34.3 percent). By comparison, GM reported a net pension expense of $146 million for 2001, based on an expected return of $7.5 billion. The actual return was a loss of $4.4 billion. If real investment experience were recorded, GM's profit would be lower by $11.9 billion (before tax)! Because GM's net income for 2001 was only $601 million, this adjustment resulted in a net loss of $7.1 billion [$0.6 billion less ($11.9 billion, or 35 percent of $11.9 billion)].

Three actuarial assumption rates are disclosed in the pension note: the discount rate, expected return on plan assets, and rate of compensation increases. These are defined in Table 10.27.

These rates are necessary for performance calculations but have the effect of smoothing the income statement results. Particularly important is the return on plan assets, because the actual return represents economic reality and is easily determined. The rationale was that actual return is particularly volatile because of the continued gyrations of the stock market, which could substantially affect annual pension cost. As demonstrated above, pension cost can be restated to substitute actual return for expected return.

Companies have almost complete control of the assumption rates used but have to disclose those rates. Based on a 2001 survey, the most common return on plan assets was between 9 percent and 10 percent. Therefore, rates of 10 percent or more could be considered relatively aggressive. Most companies used discount rates between 7 percent and 8 percent, while most companies used compensation increases of 5 percent or less (White et al. 2003, pp. 406, 413).

Blankley and Swanson (1995) found that firms do not change discount rates as often as should be done to use current market interest rates. This was particularly true when market rates were declining (based on their sample years). By avoiding lowering discount rates, firms could report lower PBO and pension costs. They also found that expected rates of return changed infrequently, but this is consistent with the SFAS No. 87 requirement that they reflect long-run expectations. Their findings showed substantial volatility in the actual rate of return experienced by firms.

The rates used by GE for the last six years are shown in Table 10.28.

Rates used by GE stayed within the "average range" over the last six years. In addition, GE announced that the 2002 return on plan assets rate would be reduced to 8.5 percent. Because the actual return for 2001 was substantially negative and prospects for 2002 looked even worse, these return rates could have been lowered sooner and by larger amounts. Note that the impact of these high rates was to overstate net income, as described above. The largest change in rates was the increase of 100 basis points in the

TABLE 10.27	THE ACTUARIAL ASSUMPTION RATES DISCLOSED IN THE PENSION NOTE
Discount rate	Interest rate used to compute the present value of benefit obligations, which should be based on current (market) interest rates
Expected return on plan assets	Projected long-term return on plan assets, used to eliminate market volatility when calculating net pension expense
Rate of compensation increase	Assumption of average annual expected compensation increases

TABLE 10.28	RATES OF RETURN USED BY GE					
	2001	**2000**	**1999**	**1998**	**1997**	**1996**
Discount rate	7.25%	7.50%	7.75%	6.75%	7.00%	7.50%
Return on plan assets	9.50	9.50	9.50	9.50	9.50	9.50
Compensation increases	5.00	5.00	5.00	5.00	4.50	4.50

discount rate for 1999, roughly consistent with increasing market interest rates. For example, the average prime rate increased from 7.75 percent at the end of 1998 to 8.5 percent by the end of 1999.

As a large conglomerate with a substantial financial component, GE has no close competitors. General Motors is used for comparison, because it has both manufacturing and financial components. The rates for GM were as shown in Table 10.29.

The rates for GM were within the ranges of the average firm but on the aggressive end. Of some concern is the return on plan assets, which was maintained at 10 percent despite the stock market downturn early in 2000 (and GM's large actual negative return on plan assets). By comparison, GE's rates do not seem aggressive.

The major cash flows associated with the pension plan include funding of the plan assets (also called employer contributions), contributions by plan participants (but not funded by the company), and benefits paid (out of plan assets). Pension costs change net income and therefore represent a noncash component of cash from operations. The major concern is the potential necessity of huge cash outflows to fund underfunded pension plans.

GE funding policy for 2001 was stated as part of Note 6:

> FUNDING POLICY for the GE Pension Plan is to contribute amounts sufficient to meet minimum funding requirements as set forth in employee benefit and tax laws plus such additional amounts as GE may determine to be appropriate. GE has not made contributions to the GE Pension Plan since 1987 because the fully funded status of the Plan precludes a current tax deduction and because any GE contribution would require payment of excise taxes.

Thus, funding is not an issue for GE. Benefits paid were $2.1 billion, not a concern given the funded status of GE's pension plans. GM had pension plans underfunded by $12.7 billion, based on funded status. There would be considerable concern that a substantial employer contribution will be needed to adequately fund GM's plans.

Pension cost for GE was a negative $1.5 billion (i.e., net income was increase by this amount) and therefore part of CFO. This is not a particular concern for cash flows, but as described above, it is a potential concern for measuring performance.

Pension plans can hold company stock. For large plans, some percentage of corporate stock may be a reasonable component of a diversified portfolio. Note that mutual funds are

TABLE 10.29	RATES OF RETURN USED BY GENERAL MOTORS					
	2001	**2000**	**1999**	**1998**	**1997**	**1996**
Discount rate	7.3%	7.3%	7.8%	7.3%	7.0%	7.5%
Return on plan assets	10.0	10.0	10.0	10.0	10.0	10.0
Compensation increases	5.0	5.0	5.0	5.0	5.0	5.0

limited to any single holding of 5 percent (based on market value) for any single corporate stock. The purpose is to ensure that these funds are well diversified. That 5 percent rule can be considered a reasonable rule of thumb for pension plans. GE stock represented 8.6 percent of pension assets for 2001 (down from 9.2 percent in 2000), higher than the 5 percent rule. Therefore, the pension plan has a somewhat increased risk associated with this relatively large holding.

In summary, there is no evidence of particular earnings manipulation by GE associated with pension plans. The plans are substantially overfunded and no aggressive assumptions were detected. However, accounting requirements for pension plans result in a number of "smoothing assumptions" that avoid "economic reality." Therefore, it is suggested that performance numbers (especially net income) be restated to eliminate the smoothing. In addition, funded status should be used as a replacement for prepaid pension asset (or liability) to determine the appropriate balance sheet amount.

OTHER POST-EMPLOYMENT BENEFITS

Historically, companies often provided early retired and other former employees certain benefits, with the costs recognized on a cash (or pay-as-you-go) basis. The most common benefits were health and other forms of insurance (with most health costs for the retired employees covered by Medicare at age 65). Particularly as health care costs rose, these obligations have increased. Because the potential obligations could be several billion dollars for large corporations, FASB increased accounting and disclosure requirements.

The accounting rules were changed with SFAS No. 106, which requires the other post-employment (entitlement) benefits (OPEB) to be recognized as liabilities, with accounting and reporting similar to pensions. SFAS No. 132 added additional disclosure requirements. OPEB can be funded (with invested assets, just like pensions) but tend to be unfunded because the contributions to OPEB plans are not deductible for tax purposes and accrued OPEB costs also are not tax-deductible (only payments for actual benefits paid are deductible).

When SFAS No. 106 was issued, companies could immediately recognize the total liability (called the transition obligation) as a write-off against net income or delay recognition and amortize the obligation over a maximum twenty years. GE chose the former and charged $1.8 billion (after tax) as a nonrecurring item (a big bath write-off). Other major corporations, including IBM and General Motors, also took billion-dollar charges to recognize the obligation immediately (in the early 1990s). Corporations that delayed recognition are likely still amortizing this smoothing item.

OPEB accounting procedures parallel those of pension plans, meaning lots of complicated assumptions and extensive disclosures. Those assumptions and disclosures are somewhat different because of the unique obligations and attempts to estimate long-run costs associated with health care and other commitments. The disclosures are basically the same as with pensions, and the focus will again be on GE. Apple did not recognize any OPEB obligations, common for relatively new high-tech companies using 401(k) plans and stock options.

GE's OPEB note (5) was similar to the pension presentation for 2001 above and had the same basic composition, including the asset portfolio valuation; calculation of the major obligation, called accumulated postretirement benefit obligation (APBO); calculation of the net liability position; and calculation of OPEB cost for the year.

The plan coverage was described this way:

PRINCIPAL RETIREE BENEFIT PLANS generally provide health and life insurance benefits to employees who retire under the GE Pension Plan (see Note 6) with 10 or more years of service. Retirees share in the cost of health-care benefits. Benefit provisions are subject to collective bargaining. These plans cover approximately 250,000 retirees and dependents.

The fair value of plan assets was as shown in Table 10.30.

The balance declined $260 million for the year, with cash contribution from GE and participants not large enough to offset benefit payments and the portfolio loss for the year. The investment portfolio included 6.4 percent GE stock, slightly overweighted for a diversified portfolio.

APBO is the actuarial present value of benefit earned and represents a "real economic obligation" (or at least an estimate). The discount rate is required to determine present value and is disclosed (the rate used could differ from the pension rate). As with pensions, the discount rate and changes in the discount rate have a major impact on the obligation calculation and the annual OPEB expense. Therefore, it is an earnings management concern. APBO has the same basic components as PBO, with service cost and interest cost the most significant items.

GE's APBO calculation is shown in Table 10.31.

The APBO increased by $374 million (5.8 percent).

Similar to pensions, the real economic net liability position (a net asset position is unlikely because of the tax requirements) is APBO less the fair value of plan assets. For GE, that's $6,796 – $1,771, or $5,025 million. This is the funded status, and to arrive at the liability recognized on the balance sheet, smoothing adjustments are added, as shown in Table 10.32.

TABLE 10.30   **FAIR VALUE OF PLAN ASSETS FOR GE**

	2001	2000
Balance at January 1	$ 2,031	$ 2,369
Actual return on plan assets	(163)	(85)
Employer contributions	466	300
Participant contributions	30	25
Benefits paid	(593)	(578)
Balance at December 31	$ 1,771	$ 2,031

TABLE 10.31   **GENERAL ELECTRIC'S APBO CALCULATION**

	2001	2000
Balance at January 1	$ 6,422	$ 4,926
Service cost for benefits earned	191	165
Interest cost on benefit obligation	459	402
Participant contributions	30	25
Plan amendments	–	948
Actuarial loss	287	534
Benefits paid	(593)	(578)
Balance at December 31	$ 6,796	$ 6,422

TABLE 10.32 SMOOTHING ADJUSTMENTS TO THE FUNDED STATUS		
	2001	**2000**
Funded status	$(5,025)	$(4,391)
Unrecognized prior service cost	909	999
Unrecognized net actuarial loss	1,393	818
Net liability recognized	$(2,723)	$(2,574)
Amounts recorded in the Statement of Financial Position:		
Prepaid retiree life plans asset	$ 66	$ 8
Retiree health plans liability	(2,789)	(2,582)
Net liability recognized	$(2,723)	$(2,574)

Unlike GE's pension plan, both funded status and the net reported amount are underfunded. The differences between the two are the annual amortized amounts for prior service cost and net actuarial loss being smoothed over several years. The net liability represents health plan costs less a small prepayment for life insurance.

The income statement reconciliation is similar to that for pension, with service cost and interest cost the major expenses. This is partially offset by expected return on plant assets (if provided—not all companies bother to provide any investment portfolio for OPEB). GE's table to calculate the net expense was as shown in Table 10.33.

GE recognized a net $615 million expense for 2001, which was "carried forward" as "net cost reduction" in the pensions note.

EARNINGS MANAGEMENT CONCERNS AND A DETECTION STRATEGY FOR OPEB

OPEB has an "off-balance-sheet" focus and presents concerns similar to those associated with pensions. These include limited information (little to none can be found on the financial statements), current and future obligations, and the various assumptions used. Earnings management concerns include those in Table 10.34.

GE's OPEB was underfunded by $5.0 billion (funded status), but GE reported a liability of $2.7 billion (1.0 percent and 0.5 percent of total assets, respectively). This is not a

TABLE 10.33 GENERAL ELECTRIC'S CALCULATION OF NET PLAN EXPENSE (MILLIONS OF DOLLARS)			
	2001	**2000**	**1999**
Expected return on plan assets	$(185)	$(178)	$(165)
Service cost for benefits earned	191	165	107
Interest cost on benefit obligation	459	402	323
Prior service cost recognized	90	49	8
Net actuarial loss recognized	60	40	45
Total cost	$ 615	$ 478	$ 318

TABLE 10.34	CONCERNS PRESENTED BY OPEB	
Topic	**Concern**	**Detection Strategy**
Economic position	OPEB "real" underfunding	Calculate as funded status; consider relative magnitude (e.g., as a percent of total assets); evaluate potential future obligations
Reported funding level	"Reported" OPEB underfunded	Note disclosure that records a net OPEB obligation; consider magnitude
OPEB expense	Large expenses recorded and potential that these will increase in future years	Note disclosure on cost; consider magnitude as a percent of net income
Expected return on plan assets compared to actual return	Actual return substantially lower than expected return	Compare based on note disclosure; consider restating earnings if significant
Actuarial assumptions	Aggressive assumptions for discount rate, expected return on plan assets, and rate of compensation increases	Compare disclosed rates to competitors' and over time
Actuarial assumption trends	Changes in rates used may suggest earnings management	Same as above
Investing in company stock	OPEB has large holdings in company stock	Percentage stated in note should be reasonable for a diversified portfolio

major concern, particularly because the pension plan was overfunded by $14.6 billion on the basis of funded status. Combining the two figures results in net overfunding of $9.6 billion ($14.6 – $5.0). This would be a major concern for companies when both the pensions and OPEB were underfunded. The OPEB investment portfolio had 6.4 percent of the total in GE stock, probably not excessive for a diversified portfolio.

GE's OPEB expense ("total cost") was $615 million, or 4.5 percent of net income (about 2.9 percent after tax), a moderate impact. Evaluating the investment portfolio usually is a minor issue, because it seldom is close to fully funding the OPEB obligation (and often is nonexistent). GE is no exception, and assets at $1.8 billion represent only 26.1 percent of APBO. Given the tax status of these funds (contributions are not tax deductible), this is expected.

The actuarial assumptions used for OPEB are similar to those for pension plans; however, the rates are not necessarily the same, and GE added a healthcare cost trend. GE's rate assumptions are shown in Table 10.35.

The discount rate, compensation increases, and return on assets are the same as for the pension plan and about average. Healthcare cost trends are large and rising and indicate a concern for future obligations.

As with the pension plan, there is no evidence of earnings manipulation by GE using OPEB. The earnings management strategy is clear—for example, significantly underfunding OPEB because of the adverse tax consequences of funding. Analysis is required to provide OPEB obligations and costs and convert the information to "economic reality."

TABLE 10.35	GE'S RATE ASSUMPTIONS WITH HEALTHCARE COST TREND ADDED		
	2001	**2000**	**1999**
Discount rate	7.25%	7.50%	7.75%
Compensation increases	5.00	5.00	5.00
Healthcare cost trend*	11.60	10.00	9.00
Return on assets for the year†	9.50	9.50	9.50

*For 2001, gradually declining to 5.0% after 2009.
†For 2002, the return on assets actuarial assumption will be 8.5%.

SUMMARY

This chapter included several important and complex topics related to management, compensation, and long-term employee benefits. The major categories were corporate governance, stock options, and retirement plans and other post-employment benefits. Corporate governance is a qualitative analysis of the top-down assessment of the earnings management environment, and the composition of the board, board members, and committee assignments represent important signals of potential problems. Executive compensation packages signal the incentives the managers have to manipulate earnings, including stock options. Stock options require substantial note disclosure but are not necessarily recorded as compensation expenses. Therefore, earnings management issues include the impact of options on both income and stock dilution. Major corporations usually provide retirement and other post-employment benefits. Defined benefit pension and OPEB plans are complex and require considerable note disclosure. This must be evaluated in detail to determine the "real economic effect" and potential earnings management issues.

QUESTIONS

1. Why are corporate governance issues important for evaluating the earnings management environment of corporations?
2. New corporate governance rules have been instituted by the SEC, PCAOB, and stock exchanges. Will these new rules increase analysts' confidence in the information presented in the financial reports? Explain.
3. Earnings management concerns associated with stock options include the incentive structure of executives and the "economic reality" of expenses and potential stock dilution. Why?
4. What is the common relationship of stock options, treasury stock, and dividends? Is this a potential problem?
5. Based on GAAP only, what are the most important earnings management issues associated with defined benefit pension plans and other post-employment benefit plans?
6. Based on "economic reality," what are the most important earnings management issues associated with defined benefit pension plans and other post-employment benefit plans?

PROBLEMS

Problem 10.1: Corporate Governance at Hilton

Evaluate the following potential concerns associated with the corporate governance environment at Hilton (based primarily on 2002 10-K and 2003 Proxy Statement).

Area of Potential Concern	Analysis
CEO and Board	Barron Hilton, son of founder Conrad Hilton, Chairman of the Board, owns 6.2 percent of common shares; 13 directors, eight independent (four up for election in 2003)
Board composition	Cash payment of $40,000 a year plus additional compensation for attending meetings; four committees: Audit, Compensation, Corporate Governance & Nominating, and Diversity
Executive compensation issues	CEO Stephen Bollenbach paid $1 million in base salary in 2002, plus $1 million bonus, and $218,000 in other compensation, has 12 million stock options (10 million exercisable); net income, $198 million for 2002, up from $166 million in 2001
Audit issues	Four-member Audit Committee, all independent, five meetings in 2002; Ernst & Young, auditor, replacing Arthur Andersen in 2002 (auditor from 1981 to 2002); 2002 audit fee, $1 million; nonaudit fees, $1.2 million; audit report dated January 27, 2003, less than one month after the end of the fiscal year; 10-K issued March 28, 2003, just meeting 90-day SEC deadline
Related-party transactions	Property sales to RLJ Development, associated with director Robert Johnson; sale of notes to GE Capital (John Myers of GE, a Hilton director)
Insider trading	One sale in May 2002 of 18,330 shares by Albrecht Marial (not a senior executive)
Other issues	Banking relationship with GE Credit

Problem 10.2: Impact of Stock Options and Equity Dilution in the Hotel and Resort Industry

a. Hotel and resort companies have the following stock options outstanding and total common shares outstanding. Calculate the options-to-shares-outstanding percentage for fiscal year 2002 (in millions).

	Stock Options Outstanding	Shares Outstanding	Options to Shares Outstanding
Hilton	36.9	376	
Marriott	6.9	236	
Mandalay	9.9	114	

b. Hotel and resort companies have the following net income and pro forma income numbers. Calculate the difference and percent difference as if stock options were treated as an expense.

	Hilton	Marriott	Mandalay
Net Income—Reported	$198	$277	$53
Net Income—Pro forma	178	222	43
Difference			
% Difference			

    c. How significant is the potential dilution of stockholders' equity for these three hotel companies? Explain

Problem 10.3: Defined Benefit Pension Plans Analysis for Hotel and Resort Companies (None Reported for Marriott)

Given below is pension information for 2002 from pension footnotes and other sources (in millions). Benefit obligation at year-end is total pension liability based on PBO; pension expense is net periodic benefit cost; prepaid pension cost/obligation is net pension asset or liability position on the balance sheet (reported as part of other assets or other liabilities if negative).

	Hilton	Mandalay*
Benefit Obligation at year-end	$257	$55.5
Fair Value of Plan Assets	253	0.0
Net Periodic Benefit Cost (Pension Expense)	18	8.3
Prepaid Pension Cost (Liability)	11	14.8
Total Assets	8,348	4,037.0
Net Income	198	53.0

*Unfunded supplemental executive retirement plan.

    a. Calculate funding status (overfunded or underfunded, based on prepaid pension cost—O or U), pension obligation/total assets; prepaid pension cost (obligation)/total assets; and pension expense/net income. Note: Net Pension Benefit Cost is a negative expense for these companies (increases net income), because of positive expected return on plan assets.

	Hilton	Mandalay
Over- or Under-funded?		
Benefit Obligation/Total Assets		
Prepaid Pension Cost/Total Assets		
Pension Expense/Net Income		

    b. Compare the pension plans of the two hotel and resort companies. Are there any concerns? Explain.

CASES

Case 1: Corporate Governance at Apple

Evaluate the following potential concerns associated with the corporate governance environment at Apple.

Concern	Analysis
Steve Jobs (cofounder) as CEO	
Board composition	
Executive compensation issues	
Audit issues	
Related-party transactions	
Insider trading	
Other issues	

Case 2: Detailed Analysis of Maytag: Stock Options, Treasury Stock, and Dividends

1. The following information comes from Maytag's 2001 Balance Sheet (in thousands):

	2001	2000
Shareowners' equity		
Common stock		
Authorized: 200,000,000 shares (par value $1.25)		
Issued: 117,150,593 shares, including shares in treasury	$ 146,438	$ 146,438
Additional paid-in capital	450,683	285,924
Retained earnings	1,164,021	1,171,364
Cost of common stock in treasury (2001: 40,286,575 shares; 2000: 40,910,458 shares)	(1,527,777)	(1,539,163)
Employee stock plans	(23,522)	(31,487)
Accumulated other comprehensive income	(186,297)	(11,400)
Total shareowners' equity	23,546	21,676
Total liabilities and shareowners' equity	$3,156,151	$2,668,924

2. Maytag reported the following information on net income and comprehensive income:

	Year Ended December 31 (in Thousands)		
	2001	**2000**	**1999**
Net income	$ 47,736	$ 200,967	$ 328,528
Other comprehensive income (loss) items, net of income taxes			
Unrealized gains (losses) on securities	1,273	(3,564)	(671)
Unrealized gains on hedges	944	–	–
Less: Reclassification adjustment for loss included in net income	–	9,097	–
Minimum pension liability adjustment	(177,123)	3,471	(4,430)
Foreign currency translation	9	(1,442)	1,187
Total other comprehensive income (loss)	(174,897)	7,562	(3,914)
Comprehensive income (loss)	$(127,161)	$ 208,529	$ 324,614

3. At the end of 2001, Maytag had 1,427,240 stock options outstanding. Net income–*pro forma* (adjusting for options expense) was $39,182 (in thousands). The company paid $55,079 (in thousands) in cash dividends during 2001 (dividends were $0.72 a share).

4. Maytag's recent stock price was $27.70, one-year-ahead EPS forecast was $2.93, actual EPS was $0.62, and five-year earnings growth rate was 15.2 percent. Intrinsic value is $125.89.

a. Calculate the following ratios for 2001:

	Ratio
Return on Equity	
Return on Assets	
Return on Assets (using comprehensive income rather than net income)	
Debt to Equity	
Dividend Yield	
Dividend Payout	
Dilution potential for stock options (as a percent of shares outstanding)	
Percent decrease in net income based on pro forma stock options	

    b. Discuss these ratios, with particular emphasis on leverage and return ratios. Why do Maytag's ratios seem unusual?

    c. Explain why stockholders' equity is so low, given that retained earnings is over $1.2 billion.

    d. Is there a relationship between treasury stock and stock options? Explain. How does this relate to the level of stockholders' equity?

Case 3: General Electric's Pension Plan and OPEB, 2002

The pension and OPEB discussion included the 2001 results for GE. The following information is available for 2002.

Amounts reported on the financial statements:

Financial Statement	Account	Amount (in Millions)
Income Statement	Income From Pensions	1,556
Income Statement	Retiree Benefit Plan Cost (OPEB)	750
Balance Sheet	Net Asset Recognized (Pension)	14,066
Balance Sheet	Net Liability Recognized (OPEB)	2,979

Additional information related to pension and OPEB:

Account	Amount (Pension, in Millions)	Amount (OPEB, in Millions)
Funded Status	$4,545	$–6,009
Expected Return on Plan Assets	4,084	170
Actual Return on Plan Assets	5,251	–225

    a. Determine or calculate the following:

Balance Sheet-Related	Amount (Pension, in Millions)	Amount (OPEB, in Millions)
Is the plan over- or under-funded?		
Amount of over- or under-funding		
The "Real" or "Economic" Value of the plan		
The difference between GAAP-Reported and Economic Amount		

Income Statement-Related	Amount (Pension, in Millions)	Amount (OPEB, in Millions)
Is "Income" or Expense reported?		
Amount reported		
Amount of income or expense if expected report on plan assets is excluded		
Amount of income or expense if actual report on plan assets is substituted for expected return on plan assets		

    b.   On the basis of the information above, evaluate the impact of GE's pension and OPEB on the financial statement information.

CHAPTER 11

Risk Management, Derivatives, and Special-Purpose Entities

This chapter includes two major components: (1) **risk management** and the use of **derivatives** to hedge certain risks and (2) **special-purpose entities** (SPEs), which are legal financial entities used with more frequency by large corporations for a variety of financial and operating purposes. Operating and financial risks are widespread and corporations are required to disclose potential risks and how they are managed. An important component of risk management is the use of derivatives for **hedging.** Unfortunately, the use of derivatives is complex and can be used for a variety of nonhedging behavior. Thus, the use of derivatives is evaluated in the context of risk management. SPEs can represent any number of separate legal entities with the major intent of keeping the assets and liabilities off-balance-sheet. Therefore, the use of SPEs is considered a direct form of earnings management and is viewed with skepticism.

RISK MANAGEMENT AND DERIVATIVES

Corporate risks are associated with various types of financial and market uncertainty. Risk management is an attempt to reduce or control the multitude of risks associated with a complex corporation. Risks include those shown in Table 11.1.

TABLE 11.1	CORPORATE RISKS
Commodity risk	Changing prices of commodities such as agricultural goods, industrial metals, oil & other energy products
Interest rate risk	Interest rate fluctuations, complicated by fixed versus variable rates and duration (maturity dates)
Market value risk	Price fluctuations for items that trade on a market, including commodities, stocks, credit instruments, and currencies
Foreign exchange risk	Currency fluctuations against all other currencies, creating substantial risks for global corporations
Event risk	Uncertainties associated with any number of potential events, including fire, strikes, hostile governments; insurance can be provided to protect against some event risk
Credit risk	Probability of default on debt or of corporate bankruptcy; problem for credit sales and holding other debt instruments
Counterparty risk	Both parties on private contracts assume the risk that the other party will default

Corporations can use hedges to manage specific risks. Thus, hedging resembles insurance. Hedging can involve natural (or economic) hedges or be artificial. Natural hedges include matching asset and liability interest rates or foreign currencies. Derivatives are the most common form of artificial hedges. Hedges can reduce most of the risks stated above; however, usually not all financial risks can be eliminated simultaneously.

Corporations describe the use of derivatives and other measures to control risk in the MD&A or notes sections of the annual report. General Electric discussed the use of derivatives for interest rate and currency risk management as follows (MD&A, 2001 annual report):

> INTEREST RATE AND CURRENCY RISK MANAGEMENT is important in the normal business activities of GE and GECS. Derivative financial instruments are used by GE and GECS to mitigate or eliminate certain financial and market risks, including those related to changes in interest rates and currency exchange rates.

One means of assessing exposure to interest rate changes is a duration-based analysis that measures the potential loss in net earnings resulting from a hypothetical increase in interest rates of 100 basis points across all maturities (sometimes referred to as a "parallel shift in the yield curve"). Under this model with all else constant, it is estimated that such an increase, including repricing in the securities portfolio, would reduce the 2002 net earnings of GECS, based on year-end 2001 positions, by approximately $189 million; the pro forma effect for GE was insignificant.

The geographic distribution of GE and GECS operations is diverse. One means of assessing exposure to changes in currency exchange rates is to model effects on reported earnings with a sensitivity analysis. Year-end 2001 consolidated currency exposures, including financial instruments designated and effective as hedges, were analyzed to identify GE and GECS assets and liabilities denominated in other than their relevant functional currencies. Under this model, management estimated at year-end 2001 that such a decrease would have an insignificant effect on the 2002 earnings of either GE or GECS.

DERIVATIVES

A derivative is a financial contract *derived* from another contract. Complex financial arrangements can be made by using derivatives, always for specific reasons. Common derivatives involve options, futures and forwards, swaps, and collars. The basic derivative strategy expected from major corporations is an attempt to reduce or manage various market risks, usually by hedging. Reducing risks on financial instruments and currency fluctuations in a complex global market is expected. However, speculating (essentially *gambling* on a specific outcome or market direction) can be the strategy actually used. The problem for the analyst is to determine to what extent derivatives exist to effectively reduce various financial and other market risks and volatility (and in some cases operating risks) and when a company is doing a poor job hedging or is in fact speculating, thereby increasing financial risks.

Derivative contracting is a huge part of financial markets and gets complex quickly. Definitions of common derivatives are listed in Table 11.2.

Financial statement items subject to derivative use for hedging include those in Table 11.3.

TABLE 11.2	COMMON DERIVATIVES
Options	Agreements that give a party the right to buy (call) or sell (put) a specific quantity at a specific price (exercise price) until a specified maturity date; examples include commodities, currencies, and stocks
Forward Contract	Agreement between buyer and seller to deliver an asset in exchange for cash (or financial instrument) at a fixed price on a specific future date; examples include commodities, currencies, and stocks
Futures Contract	Standardized forward contract traded on an organized exchange; same examples as above
Swaps	Contracts to exchange one series of payments for another
Interest Rate Swaps	Contracts to exchange fixed for floating interest payments on bonds and other credit agreements
Currency Swaps	Agreements to make payments in one currency in exchange for the obligations in another currency
Collars	Derivatives that limit the effects of fluctuations beyond a set range, usually for foreign currency or interest rates

TABLE 11.3	FINANCIAL STATEMENT ITEMS SUBJECT TO DERIVATIVE USE FOR HEDGING	
Type	**Risk**	**Hedge**
Physical assets	Price changes	Forward or futures contracts, options
Financial assets	Interest rates	Interest rate swaps
Foreign currency	Relative currency prices	Foreign exchange swaps
Stocks	Price changes	Stock options

An airline might use forward contracts to fix the future price it will pay for jet fuel. Alternatively, call options could be used; the options would be exercised if fuel prices rose sufficiently (and not exercised if fuel prices dropped). Banks and other financial institutions have large portfolios of credit instruments both on the asset and liability side. These institutions match relative interest rates, including fixed versus variable rates and relative duration (maturity schedules). Mismatches can be offset by using interest rate swaps (e.g., swapping fixed for variable rates). Firms with multinational operations can do much the same with foreign currency swaps.

ACCOUNTING FOR DERIVATIVES

Accounting for derivatives is based on SFAS Nos. 133 and 138; these are relatively recent standards, issued in 1998 and 2000, respectively. Basic accounting rules are that derivatives are recorded in the financial statements and measured at fair value (marked-to-market). Holding gains and losses are recorded either as part of net income or as other comprehensive income. Derivative prices also affect how the "hedged items" are measured.

There are three categories of hedges, which determine how holding gains and losses are recorded. These are shown in Table 11.4.

Derivatives used to hedge for price-change risks are fair value hedges. The purpose is to control the risk exposure to market value changes, such as the value of inventory items or fixed income investments or obligations. For example, a futures contract can be used to hedge the value of current inventory (e.g., fuel, basic metals). If the inventory declines in value for the period, the derivative would record a gain on the income statement; at the same time (this assumes an effective hedge), a loss would be recorded on the income statement for the declining inventory value as the inventory item is written down on the balance sheet.

Cash flow hedges are used to control the volatility of future cash flows and include interest exposure on variable debt and certain types of forecasted transactions. Most foreign exchange hedges effectively are equivalent to cash flow hedges. Gains and losses for both cash flow and most foreign exchange hedges are recorded as other comprehensive income. The rationale is that market value is not at risk—only the level of cash flows. For example, a future payment denominated in a foreign currency can be hedged by using a foreign exchange forward contract. If the value of the foreign currency declines over the period, a gain would be recorded as an increase in the forward contract (on the balance sheet), offset as an increase in other comprehensive income.

TABLE 11.4	CATEGORIES OF HEDGES	
Category	Definition	Measuring Gains & Losses
Fair value	Hedge on exposure to changes in market value of existing asset or liability or firm commitment (e.g., commodity pricing, interest rate exposure on fixed rate debt)	Income statement as part of income from continuing operations
Cash flow	Anticipated transactions (e.g., futures contract) or interest rate exposure on floating rate debt	Other comprehensive income
Foreign exchange exposure	Hedge on changes in currency rates (e.g., foreign exchange swaps)	Other comprehensive income

Hedging a fixed-rate interest contract is a fair value hedge, while hedging a variable rate interest contract is a cash flow hedge. That's because interest rate changes affect the market value of fixed rate contracts of the interest agreement (but not cash flows if held to maturity). Changing interest rates have no effect on the market value of variable rate contracts, but they do change the amount of cash actually paid or received.

General Electric described hedging activities and defined specific use of derivatives in its 2001 annual report as follows:

> DERIVATIVES AND HEDGING. GE and GECS global business activities routinely deal with fluctuations in interest rates, in currency exchange rates and in commodity and other asset prices. GE and GECS apply strict policies to managing each of these risks, including prohibitions on derivatives trading, derivatives market-making or other speculative activities. These policies require the use of derivative instruments in concert with other techniques to reduce or eliminate these risks.
>
> CASH FLOW HEDGES. Under SFAS 133, cash flow hedges are hedges that use simple derivatives to offset the variability of expected future cash flows. Variability can appear in floating rate assets, floating rate liabilities, or from certain types of forecasted transactions and can arise from changes in interest rates or currency exchange rates. GE uses currency forwards and options to manage exposures to changes in currency exchange rates associated with commercial purchase and sale transactions. These instruments permit GE to eliminate the cash flow variability, in local currency, of costs or selling prices denominated in currencies other than the functional currency. In addition, GE and GECS use these instruments, along with interest rate and currency swaps, to optimize borrowing costs and investment returns. For example, currency swaps and non-functional currency borrowings together provide lower funding costs than could be achieved by issuing debt directly in a given currency.
>
> FAIR VALUE HEDGES. Under SFAS 133, fair value hedges are hedges that eliminate the risk of changes in the fair values of assets, liabilities and certain types of firm commitments. For example, GECS will use an interest rate swap in which it receives a fixed rate of interest and pays a variable rate of interest to change the cash flow profile of a fixed rate borrowing to match the variable rate financial asset that it is funding. Changes in fair value of derivatives designated and effective as fair value hedges are recorded in earnings and are offset by corresponding changes in the fair value of the hedged item. GE and GECS use interest rate swaps, currency swaps and interest rate and currency forwards to hedge the effect of interest rate and currency exchange rate changes on local and nonfunctional currency denominated fixed-rate borrowings and certain types of fixed-rate assets. Equity options are used to hedge price changes in investment securities and equity-indexed annuity liabilities at GECS.
>
> NET INVESTMENT HEDGES. The net investment hedge designation under SFAS 133 refers to the use of derivative contracts or cash instruments to hedge the foreign currency exposure of a net investment in a foreign operation. At GE and GECS, currency exposures that result from net investments in affiliates are managed principally by funding assets denominated in local currency

with debt denominated in that same currency. In certain circumstances, such exposures are managed using currency forwards and currency swaps.

DERIVATIVES NOT DESIGNATED AS HEDGES. SFAS 133 specifies criteria that must be met in order to apply any of the three forms of hedge accounting. For example, hedge accounting is not permitted for hedged items that are marked to market through earnings. GE and GECS use derivatives to hedge exposures when it makes economic sense to do so, including circumstances in which the hedging relationship does not qualify for hedge accounting. GE and GECS use option contracts, including caps, floors and collars, as an economic hedge of changes in interest rates, currency exchange rates and equity prices on certain types of assets and liabilities. For example, GECS uses equity options to hedge the risk of changes in equity prices embedded in insurance liabilities associated with annuity contracts written by GE Financial Assurance. GECS also uses interest rate swaps, purchased options and futures as an economic hedge of the fair value of mortgage servicing rights. GE and GECS occasionally obtain equity warrants as part of sourcing or financing transactions.

EARNINGS MANAGEMENT CONCERNS AND A DETECTION STRATEGY

The use of derivatives as part of corporate strategy gets complex quickly, and detecting earnings management strategies that increase risk is difficult. Risk management and derivatives use disclosures that can be evaluated for relative effectiveness. Certain signals may result in earnings management concerns, which are summarized in Table 11.5.

The typical financial analysis strategy is to consider basic points of derivative use. This includes the evaluation of objectives of derivatives used, the risk exposure of the corporation, hedging effectiveness, and whether derivatives are used for trading or speculation. GE has extensive disclosures and states in the 2001 annual report: "As a matter of policy, neither GE nor GECS engages in derivatives trading, derivatives market-making or other speculative activities." The evaluation of GE's risk management disclosures should support this assertion.

Hedge effectiveness is a measure of a hedging instrument's ability to offset the specific risk involved. Many derivatives exactly match the risk, such as direct currency or interest rate swaps or forward contracts on the specific commodity being hedged for price changes. However, direct hedges are not always available and substitutes are used, such as similar commodity forwards or using an interest index derivative to hedge a specific debt contract. GE disclosed the noneffective hedges for 2001 (Table 11.6).

With total assets of $495 billion at year-end, GE's disclosure suggests that ineffectiveness was only a minor factor in evaluating risk management. The gains and losses on cash flow and most foreign exchange exposure derivatives are recorded as other comprehensive income and therefore have no direct impact on income statement performance. Gains and losses of all other derivatives are recognized in the income statement. Therefore, some level of earnings management is possible by switching from one category to another. For example, a strategy could be to recognize gains as income but losses as other comprehensive income. Because of limited disclosure, this strategy is hard to detect. The statement of stockholders' equity should be analyzed, comparing relative foreign currency gains and

TABLE 11.5	**EARNINGS MANAGEMENT CONCERNS POSED BY RISK MANAGEMENT**

Topic	Concern	Detection Strategy
Risk Management	Effectiveness of risk management strategy questionable; strategies seem to increase risk rather than control it	Review risk management discussion in MD&A & evaluate compared to business strategy; compare to other companies
Hedge Effectiveness	Ineffective derivative effectiveness disclosed	MD&A or note disclosure on hedging effectiveness
Fair Value vs. Cash Flow Hedges	Evidence of earnings management on reporting gains & losses between income statement & other comprehensive income, e.g., reporting gains as fair value hedges and losses as cash flow hedges	Note disclosure of gain & loss recognition; compare gain & loss recognition in the income statement and statement of stockholders' equity; evaluate trends over time to determine unexpected patterns
Magnitude Changes	Large fluctuations (especially increasing) in derivative activity	Note disclosure, especially tables or other risk disclosures; calculate changing amounts
Counterparty Risk	Counterparties have below-investment-grade credit ratings	Note disclosure on counterparty risk; evaluate for default risk potential
Trading & Speculating	Disclosure of unexpected trading &/or speculation activity	MD&A disclosures; evaluate expected use of derivatives
Stock derivatives	Corporation using derivatives (usually puts) to "speculate" on company stock	MD&A and note disclosure; evaluate rationale for use

TABLE 11.6	**NONEFFECTIVE HEDGES USED BY GE IN 2001 (MILLIONS OF DOLLARS)**

December 31	Cash Flow Hedges	Fair Value Hedges
Ineffectiveness	$ 1	$ 26
Amounts excluded from the measure of effectiveness	$(1)	$(16)

losses reported as other comprehensive income. Consistently recording losses rather than gains suggests the earnings strategy above. GE had exactly that pattern. Currency translation adjustments showed losses for the last three years ($562 million in 2001, $1.2 billion in 2000, and $632 million in 1999). Also reported were "derivatives qualifying as hedges," with an additional other comprehensive loss of $955 million for 2001. Losses were more common than gains. As GE reported,

> At December 31, 2001, the fair value of derivatives in a gain position and recorded in "All other assets" is $2.3 billion and the fair value of derivatives in a loss position and recorded in "All other liabilities" is $3.8 billion.

The relative magnitude of derivative instruments is expected to stay relatively constant, since the purpose of hedging is reducing risk management. Large changes, especially increases, may be a cause for concern. For example, Enron reported that assets from price risk management activities increased from $4.1 billion in 1998 to $21.5 billion in 2000. Because the last balance sheet issued by Enron (3rd quarter 2001) showed $64.9 billion in total assets, the increase of $17.4 billion (or 424.4 percent) resulted in price risk management assets equal to 33.1 percent of total assets.

Credit risk of counterparties can be significant, representing the potential for default. As reported by GE,

> Counterparty credit risk is managed on an individual counterparty basis, which means that gains and losses are netted for each counterparty to determine the amount at risk. When a counterparty exceeds credit exposure limits in terms of amounts due to GE or GECS, typically as a result of changes in market conditions, no additional transactions are executed until the exposure with that counterparty is reduced to an amount that is within the established limit. All swaps are executed under master swap agreements containing mutual credit downgrade provisions that provide the ability to require assignment or termination in the event either party is downgraded below A3 or A–.

Thus, credit risk is relatively low at GE. Such was not the case for Enron, again according to assets from price risk management activities. Not only did assets increase over 400 percent, but the credit risk of counterparties dropped. In 1998, 16.5 percent of transactions were with counterparties with non-investment-grade status. This increased to 22.1 percent in 2000. The combination of rising derivative-based assets and declining counterparty credit status should have been recognized as a red flag and a major earnings management concern.

The focus of accounting for derivatives is on hedging as part of a risk management strategy. Derivatives may also be used for speculating, which can substantially increase financial risks. Beyond what companies disclose on speculation, it is difficult to evaluate the potential for speculation. As noted above, GE disclosed "derivatives not designated as hedges." GE claimed that certain hedges not specifically tied to specific assets or liabilities were a useful part of the risk management strategy. Thus, this use did not qualify for hedge accounting. The difficulty is determining when that is correct versus when the company is, in fact, speculating.

Somewhat related are companies that trade in derivatives. Investment banks often "make markets" in specific derivative instruments and record these as income from continuing operations. They also may trade for their own accounts, very likely speculating. The extreme examples of this were the failures of Long-Term Capital Management and Barings Bank in the 1990s because of derivative trading.

Derivatives can be indexed in a company's own stock. Several high-tech companies such as Microsoft and Dell sold put options in their stocks. The usual rationale was the relationship of these puts to employee stock purchase programs. As long as the stock prices were rising, the puts expired and the company pocketed the fee. However, when stock prices declined, the companies were forced to buy the stock in the open market to fulfill the option contracts. This resulted in losses—recorded directly to income. Thus, Microsoft recorded a $472 million gain in 2000, followed by a $1.4 billion loss in 2001. This is an unusual way to "participate" in the stock price success of a company, but it magnifies the risk. Additional gains are recognized in "good years," but losses follow in "bad years."

SPECIAL-PURPOSE ENTITIES AND STRUCTURED FINANCING

The topic of SPEs became particularly important with the financial collapse of Enron in 2001. In the October 2001 quarter 10-Q, Enron consolidated three SPEs in its financial statements, and income (a net loss of $569 million) and equity (a net reduction of $1.2 billion) were restated. Then Enron filed for bankruptcy. Enron's financial collapse revolved around SPEs. Enron had several partnerships using hundreds or perhaps thousands of SPEs, which were off-balance-sheet and unreported by the company prior to the 3rd-quarter 10-Q. What are SPEs? Can they be used to manipulate earnings on a massive scale? Are they common among America's largest corporations?

According to Financial Executives International, an SPE is a separate legal entity established by asset transfer to carry out some specific purpose. This entity could be a partnership, trust, or corporation. SPEs are a form of structured financing to achieve a specific purpose based on some set of financing or operating needs. These can be used to access capital or manage risk. Examples include leasing, sales, and transfer of assets to an SPE, which then issues debt obligations or equity for these assets, financing arrangements with third-party financial institutions, or various project development activities.

General Motors created SPEs to redevelop closed factories with environmental problems. Airlines created SPEs to hold airplane leases, keeping the liabilities off the balance sheet or even in the lease notes. Mortgage companies used them to consolidate and sell mortgages to investors. AOL Time Warner and Microsoft used SPEs to create synthetic leases (using sales-and-leasebacks through the SPEs) to borrow funds from financial institutions to finance fixed assets or other asset acquisitions. Even Dell dabbled in SPEs, creating a joint venture with Tyco International for computer financing of customers.

SPE accounting is difficult because the contracts and rules are complex and cover extremely diverse transactions. A key component is determining when they have to be consolidated in the financial statements rather than off-balance-sheet (and unreported). Generally, a third party has to maintain a 10 percent equity interest (up from 3 percent in January 2003) at market value for the SPE to be off-balance-sheet. The lack of a large enough third-party equity position was one of the violations at Enron, causing the restatements in the company's 10-Q.

SPECIFIC TYPES OF SPES AND HOW THEY'RE USED

The use of SPEs began in the early 1980s as a means of achieving specific financial benefits. Banks started moving loan receivables and mortgages into SPEs to get them off the books (that is, to reduce their reported liabilities) and then "securitize" them for resale as bonded debt instruments. Many companies started using synthetic leases primarily for tax advantages and the related off-balance-sheet treatment. American Express moved high-interest-cost debt into an SPE and, as a result, removed the liabilities from the balance sheet and recorded a gain of over $150 million on the transaction (using a process called **in-substance defeasance**).

A summary of the major uses of SPEs is provided in Table 11.7.

SPEs use structured financing, placing assets and corresponding liabilities into a separate legal structure, such as a corporation, partnership, trust, or joint venture. These are all common legal entities, but when used as SPE vehicles they have a limited life, a unique formal structure, and a specialized purpose. The SPE has relatively high transactions costs. Benefits must be substantial enough to fund these costs. Hopefully, the benefits represent legitimate business "savings" such as lower interest costs or tax savings rather than hiding excessive debt or camouflaging fraudulent activities.

The SPE has at least one equity investor, a trustee, and a servicer. The SPE must have an outside equity investor contributing assets (usually cash) of at least 10 percent of the fair value of assets. This is required for the originator (that's the corporation being evaluated)

TABLE 11.7	**MAJOR USES OF SPES**
Synthetic Leases	An asset (e.g., office building) is "sold" to the SPE and then leased back (sale-and-leaseback for accounting) to the originator. This is then treated as an operating lease for accounting purposes and as a loan for tax purposes. The company gets the tax benefits of interest and depreciation expense and the accounting benefits of off-balance-sheet treatment.
Securitize Loans & Mortgages	A bank "sells" outstanding loans or mortgages to the SPE; these receivables serve as collateral and the SPE repackages these and sells them as bonds or notes to investors. The bank remains as servicer and charges a fee to manage the original loans or mortgages, while the receivables are no longer on the books.
"Sell" Receivables	A manufacturing firm making credit sales eliminates some percent of the receivables by "selling" them to an SPE. The SPE uses the receivables as collateral to borrow the cash to fund the receivables, which is paid back to the company. The company now has cash and a lower receivables balance (suggesting that credit terms are more stringent than they really are).
Take-or-Pay Contracts	A take-or-pay contract requires the buyer to take some amount of product or pay a specific amount if refused. The contract can be used as collateral to fund a new manufacturing plant using an SPE.
Throughput Arrangements	Similar to take-or-pay, used primarily by gas or oil pipelines and requiring a specific guaranty of acquisition. The throughput contract (similar to a forward contract) can be used as collateral to fund the construction of a pipeline using an SPE.
Asset Construction Projects	An SPE can be set up to finance future construction projects by using a forward contract on the project, which is then used as collateral by the SPE to fund the construction. The construction costs and corresponding debt are off the books of the builder. Upon completion, the company can then lease back the fixed assets as a synthetic lease for additional tax benefits.
In-Substance Defeasance	An existing debt agreement is placed in trust with an SPE against specific assets (e.g., government bonds with essentially equal terms). Usually established to take advantage of lower interest rates than on existing debt.
R&D Costs	An SPE can be established to fund R&D, transferring the risk and avoiding recognition of either the expense involved or liabilities used to fund the ongoing R&D.

to avoid consolidation (i.e., to keep it off the books). The trustee is an independent third party paid a fee to advocate the interests of the SPE. The servicer provides the basic accounting and other administrative requirements, for a fee. This often is the originator, such as a bank servicing the loans or mortgages that have been securitized.

Supporters of the use of SPEs point out the obvious advantages. As stated by Kahn (2002),

> Like many complex instruments, SPEs were created to perform a straightforward, necessary task—isolating and containing financial risk. Businesses that wanted to perform a specialized task—an airline buying a fleet of airplanes; a company building a big construction project—would set up an SPE and offload the financing to the new entity.

In theory, SPEs protected both sides of the transaction if something went awry. If the project went bust, the company was responsible only for what it had put into the SPE; conversely, if the company went bankrupt, its creditors couldn't go after the SPE's assets.

Over time, SPEs became essential components of modern finance. Their uses expanded wildly—and legitimately. For example, virtually every bank uses SPEs to issue debt secured by pools of mortgages. And companies as diverse as Target and Xerox use SPEs for factoring—the centuries-old practice of generating cash by selling off receivables.

SPEs are also a good way to keep money away from Uncle Sam. Most tax-avoidance techniques using SPEs cleverly exploit discrepancies between accounting rules and tax laws. Synthetic leases are a good example.

AOL Time Warner (AOL) used SPEs for synthetic leases, receivables, and licensing contracts (e.g., network broadcasting). Outstanding balances at the end of 2001 are shown in Table 11.8.

AOL had substantial properties, the majority under operating leases. The company used a synthetic lease to fund the future corporate headquarters in New York (AOL Time Warner Center at Columbus Circle), at an expected cost of $800 million. As is typical of synthetic leases, this allows operating lease procedures for accounting but a financing arrangement for the IRS. AOL gets to deduct depreciation and interest paid for tax purposes.

GE and its financial arm General Electric Capital Services (GECS) reported the use of SPEs to dispose of credit card and trade receivables. As stated in the MD&A section of the 2001 annual report:

> GE and GECS are selling high-quality, low-yield financial assets to highly rated entities that have financed those purchases using low-cost commercial paper. ... Qualifying entities raise cash by issuing beneficial interests—rights to cash flows from the assets—to other GECS-sponsored special purpose entities that issue highly rated commercial paper to third-party institutional investors. These entities use commercial paper proceeds to obtain beneficial interests in the financial assets of qualifying entities, as well as financial assets originated by multiple third parties. The following table summarizes receivables held by special purpose entities:

TABLE 11.8	**OUTSTANDING BALANCES OF AOL SPEs AT THE END OF 2001 (MILLIONS OF DOLLARS)**		
	Committed Capacity	**Unused Capacity**	**Outstanding Utilization**
Accounts receivable	$1,480	$330	$1,150
Backlog securitization (licensing contracts)	500	58	442
Real estate and aircraft	480	93	355
Total	2,428	481	1,947

	December 31 (in Millions)	
	2001	**2000**
Receivables—secured by		
Equipment	$ 12,781	$ 7,993
Commercial real estate	9,971	7,445
Other assets	7,761	6,249
Credit card receivables	9,470	6,170
Trade receivables	3,028	3,138
Total receivables	$ 43,011	$ 30,995

These are substantial amounts of structured financing arrangements. Securitizing receivables is a standard operating procedure in financial organizations such as GECS. On the other hand, it's not clear to what extent analysts should view these as standard financing practices versus eliminating troublesome assets.

Lucent used SPEs to sell trade receivables and real estate financing. Problems arose because of Lucent's deteriorating credit risks, with bond ratings (for long-term debt) downgraded to B- by Standard & Poor's and Caa1 by Moody's. As stated in the 2001 annual report: "As a result of past downgrades, we no longer have the ability to participate in the commercial paper market and are unable to sell trade and notes receivables to the Trust."

Alcoa used take-or-pay contracts at its Australia subsidiary, which represented a $3.1 billion off-balance-sheet obligation as of 2001. This was equivalent to 18.9 percent of total liabilities. The contracts required the company to purchase minimum amounts of natural gas and electricity through 2022.

ENRON—EXTREME USE OF SPES

Enron used SPEs on a vast and fraudulent basis—and made SPEs infamous. Not only were Enron's financial statements misstated, but CFO Andrew Fastow and other executives enriched themselves by acting as the so-called independent third party trustees. At a minimum, these should have been disclosed as related-party transactions and, in many cases, consolidated in the Enron financial statements. The degree to which the SPEs were mishandled and CFO Fastow was allowed to manipulate these by both the audit committee and auditor Arthur Andersen is quite remarkable.

By the early 1990s, Enron had the largest natural gas transmission network in the United States, a 38,000-mile pipeline system. It also had substantial debt, which limited its ability to grow. The use of SPEs, partnerships, and joint ventures, rather than new debt, represented major vehicles to fuel new operations, especially into energy trading and other "new economy" businesses. The ethics of Enron at this time were questionable and declined. To meet quarterly analysts' earnings targets, Enron relied more and more on the magic of proclaiming revenues from SPEs, for example, when traders bet wrong on speculations (Swartz and Watkins 2003).

The two primary sources of information on Enron's use of SPEs are the 3rd Quarter 2001 10-Q and a report by the Special Investigation Committee of Enron's directors, called the Powers Report (after Chair William Powers of the University of Texas School of Law). Both focus on a few of the multitude of SPEs used by Enron and indicate the complexity used by Fastow and other insiders to dramatically misstate Enron performance and reward themselves, even for sham transactions.

Enron was a high flyer until 2000. The company had been transformed from a stodgy gas transmission company to a high-tech energy trading company. It expanded trading to include almost anything, including weather futures. The market agreed with this business strategy and, at its peak, the stock price hit $90 a share, giving it a market value of $80 billion.

The company's reports failed to explain the high-risk nature of the business or how much of the business was funneled through partnerships, joint ventures, and other structured finance contracts using SPEs. Of course, the related-party deals, massive off-balance-sheet liabilities (with high-risk compounded by side agreements using, among other things, Enron stock as the asset guarantying payment), and fraudulent transactions were not disclosed.

Other companies gained expertise in energy trading, driving down Enron's profitability and pushing it to assume greater risks and to venture into trading areas it had no expertise in. The end result was obvious. Losses, side deals gone bad, and other shady practices caught up with Enron—although complex, fraudulent transactions using SPEs hid the problems for a while. In mid-2001, the stock price started dropping, executives bailed out of their options, and SPEs "with no skin" (that is, no hard assets) could not be kept off the balance sheet (even with accommodating attorneys, auditors, and board members).

Enron had recorded net income of about $1 billion for both 1999 and 2000 and had total assets of $65.5 billion at the end of 2000. Enron announced in late October 2001 that it was reducing net income, and in early November the company announced that it was restating financial statements from 1997 to 2000. This reduced stockholders' equity by $1.7 billion (18 percent of equity). Then on December 2, 2001, Enron declared bankruptcy. A set of SPEs and partnerships by such names as JEDI, LJM, and Raptors proved to be central to the restatements. Somewhat like the utility pyramiding schemes of the 1920s, Enron had created a partnerships-and-SPE pyramiding scheme that collapsed.

Benston and Hartgraves (2002) pointed out six areas of accounting and auditing concerns with Enron:

> (1) The accounting policy of not consolidating SPEs that appear to have permitted Enron to hide losses and debt from investors. (2) The accounting treatment of sales of Enron's merchant investments to unconsolidated (though actually controlled) SPEs as if these were arm's length transactions. (3) Enron's income recognition practice of recording as current income fees for services rendered in future periods and recording revenue from sales of forward contracts, which were, in effect, disguised loans. (4) Fair-value accounting resulting in restatements of merchant investments that were not based on trustworthy numbers. (5) Enron's accounting for its stock that was issued to and held by SPEs. (6) Inadequate disclosure of related party transactions and conflicts of interest, and their costs to stockholders (pp. 106–107).

Although Enron's 2000 10-K was long and complex, very little was mentioned about SPEs. In fact, they weren't called SPEs. Note 16 on related-party transactions stated:

> In 2000 and 1999, Enron entered into transactions with limited partnerships (the Related Party) whose general partner's managing member is a senior officer of Enron. The limited partners of the Related Party are unrelated to

Enron. Management believes that the terms of the transactions with the Related Party were reasonable compared to those which could have been negotiated with unrelated third parties. In 2000, Enron entered into transactions with the Related Party to hedge certain merchant investments and other assets. As part of the transactions, Enron (i) contributed to newly-formed entities (the Entities) assets valued at approximately $1.2 billion, including $150 million in Enron notes payable, 3.7 million restricted shares of outstanding Enron common stock and the right to receive up to 18.0 million shares of outstanding Enron common stock in March 2003 ... [complex disclosures continue]

The SPEs were more or less disclosed, although the type of "limited partners," the fact that the Related Party was usually Fastow or a Fastow crony, and how these were reported relative to Enron's financial statements were not stated.

The 3rd Quarter 2001 10-Q disclosed that the restatements were based on the following related-party entities:

The financial activities of Chewco Investments, L.P. (Chewco), a related party which was an investor in Joint Energy Development Investments Limited Partnership (JEDI), should have been consolidated into Enron's consolidated financial statements beginning in November 1997; The financial activities of JEDI, in which Enron was an investor and which were consolidated into Enron's financial statements beginning in the first quarter of 2001, should have been consolidated beginning in November 1997; and The financial activities of a wholly-owned subsidiary of LJM Cayman, L.P. (LJM1), a private investment limited partnership for which the general partner's managing member was Andrew S. Fastow, former Executive Vice President and Chief Financial Officer of Enron, should have been consolidated into Enron's consolidated financial statements beginning in 1999.

Restatements of earnings were summarized as follows for 1997–2000:

	1997	1998	1999	2000
Net income as reported	$ 105	$ 703	$ 893	$ 979
Restatements:				
Consolidation of JEDI and Chewco	(28)	(133)	(153)	(91)
Consolidation of LJM1 subsidiary	–	–	(95)	(8)
Prior period proposed audit adjustments and reclassifications	(51)	(6)	(10)	(38)
Net Income Restated	$ 26	$ 564	$ 635	$ 842

JEDI was a joint venture with the California State pension plan (CalPERS), created in 1993 to invest in energy projects. Enron reported JEDI as an unconsolidated affiliate using the equity method. Enron bought out CalPERS in 1997 by setting up an SPE, Chewco, to take over CalPERS' share, with borrowing from Barclay's Bank. Enron employee Michael Kopper became manager. CFO Andrew Fastow, as a senior executive, would have had to disclose the related-party transaction in the proxy statement if he were the manager, according to auditor Arthur Andersen. (It's not clear why this wouldn't be disclosed as a related-party transaction, even with Kopper as manager.) Side agreements provided Kopper's "investment." Chewco was consolidated with Enron as part of the 2001 restatements, because it was an Enron subsidiary (it failed the 3 percent equity at-risk requirement then in force).

LJM1 and LJM2 were established in 1999 with Fastow as managing partner (later sold to Kopper). As stated in the 10Q: "Enron now believes that Mr. Fastow earned in excess of $30 million related to his LJM management and investment activities" (note 4). Many activities used SPEs relying on restricted Enron stock (which was substantially discounted—part of the "profit" claimed by Fastow and other partners). One SPE, LJM Swap Sub, was capitalized with liabilities greater than assets by $20 billion. This was an obvious violation for nonconsolidation. LJM2 also used SPEs called Raptors that used Enron put options to allow Enron to avoid recognizing losses on investments (i.e., these were "offset" by the put options)—a convoluted manipulation process without economic substance. Since the Raptors' major asset was Enron stock, the decline in Enron market price eliminated all pretenses that these SPEs could be used to avoid disclosing massive losses.

EARNINGS MANAGEMENT CONCERNS AND DETECTION STRATEGY

SPE use is widespread and justified as a viable approach for various financial and operating procedures. From an analyst's perspective, SPEs raise substantial concerns because of their ability to hide liabilities and certain types of operations. Even with substantial disclosure, it can be difficult to determine the true impact of structured financing activity on the balance sheet and other implications to earnings and cash flows. As demonstrated by Enron, the potential for blatant manipulation is present and can be hard to detect beyond basic signals of questionable activities. Specific concerns and possible detection strategies are summarized in Table 11.9.

Most corporations use SPEs for a limited number of peripheral operations. They should have legitimate purposes and be fully explained in the annual report, so that investors can evaluate the real impact of these operations and underlying obligations. Because the primary purpose of SPEs is to keep these items off-balance-sheet, they should be viewed skeptically. The use of SPEs represents a type of earnings management. The question is to what extent their use signals an environment of potential manipulation.

SPE disclosure should be in both MD&A and appropriate notes. This disclosure tended to be limited or nonexistent in the past, with Enron the most notable example. Therefore, the first step is to find the disclosure (there may not be a separate category called "special purpose entities"). The key question is the fit of SPE use to the overall business strategy. As noted above, their use fits certain categories. Most of these relate to financial services, so banks, other financial institutions, and other firms with substantial financial operations (such as GE) are likely to use SPEs. GE and GECS use SPEs to securitize receivables, an expected use of SPEs. On the other hand, the reported magnitude at $43 billion is large even by GE standards.

The problem of SPEs being used by companies struggling to survive is well illustrated by Lucent. A high credit rating is needed to effectively use SPEs to securitize various receivable categories. When Lucent's credit rating deteriorated, it was forced out of the commercial paper market, a significant part of its SPE usage. On top of a host of other problems, the failure of SPE use compounded the problem of raising funds as the credit rating declined.

TABLE 11.9	EARNINGS MANAGEMENT CONCERNS POSED BY SPES	

Topic	Concern	Detection Strategy
Fit to business strategy	No obvious reasons for using SPEs	Evaluate MD&A and note disclosures on SPE uses; compare to competitors
Relative magnitude of off-balance-sheet SPEs	SPEs result in substantial reduction in liabilities, understating the true financial position of the corporation	Evaluate debt levels and composition trends and compare to SPE disclosures for signs of a deteriorating liability position
Ambiguous disclosures	In the Enron category, may suggest an attempt to hide manipulation	Evaluate MD&A and note disclosure; compare to business strategy
Impact on financial ratios	Substantial negative effect on debt-to-equity, return on assets, performance, and financing costs	Calculate ratios based on financial statements and estimate revised amounts based on SPE disclosures
SPE use relative to credit rating and other credit risk characteristics	Firm with operating problems and declining bond ratings and credit risk resorts to SPE use	Evaluate bond ratings, ratings changes, and other measure of credit risk; then compare this to recent SPE use
Accounts receivable	SPE used to move substantial receivables off the balance sheet, making it difficult to determine credit terms and impact on sales	Determine receivables trends and relationship to sales over time; evaluate MD&A and note disclosure on receivables, SPE activity, and attempt to reevaluate receivables

SPE use to "factor" receivables has been a favorite off-balance-sheet strategy, but it suggests further evaluation related to credit terms, revenue recognition, and potential for rising bad debt rates. Removing receivables gives the appearance of an effective and disciplined customer credit strategy when, in fact, it may mean that credit standards are being relaxed to increase sales. The rising receivables and bad debt rates are then camouflaged by SPE use. This may be difficult to determine unless the note disclosure is comprehensive.

SUMMARY

This chapter included two complex components, both of which are difficult to fully evaluate for earnings management: risk management and special purpose entities. Given the complex global risks faced by major corporations, risk management is an essential component of accounting analysis. A company is expected to hedge major risk categories, often by means of derivatives. The derivative markets are complex and have been expanding rapidly. Derivatives can be used to hedge against specific risks and can be accounted for as fair value hedges (with gains and losses recorded to the income statement) or cash flow or equivalent hedges (with gains and losses recorded as other comprehensive income). The earnings management detection strategy focuses on the expected effectiveness of the hedging strategies and the potential for speculation (that is, increasing risks) rather than hedging.

Special purpose entities are separate legal entities established for some specific purpose and legally separated from the "parent" company. They are used for legitimate purposes, usually for off-balance-sheet reporting, tax benefits, and improved credit terms. From an earnings management perspective these are all suspect activities, because they mask economic reality and make a thorough analysis of operating, financing, and credit risk more difficult. Thorough disclosure is expected, but the actual information provided varies substantially by company. Enron was the most extreme example and indicated the potential for outright fraud with the use of SPEs.

QUESTIONS

1. How useful are MD&A disclosures on risk management for determining the fundamental risk levels of a corporation?
2. How can a derivative be used for hedging? For speculating? Can the analyst effectively determine the difference? Explain.
3. Why do cash flow derivatives differ from all other kinds of derivatives? What are the earnings management considerations?
4. Why are special purpose entities a particular earnings management concern?
5. Securitizing receivables may be the most common use of SPEs. Does this seem a legitimate use for SPEs or does it raise additional earnings management concerns?
6. Enron represented an extreme use of SPEs. Are there warnings signs for this type of fraudulent activity? Explain.

PROBLEMS

Problem 11.1: Financial Leverage and Solvency Ratios in the Hotel and Resort Industry

Below are financial numbers for three hotel/resort companies (in millions of dollars).

	Hilton	Marriott	Mandalay
Net Income, 2002	$ 198	$ 277	$ 53
Total Equity, 2002	2,053	3,573	941
Total Equity, 2001	1,783	3,478	1,068
Total Assets, 2002	8,348	8,296	4,037
Total Assets, 2001	8,785	9,107	4,248
Common Equity, 2002	2,053	3,573	941
Common Equity, 2001	1,783	3,478	1,068
Total Liabilities, 2002	6,295	4,723	3,096
Long-term Debt, 2002	4,554	1,492	2,787

a. Calculate the following ratios for 2002:

	Formula	Hilton	Marriott	Mandalay
Financial Leverage Index	ROE/ROA			
Financial Structure Leverage Ratio	Average Total Assets/ Average Common Equity			
Debt/Equity	Total Liabilities/ Total Equity			
Long-term Debt Equity	Long-term Debt/ Total Equity			

b. Evaluate the financial leverage and credit risk of these companies, including a rating from 1–10.

	Hilton	Marriott	Mandalay
Financial Leverage			
Credit Risk			

Problem 11.2: Risk Management, Derivatives, and SPEs at Hilton

Evaluate the following summary information from Hilton's 2002 10-K:

Topic	Analysis
Financing for franchisees	Provide secondary financing for franchisees, through loans of $48 million; provides mortgage construction financing through Hilton Managers Acceptance Corp., including loan guarantees
Timeshares	Sale of notes receivable to GE Capital for $125 million
Commitments	Guarantor on 12 operating leases to West Coast Hospitality; various performance guarantees to hotels operating by Hilton, $215 million
Derivatives	Interest rate swaps on long-term debt; foreign currency swaps
Unconsolidated affiliates	Joint ventures for Hilton HHonors Worldwide & Hilton Reservations Worldwide; investments of $291 million in affiliates, primarily using the equity method
SPEs	MD&A states specifically that Hilton does not use SPEs

CASES

Case 1: Risk Management, Derivatives, and SPEs at Apple

Evaluate the following summary information from Apple's 2002 10-K:

Topic	Analysis
Credit risk	Accounts receivable through third party resellers associated with bad debts risk.
Investments	Long-term equity & debt investments of $39 million
Derivatives	Interest rate swaps and collars on long-term debt; foreign currency forwards & options
Inventory risks	Orders for components placed in advance of customer orders; some components potentially in short supply; firm often dependent on specific third party suppliers located in foreign countries
SPEs	Not mentioned in 10-K

Case 2: Pepsi's Risk Management Strategy

PepsiCo presents substantial information on market risks and derivative use in their 2002 10-K. As stated in Note 10,

> We are exposed to the risk of loss arising from adverse changes in: commodity prices, affecting the cost of our raw materials and fuel; foreign exchange risks; interest rates on our debt and short-term investment

portfolios; and stock prices. In the normal course of business, we manage these risks through a variety of strategies, including the use of derivative instruments designated as cash flow and fair value hedges.

Fair Value: All derivative instruments are recognized in our Consolidated Balance Sheet at fair value. The fair value of our derivative instruments is generally based on quoted market prices. Book and fair values of our derivative and financial instruments are as follows:

	2002		2001	
	Book Value	Fair Value	Book Value	Fair Value
Assets				
Cash and cash equivalents	$1,638	$1,638	$ 683	$ 683
Short-term investments*	$ 207	$ 207	$ 966	$ 966
Forward exchange contracts†	$ 2	$	$ 6	$ 6
Commodity contracts†	$ 6	$ 6	$ 1	$ 1
Prepaid forward contracts†	$ 96	$ 96	$ 65	$ 65
Interest rate swaps†	$ 1	$ 1	$ 32	$ 32
Liabilities				
Forward exchange contracts‡	$ 3	$ 3	$ 2	$ 2
Commodity contracts‡	$ 2	$ 2	$ 17	$ 17
Debt obligations	$2,749	$3,134	$3,005	$3,270

Included in the Consolidated Balance Sheet under the captions noted above or as indicated below.
*Includes $82 million at December 28, 2002 and $89 million at December 29, 2001 of mutual fund investments used to manage a portion of market risk arising from our deferred compensation liability.
†Included within prepaid expenses and other current assets.
‡Included within accounts payable and other current liabilities.

Included in the Consolidated Balance Sheet under the captions noted above or as indicated here:

a. Includes $82 million at December 28, 2002 and $89 million at December 29, 2001 of mutual fund investments used to manage a portion of market risk arising from our deferred compensation liability.

b. Included within prepaid expenses and other current assets.

c. Included within accounts payable and other current liabilities.

The following information is presented on Commodity Prices:

Rationale (Note 10): We are subject to commodity price risk because our ability to recover increased costs through higher pricing may be limited in the competitive environment in which we operate. This risk is managed through the use of fixed-price purchase orders, pricing agreements, geographic diversity and cash flow hedges. We use cash flow hedges, with terms of no more than two years, to hedge price fluctuations in a portion of our anticipated commodity purchases, primarily for corn, natural gas, oats, packaging materials and wheat. Any ineffectiveness is recorded immediately.

Finances (MD&A): Our commodity derivatives totaled $70 million at December 28, 2002 and $252 million at December 29, 2001. These derivatives resulted in a net unrealized gain of $6 million at December 28, 2002 and a net unrealized loss of $16 million at December 29, 2001. We estimate that a 10 percent decline in commodity prices would have resulted in an unrealized loss of $2 million in 2002 and increased the unrealized loss by $18 million in 2001.

a. Evaluate the effectiveness of Pepsi's risk strategy for using commodities. Note that inventories totaled $1,342 at the end of 2002 and $1,310 in 2001.

The following information is presented on Foreign Exchange:

Rationale (Note 10): Our operations outside of the United States generated 34 percent of our net sales of which Mexico, the United Kingdom and Canada contributed 19 percent. As a result, we are exposed to foreign currency risks from unforeseen economic changes and political unrest. On occasion, we enter into fair value hedges, primarily forward contracts, to reduce the effect of foreign exchange rates. Ineffectiveness resulting from our fair value hedges was not material to our results of operations.

During 2002, the impact of declines in the Mexican peso was substantially offset by increases in the British pound and the euro. However, if future declines in the Mexican peso are not offset by increases in the British pound and the euro, our future results would be adversely impacted.

Finances (MD&A): Our foreign currency derivatives had a total face value of $329 million at December 28, 2002 and $355 million at December 29, 2001. These contracts had a net unrealized loss of less than $1 million at December 28, 2002 and a net unrealized gain of $4 million at December 29, 2001. We estimate that an unfavorable 10 percent change in the exchange rates would have increased the unrealized loss by $34 million in 2002 and would have resulted in an unrealized loss of $31 million in 2001.

In 2002, we hedged 2.1 billion Mexican pesos related to our net investment in Pepsi-Gemex which resulted in a $5 million gain upon our disposal of Pepsi-Gemex described in Note 8.

b. Evaluate the effectiveness of Pepsi's risk strategy for using Foreign Exchange. Note the exposure in British pounds versus the Mexican peso. Will the strategy used be effective in the future?

The following information is presented on interest rates:

Rationale: We centrally manage our debt and investment portfolios considering investment opportunities and risks, tax consequences and overall financing strategies. We have used interest rate swaps to effectively change the interest rate of specific debt issuances, with the objective of reducing our overall borrowing costs.

Finances: Late in 2002, we terminated the majority of our interest rate swaps used to manage our interest rate risk. As a result, 12 percent of our debt is exposed to variable interest rates compared to approximately 45 percent in 2001. Assuming year-end variable rate debt and investment levels, a 1 percentage point increase in interest rates would have reduced net interest expense by $11 million in 2002 and increased net interest expense by $3 million in 2001. The impact of the 1 percentage point increase in rates at year-end 2002 reflects higher investment balances and lower variable debt balances. This sensitivity analysis includes the impact of existing interest rate swaps during these years.

c. Evaluate the effectiveness of Pepsi's risk strategy for using interest rates.

The following information is presented on stock prices:

We manage the market risk related to our deferred compensation liability, which is indexed to certain market indices and our stock price, with mutual fund investments and prepaid forward contracts for the purchase of our stock. The combined losses on these investments are offset by changes in our deferred compensation liability which is included in Corporate selling, general and administrative expenses.

d. Evaluate the effectiveness of Pepsi's risk strategy for stock prices.

Case 3: More on Enron

The stock chart indicates the market reaction to Enron in 2001.

Period: June 13, 2001 – June 13, 2002

From a high over 90 in August 2000 the stock continued down over the entire second half of the year, until Enron declared bankruptcy in early December, when the price essentially went to zero. What happened? Until the 3rd quarter 10-Q, the financial statements weren't much help. They showed a profitable company, although leverage was high.

What was not obvious was earnings manipulation on a vast scale. The third-quarter results were announced October 16 and the 10-Q was released November 19. The SEC announced a formal investigation on October 31. Financial statements were restated from 1997, resulting in a decrease in stockholders' equity over $1 billion. The company filed for Chapter 11 bankruptcy December 2. Note the large drop-off in price beginning around the October 16 announcement.

Highlights of the 3rd quarter 10-K: First, the restated net income and stockholders' equity since 1997 (in millions). Calculate the difference and percentage difference for each year.

	1997	1998	1999	2000	2001*
Net Income, Reported	$105	$703	$893	$979	$829
Net Income, Restated	26	564	635	842	869
Difference					
% Difference					

*First two quarters only.

	1997	1998	1999	2000	2001*
Equity, Reported	$5,618	$7,048	$9,570	$11,470	$11,740
Equity, Restated	5,309	6,600	8,724	10,289	10,787
Difference					
% Difference					

*First two quarters only.

a. The third-quarter earnings summary, compared to same quarter, 2000 (in millions, restated) is as follows. Calculate common-size percentages.

	Third Quarter 2001	Third Quarter 2001, Common-Size	Third Quarter 2000	Third Quarter 2000, Common-Size
Revenues	$46,877		$29,834	
Operating Income	–917		–513	
Net Income	–644		–282	

b. The third-quarter balance sheet summary, compared to December 31, 2000 (in millions, restated) is as follows. Calculate common-size percentages.

	Third Quarter 2001	Third Quarter 2001, Common-Size	12/31/2000	12/31/2000, Common-Size
Cash	$ 1,001		$ 1,240	
Current Assets	24,847		30,027	
Total Assets	61,783		64,926	
Current Liabilities	27,003		28,741	
Total Liabilities	17,407		18,452	
Stockholders' Equity	9,598		10,289	

    c. Calculate basic financial ratios, including cash, current, debt to equity, return on sales, and return on equity.

	Third Quarter 2001	Earlier Period
Cash Ratio		
Current Ratio		
Debt to Equity		
Return on Sales		
Return on Equity		

    d. Rate Enron from 1 to 10 based on this abbreviated quantitative analysis. How useful are the financial numbers in predicting the potential for bankruptcy for Enron? On the basis of the information presented, what was the most useful indicator of severe financial problems?

Appendix: An Earnings Management Checklist and Comprehensive Case

This appendix summarizes the information available throughout the book for developing a detection strategy and evaluating economic reality. The analyst should expect relative "conservative accounting," full disclosure (ideally well beyond the minimum requirements), and a corporate governance structure that provides confidence of competence and independence.

APPLE COMPUTER: COMPREHENSIVE REVIEW

(Concerns in bold, RF for Red Flags)

Overview: Quantitative Analysis and Corporate Governance (Chapters 3 and 10)

Topic	Analysis
Evaluation of Business Strategy	Proprietary hardware and software in competitive PC industry, strategy to maintain unique product and maintain market share; importance of R&D and marketing stressed; competing against IBM, "Wintel" standard.
Evaluation of Industry and Economic Conditions	Extremely competitive industry, with "commoditization" of products, competitors both large and small with diverse niches; poor performance expected in down economy.
Role of the CEO	**Steve Jobs, cofounder, extraordinary power and unusual compensation package;** new board rules should limit potential problems.
Composition of the Board	Small board, with only five members (Larry Ellison of Oracle resigned in Sept. 2002), all CEOs; problems with independence issues: **Jeremy York, CEO of Micro Warehouse, a major customer of Apple;** interlocking directorship with Millard Drexler, CEO of Gap, until Jobs resigned from Gap board.
Board Committees	Audit, Nominating ,and Compensation Committees new, mandated by NASDAQ rules; this should improve future corporate governance.
Executive Compensation	**Jobs given a Gulfstream airplane as a perk plus tax assistance, grant of 7.5 million stock options (previous options were "underwater").**
Auditing	Three-member audit committee, **chaired by Jerome York—interrelated party,** but former CFO; met eight times in 2001, written charter. Auditor: KPMG; audit fee $1.8 million; **nonaudit fees $16.1 million, 90% of total fees.** Future nonaudit function limited; unqualified opinion, report issued 15 days after end of fiscal year.
Related-party Transactions	Role of Jeremy York previously noted. Relocation loan to SVP Ronald Johnson of $1.5 million; reimbursement agreement with Jobs for operating private plane.
Insider Trading	**Substantial selling of Apple stock by several executives in April and May of 2002.** Stock price drop of Apple roughly from May to July (note that market also dropped in same period).
Regulatory, External	Thirteen 8-K filings in last 5 years, but none considered serious.

Balance Sheet (Chapters 4 and 8)

Topic	Analysis
Overview Issues	High cash balance, current assets, and working capital; low receivables and inventory; low leverage.
Cash and Cash Equivalents	$2.3 billion (41.8% of current assets).
Working Capital	Current ratio of 3.2, large working capital amount.
Short-term Marketable Securities	$2.1 billion (38.7% of current assets), available-for-sale, small gain of $7 million, reported as other comprehensive income.
Inventory	FIFO, $45 million (0.8% of current assets), 2.5 days of inventory.
Accounts Receivable	10.5% of current assets, 32.9 days receivables; bad debts of $51 million, 8.3% of gross receivables); **10.8% of receivables from one customer, Ingram Micro.**
Relationship of Inventory and Receivables to Sales	Inventory levels have remained small since 1999 (e.g., declining from $78 million in 1998 to $45 million in 2002); inventory in days ranged from 1 to 4 days in last 3 years. Accounts receivable balances have fluctuated from a high of $955 million in 1998 to $565 in 2002 (the lowest balance was $466 in 2001). Receivables in days: 46 in 2000, 29 in 2001, and 36 in 2002.
Accounts Payable	54.9% of current liabilities, 54.5 days payable.
Other Current Assets and Liabilities	Other current assets of $275 million (5.1% of current assets); accrued expenses of $747 million.
Property, plant, and equipment (PPE)	9.9% of total assets, average age 3.7 years; **capitalized software development costs of $184 million (26.6% of ending gross investment),** part of PPE.
Intangibles	$119 million in 2002 (see business combinations).
Long-term Investments, Debt and Equity	$39 million (vs. $2.1 billion short-term) combining both debt and equity, including Earthlink, Akamai, ARM Holdings, and Samsung.
Long-term Liabilities	$316 million ($300 million in long-term 6.5% unsecured notes, due in 2004); $229 million deferred tax.
Warranties	$745 million accrued (1.1% of total assets), $69 million actual costs in 2002.
Commitments, Contingencies	Commitments from contract manufacturers for components, $525 million outstanding; lawsuits outstanding, considered immaterial.
Off-balance-sheet Items	Operating leases of $464 million for facilities and equipment (equivalent to 7.4% of total assets).
Equity, Composition	Paid-in capital, retained earnings, acquisition-related deferred stock, other comprehensive income. Equity has increased over the last six years. No dividends paid.
Treasury Stock	$116 million reported under paid-in capital in 1999; forward purchase of 1.5 million shares for Sept. 2003.
Other Comprehensive Income	Negative $49 million (1.2% of stockholders' equity).
Statement of Stockholders' Equity	Reconciled by year, beginning in 1999; unrealized loss on marketable securities of $267 million reported in 2001.

Income Statement (Chapters 5, 6, and 8)

Topic	Analysis
Overview	A major struggle to maintain market share and profitability in the last 2 years (after a successful fiscal year 2000). Net loss in 2001, followed by a small net income in 2002.
Revenue Recognition Policy	Product is considered delivered to the customer once it has been shipped and title and risk of loss have been transferred. Revenue for consulting and implementation services is recognized upon performance and acceptance by the customer. Revenue from extended warranty and support contracts is recognized ratably over the contract period (considered conservative).
Revenues	$5.7 billion in revenues for 2002, up 7.1% from 2001. However, revenues were almost $8 billion in 2000.
Revenues, Long-term trends	**Revenue patterns erratic over the last 6 years, dropping in 1998 and 2001. Revenue declined $1.3 billion from 1997 to 2002 (18.9%).**
Evidence of Aggressive Revenue Recognition	None.
Cost of Sales	$4.1 billion for 2002, 72.1% of revenues; gross profit $1.6 billion.
Operating Expenses	$1.6 billion in 2002; major expense categories (% of revenues) were research and development (7.8%); selling, general, and administrative (SG&A) expense (19.3%); and special charges (0.5%).
Selling, General, and Administrative (SG&A)	**SG&A, at $1.1 billion, was 19.3% of sales,** down slightly from the previous year (21.2% for 2001). MD&A emphasized the importance of marketing to maintain the competitive position of Apple products.
Research and Development (R&D)	$446 million in 2002; expensed as incurred, except for software development costs of $25 million, which were capitalized (6% of R&D). Apple has increased R&D spending slightly in dollar amounts since 1998 and considerably as a % of revenues (e.g., from 4.8% in 2000 to 7.8% in 2002).
Special Charges	**Special charges for 2002: restructuring charges totaled $30 million in 2002 and executive bonus of $90 million was made (primarily for the cost of an airplane) to the CEO in 2000. Apple has recorded special charges each of the last 6 years.**
Income Before Tax	$87 million in 2002 (1.5% of revenues).
Provision for Taxes	$22 million, 25.3% effective tax rate.
Operating Loss Carry-forwards	Operating loss carry-forwards for federal tax purposes of approximately $72 million, which expire from 2009 through 2021.
EBIT, EBITDA	EBIT of $98 million for 2002 (51% above net income); EBITDA of $216 million (232% above net income).
Nonrecurring Items	$12 million gain in 2001, for adoption of SAB 101.
Net Income	**$65 million (1.1% of sales), up from a $25 million loss in 2001.**
Net Income, Long-term Trends	**Erratic pattern in net income, with loss years in 1997 and 2001, a $1 billion loss in 1997, and $25 million loss in 2001; largest net income $786 million in 2000.**
Net Income, Quarterly	**Erratic pattern in recent quarters, including losses of $45 million for the Sept. 2002 quarter and $4 million for the Dec. 2002 quarter.**
Earnings per Share	18¢ a share, both basic and diluted.
Comprehensive Income	$38 million (58.5% of net income) for 2002.

Cash Flows (Chapters 7 and 8)

Topic	Analysis
Cash From Operations	$89 million (36.9% above net income) for 2002, down from $185 million in 2001.
Net Change in Cash	$-58 million for 2002; however, cash balance still above $2 billion. Cash balances have generally increased over the last 6 years.
Free Cash Flows (FCF)	**FCF of $-252 million in 2002** (defined as CFO minus CFI) or **$-85 million** (defined as CFO minus capital expenditures). Apple is not generating enough operating cash to maintain and expand operating capacity. Apple's FCF for the previous 2 years were positive under either definition.

Business Acquisitions and Related Issues (Chapter 9)

Topic	Analysis
Acquisitions	Three acquisitions in 2002: EMagic, Space Technologies, and Power School, total acquisition price of $107 million (1.7% of total assets).
Allocations	$27.7 million allocated to "real net assets" (26%), $11.3 million to in-process R&D (10.6%), and $68 million (64%) to goodwill.
Allocation Strategy	**Allocate as much as possible to goodwill**—benefit of no amortization; given the difficulty of Apple to be profitable, this is the expected strategy. Potential for future "big bath" write-offs.
Use of Equity Method	None reported.
Joint Ventures	None reported.
Divestitures	None reported.
Segment Reporting, Disclosure	**Limited disclosure: only sales for industrial segments listed (in MD&A); no performance data available for analysis;** geographic segment listed essentially for five areas.
Relative Performance	America's largest at $3.1 billion (54% of total net sales); return on sales (operating income/net sales) 9.1%; **U.S. Retail, -7.85% return on sales (RF);** Europe, 9.8%; Japan, 19.7%, Other, 21.5%.

Stock Options (Chapter 10)

Topic	Analysis
Stock Options Outstanding	**109 million shares outstanding at year-end 2002; 30.4% of outstanding shares,** substantial dilution potential.
Pro forma Net Income	Net income reported, $65 million; **Net income pro forma, $-164 million (RF), % difference of 352.3%.**
Relationship to Dividends and Treasury Stock	Apple pays no dividends, despite substantial cash balance; purchased 2.55 million Apple shares for $116 million in 2000, less than 1% of outstanding shares (repurchase plan allows up to 6 million shares of Treasury stock); recorded as a reduction of paid-in capital rather than separately as Treasury stock.
Forward Purchase	During 2002 Apple engaged in a forward purchase for Sept. 2003 of Apple stock of 1.5 million shares, at an average cost of $16.64 ($25.5 million).
Revaluing Options	**Steve Jobs reissued 7.5 million stock options to replace "underwater" options.**

Pensions and Other Post-Employment Benefits (Chapter 10)

Topic	Analysis
Pension Plans	401(k) plan, a defined contribution plan (savings plans with company matching employee contributions, $19 million contribution in 2002)—no further obligations on the part of the company.
OPEB	None reported for Apple.

Risk Management, Derivatives, and Special Purpose Entities (Chapter 11)

Topic	Analysis
Foreign Currency and Interest Rate Risks	To ensure the adequacy and effectiveness of the Company's foreign exchange and interest rate hedge positions and option positions.
Interest Rate Swaps	Company has entered into interest rate swaps with financial institutions in order to better match its floating-rate interest income on its cash equivalents and short-term investments with its fixed-rate interest expense on its long-term debt. As of September 28, 2002, the Company had no interest rate derivatives outstanding.
Foreign Currency Hedges	Company enters into foreign currency forward and option contracts with financial institutions primarily to protect against foreign exchange risks.
Other Derivative Use	None reported.
Credit Risk	Altman's Z-score, 7.15 (healthy).
Credit Risk, Accounts Receivable	A substantial majority of the Company's outstanding trade receivables are not covered by collateral or credit insurance. The Company also has nontrade receivables from certain of its manufacturing vendors.
Special-Purpose Entities (SPEs)	None reported.

SUMMARY OF EARNINGS MANAGEMENT FINDINGS FOR APPLE

Key concerns include corporate governance issues, problems with sales levels and profitability, and stock options. Corporate board practices have been poor in the past but are improving with new regulations. Minor concern with Jeremy York as CEO of a major customer. Some concern with compensation for Steve Jobs and insider trading by executives. Other issues: Ingram Micro represents almost 11% of outstanding receivables; purchases of Treasury stock; high SG&A and R&D; special charges recorded each of the last 6 years; limited industrial segment disclosures and loss at U.S. Retail.

EARNINGS MANAGEMENT CHECKLIST FOR HILTON HOTELS

On the basis of the problems involving Hilton and competitors Marriott and Mandalay Resorts, summarize the earnings management findings for Hilton.

Accounting Policies and Balance Sheet (Chapters 3 and 4)

Topic	Analysis
Accounting Policies	
Business Strategy	
Overview Issues, Quantitative Analysis	
Inventory	
Property, Plant, and Equipment (PPE: Average Age)	
Operating Leases	

Income Statement (Chapters 5, 6, and 8)

Topic	Analysis
Overview, Quantitative Analysis	
Earnings Forecast	
Revenue Composition	
Income Tax Allocation	
Segment Reporting	
Altman's Z-score	
Interest Expense	
Revenue and Earnings Trends	
Quarterly Trends	

Cash Flows, Bottom Line (Chapters 7 and 8)

Topic	Analysis
Cash from Operations	
Other Cash Flow Issues	
EBIT, EBITDA	
Bottom Line Reconciliation	

Business Acquisitions and Related Issues (Chapter 9)

Topic	Analysis
Goodwill	
Segment Reporting	

Corporate Governance, Compensation (Chapter 10)

Topic	Analysis
Corporate Governance	
Stock Options	
Pension	

Risk Management and Derivatives (Chapter 11)

Topic	Analysis
Financial Leverage and Credit Risk	
Risk Management, Derivatives, and SPEs	

Glossary

8-K Form submitted to the SEC for specific events, including auditor changes and acquisitions

10-K Annual financial report submitted to the SEC

10-Q Quarterly financial report submitted to the SEC

above the line Focus on income from continuing operations, ignoring nonrecurring items and other gains and losses associated with comprehensive income

abusive earnings management Term used by the SEC to indicate the intentional misstatement of financial information; equivalent to earnings manipulation

accounting choice Discretionary alternatives for reporting various financial items, such as depreciation or inventory method

accumulated benefit obligation Pension calculation under defined benefit plan: present value of amounts employer expects to pay retired employees based on employee service to date and current salary levels

acquisition Acquiring the right to manage a company through a business combination or acquisition of enough voting shares to have effective management

activity ratio Financial calculation to evaluate how effective corporate operations are

affiliates Firms with a substantial equity interest but not consolidated

aggressive accounting Accounting choices made to increase revenues, decrease expenses, or effect other desired results, usually within GAAP limits

all-inclusive earnings Earnings measurement based on all factors associated with revenues, expenses, gains and losses; equivalent to comprehensive income

Altman's Z-Score Financial ratio model used to evaluate bankruptcy potential; can also be used to assess relative financial health

analysts' forecasts Specialist predictions of earnings per share (or other definitions of performance) for the forthcoming quarters and years

assets Assets are economic resources ("probable future economic benefits based on past transactions or events," according to the Statements of Financial Accounting Concepts (SFACs) No. 6)

asset reserve Contra-asset (or liability) account to reduce the value of the asset based on likely impairment to value such as allowance of doubtful accounts

audit The financial audit is an external audit performed by licensed professional to ensure that the accounting information is in conformance with GAAP

bankruptcy risk The probability that a firm will file for bankruptcy in the near future

base year analysis Multiple-period analysis by setting a base year equal to 100 and comparing financial statement items relative to the base year

basic earnings per share (EPS) EPS measured as net income/(weighted average number of common shares outstanding)

below the line Focus is on all-inclusive definition of earnings, therefore including nonrecurring items

benchmark A standard of comparison based on rules of thumb, industry averages, market averages, and so on

big bath write-off Large loss (or other reduction to earnings) for a specific purpose, often when losses are recorded to that period anyway; this can increase the changes of better earnings in future periods

Big Four The largest accounting firms (KPMG, Ernst & Young, Deloitte & Touche, and PricewaterhouseCoopers) that audit most major corporations

bill and hold Product sold with the stipulation that delivery will occur in a later period

boiler plate A standard description or analysis; in other words, to an experienced analyst this adds no new information

bond ratings Relative grades of "financial health," from highest (AAA for Standard & Poor's, Aaa for Moody's) to lowest (D for Standard & Poor's, C for Moody's)

capital structure The composition of long-term debt and equity, measuring relative leverage

cash burn rate The amount of cash available to fund future operations and capital expenditures (usually of a start-up company before profitability)

cash from operations Cash flows directly associated with net income and other operating transactions, as reported on the Statement of Cash Flows

channel stuffing Shipments to wholesalers or others using deep discounts to encourage acceptance, usually at the end of the accounting period; they have right of return

closing stock price The ending (last) stock price of the day for a security trading on a stock exchange

comprehensive income Change in equity during a period from all nonowner sources

conceptual framework Attempt of the Financial Accounting Standards Board (FASB) to describe financial accounting theory in a coherent body, as stated in Statements of Financial Accounting Concepts (SFACs)

conglomerate merger Acquisition of a firm from an entirely different industry

conservative accounting Standard approach to GAAP accounting, but possibly understating operating results

consolidation The accounts of a subsidiary are included directly in the books of the parent company

cookie jar reserves Establishing reserve accounts to smooth earnings, increasing reserves (reducing earnings) when performance is strong and decreasing reserves (increasing earnings) when performance is weak

corporate governance The board of directors and the structure in place to oversee the management of an organization

credit analysis The financial analysis process associated with evaluating the investment prospects in a debt instrument

credit risk The probability that a firm will default on paying liabilities and/or declare bankruptcy

credit-worthiness Analysis of credit risk and other factors to determine if the customer is acceptable for a loan (or other debt instrument) and under what terms

currency swaps Agreement to make payments in one currency in exchange for the obligations in another currency

current operating performance Earnings based on "core earnings," those that are part of normal operations—also called sustainable earnings

debt covenants Contract terms mandated by the creditor to protect against possible loan default, such as minimum financial ratios or limitations on dividends

default risk The probability that a firm will not pay interest and principal when they come due

defined benefit plan Pension plan committing employer to pay specific benefits at employees' retirement

defined contribution plan Pension plan committing employer to make specific cash payment to the employees' retirement accounts

derivatives Financial contract derived from another financial instrument, including options, futures, and swaps

diluted earnings per share (EPS) EPS with number of shares adjusted for potential dilution (e.g., from stock options), which reduces EPS

dirty surplus Gains and losses recorded directly to equity and not in the income statements, such as marketable securities and foreign currency translations adjustments

diversification Investment portfolio holding a broad base of securities, in an attempt to maximize the risk-return tradeoff

divestiture Sale or disposition of part of a business, usually a subsidiary

dividend yield Dividends per share divided by stock price, a measure of direct cash return on investment

Dow Jones Industrial Average A stock price average based on 30 of the largest industrial companies in America, the most well-known stock average

earnings-based growth models Model for the valuation of the firm, based on dividend payout relative to earnings, discounted by some interest rate net of earnings growth rate; also called the dividend discount model

earnings management Operating and discretionary accounting methods to adjust earnings to a desired outcome; the incentives of management to modify earnings in their own best interests

earnings manipulation Opportunistic use of earnings management to effectively "modify or misstate" earnings to benefit managers

earnings per share (EPS) Net income (or some other measure of earnings) converted to a per-share basis (annually or quarterly), which can be calculated as basic EPS or diluted EPS

earnings power The sustainable earnings of a company, often associated with earnings persistence; income from continuing operations or operating income may be useful measures of earnings power

earnings quality The extent to which earnings represent economic reality, associated with conservative accounting and full disclosure

earnings restatements Company revises public financial information that was previously reported; also called financial statement restatements

EBIT Earnings before interest and taxes (also called "operating earnings"), used to evaluate the firm's ability to service debt

EBITDA Earnings before interest, taxes, depreciation, and amortization (also called "cash earnings"), used to evaluate cash flows

economic reality Financial information free of distortions that tend to hide the actual results of sales, expenses, and other transactions

enforcement actions Legal actions taken by the SEC Enforcement Division, based on regulatory violations by corporations

equity Residual interest in the assets after deducting liabilities; i.e., ownership

equity method Accounting method used when patent owns roughly 20%–50% of an affiliate; consolidation is not used

expenses Outflows from incurring liabilities or using up assets associated with sales and other central operations

Financial Accounting Standards Board Authoritative body that now establishes accounting standards for commercial and nonprofit accounting

financial leverage index A ratio of the impact of financial leverage on the performance of the firm, measured as return on equity/return on assets

first in, first out (FIFO) Inventory method where the first items recognized in inventory are released (sold) first

fixed assets Property, plant, and equipment (PPE), the basic infrastructure of the corporation

fluctuating currencies All currencies "float"; that is, their value is based on current market conditions compared to all other currencies

foreign currency translation Amount of gains and losses based on relative currency values of foreign operations of financial statement items and reported directly to stockholders' equity

forward contract Agreement between buyer and seller to deliver an asset in exchange for cash (or financial instrument) at a fixed price on a specific future date; examples include commodities, currencies, and stocks.

fraud Intentional act or omission to materially misstate financial information

free cash flows (FCF) A measure of cash available for discretionary uses after certain cash outlays; a common calculation of FCF is cash from operations minus cash from investments (CFO–CFI)

futures contract Standardized forward contract traded on an organized exchange; examples include commodities, currencies, and stocks

gains Increase in net assets from peripheral transactions

Generally Accepted Accounting Principles (GAAP) Comprehensive set of accounting standards established by the FASB and predecessor bodies

geographic segments Foreign operation footnote disclosure, including sales and identifiable assets

Gold Standard Historical system (no longer in use) in which currencies were pegged to gold by weight and currencies were redeemable in gold

goodwill Acquisition price of a target company less the fair value of the net assets of the target, used with the purchase method

growth analysis Multiple-period (usually by year) comparisons of specific financial statement items (or ratios) to calculate periodic growth rates

hedging Techniques used to protect against adverse movements in prices, interest rates, foreign currency, or other risks

held-to-maturity securities Marketable securities that will be held to maturity and recorded at cost (or amortized cost)

horizontal merger Acquisition of a direct competitor, thus increasing market share and reducing direct competition

hybrid securities Securities that have characteristics of both debt and equity, such as convertible bonds

income from continuing operations Operating income as measured before nonrecurring items; a standard measure of current operating performance

income smoothing Earnings management to smooth out erratic revenue and earnings behavior

industry analysis Identifying the industry in which a corporation competes and evaluating the key characteristics and prospects of that industry

industry segments Industry or department segment disclosure for major divisions, including sales, operating income, and identifiable assets

initial public offering The first sale of stock in the open market, with the stock to be publicly traded, often on an exchange (and subject to SEC oversight)

in-process research and development (R&D) R&D costs of an acquired firm (under the purchase method) for ongoing projects. Difficult to value and subject to earnings manipulation by acquiring firm

insider trading Buying and selling of securities by board members, executives, and other insiders; potentially illegal if they acted for personal gain on the basis of insider information

in-substance defeasance An existing debt agreement is placed in trust with use of an SPE (special-purpose entity) against specific assets (e.g., government bonds with essentially equal terms)

interest rate swaps Contract to exchange fixed for floating interest payments on bonds and other credit agreements

interperiod tax allocation Deferred tax items recorded as separate assets or liabilities on the balance sheet

intraperiod tax allocation The tax effect associated with specific nonrecurring items; these items are reported net of tax (i.e., the intraperiod tax allocation) on the income statement

investment grade bond rating The four highest bond-rating categories (Standard & Poor's AAA to BBB), considered to have relatively low credit risk

joint venture Contractual arrangement between two or more corporations (or other entities) for a particular purpose, including supplies and sales

junk bonds Bonds with below-investment-grade ratings

last in, first out (LIFO) Inventory method in which the last items recognized in inventory are released (sold) first

lease Contract agreement for the use of assets on a rental or fee basis for a set period of time

liabilities Claims against the resources of a company ("probable future economic sacrifices from present obligations," according to Statement of Financial Accounting Concepts [SFAC]. No. 6)

losses Decrease in net assets from peripheral transactions

market-to-book A comparison of market value to book value (total stockholders' equity, also called net assets)

market value Also called market capitalization or market cap, stock price × number of shares outstanding, a measure of how the stock market values companies

marketable securities Debt and equity securities that are market-traded and typically held for a short period of time as a cash equivalent

matching principal Recording expenses that are related to revenues recognized, both product and period costs

merger A combination of two companies into a single corporate entity

monetary items Assets and liabilities that are denominated in dollars (or other currencies) such as accounts receivable and corporate bonds

net assets Total assets minus total liabilities, equal to total stockholders' equity

nonmonetary items Assets and liabilities that are not denominated in currency such as inventory or fixed assets

nonrecurring items Gains and losses from peripheral transactions that are recorded as separate line items on the income statement and reported net-of-tax, such as extraordinary items and discontinued operations

normalizing income Restating earnings results to better reflect economic reality

off-balance-sheet financing Contractual arrangements so that assets and liabilities are not recorded on the balance sheet; a likely source of earnings management

operating lease Short-term lease, with lease payments recorded as a periodic expense and obligation is off-balance-sheet

opportunism Individual behavior associated with self-interest with guile, that is, beyond the standard ethical norms

option Agreement that gives a party the right to buy (call) or sell (put) a specific quantity at a specific price (exercise price) until a specified maturity date; examples include commodities, currencies, and stocks

other post-employment benefit obligations Contractual obligations to retired or terminated employees, such as health insurance; must be recognized as liabilities

out-of-period sales Revenue recognized this period for sales legitimately for the next period

pensions Retirement plans to provide employees income after retirement

period costs Expenses that are charged to a specific accounting period rather than directly matched to specific sales, such as advertising

permanent tax difference A difference between financial accounting and tax accounting that never washes out and is not recorded on the balance sheet

phantom stock A promise to pay a bonus in the form of the equivalent of either the value of company shares or the increase in value over a period of time

political costs Political issues may impact on economic and financial decisions, usually encouraging companies to report lower earnings for some political purpose

pooling of interests Accounting procedures for business acquisition meeting specific criteria; no longer allowed by GAAP

price earnings (PE) ratio Stock price divided by annual earnings per share (EPS), a measure of the "market premium" for earnings

PEG ratio PE divided by earnings growth rate, a measure of "reasonableness" of the PE ratio; a possible rule of thumb is a PEG equal to or less than one

primary market Capital market where new securities are initially issued

product costs Expenses that are recognized directly for sales and other revenue; cost of goods sold is the obvious example

pro forma earnings Hypothetical earnings measurement based on the method and assumptions of the preparer

projected benefit obligation Pension calculation under defined benefit plan: present value of amounts employer expects to pay retired employees, based on employee service to date and expected salary at retirement

proxy statement Annual report issued by the company in advance of the annual stockholders' meeting, which includes information on audit fees, compensation, and board members

purchase method Accounting procedures now required for all business acquisition; target is stated as actual market price

quantitative Financial Analysis A host of ratios, models, time series, and forecasts to identify key financial characteristics, which can be compared to competitors' or other standards

quarterly Analysis Financial analysis on a quarterly rather than an annual basis, almost always with a multiple-period approach

related-party transaction An exchange or transaction with an executive, board member, relative, or other individual directly connected with the company

restricted stock A grant of stock to an employee in which the employee's rights to the shares are limited until the shares vest

revenues Inflows and other asset enhancements from sales and other central operations

revenue recognition Criteria for recognizing revenues when revenue is (1) realized or realizable and (2) earned; timing (when revenue is recognized) usually is the key issue

risk management Techniques used by corporations to reduce or control for potential adverse consequences (uncertainty), primarily related to prices, interest rates, and foreign currency

round-trip transaction Simultaneous purchase and sale between colluding (related-party) companies

Sarbanes-Oxley Act Federal law passed in 2002 to increase the regulations on auditors and securities markets

Securities & Exchange Commission (SEC) Established by the SEC Act of 1934 to regulate U.S. securities markets, including accounting and auditing

segment reporting Footnote disclosures on industry and geographic segments, particularly important for major corporations with multiple industry segments and global operations

sham rebates Order from supplier that inflates costs but includes a "rebate" that is treated as revenue

special purpose entities (SPEs) A unique legal entity to be used for a specific purpose, such as leasing arrangements or project development activities; the purpose is to treat this as an off-balance-sheet item

spin-off A new business is created from an existing part of the business, usually through the distribution of shares to the stockholders on a pro rata basis or sale of new shares

stock appreciation rights A promise to pay a bonus in the form of the equivalent of either the value of company shares or the increase in that value over a period of time

stock options Employee benefits that allow employees to acquire a set number of shares or firm stock at a set price; options will be exercised only if stock price is higher than the exercise price

sustainable earnings Measure of operating earnings that best captures the ability to maintain earnings from the basic operation of the corporation; gross margin, operating income, and income from continuing operations are the most common measures used

swap Contract to exchange one series of payments for another

temporary tax difference A tax difference between financial accounting and tax accounting that represents a timing difference and is recorded on the balance sheet (see deferred tax)

time series analysis The analysis of financial data over time, usually to determine basic characteristics over time, also called trend analysis

tracking stock Stock issued by a public company to track the value of a subsidiary, with the parent maintaining control

trading securities Marketable securities that are held (usually by a financial institution) for resale to another organization or individual; holding gains and losses are recognized on the income statement

treasury stock Common stock acquired by the company in the open market and recorded as a negative equity item

trend analysis Any multiperiod quantitative analysis, used to analyze longer-term trends

vertical merger Acquisition of an "indirect" competitor, that is, in the same basic industry but generally in a different market segment

whistle-blower Employee of a company who comes forward with information (usually to senior executives, board members, the auditor, or regulators) that may be incriminating to the company

References

Bentson, G. and A. Hartgraves, "Enron: What Happened and What We Can Learn From It," *Journal of Accounting and Public Policy*, Summer 2002, pp. 105–127.

Blankley, A. and E. Swanson, "A Longitudinal Study of SFAS 87 Pension Rate Assumptions," *Accounting Horizons*, December 1995, pp. 1–21.

Botosan, C., "Disclosure Level and the Cost of Equity Capital," *The Accounting Review*, 72(1997), pp. 323–349.

Charan, R. & J. Useem, "Why Companies Fail," www.fortune.com, 2002.

Committee of Sponsoring Organizations of the Treadway Commission (COSO), *Report of the National Commission on Fraudulent Financial Reporting*, New York: COSO, 1987.

COSO, *Fraudulent Financial Reporting: 1987–1997—An Analysis of US Public Companies*, New York: COSO, 1999.

Dechow, P., and D. Skinner, "Earnings Management: Reconciling the Views of Accounting Practitioners, and Regulators," *Accounting Horizons*, 14 (2000), pp. 235–250.

Fields, T., T. Lys, and L. Vincent, "Empirical Research on Accounting Choice," *Journal of Accounting and Economics*, 31 (2001), pp. 255–307.

Foster, J., "Observations on the Current Crisis and its Affect on the Development of Accounting Standards," *Speech at Texas A&M Profession at a Crossroads Series*, November 14, 2002.

France, M., "What About the Lawyers?" *Business Week*, December 23, 2002, pp. 58–62.

France, M., "The SEC's Plan Shouldn't Make Lawyers Squawk," *Business Week*, January 27, 2003, p. 54.

Friedman, T., *The Lexus and the Olive Tree*, New York: Anchor Books, 2000.

Gibson, C., *Financial Reporting & Analysis, Eight Edition*, Cincinnati: South–Western College Publishing, 2001.

Giroux, G., "Annual Reports of the Minehill and Schuylkill Haven Railroad Company: 1844–1864," *The Accounting Historians Notebook*, April 1998, pp. 9–10, 30–33.

Giroux, G., *Financial Analysis: A User Approach*, New York: John Wiley & Sons, 2003.

General Accounting Office: *Financial Statement Restatements: Trends, Market Impacts, Regulatory Responses, and Remaining Challenges (GAO 03–138)*, Washington: GAO, October 2002.

Healy, P., "The Impact of Bonus Schemes on the Selection of Accounting Principles," *Journal of Accounting and Economics*, 7 (1985), pp. 85–107.

Healy, P. and J. Wahlen, "A Review of the Earnings Management Literature and its Implications for Standard Setting, *Accounting Horizons*, December 1999, pp. 365–383.

Henry, D., "Mergers: Why Most Big Deals Don't Pay Off," *Business Week*, October 14, 2002, pp. 60–70.

Himmelstein, L. and B. Elgin, "Tech's Kickback Culture," *Business Week*, February 10, 2003, pp. 74–77.

Jones, J., "Earnings Management During Import Relief Investigations," *Journal of Accounting Research*, 29 (1991), pp. 193–228.

Kahn, J., "Off Balance Sheet—and Out of Control; SPEs are Ripe for Abuse, but Few Went as Far as Enron's Fastow," *Fortune* (www.fortune.com), February 18, 2002.

Levitt, A. and P. Dwyer, *Take on the Street: What Wall Street and Corporate America Don't Want You to Know*, New York: Pantheon Books, 2002.

Maremont, M., "Tyco Reveals $8 Billion of Acquisitions Made Over Three Years, but Not Disclosed," *Wall Street Journal*, February 4, 2002, p. A3.

McNichols, M., "Research Design Issues in Earnings Management Studies," *Journal of Accounting and Public Policy*, 19 (2000), pp. 313–345.

Mulford, C. and E. Comisky, *The Financial Numbers Game: Detecting Creative Accounting Practices*, New York: John Wiley & Sons, 2002.

Paton, W. and A. Littleton, *An Introduction to Corporate Accounting Standards*, New York: American Accounting Standards, 1940 (reprinted in 1974).

Penman, S., *Financial Statement Analysis & Security Valuations*, Boston: McGraw-Hill Irwin, 2001.

Revsine, L., D. Collins, and W. Johnson, *Financial Reporting & Analysis, Second Edition*, Upper Saddle River, NJ: Prentice Hall, 2002.

Schilit, H., *Financial Shenanigans: How to Detect Accounting Gimmicks & Fraud in Financial Reports, Second Edition*, New York: McGraw-Hill, 2002.

Schipper, K., "Commentary: Earnings Management," *Accounting Horizons*, December 1989, pp. 91–102.

Sengupta, P., "Corporate Disclosure Quality and the Cost of Debt," *The Accounting Review*, 73 (1998), pp. 459–474.

Swartz, M. and S. Watkins, *Power Failure: The Inside Story of the Collapse of Enron*, New York: Doubleday, 2003.

Symonds, W., "Behind Tyco's Accounting Alchemy," *Business Week*, February 25, 2002.

Watts, R. and J. Zimmerman, *Positive Accounting Theory*, Englewood Cliffs: Prentice-Hall, 1986.

Weiss, G., "Just a Minute Mr. Donaldson," *Business Week*, February 10, 2003, pp. 66–67.

White, G., A. Sondhi, and D. Fried, *The Analysis and Use of Financial Statements, Second Edition*, New York: John Wiley & Sons, 1998; *Third Edition*, 2003.

SPECIFIC PRONOUNCEMENT & REGULATIONS CITED IN THE BOOK

Accounting Principles Board

Opinion No. 20, *Accounting Changes*
Opinion No. 30, *Reporting the Results of Operations*

Financial Accounting Standards Board

Statements of Financial Accounting Standards (SFAS)
SFAS No. 4, *Reporting Gains and Losses from Extinguishment of Debt*
SFAS No. 5, *Accounting for Contingencies*
SFAS No. 13, *Accounting for Leases*
SFAS No. 14, *Financial Reporting for Segments of a Business Enterprise*

SFAS No. 34, *Capitalization of Interest Cost*
SFAS No. 52, *Foreign Currency Translation*
SFAS No. 87, *Employers' Accounting for Pensions*
SFAS No. 95, *Statement of Cash Flows*
SFAS No. 106, *Employers' Accounting for Postretirement Benefits Other Than Pensions*
SFAS No. 109, *Accounting for Income Taxes*
SFAS No. 123, *Accounting for Stock-based Compensation*
SFAS No. 128, *Earnings Per Share*
SFAS No. 130, *Reporting Comprehensive Income*
SFAS No. 131, *Disclosures About Segments of an Enterprise and Related Information*
SFAS No. 132, *Employers' Disclosures about Pensions and Other Postretirement Benefits*
SFAS No. 133, *Accounting for Derivative Instruments and Hedging Activities*
SFAS No. 138, *Accounting for Certain Derivative Instruments & Certain Hedging Activities*
SFAS No. 141, *Business Combinations*
SFAS No. 142, *Goodwill and Other Intangible Assets*
SFAS No. 144, *Accounting for the Impairment or Disposal of Long-lived Assets*

Statements of Financial Accounting Concepts (SFAC)

SFAC No. 1, *Objectives of Financial Reporting by Business Enterprises*
SFAC No. 6, *Elements of Financial Statements*

Security & Exchange Commission, Staff Accounting Bulletins (SAB)

SAB No. 99, *Materiality*
SAB No. 100, *Restructuring and Impairment Charges*
SAB No. 101, *Revenue Recognition in Financial Statements*

Federal Laws

Securities Act of 1933
Securities and Exchange Commission Act of 1934
Employee Retirement Income Security Act of 1974 (ERISA)
Sarbanes-Oxley Act of 2002

USEFUL WEBPAGES

www.cnnfn.com: This is one of my favorite sites; by using the ticker symbol, substantial financial information is made available from CNNFN and other sites like quicken.

www.hoovers.com: Another useful site, especially information on specific companies such as simplified financial statements (more information is available to members).

www.fortune.com/fortune: Fortune Magazine, includes Fortune 500 list.

www.fool.com: Motley Fool's site, long list including Fool's School.

www.rutgers.edu/Accounting/raw: Rutgers accounting web. Extensive list of accounting sites.

www.sec.gov: Useful SEC site, includes Edgar database.

www.fasb.org: FASB site, useful for recent actions.

www.wsj.com: Wall Street Journal site.

www.businessweek.com: Business Week's site.

www.thestreet.com: The Street, another big site.

www.labpuppy.com: "Retriever" for investment information.

cbs.marketwatch.com: CBS contribution to investment information.

www.morningstar.net: Morningstar ratings and other useful information.

www.dnb.com: Dun & Bradstreet.

www.moodys.com: Moody's Investor Service.

www.standardpoors.com: Standard & Poor's.

quote.yahoo.com: Yahoo's finance site.

moneycentral.msn.com: Microsoft (msn) site.

www.quicken.com: Quicken's site, considerable information available.

www.10kwizard.com: Search engine for SEC filings.

www.marketplayer.com: Stock screening & stock chartings, etc.

www.easystock.com: Stock charts & other financial data available.

www.stockselector.com: Useful stock & industry information & recommendations.

www.bloomberg.com: Considerable information on stocks & other finance topics.

www.zacks.com: Particularly useful for analyst earnings forecasts.

www.investorama.com: Links to hundreds of sites.

www.census.gov: U.S. Census Bureau.

www.bea.doc.gov: Bureau of Economic Analysis, useful for economic updates.

www.federalreserve.gov: Federal Reserve Board.

WEB PAGES OF COMPANIES CITED

www.dell.com
www.gateway.com
www.hp.com

www.ford.com
www.gm.com
www.dcx.com
www.dupont.com
www.dow.com
www.ppg.com
www.hilton.com
www.marriott.com
www.mandalayresortgroup.com
www.amazon.com
www.ebay.com
www.cdnow.com
www.duke-energy.com
www.pgecorp.com
www.utilicorp.com
www.txu.com
www.southern.com
www.alcoa.com
www.americanexpress.com
www.att.com
www.boeing.com
www.cat.com
www.citigroup.com
www.cocacola.com
www.disney.com
www.kodak.com
www.exxon.mobil.com
www.ge.com
www.hp.com
www.homedepot.com
www.honeywell.com
www.ibm.com
www.intel.com
www.ipaper.com
www.jnj.com
www.mcdonalds.com
www.merck.com
www.microsoft.com
www.mmm.com
www.jpmorgan.com
www.philipmorris.com
www.pg.com
www.sbc.com
www.utc.com
www.walmart.com

Index